The Supervisor's Infobank

The Supervisor's Infobank

1000 Quick Answers to Your Toughest Problems

Arthur R. Pell, Ph.D.
Consultant, Human Resources Development

McGraw-Hill, Inc.

New York   San Francisco   Washington, D.C.   Auckland   Bogotá
Caracas   Lisbon   London   Madrid   Mexico City   Milan
Montreal   New Delhi   San Juan   Singapore
Sydney   Tokyo   Toronto

Library of Congress Cataloging-in-Publication Data

Pell, Arthur R.
    The supervisor's infobank : 1000 quick answers to your toughest
problems / Arthur R. Pell.
         p.   cm.
    Includes index.
    ISBN 0-07-049185-2
    1. Supervision of employees.   I. Title.
HF5549.12.P45   1994
658.3'02—dc20   94-2702
                                            CIP

1 2 3 4 5 6 7 8 9 0 DOC/DOC 9 0 9 8 7 6 5 4

ISBN 0-07-049185-2

*The sponsoring editor for this book was Betsy N. Brown, the editing super-
visor was Caroline R. Levine, and the production supervisor was
Donald F. Schmidt. It was set in Garamond by McGraw-Hill's Professional
Book Group composition unit.*

Printed and bound by R. R. Donnelley & Sons Company.

To Erica,

My life-partner and best friend
for more than half a century

Contents

Preface   xi

1. Getting Started As a New Supervisor   1
Breaking In   2
Overcoming Resentment   5
Friends As Subordinates   9
Special Problems Faced by New Supervisors   12

2. Selecting the Right People   23
Job Specifications   23
Sources of Personnel   24
Screening Applicants   30
Giving Information   41
Problem Applicants   43
Remembering the Applicant   46
Making the Hiring Decision   47
Testing Applicants   53
Checking References   56
Making the Offer   64

3. Complying with Equal Employment Laws   70
Overview of Equal Employment Opportunity Laws   71
Americans with Disabilities Act   81
Criminal Records   84
Sex Discrimination   85
Hiring and Working with People from Other Cultures   93
Applying EEO on the Job   96

Age Discrimination   99
Affirmative Action   101
Dealing with Complaints   102

4. Training   **107**
Systematic Training   107
Setting the Training Schedule   113
Using Other Employees As Trainers   116
Training Methods   118
Continuing Training   123

5. Delegation   **135**
Importance of Delegation   135
Communicating What You Delegate   138
Maintaining Control   140
Day-to-day Problems in Delegation   143

6. Communicating with Your People   **151**
The Words We Choose   152
The Way We Speak   155
Nonverbal Communication   158
Listening   160
Feedback   163
Attitudes, Biases, and Emotions   165
Communication Problems on the Job   170
Giving Orders   176
Improving Written Communication   177

7. Upward Communication   **185**
Upward Communication from Individuals   185
Suggestion Systems   190
Meetings   194
Developing Creativity in Your People   197

8. Motivation and Morale   **204**
Motivation Principles and Techniques   204
Goals   215
Getting More from Your People   218
Motivating a Diversified Work Force   225
Building Teams   229
Other Motivational Problems   232
Morale   240

9. Dealing with Problem Employees   **244**
    Attitude   244
    Dealing with Personal Problems   251
    Alcohol and Drugs   258
    Problem People   261
    Boss–Subordinate Relations   270

10. Day to Day on the Job   **281**
    Work Assignments   281
    Interpersonal Relations   294
    Absenteeism and Tardiness   301
    Work Habits   309

11. The Supervisor As a Counselor   **314**
    Conflict Resolution   314
    Gripes and Grievances   322
    Counseling   336

12. Employee Evaluation   **345**
    Purposes of Employee Evaluation   346
    Trait Rating   352
    Other Evaluation Systems   356
    The Performance Appraisal Interview   358

13. Discipline   **368**
    Progressive Discipline   369
    Affirmative Discipline   379
    Legal Implications of Discipline   381
    Discipline on the Job   384

14. Layoffs, Quits, and Termination   **394**
    Layoffs   395
    Voluntary Quits   401
    Firing Employees Legally and Tactfully   406
    Employment at Will   416

15. Time Management   **420**
    Planning   421
    Interruptions   426
    Handling Mail   434

Meetings   436
Personal Barriers to Efficient Use of Time   437
Time Management on the Job   440

16. Your Boss and Your Career   **444**
The Relationship Between You and Your Boss   445
Policy   450
Assigning Work   452
Personality Problems   455
Your Career   462

Afterword   466
Index   467

Preface

My first exposure to leadership training was as an officer in the United States Army during World War II. My immediate reaction was, "An officer tells his men what to do and they do it." But even in that highly disciplined situation, we were taught that the way to truly lead people was to elicit from them their willing cooperation. If people are led by an officer, a supervisor, or a manager who has earned their respect and confidence, they will extend themselves to accomplish the objectives desired.

In my first job after the war, as the personnel manager of a manufacturing company, I was asked to develop a program to train foremen (a title used in those ancient days for supervisors) in the techniques of supervision. In researching the literature in the field, I learned that much of what I had been taught in the Army was applicable to the world of work.

In the following years, as a consultant in human resources, I designed training programs for supervisors in a variety of organizations, including police and fire departments, hospitals, not-for-profit organizations, and all types of businesses.

To ensure that my material was always correct, current, and pragmatic, I surveyed the supervisory practices at my client companies—observing men and women who were very successful as supervisors as well as those who were not at all successful—to learn the differences in supervisors' approaches to their jobs. Of course, I kept up with the literature in the field. It was during these years that seminal works in human resources were written by such gurus as Peter Drucker, Abraham Maslow, Douglas McGregor, Rensis Likert, and Frederick Herzberg.

Some people feel that all that is needed to be a good supervisor is common sense. There is no question that "common sense" is essential in all management matters, but unfortunately there is no universal understanding of this term. How it is interpreted depends on the background, previous experience, psychological mindset, and basic philosophy of each individual. What appears to be logical to one person may seem totally irrational to another. Successful supervision requires more objective guidelines than a vague "commonsense" approach.

Others say that adhering to the golden rule, "Do unto others as you would have others do unto you," is all that is needed to be a good supervisor. Indeed, the golden rule in various forms appears in almost every culture. However, it may be too simplistic a guideline. People do not necessarily want to be treated the same way you do. For example, Jonathan likes to be given assignments in broad terms with the authority to take whatever steps are necessary to complete it successfully. Jessica prefers to be given detailed instructions as to how to perform every aspect of the project. If Jonathan followed the golden rule and assigned Jessica work in the way he liked to receive it, Jessica would be frustrated and unhappy and probably fail.

Perhaps we should follow a variation of the golden rule: Do unto others as you believe they want to be treated. This makes the job of the supervisor much more difficult. To succeed you must take the time and effort to learn as much as you can about your people so you can tailor the way you deal with each of them to their individualities. There is no magic formula when it comes to how you relate to others. The Know Your People Worksheet in Chapter 1 will help you focus on this task.

Over the past 20 years, I have presented seminars on supervision to thousands of supervisors and managers. As I looked back over my seminar notes, workbooks, and research materials, I noted significant changes in what I taught the participants over the years. What I present now is quite different from what I presented in the 1970s. Has the field changed that much? Have so many new techniques been introduced? Of course, there have been some significant changes of emphasis. Certain laws have been passed or re-interpreted which require people to conduct themselves differently on the job. However, this is not the main reason for the changes. The main reason is the evolving focus of seminar participants. In the early 1970s, there was considerable concern over the new equal employment opportunity laws. Today, although EEO is still very important, most people are aware of its implications and display more interest in such things as empowerment, team development, and motivation.

How do I know what participants want? Chiefly from the questions they ask in my seminars. In most seminars, the leader provides an open-ended segment in which questions can be asked. By analyzing these questions, the leader can determine the areas in which real interest lies. Changes can then be made in the basic seminar material to incorporate these areas into the program.

Often the question-and-answer period is the best part of the seminar. It occurred to me that if these questions and answers could be set down in one place, they would provide a ready reference for supervisors. That was the genesis of this book. At first, I guessed that I could put together 500 different questions that supervisors ask. In order to determine if this was feasible, I changed my approach to the Q&A segment. Instead of asking for oral presentations from the floor, I had the participants put their questions in writing. I studied the questions and selected those that I believed were of the most interest to supervisors.

After a few months, it became apparent that I could assemble not 500 but 1000 different questions. In fact, the challenge became selecting which 1000 would be the most useful. I divided the questions into the 16 subjects that make up the chapters of this book, and added a variety of forms and charts to supplement the text.

This is a reference book. Of course, it can be read from cover to cover as an overview of the field for newcomers or as a refresher for experienced supervisors. As a reference tool, it should be kept on the desk with your dictionary and company policy manual. By using the index for specific problems or the table of contents for more general information, you will gain immediate access to the answers to many of the questions that supervisors face in the performance of their jobs.

The focus of the book is *people*—not administrative or technical matters. The table of contents provides a capsule view of what is in the book. Glance through it. Look up a few of the problems you are facing today. This will give you the flavor of the book. You will find that the questions are succinct and the answers practical and easy to put into effect. Theoretical concepts have been avoided except when they are essential to explain a practical application.

Many of the actions that supervisors take have legal implications. Inasmuch as such matters are often complex, I strongly recommend that you consult your company's legal advisors.

Arthur R. Pell, Ph.D.

Acknowledgments

I want to express my thanks to those people whose assistance and support made this book possible: to William D. Frohlich and Elinor Basso of Dun & Bradstreet's Business Education Services for giving me the opportunity to conduct my seminars; to David Katz, my agent, for introducing me to McGraw-Hill; to Betsy N. Brown, senior editor at McGraw-Hill, for her enthusiastic support and editorial suggestions; and to my wife, Erica, for her patience and support over the months in which I researched, wrote, and put this book into its final shape.

Arthur R. Pell, Ph.D.

The Supervisor's Infobank

1

Getting Started
As a Supervisor

People promoted to their first job as supervisors immediately face a wide variety of new problems and situations. Unfortunately, all too often, companies do not prepare supervisors for the new challenges they must meet.

Most people, when raised to the ranks of management, still must perform many of the duties they had before promotion as well as assume the added responsibilities of dealing with the people they must now direct. For example, the new chief accountant might continue to devote many hours to accounting, but will also be accountable for the work of the people supervised.

Making this transition is never easy. New supervisors must be prepared to allow others to do work which they may well be able to do better themselves—and with which they are more comfortable—so that they can gain the time to learn and perform their managerial functions. Although many courses and seminars are available on how to make this transition, for the most part new supervisors have to "play it by ear," learning through trial and error. Here are some of the most commonly asked questions concerning the initial "breaking-in" period.

Breaking In

1-1   For the past 7 years I have been an accounting clerk and I've been very good at it. Recently I was promoted to supervisor. In the past I've always felt very confident about my ability to do my job, but now I find that I'm a bit scared.

That's normal, don't worry. Most people who are promoted from within the ranks are chosen because they are good performers and have developed plenty of self-confidence because of their proven ability to perform. But what it takes to be a good performer and what it takes to be a good supervisor are not necessarily the same thing. You will have to learn different skills—and they are learnable. Once you acquire them, your self-confidence to do your new job will grow.

1-2   What skills are needed to succeed as a supervisor?

A supervisor by definition plans the work of the department, organizes the resources needed to do the job, directs the work of the people, coordinates with other departments, and assures higher management that what is supposed to be accomplished will be accomplished. To do these essential tasks, you must first enlist the willing cooperation of the people you supervise.

1-3   How do I know if I really want to be a manager? Why not remain where I am, doing a good job in my specialty?

There are advantages on either side. Some people are much more comfortable performing jobs rather than supervising others. Being happy in what you do is, of course, important. Here are some of the pragmatic advantages of remaining in the rank and file.

- *Overtime pay.*   Most supervisory jobs are exempt from the requirement that work in excess of 40 hours a week be paid at time and one-half. Some companies, however, voluntarily give supervisors additional compensation (not necessarily time and one-half) for overtime work. If you have been making a considerable amount of overtime, you may sacrifice some earnings in taking a promotion.

- *Responsibility for the work of others.*   Once you are promoted to a supervisory position, you are held responsible for the work of the people you supervise. This means that often you will be "on the carpet" for mistakes or misjudgments of your people.

- *More paperwork.* Some people do not like the administrative tasks associated with most supervisory jobs. They are happier doing "hands on" work.
- *Loss of job security.* Most union contracts cover only rank-and-file workers. Once promoted, you must leave the union and lose its protection.

The advantages of accepting a promotion begin with your desire to get ahead. In most companies, the only way to move up the ladder is to take on supervisory responsibilities. The first rung of this ladder is the first-line supervisory job. Here are some other advantages of becoming a supervisor.

- It is clear recognition by the company of your capabilities.
- It usually brings with it an increase in your pay and moves you from the hourly payroll to the salaried payroll, with its many advantages.
- If you are ambitious, it is the beginning of what might lead to additional promotions.
- It gives you the opportunity to learn new skills and to exercise them in your new job.
- It may lead to a new and improved lifestyle based not only on added income but on exposure to new training and contacts and on closer association with men and women at higher levels in your organization.

1-4   How do I stop being a hands-on person? For 20-plus years I did things myself and I am having problems with not being able to stop!

It sure is hard to change any habits after so many years. It may seem impossible, but change starts with your mental attitude. View yourself as a supervisor—not as a performer. Break away from thinking (even if correctly), "By the time I show Lisa how to do it, let her do it, check it and find it's wrong, and then show her again, I could do it myself." Accept the fact that the only way you can succeed in your new job is to get Lisa to do what you can do better. It takes patience on your part and the resolve that you do want to be a supervisor and are willing to break from the past.

1-5   What is the first step I should take to make a successful start as a new supervisor?

Start thinking of yourself as a supervisor instead of as a worker. Up to now you have been measured by how well you did your specialty. From now on you will be measured by how well you keep your department, as a whole, functioning. You will undoubtedly still be required to perform a good deal of the same type of work you had been doing (e.g., bookkeeping), and it is easy to fall into the trap of neglecting your supervisory responsibilities and sticking to what you know best. Your mindset and approach must change from that of worker to supervisor if you are to succeed.

1-6   How can I learn the techniques of supervision?

Study all you can about supervision. Take seminars, read books, listen to tapes. Most of all, speak to experienced supervisors in your company and people who are supervisors in other companies. Don't be afraid to ask them how they handle specific problems. Remember, you are not the first person to be promoted to a supervisory position. Others have faced the same problems you now face, and they are usually happy to share their experiences with you. So dig in and do your research!

1-7   When I start on my new assignment, how should I let the others know that I'm their new boss?

Your promotion should be announced by the person who made the decision to promote you in the first place—your boss. If an announcement has not yet been made, it's a good idea to ask your boss to do so a few days before you take over. Then others will have a chance to get used to the idea.

Some new supervisors start their job by calling a meeting of all the people in the department and saying: "I'm the new manager here and from now on we will be running this department *my* way." Don't. This is not the way to win friends and influence people!

What you should do is to sit down with each of your people over the first few days and talk. Share some of your ideas; elicit some of theirs. Let them know that their cooperation is essential for the success of the department. Show them that you are their team leader and tell them that you expect to work with them to achieve the goals of the company.

1-8   I have just been transferred to supervise another department in my company. What special problems will I face?

When you are transferred to another department or hired from the outside, you face additional problems as a new supervisor. Not only are you a stranger to your people, but they may be resentful. They may be thinking, "Hmm, why somebody from outside? Aren't any of us good enough?" "How does this bode for my future?"

The only person who can bridge the gap is the manager who made the decision. It is that person's responsibility to prepare people for your arrival. He or she might say something like this to ease the transition: "Ever since Tim told us he planned to retire, we have been seeking a new supervisor for this department. Our major concern in making the decision were the plans we have for the department's development. These plans include a big move into computerization. Unfortunately, we have nobody within the company with the background to do this, so we had to go outside for someone. We have hired Michael Kim, who will start on Monday. His background is...and we can all learn much from him. I would appreciate you doing your best to give him your full cooperation."

One helpful hint before you start on the job is to try to look at the personnel files of the people you will supervise. The information you pick up will help you relate to them. For example, one supervisor reported that she took her present job a year and a half ago and did look at the files. She noted that one of the young men in her department had never held a job for more than 2 years, and he had been with her company for 18 months. She thought: "Six months and he'll be gone." So when she sat down with him, she didn't mention that she had read the file but instead probed and found that he was getting restless. She also realized that he was a very talented person. By giving him some special attention and special assignments in his areas of interest, she rekindled his enthusiasm for the job. A year and a half later, he was still there and had become one of her most valuable workers.

Overcoming Resentment

1-9 Some of the people in my department seem to resent me. I didn't do anything to them. Why should they resent me?

There could be many reasons for resentment. One of the most usual is jealousy. A worker might rationalize, "I should have had that job." Or maybe, "One of my friends should have gotten it." The reasons for resentment may not always be clear or rational.

1-10   How can I overcome resentment?

Keep in mind that there are no magic formulas in dealing with people. What works for one may not work for another. One useful approach is to ask people for their advice. Most people like to give advice and are flattered when asked. Often because of their experience, they come up with good ideas. When you seek others' advice, people recognize that you respect them. Mutual respect mitigates resentment.

1-11   Suppose a person's advice is not any good and I have to reject it. Won't that cause even more resentment?

If you solicit advice and then don't take it, you reinforce the resentment. First, reject it privately. Never embarrass a person by turning down his or her suggestions in front of others. Second, do it diplomatically. Instead of telling Carlos that his advice is not good, ask further questions about it. Good questions will enable Carlos to find the weaknesses in his advice and reject it himself without your having to make a negative comment.

1-12   I'm much younger than many of my people.
I'm a woman. Most of my subordinates are men.
I'm a member of a minority group. Most of my people are white.
How can I overcome their resentment?

Whether the issue is age, sex, or race, you are dealing with an emotional problem, not a logical one—and you can't tackle emotion with logic. The key word in handling resentment is *respect*. You must earn the respect of your people and at the same time give them respect.

1-13   What can I do to earn respect?

Here are four ways to earn the respect of your people.

1. *Be good in what you do.*   People respect professionalism. This does not mean that you have to do every job better than your people do it themselves. As a matter of fact, the higher you rise in management, the less likely it is that you will be able to do many of the jobs performed by your subordinates. Rarely can the president of a company operate every piece of equipment or program every computer. Even in the lower echelons, first-

line managers may have to supervise specialists in areas out-side their specialty. But if you perform your job in a profes-sional manner, you will be respected.

2. *Treat your people fairly.*   This is self-explanatory.

3. *Stick up for your people.*   If there's a dispute between your department and another department, and your people are right (but make sure they *are* right), stick up for them even if it is not politically expedient.

4. *Give your people credit.*   One of the most devastating things supervisors can do is to take credit for something one of their people has done and claim it as their own. If you claim false credit, you destroy any relationship you have with that one employee as well as with everybody in the department.

1-14   You said we must also give respect to our people. How can we do that?

1. *Ask for their advice.*   (See question 1-10.)

2. *Listen to them.*   Be an active listener. Active listeners do not only sit or stand with ears open; they let the other person know that they are listening. They ask questions about what has been said; they paraphrase. They show with nonverbal lan-guage that they are listening. They listen empathetically, putting themselves in the other person's shoes. An empathetic listener not only hears what a person is saying but feels what that person is feeling when it is said. When your people realize that you are truly listening, they will know you respect them.

3. *Give them responsibility.*   When you give people assignments which utilize their talents and also give them authority to carry out those tasks, people trust that you respect them.

4. *Be there for your people.*   In survey after survey of what work-ers want from their bosses, this one item always shows up at the top. A boss who is there for people is a boss who cares about people as individuals, one who does not jump on them when they bring up a problem, one who gives them the sup-port—tools and training—they need to do their work.

1-15   I supervise a department where I had been a worker for several years. My people still treat me as a co-worker and do not take my orders and directions seriously. No mat-ter what I say, they continue to ignore my orders and do

things the way they always did them. How can I change this?

It's never easy for newly promoted people to make the transition from worker to supervisor. Though you don't want to appear "bossy," at the same time you must be the leader. Think of yourself as a facilitator, rather than as a boss. When a new project arises, get your people to contribute their ideas on how it should be done. If you seek their input before making your decision, people will recognize that you have respect for them. You are interested in their ideas, not just in imposing yours on them.

If it becomes necessary to make immediate decisions or to give an order on urgent matters, do what you feel must be done. If you meet resistance, explain your reasoning. If some of your people go along only reluctantly, make a special effort to thank them for their cooperation. If others still insist on doing things their way, do not criticize or threaten. ("Do it my way or else!") Instead, suggest that they try your way and give them positive reinforcement when they do. You will build up their self-esteem and reduce their need to defy you.

1-16   I'll soon be taking on a new area where I have limited job knowledge. Is it wise to ask my new subordinates to teach me what they know?

It is not uncommon for workers to have more job knowledge than their supervisors in certain areas. The only way you can learn those skills is from your people. When you start the job, explain that because you come from another area, you are depending on your people to teach you the specifics of the work they do. You may meet resistance: "Why did they give you this job if you don't know the work?" Be prepared to answer diplomatically: "Of course, the company knew I had to learn the specifics of this work. But the experience I bring to the job (administrative, computer, or whatever) together with the specific job skills you offer will make this department even more effective."

1-17   I recently made the upward transition from bedside staff nurse to shift supervisor. But the staff nurses still expect me, the supervisor, to help them with the various bedside tasks. The nurses just don't understand what I do all night. They say things like, "Oh, she forgot what it's like to be a staff nurse." Or "It must be nice to do clipboard work all the time!" This infuriates me, but what can I do?

This situation is not unique to nurses. Your former peers just don't realize that your new duties are time-consuming, and even if you would like to help with patient care, your new responsibilities are important. Don't make a big issue of this. What you can do is describe what some of these new activities are and why they take so much of your time. Point out that the "clipboard work" is designed to make their work easier. You might mention that it is more satisfying to work with patients, but in this complex world of big government and mountains of insurance company paperwork, what you are doing is vital to keep the hospital in business.

Friends As Subordinates

1-18   When I was a rank-and-file worker, I had some special friends in my department. We went to lunch together every day and socialized after work. Now that I am their boss, should I continue this close personal relationship?

In general, it's not a good idea to have close friends among your subordinates. The reason is that you may subconsciously favor your friends, or the friends may take advantage of your friendship. Even if you don't favor them in assigning work or in other ways, it may appear to outsiders that you do. It is best to break off these friendships.

1-19   But they are my friends. How can I break away?

I'm not suggesting that the day you get your promotion you say, "As of this date, we don't see each other any longer." You must do it gradually. Instead of eating lunch with the same people all the time, start eating with others. Gradually move up to the point where you are lunching chiefly with your new peers—the other supervisors with whom you must interrelate. Don't do it too suddenly, however, or you'll look like a snob.

1-20   What do I do when some of my people suggest I go to lunch with them? I can't keep turning them down.

You can still occasionally lunch with your subordinates, but not all the time. When asked, you can decline by mentioning that you must meet with the other supervisors to discuss business matters.

1-21   What about outside of work? In some cases our spouses have become friendly and we are invited to employees' homes.

It's never easy to handle this issue. Of course, you do not want to antagonize your people. You need their cooperation. It may take several months to phase out old friendships, but if you want to be an effective supervisor it eventually must be done. Senior executives who have moved steadily up the career ladder often make this point. They say that breaking off friendships with people who are now their subordinates was one of the most difficult things they had to do. But all agree it was necessary.

1-22   Michelle and I have been friends and co-workers for years. I really don't want to break this off.

Suppose you have to give Michelle an unpleasant assignment, a reprimand, a less than satisfactory performance review. Could you do it? Some people have the strength of personality to be an objective supervisor and still maintain a friendship—but not many. Each of us must make our own decision as to whether we can do it.

1-23   On a more general note, how friendly should a supervisor be with his or her subordinates—totally aloof or buddy-buddy?

Obviously, somewhere in between. But determining where in between is not always easy. It depends on the type of environment in which you work. In professional and technical areas, people work on a collegial basis—they are colleagues. In this case, a closer relationship is permissible Sure, the supervisor has responsibility for the department, but this person is the first among equals. However, in the more typical boss-subordinate situations, relationships must be more distant. People tend to take advantage of supervisors who socialize with them on a regular basis.

1-24   Does that mean that I must never socialize with my people?

Of course, there are times when socializing is fine—a retirement party, a birthday party, a Christmas gathering, or some other special occasion. Socializing is simply not a good idea on a regular basis.

1-25   How do you undo something that has already been established by a previous supervisor? In my case it is too much social familiarity and a too strong buddy-buddy attitude between subordinates and the one in charge. I realize now—possibly when it's too late—that this type of familiarity is detrimental to my authority.

Do it gradually. As a new boss, don't change things too radically too soon. Make the necessary changes over a few months. Follow some of the suggestions made in answer to the previous questions. Over time your people will begin to accept your style of management.

1-26   Before assuming my present position, I was friendly with one of my co-workers. Since my promotion, however, when that person arrives at work each morning he is noticeably angry with me and challenges my judgment throughout the day. How should I handle this situation?

Your "friend" resents your new authority. Perhaps he is jealous, having expected the promotion for himself. Or perhaps he feels that your promotion has ended the friendship and is angry about that.

Speak to your subordinate about this. Point out that he is one of your most valued people and you depend on his cooperation. As noted earlier, it is not a good idea to have close friends among your subordinates, but this doesn't mean you can't be friendly. So chat with him from time to time about the things you chatted about when you were peers. Let him feel that you still like him.

1-27   I've been supervising two people who worked with me before I became a supervisor. One thinks I pick on her, because I tell her that she has made mistakes. She says, "I'm your friend." How can I speak to her in a way that will not hurt our friendship?

Fact number one: Nobody likes to be criticized—even constructively. So the best way to deal with this type of person is to praise her for some of the good things she has done. Then you can add "*and* here are some ideas on how you can do them even better." Note the emphasis on the word *and*. Many supervisors start a criticism with praise, reach the word *but,* and then pour on the negatives. People expect this and wait for the *but*. Then they either stop listening or prepare to rebut the criticism. However, in using *and* instead of *but,* you become more positive.

Special Problems Faced by New Supervisors

1-28   I can't say no without feeling guilty. *What should I do?*

Many people feel this way. The basic reason is probably the desire to be popular. Of course, it's nice to be liked by others, but it is rarely possible to be liked by everybody—all the time! If you allow people to do everything they want, they will walk all over you. So you have to face reality and say no when necessary.

There are many ways to say no diplomatically. For example, your employee asks for time off to handle a personal matter. You have a rush project that must be completed. In this case, you can say: "I know it is important for you to take care of that, but the boss is really pressing to have this project done by tomorrow. It just isn't the right time for any of us to take time off. Once this is completed, we'll work something out."

1-29   Are there any positive or negative effects of sharing an office with several people I directly supervise?

In most organizations, supervisors do work in the same space as their subordinates. There are many advantages to this. For one, you have closer contact with them and they have easy access to you. You can observe them easily and can control situations as they arise. When the boss is right there with his or her people, they are less likely to come in late, take long breaks, or goof off on the job.

The major negative of working in the same facility as your people is lack of privacy. There is nowhere to talk discreetly with a subordinate or meet with people from other departments. If you do not have a private place for such meetings, use a conference room. Otherwise your people will be listening to your conversations instead of working—and if the matters are confidential, the problem could become serious.

Another negative is that when you are too easily available to your people, they interrupt you with constant questions or comments, keeping you from getting your work done. Separate facilities help minimize interruptions.

1-30   The morale in the department I just took over is poor. What is the best way for me to initiate a good motivation and morale program? Is it best to start one on one with individuals, to break off with smaller groups, or to take into consideration the entire department?

Your first step should be to determine why morale is low. If you discover that the problem lies with the actions or attitudes of your predecessor, meet with the entire group. Find out what caused the discontent and promise to study the issues and do your best to resolve them. This will set the stage for a new beginning. If you learn (from discussions with your boss and with some of your people) that the poor morale is a reflection of one or two discontented workers, then one-on-one meetings are more appropriate. Talk with each of these people to determine the cause and possible solutions. More specific suggestions on dealing with morale problems are presented in Chapter 8.

1-31   One of the reasons I was transferred to supervise my department is the lack of productivity under my predecessor. My major function is to increase the amount of work each person is doing. But my people think they are doing as much as they are able to. Apparently, my predecessor reinforced this belief by his lax acceptance of lower production standards. What can I do to get my people to put out more work?

The first step is to make sure that the performance standards expected from your people are reasonable. If the company does expect more than can be attained, perhaps your predecessor was right and you will have to adjust the standards. More likely, however, the standards are reasonable and attainable and the problem lies with your people. Sit down with them and discuss the standards. Ask what they think they can do to increase their productivity so that the standards will be met. Point out that you have confidence in them and that other units of the company (or of competitors) are meeting these standards, so you are sure they can as well.

Tell your people that you agree they are working as hard as they can, but are they working as smart as they can? Brainstorm for ideas on how the work can be simplified, how new approaches might help, how those who are working more effectively than others can share their know-how and teach refinements of the work to those who are less effective. Promise them support and keep that promise by learning all you can about the work and making your own suggestions on how it can be improved.

If there is a financial incentive plan—based either directly on improved productivity or indirectly on profit sharing—let your people know how they can earn more money through improved productivity. But do not try to raise standards too high too fast. Do it incrementally. Give people reachable goals, offer praise when goals are accomplished, and set new goals together.

1-32   How would you handle a situation in which a previous supervisor "talked down" to his people? It seems apparent to me that he himself was the problem. For example, the supervisor told me that his people had a poor attitude. I found out later, however, that the supervisor was the one with the attitude problem.

Let your people know from the start that you have confidence in them. Encourage them to bring any grievances left over from your predecessor to you so you can deal with them. Augment this approach by handling any new problems speedily so your people know you have their interests at heart.

1-33   Being relatively new to the job of supervisor, I looked to my immediate boss as a role model. However, I find the boss's style to be one I don't like. How can I learn to develop a style of management that will be more positive than what I currently see?

If you work in a large organization, seek out other supervisors and study their styles of management. If there is one you particularly admire, ask him or her to be your mentor—your guide and model. Learn from that person how to set your management style.

If there is nobody in your company you wish to emulate, seek out friends or acquaintances who are supervisors in other organizations for advice and guidance. Take courses or seminars; read books on supervision and management. Most important, try different approaches and see what works best for you.

1-34   As an assistant manager recently promoted to manager, and a person who has been brought up through the ranks, I am primarily concerned, not with my subordinates, but with "fitting in" with a new peer management group. I don't necessarily want to be considered as "one of them." My management style—and the way in which I wish to be

perceived—is not necessarily the way my peers (management) think it should be. Is it possible to maintain my unique style and independence, yet still be considered part of the management team?

Anybody who is different in any aspect of life or work is not perceived to be a member of the team. However, this does not mean you have to conform to everything your peers do. I would move very slowly to the type of management style that best fits you. Perhaps as other managers see your success, they will want to emulate what you have done. You can still have a good relationship with them without managing exactly the way they do—provided you do not flaunt your style or derogate theirs.

1-35 When I took my job as supervisor, I had the misfortune of having to replace a "Mr. Nice Guy" (who retired). He was very popular and had stayed with the company for many years. The problem is that when he ran the department, he let employees do whatever they liked. He could never say no, and he practically "gave the shop away" to our customers. He kept very poor records, and no one ever checked them. People always took his word for it. Now everybody wants proof of completed work, and no records seem to be available. I get a lot of the "we never used to do it this way" defense, instead of the type of cooperation I am looking for. What can I do?

The first thing you have to do is to meet with all your people and set the stage for change. Start with tangible matters like improving the records before getting into the less tangible aspects of the problem. Point out that when a person (like your predecessor) has been in a job for a long time, that person can manage a department with minimum records, relying solely on experience and memory. With new management, however, it becomes more important to keep accurate records. Indeed, the company insists on it. Therefore: "Let's set up a records system with which we can all live." Present the type of information the company needs and invite people to suggest how the information can be provided in the most expeditious manner. Set up a system that everyone can manage and follow through to see that it is adhered to.

Once the records have been straightened out, work with each of your people to make the necessary changes in work style to meet the company's demands. Resistance to change is normal, so expect it. People do not want to be compelled to change work habits. Change hurts. If you change the way you do something physically, you use different muscles and it hurts. Making mental changes can cause headaches and psychological disruption. Explain the reasons and need for the changes. But do not change things suddenly. Think evolution—not revolution—and exercise plenty of patience. Only in time do people adjust.

1-36   What is the best way to instill accountability for employees' work so that I (the immediate supervisor) am not always the "fall guy"?

Every person should know what is expected of him or her. A good job description should spell out the performance standards expected in that job. All employees should be thoroughly familiar with these standards and in what manner they will be measured. Performance reviews should be made periodically and should be the basis of the employee evaluation system. Do not restrict evaluation to the annual review. From time to time during the year, hold an informal meeting with each employee and go over how she or he is doing in relation to these standards.

Whenever specific assignments are discussed with employees, the standards to be met must be outlined and timetables for reviewing progress established. In this way, each person can check his or her own work against the standards. When employees know what is expected of them and understand that they are accountable for its accomplishment, they will monitor their progress and make corrections as the need develops.

1-37   I am in a kind of role reversal with my former supervisor. He voluntarily stepped down, although he still works in the department. Meanwhile, my subordinates still look to him for direction and go to him with their problems instead of to me. He likes to influence them and seems to hold no animosity toward me. But how can I get him to stop? My people don't take me seriously.

You can start by having a heart-to-heart talk with him. Keep in mind that he voluntarily took the demotion because he probably did not want the full responsibility of running the department—though he tacitly still runs it, leaving you with the responsibility! Air this dilemma and ask him what he can do to help you gain the respect and support of your employees. Right off the bat he might suggest that he stop what he is doing and ask the employees to refer their questions and their problems to you. If he doesn't suggest this, then you should. As a final recourse—if the heart-to-heart approach does not work—get your boss to intervene. Sometimes the only one who can get through to a demoted employee is the person who was his or her boss before.

1-38   I realize it's important to know the people who work for me as total people. How do I learn who my people really are?

In order to deal effectively with people, you need to learn as much about them as possible. Find out what is important to them: their families, interests, hobbies, and so on. The more you know about them, the easier it will be to determine how to deal with them on the job. It is not enough just to know how well a person performs on the job; you must also learn as much as you can about the *whole* person.

In most departments, there are times when things slow down. Use that time to converse with your people. Learn about the things they are involved in. Be discreet—some people are very sensitive about their privacy. A seemingly innocuous question can cause them to blow up. You may ask "Hey, do you have any kids?" and get this response: "None of your damn business." Wait a few days after somebody starts work and just keep your ears open. Quite often you can learn a lot about a person by listening. After a while you'll find out just how far you can probe.

Listen when your people speak to you. Listen to what they say. Listen to what they don't say. Listen when they speak to other people. Eavesdropping may not be polite, but you learn a lot!

Observe the way they do their work, the way they act and react. Learn their MOs (modis operandi)—the manner in which they operate in their lives. Psychologists call this their patterns of behavior.

Find out their goals and aspirations. It is important to know what each of them wants from the job—immediately, and in the future. Of course, some people do not have any goals—all they want is to have a job and not get fired. But even knowing that will help you deal with them.

If you have more than a few subordinates, it may be difficult to remember everyone's characteristics and interests. It is good to keep a file for each of your people. A prototype form is presented in Figure 1-1.

Know Your People Worksheet

Name _____

Position _____

Date employed _____

Spouse's name _____

    Child's name _____   Age _____

    _____   _____

    _____

Hobbies _____

_____

_____

Interests _____

_____

_____

Schools/college, etc. _____

_____

_____

Other pertinent information _____

_____

_____

Patterns of behavior _____

_____

_____

Figure 1-1

1-39   Can't knowing certain things about people work against them? One of my people is taking a computer course. We don't use computers in my department. Because I learned this, I feel that the man is not interested in what we are doing and I have developed negative feelings toward him.

Even though learning about computers won't help in your department, it shows that the employee is ambitious and has· other interests. A few questions might bring out whether he is taking the course for personal reasons, such as using his home computer more effectively, or whether he plans to study other business-oriented subjects. This knowledge could be of value to you in motivating the employee, particularly if your department may become computerized in the future. Is the employee planning to change jobs once he masters the computer? Although computer skills may not help you, they are probably valuable to the company. You could arrange for an in-company transfer when the employee has completed the training rather than lose him to another company.

1-40   My company has developed long-term and intermediate-term plans to meet its objectives. As a supervisor, I am responsible for developing short-term plans for my department. What suggestions do you have to help make planning more effective?

Your first step is to understand the long-term and intermediate-term plans so that what you develop will be congruent with them. Discuss them with your boss. Then study the project. If you or any others have had to plan for similar projects in the past, perhaps the plan used before will be appropriate and it will not be necessary to design a new one. If the current situation is not exactly the same, study any aspects of the former plan that can be used. Use the talents of your people and other resources to help design a new plan. An open mind for suggestions and ideas will help make your plan more successful.

Once all the suggestions are studied, evaluated, and synthesized, put a draft of the plan (old one or new one) in writing. Review it with your boss and with the people who will implement it. Set a timetable that is realistic and attainable. Set control points at which you will be able to check how close you are adhering to the plan and make sure that everybody knows what must be done and when.

1-41   How many subordinates can a manager manage effectively?

Too wide or too narrow a span of responsibility can weaken the management structure. To set an appropriate span, review the following questions.

1. How much time will you be devoting to supervision? Most supervisors still do a great deal of technical, specialized, or administrative work. Supervisors whose job is primarily directing the work of the department can supervise more people than those who spend a great deal of time in other activities.

2. How complex are the problems you will be handling? If they are of a highly technical nature or involve a great deal of administrative work, it is better to have fewer people reporting to you. Because higher-level managers generally need more time for policymaking, they cannot devote much time to directing the work of others. Lower-level supervisors whose job is primarily to supervise can handle more people.

3. Are the problems and activities you will be managing repetitive or unusual? Managers who work chiefly with repetitive situations can supervise more people than those who handle more varied types of activities.

4. How well trained and capable are your subordinates? A manager with a highly competent team can control more people than one who must spend a great deal of time training and checking workers.

5. Over how wide an area are your subordinates spread? If people are spread over too wide an area, it is difficult to supervise them. Whenever possible, supervisors should be close to the people they direct.

6. What kind of staff assistance is provided? If subordinates can seek aid from staff personnel on technical matters rather than go to their immediate supervisor, the line supervisor is freed to handle more people.

1-42   Our company does not have supervisors and subordinates. It has team leaders and associates. I have just been named team leader. How does this differ from being a supervisor?

The use of teams has been growing in American industry. What this means exactly depends a lot, however, on the company. In some companies it is just a change in titles and the team leader's role is not very different from that of any other traditional supervisor who makes decisions and gives orders. However, if the team concept is truly utilized, there are significant differences. The main one is that the team leader acts as a facilitator. Decisions are made through group participation and plans of action are decided on by the team. Furthermore, team leaders are coaches who work with their people—guiding, motivating, teaching, and supporting them. (See the section on building teams in Chapter 8.)

1-43   I have just been hired as a regional supervisor for a retail chain. The individual stores are scattered over three states. I visit each store at least twice a month—more if problems develop. How can I get to know my people—the store managers and their staffs—when I have so few opportunities to observe them and speak to them?

Managers who supervise people in areas remote from their home base find supervision to be very challenging. Here are the suggestions of some veterans in the field:

- Before you make your first visit to a local outlet, study the personnel files of the manager and assistant manager. Get an idea of their backgrounds and of how they have been viewed by your predecessors. Talk to people in the organization who have worked with them in the past and learn as much as you can about these key people. One word of caution: Some people may be biased for or against certain managers. If their comments reflect too high or low an opinion, reserve your own judgment until you find out for yourself.

- At your first visit to the store, give yourself enough time to chat with the manager and the assistant manager and let them do most of the talking. Don't dominate the conversation or spend much time touting your own high qualifications (for your new job). Listen attentively to them and remember what you learn. Immediately after leaving the store, make notes or dictate your comments into a recorder so you will not forget any key points.

- Write a brief note to the people you spoke to, thanking them for their time and letting them know that you are there to help.

- Do not make any major changes until you have had the opportunity to study the current situation thoroughly. Radical changes made too soon can cause unrest and erode future good relationships with your people.

1-44   When my boss hired me, he told me that I had to get the department into decent shape within 6 months.

However, immediately after I started, I recognized that this would involve radical surgery. How can I complete the process without instigating a revolt in the ranks?

First, be sure you know what has to be done. Get as much input as possible—from your boss, from the people you deal with in the organization, and from the employees themselves—on what must be changed. Let your people know the importance of making changes fast, so that company goals can be met. Point out how it is to their benefit to go along with your plans.

1-45   My predecessor was fired because she couldn't keep the department within its budget. The only way to cut costs, however, is to reduce staff. Since I must do this during my first month on the job, how can I maintain morale and not be looked upon from the beginning as a "hatchet man"?

When a couple of people are laid off, everybody in a department becomes concerned. It is only natural to wonder, "Is it my turn next?" To avoid this kind of confusion and unnecessary paranoia, once the decision is made as to who will be cut, bring all your people together and explain the need for the layoffs. Point out that the process started long before you came on board and that, as their supervisor, you can work together with them to bring the department up to budget—so further layoffs need not happen in the foreseeable future.

2

Selecting the Right People

In companies that have a human resources department, personnel specialists will locate and screen applicants for employment. In smaller companies or in branches of larger companies that have no such department, the supervisor must locate, screen, and hire applicants for positions in his or her department. Usually, even when the specialist completes the initial screening, the supervisor will interview and either make or participate in making the hiring decision.

Many supervisors are uneasy about this function, since they have received little or no training in hiring. In this chapter, we will tackle some of the most frequent problems supervisors face in interviewing applicants and selecting personnel. A good number of these problems relate to complying with the various laws on equal employment—a topic covered in Chapter 3.

Job Specifications

2-1   How can I determine what the requirements are for the jobs I have to fill?

The first step is to make a good job analysis. This consists of two parts: the *job description*—a detailed summary of duties, responsibilities, and other job factors; and the *job specification*—a description of the skills and aptitudes needed to perform the job (education, previous training and experience, and physical, mental and psychological factors). Both are needed in order to ensure that you select the right person for each job opening.

Writing a job description requires a thorough knowledge of the job—either from your own experience or from careful observation of the work and discussions with the people performing it. A guideline to what to look for and what questions to ask is provided in Figure 2-1.

To identify the skills and abilities of qualified candidates, review the backgrounds of current employees and determine what factors in their backgrounds are essential to success on the job.

2-2   Many of the jobs I hire for are entry-level positions, and we need people who not only can do the current job but are qualified for promotion. Should this factor into my job specification?

Sometimes this is an important consideration. Suppose that a high school diploma is sufficient for the entry-level job but college is needed for promotion. It appears to be sensible to require some college for the entry job. However, in doing so you may eliminate some excellent candidates, people who could acquire the added education while employed in the lower job. It is best to determine educational specifications on what is actually needed for the job at hand.

2-3   More important than education or experience are intangible factors like integrity, initiative, work ethic, and ability to work with others. How can they be incorporated into a job specification?

It is difficult to define these intangibles when writing a job specification. You can (and should) incorporate them in the job spec, but determining them in an applicant is not easy (see questions 2-25 to 2-28).

Sources of Personnel

2-4   My company does not have a personnel department. I'm the office manager and have to hire all clerical personnel. What sources should I use to locate high-quality applicants?

Job Description Worksheet

Job Title_____

Reports to _____ Dept. _____

Duties performed _____

_____

_____

_____

_____

Tools used _____

Skills used_____

_____

Responsibility for people _____

_____

Responsibility for equipment _____

_____

Responsibility for money _____

_____

Other aspects of job _____

_____

Special working conditions _____

_____

Comments_____

_____

Number of people performing job_____

Analysis made by_____ Date_____

Figure 2-1

If you are willing to train employees who have little experience, your best source is your local high school. Many high schools give courses in office skills, including typing, word processing, basic computer operations, and office practices. Community colleges and special business schools also are sources. Seek out schools which have internship programs in which students spend part of their time working in offices. These students bring some experience as well as school-learned skills to the job.

If you need experienced people, your best source may be public or private employment agencies. Public employment agencies do not charge fees, as do private agencies. (see question 2-5). You might also place ads in the help-wanted columns of your local paper (see question 2-9).

2-5 Most private employment agencies require the employer to pay a substantial fee if one of their referrals is hired. Is this a sound investment?

Employer-paid fees to agencies may range from 10 to 20 percent of the annual salary of an office employee (even more for technical and management jobs). Agencies are expensive. However, what are you getting for their fee? Most agencies have files of applicants who are immediately available and can match them against your job specs, enabling you to fill the job quickly. Since agencies screen applicants before referring them, you will see only qualified candidates and avoid the wasted time of interviewing countless unqualified people. Once you have established a relationship with one or two agencies, you will have a ready source of personnel when needed.

2-6 State employment services don't charge any fees. Wouldn't it be better to use them?

All states have an employment or job service which can recommend applicants. You certainly should list your jobs with the local office of this agency. State services also often provide testing and other screening facilities. Some companies have developed excellent relations with these agencies. Other firms have not been happy because state placement services are concerned primarily with placing unemployed people. They feel that the better applicants may be currently employed and not registered with these agencies.

2-7   Are school-affiliated employment services a good source of applicants?

High school, college, technical, and specialized school employment services are excellent sources for recruiting people with little or no experience. Most do not charge a fee and are anxious to place their graduates. (Schools that prepare students for jobs in which trained people are in short supply may charge a fee.) Also, some schools keep files of alumni who do have work experience.

2-8   The people I hire are highly specialized and very difficult to locate. Any ideas on how I can find qualified people for these hard-to-fill jobs?

Your first move is to tap the resources you have on hand—your current staff. Most people in technical and other specialized work have friends and acquaintances in their own field. They belong to professional associations, keep up with classmates, and attend conventions. Ask them for referrals. Some companies have formal programs that offer rewards for referrals which result in a hire.

Another approach is to contact the placement committees of appropriate professional associations. Place ads in professional journals. Also, contact employment agencies which specialize in your type of work. You can identify these agencies by studying the ads that they place in general and professional journals. If you note that certain ads cover a variety of jobs in your area of interest, contact the agencies even if they do not have a specific listing in which you are interested. They may know people who fit your needs.

2-9   What can I do to make my help-wanted ads more effective?

Newspapers and many professional journals publish help-wanted advertisements for companies seeking employees. Typically these ads appear in a classified section, in which all jobs are listed (usually alphabetically by title) in one part of the paper. Some papers also publish larger display ads, which may appear anywhere in the paper: the help wanted section, the financial section, or even the sports or news section.

If you have a hard-to-fill job, it probably is best to use a display ad. Ask an agency to design the ad for you. Most ad agencies will not charge a fee unless a good deal of artwork is involved. They earn their money from commissions from the publication. The advantages of display ads are that you can use a variety of typefaces, diagrams, boxes, logos or other artwork. The disadvantages are that display ads are much more expensive than classified ads and are not grouped by type of job. Thus the reader seeking a specific type of work has to read through all the display ads to find yours. It must be attractively designed to catch the eye of the reader.

Classified ads allow very little opportunity for differentiation. All ads are generally in the same typeface. No artwork is usually permitted. You can design the ad yourself. Fees are based on the amount of space utilized. Each line of white space (i.e., where no printing is used) is charged as if it were printed, but white space sets your ad apart from others. The major advantage of a classified ad is that it will be placed by job category so a person seeking a certain type of work will know where to locate the ad.

2-10   What should I say in the ad to attract qualified applicants?

In writing copy for your ad, be sure to list only the key requirements. Remember that the more requirements you place in the ad, the fewer responses you will receive. For example: the job calls for a degree in accounting; an MBA is desirable. Just list the accounting degree in the ad. Although the MBA is *desirable,* many good accountants who do not have that degree may not answer the ad. It is better to view the MBA factor as an extra during the interview rather than miss seeing the best candidate for the job who happens to lack that "desirable," but not essential qualification.

Be sure to state some of the advantages of the job, not just the requirements. In determining which of several positions to respond to, job seekers will pick the ones which offer the most opportunities.

Ads may include the name of the company or may be listed blind—that is, using a box number. The advantage of including your name is that it might attract people who know your company's reputation. In addition, currently employed people are often reluctant to answer a blind ad for fear it may be from their own company or one affiliated with it. The disadvantage is that you may be bothered with phone calls from unqualified people trying to sell themselves.

Here is an example of a good classified ad:

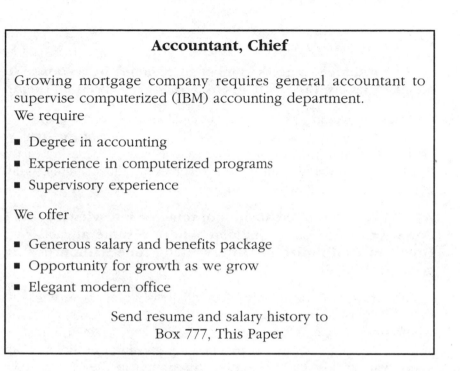

Accountant, Chief

Growing mortgage company requires general accountant to supervise computerized (IBM) accounting department.
We require

- Degree in accounting
- Experience in computerized programs
- Supervisory experience

We offer

- Generous salary and benefits package
- Opportunity for growth as we grow
- Elegant modern office

Send resume and salary history to
Box 777, This Paper

2-11   Should I specify salary in a help-wanted ad?

The advantage of including salary is that you eliminate having to read the résumés of people who want much more (or less) than you are willing to pay. However, many people are flexible on salary and so are many companies. By asking applicants for a salary history, you can get a good idea of whether they are in line with what you are willing to pay.

2-12   Our company benefits are not at all competitive. How can we attract good people?

Although most companies provide health insurance and other basic coverage, benefits packages vary considerably. If your company does not offer as many benefits as others seeking the same type of personnel, you will have to show how the advantages of working for you make up for it. For example, your company has a history of rapid promotion for its people, or you give employees opportunity to work on projects in which they are particularly interested. Many excellent workers are more interested in the work they will do than in the benefits.

Screening Applicants

2-13   I often get a good number of résumés in response to an ad. What are the key items to look for in screening them?

Start by making a list of the principal requirements for the job. If the job calls for a specific type of education and/or experience, list that first, followed by any other salient factors, including salary range. Then quickly scan all the résumés for these items. Only those which survive the screening will have to be read in detail.

2-14   I have a limited amount of time for interviewing, yet I don't want to miss a candidate whose résumé attracts me. How can I minimize my interviewing time without losing good people?

Careful screening of résumés will help target those who are most likely to fit your job. However, since résumés do not tell the whole story, it is helpful to prescreen candidates by telephone.

Before calling an applicant, prepare specific questions about items that are not clear or extensive enough in the résumé. List them on a paper with room to write the responses. For example, suppose the résumé reads: "Improved productivity by 30 percent." Ask: "What did you do to accomplish this?" Then tell the applicant a little about the job (not too much detail at this point). If you are both interested in pursuing it, invite the applicant to come for an interview.

2-15   Most of my applicants have résumés. Is it necessary for them to fill out a company application form?

Yes. Résumés are designed to sell the applicant to you. Most will not have all the information you want. For example, many résumés do not list every employer—only those a candidate wants you to know about—and do not give specific dates of employment, salary history, and other information you may need. The application form enables you to compare all candidates on the same basis. Even if a résumé is satisfactory, ask the applicant to complete your form.

Many companies make the application form part of their permanent personnel file, which may also include authorizations for reference checks and other legal matters.

2-16   As a small firm, we don't hire many people and we don't have a formal application form. What information should we have on this form?

The application form should include only basic information about education, experience, and skills. Because of equal employment and other laws, many of the questions that have previously been routinely asked (such as age and marital status) may not be appropriate. (More on this in Chapter 3). A good basic application form is presented in Figure 2-2. If you hire specialized personnel such as technical, professional, or salespeople, special forms should be designed for them.

2-17   In interviewing applicants, what types of questions should I ask to get the most valuable information?

Questions should be based on job requirements, so reread the job specifications and job description before planning the interview. Your objective is to get a thorough perspective on the applicant's background. Some of this information can be obtained from the application form and résumé, so use them as guides.

Structure the interview so that you will not forget to ask important questions. There are five major areas of inquiry.

Education: Does the applicant have the requisite educational requirements? What about additional education which may be of value in this job?

Experience: What is the type and length of the applicant's experience?

Accomplishments: What has the applicant done that makes him or her more than just an average worker?

Skills: Can the applicant perform any special tasks (e.g., computers, machinery, crafts, office skills, health-care skills)?

Personal characteristics: Does the personality of the applicant fit the job?

2-18   How important is it to discuss education in the interview when people have been out of school for many years?

The longer a person is out of school, the less important high school and college education is. To discuss extracurricular activities and grades when a person has 20 years' experience is not appropriate. Ask questions about what courses, seminars, or other activities the applicant has engaged in to keep up with the state of the art in the field.

For recent graduates and people who have limited experience, ask questions about school, part-time work while in school, and extracurricular activities to gain some insight into the person's abilities and potential.

2-19　I never know how to get started when interviewing an applicant. Do I just barge in with questions?

People who are applying for a job may be nervous. An interview is not a routine experience, and they may be very anxious to get the job. You first have to put the applicant at ease. This is known as developing rapport.

A nice way to start is to go out and greet the applicant in the reception area rather than have him or her brought into your office by a secretary or receptionist. A greeting makes the person feel welcome. Open the conversation with a noncontroversial question, such as "Did you have trouble finding our building?" If the person was referred by a friend or business associate, talk a bit about that person.

The résumé or application offers a good source of information for conversational questions. For example, "I notice you went to Downtown Tech. Did you know Professor Kingston in the math department?" Or "I see you live in Chelsea. Have you ever eaten at Su Lee's Kitchen?"

2-20　Some of the applicants I interview are very nervous. Even when I do take time to develop rapport, they are not at ease. They may be good at their work, but if I can't get through to them how can I find out?

One way to overcome nervousness is to mention a shared experience. Do you and the candidate have the same hobbies, education, or professional associations? Referring to past successes noted in the résumé either in previous jobs or outside the work field—also helps.

Avoid beginning an interview with a challenge: "What makes you think you can handle this job?" You will put the applicant on the defensive and cut off the flow of information.

2-21　Any suggestions on getting really into depth about the applicant's background?

Refer to the job description and plan in advance. Write down specific questions on each aspect of the job and make them the basis of your interview. Use an open-ended format. Avoid ques-

Application for Employment

Date _____

Name _____ Soc. Sec. No. _____

Address _____

City/State/Zip _____ Phone _____

Position Sought _____ Salary Desired _____

Education

Level	School/ Location	Course	No. of Yrs.	Degree/ Diploma
High school				
College				
Other				

Employment Record

1. Company/Address   Dates   Salary   Supervisor
_____

_____

Duties _____

_____

Reason for leaving _____

_____

2. Company/Address   Dates   Salary   Supervisor

Duties _____

_____

_____

Reason for leaving _____

_____

Figure 2-2

(Continued)

Figure 2-2 (Continued)

3. Company/Address	Dates	Salary	Supervisor

Duties _____

_____

Reason for leaving _____

How were you referred to this company? _____

Are you 18 years of age or older? _____

If hired, can you provide written evidence that you are authorized to work in the United States? _____

Is there any other name under which you worked that we would need to check your work record? _____

APPLICANT'S STATEMENT

I understand that nothing in this application is intended to create or imply a contractual relationship: if hired, I understand that my employment is at will—i.e., not for any specific time period or duration—and can be terminated at any time, or for any reason consistent with applicable federal and state laws. This employment-at-will policy cannot be changed verbally or in writing unless specifically authorized by the president or executive vice president of this company. I understand that this application is not a contract of employment. I understand that the federal government prohibits the employment of unauthorized aliens; all persons hired must provide satisfactory proof of employment authorization and identity. Failure to submit such proof will result in denial of employment.

I understand that the employer may investigate my work and personal history and verify all information given on this application, on related papers and in interviews. I hereby authorize all individuals, schools, and firms named therein, except my current employer (if so noted), to provide any information requested about me and hereby release them from all liability for damage in providing this information.

Figure 2-2 (Continued)

> I certify that all the statements in this form and other infor-
> mation provided by me in applying for this position are true
> and understand that any falsification or willful omission shall
> be sufficient cause for dismissal or refusal of employment.
>
> Signed _____

tions that can be answered yes or no. Instead of asking, "Have you
prepared financial statements?" say, "Tell me about the work you
have done in preparing financial statements." Then probe for
details. Don't be satisfied with vague responses, such as "I put out
weekly and monthly statements." Ask for details: "What was included?" "What information did you have to develop?" "How did you
do this?" "What computer programs did you use in your analysis?"

Do not limit your interview to the questions on your list.
Listen carefully to the answers and ask follow-up questions to
obtain as much information as you need about a given point.

2-22   I see many applicants who meet the job requirements. How can I tell which candidate is best qualified?

Ask about personal accomplishments. Many people have
years of experience in a type of work, but may not be as good as
others with less experience. They have worked on the job, but
have been only average workers. Accomplishers have made suggestions that improved quality or quantity; they have exceeded
quotas by significant amounts; they have sold more product, initiated programs, created concepts. Ask: "What do you consider to
be your most significant accomplishment?" Then probe to determine how significant it was.

If the applicant answers, "I introduced a system that cut costs
by 10 percent," follow up with specifics: "Describe the original system" "What changes did you make in it?" "What problems did you
have putting those changes into effect?" "How did you solve them?"
"What were the results?" "How did you measure the savings?"

2-23   Learning about specific skills is easy. I need bright people. Other than giving intelligence tests, how can I tell if a person is bright?

Intelligence is a nebulous term. There are all kinds of intelligence. If the job calls for somebody who can think fast under

pressure, ask a series of tough questions and observe how rapidly the candidate responds. If the job calls for deliberative, analytical thinking, quick answers to complex questions are a bad sign. Problem-solving intelligence is best determined by posing questions that test an applicant's logic.

For recent graduates, grades attained in school give some indication of a conceptual intelligence. If grades were poor, probe for extenuating circumstances.

2-24 All our jobs require a good deal of physical energy. Any suggestions on determining this?

Observe the way the applicant moves when walking into your office. Active people move rapidly and forcefully. Those with little energy move more slowly. Ask about their health-building regimens. Energetic people engage in swimming, tennis, jogging, or some other regular exercise program.

2-25 What questions can I ask to determine the maturity of a candidate?

Ask: "What goals have you set for yourself?" Seek out both career and personal goals. Mature people usually have realistic goals for themselves and their families.

Ask: "What is the most important decision you've had to make in the past 5 years?" Ask for details as to why it was important, how it was made, and how it affected the candidate's life.

Ask: "If you were to start your career again, what changes would you make?" Look for a realistic response. If the answer is "I'd be a rock star," you might be concerned about maturity. The response should also show attitude toward work. If the candidate indicates a real interest in areas other than the one applied for, he or she may be wrong for the job.

2-26 In our company, we have to be prepared to face the unexpected. How can I determine a candidate's resourcefulness?

Ask: "How did you solve some of the more difficult problems you faced on your current (last) job?"

Ask: "What are some of your major failures and how did you handle them?"

Ask: "How did you change the scope of your job?

From the answers to these questions, you can determine whether the applicant has the ability to deal with difficult situations, make changes when needed, and roll with the punches.

2-27   How can I tell in an interview whether an applicant has a leadership style that is congruent with ours?

Leadership styles vary from autocratic ("I'm the boss; do as you are told") to permissive ("Let's discuss this and determine what to do").

Ask: "When you got a rush job, how did you get your people to meet the deadline?" Follow up by asking how the people reacted and what resulted.

Ask: "How much turnover did you have in your department?" Good leadership results in lower turnover.

If the candidate has had no previous supervisory experience, ask about leadership roles in school, the community, and other nonbusiness areas.

2-28   Leadership is important for some jobs, but I want people who can follow directions. How can I screen candidates for "followership"?

How a person works under supervision is an essential ingredient of most jobs. If the candidate has worked for several supervisors in past positions, say: "Of all the supervisors you worked for, describe the supervisory methods of the one you enjoyed working for most; least." If the candidate has had only one supervisor, ask about that person's supervisory methods and how the applicant related to them.

If the answers to these questions show that the candidate's preferred style of followership is congruent with yours, he or she may be a good match. If the answers point in another direction, you may have difficulty supervising that person.

2-29   I tend to talk about half the time when I interview. I know that's too long. Any guidelines as to how much I should be talking?

If you talk more than 50 percent of the time, you are monopolizing the interview. Even if the figure is 25 percent, you are talking too much. Your job is to listen and evaluate. The only talking you should do is to establish rapport, ask questions, probe deeper, and keep the applicant talking. At various times during the interviewing process you will need to describe the job, but keep the description brief (see questions 2-38 and 2-39).

2-30   Every job is different and the questions an interviewer asks obviously must relate to the job. Are there any "generic" types of questions that can be used?

One effective way of obtaining the information you need, and of keeping the applicant talking is to use the *w* words: *what, when, where, who,* and *why.* With the addition of *how,* you can draw out most of the information you need about your applicant's background. For example:

- What skills were needed?
- When did you do this kind of work?
- Where was this applicable?
- Why did you reach that conclusion?
- How did you solve that problem?

2-31   Often when I interview applicants, I get a rehash of what I read in the résumé. How can I elicit more detailed answers?

Use the résumé as the nucleus for structuring the interview. Take each point that you want to expand and ask specific questions about it. For example, the résumé reads: "Developed new system for handling faxes." Ask for details as to why the system was needed, what was done, and what resulted. Get specifics as to time and/or money saved and any other benefits to the company. Many "accomplishments" listed in a résumé are actually the result of a team effort. Ask the applicant to discuss exactly what his or her part was in that activity.

2-32   Many of my applicants do not have résumés. Our application form provides little space for details of work experience. What are some good questions to ask to get the applicant talking about his or her work?

Use an open-ended format. For example:

- Please describe your present responsibilities and duties.
- How do you spend an average day?

- How did you change the content of your job from when you assumed it until now?
- Discuss some of the problems you encountered on the job.

2-33   Discussion of work experience is a major component of an interview. But how can I find out what applicants think about the job for which they are applying?

Ask questions like these:

- How do you view the job for which you are applying?
- What in your background particularly qualifies you to do this job?
- If you were to obtain the job, in what areas could you contribute immediately? Where would you need additional training?
- In what ways have your education and training prepared you for this job?

Follow up on all answers with probing questions to obtain more details.

2-34   Applicants always stress their strengths. How can I probe for their weaknesses?

Ask questions about sensitive areas in the jobs they held that are likely to have caused problems. Find out how the problems were handled. For example:

- What aspects of your previous jobs gave you the most trouble?
- What are some of the disappointments you have had in your jobs?
- In what areas did you need help or guidance from your boss?
- For what things have your superiors complimented you? Criticized you?
- What did you like most about your past jobs? Least?

Note that the last two questions ask first about positive factors, then lead into the negatives. From the answers to the negatives you can identify weak points which may be pertinent to the candidate's ability to do the job.

2-35   It takes us a long time to train our people and make them productive. We must avoid hiring people who are unlikely to stay for a reasonable time. How can we find out if they are stable?

Usually, a record of job hopping is an indicator of instability. However, some people with such records have just had bad luck. Ask about the reasons for leaving each job and determine if they were signs of instability or reasonable decisions.

If candidates are employed, ask why they want to leave at this time. People who seek to leave their jobs after a short period may get bored easily and may become bored with your job as well. People who cite "lack of opportunity for advancement" as a reason for leaving may want advancement more rapidly than your company can offer.

Ask about career goals. If your work cannot help people meet their career goals, it is likely that they will not stay with you for too long.

2-36   An old-timer told me that the best way to interview is to say "Tell me about yourself" and let the applicant ramble on. I tried it, but it took forever and although I got some good information, I had to listen to a lot of irrelevant things. Is there a better way?

"Tell me about yourself" is an inefficient way to open an interview. However, it is not always possible to get all the information you want by direct questioning. You may not know the right questions to ask. A variation of "Tell me about yourself" is nondirective interviewing. Use an open-ended approach: "Tell me how you prepared for new projects." The applicant will then tell you whatever he or she feels is important in this area. You should make no comments during the response other than an occasional noncommittal reaction ("yes," "uh-huh," "mmmm"). In this way, you encourage the applicant to keep talking without giving any hint as to what you are seeking. The applicant may bring up problems, personality factors, attitudes, or weaknesses that would not have been uncovered directly. You may also discover some positive factors or strengths that were missed in direct questioning.

Nondirective questioning is time-consuming, so you should not use it extensively in an interview. Instead, interlace it with direct questions when they are appropriate.

2-37   Sometimes I feel that an applicant is holding something back in answer to a question. How can I dig it out?

Silence. It is difficult for most people to tolerate silence. If you do not respond instantly, the applicant may keep talking. Try this: After listening to the applicant's response to your question, count to 5 slowly (to yourself, of course) before asking the next question. If you wait 5 seconds, you will be surprised at how often an applicant adds something—positive or negative—to a response.

Giving Information

2-38   I know it is important to tell the applicant about the company and the job. When is the best time to do so?

Some interviewers start the interview by describing the job duties. Some give the applicant a copy of the job description in advance of the interview. This is a serious error. If the applicant knows too much about the job too soon, he or she is likely to tailor the answers to your questions to fit the job. For example, you tell a prospect that the job calls for selling to department store chains. Then you ask: "What types of markets have you called on?" Even if the applicant has only limited experience in this area, guess which market she or he will emphasize?

The best way to give information about duties and responsibilities is to feed it to the applicant throughout the interview *after you have ascertained the applicant's background in that phase of the work.* For example

INTERVIEWER: What types of markets did you call on?

APPLICANT: Drug chains, discount stores, department stores, and mail-order houses.

Then ask specific questions about the candidate's experience in each of these markets. If the department store background is satisfactory, say: "I am glad you have such a fine background in dealing with department store chains, because they represent about 40 percent of our customer list. If you should be hired, you would be working closely with those stores." If the applicant's department store background is weak, you might say: "Since a great deal of our business is with department store chains, if you should be hired we would give you added training in this area."

By the end of the interview, you should have a fairly complete knowledge of the applicant's background and the applicant should have a good idea of the nature of the job.

2-39   Should I encourage applicants to ask questions about the job and the company?

To save time, it is a good idea to give the applicant a brochure or other printed matter describing the company's history, type of business, and other background. Some companies provide written information on benefits as well. Others discuss benefits only at subsequent interviews—with applicants who are seriously being considered for the job.

Encourage the applicant to raise questions related to the job itself—usually at the end of the interview. In addition to satisfying the applicant's concerns, the questions will give you some insight into her or his personality and help you in your evaluation.

Pay close attention to the nature of the questions. Are they primarily about personal issues (vacations, time off, raises) or are they about the job? People who focus on personal issues are less likely to be as highly motivated as job-oriented applicants. The questions can also give you clues on an applicant's real interest in the job. If the questions suggest that a good candidate is not too enthusiastic about the job, you will have another chance to "sell" him or her.

2-40   Should I try to sell a person on a job? Isn't it better to hire someone who really wants it?

In many situations, good candidates are scarce and may have offers from other firms. You do have to persuade such candidates that your job is the one they should take. Even if you are not sure that you want to hire a person, you should be selling your company. It is important that you present your company and the job in a positive and enthusiastic manner. This does not mean that you should exaggerate or mislead the applicant. Try to determine what the applicant wants from a job and show how what you offer will help him or her achieve it. Even if you do not hire the person, he or she will leave with a positive feeling. That person may someday be a customer or in some other way be important to the company. The image developed at the interview will influence a prospect in any future contact with your organization.

2-41   If there are negative aspects of the job, should I tell them to an applicant?

Every job has its negative aspects and if you hide them, the applicant will find out sooner or later. This could lead to rejection of your offer or, worse, acceptance and early resignation.

Tell the applicant the negatives at the interview, but show how the positives outweigh the negatives: "Our company does require its technicians to put in a great deal of overtime because we are working on very urgent matters. However, not only can you earn more money, but I'm sure you will get as much satisfaction as we do from the challenges of the work."

Problem Applicants

2-42   What do I do if someone just won't stop talking? I ask a question and the applicant goes on and on.

Unfortunately, there are many loquacious people who want to tell you much more than you want to hear. You ask what time it is and they describe in detail how to make a clock. If such an interview is to be brought to a successful conclusion before nightfall, you must assume control. The best approach is to interrupt the candidate frequently with questions on specific points. Use close-ended questions. When the applicant pauses for breath, ask a very specific question which must be answered in one or a few words: "Which Macintosh model did you use?" Follow up with a series of similar questions.

2-43   Some applicants know all the right words. They talk a great game, but how can I tell if they can really do the job?

True. Often people with superficial knowledge of a job can impress an interviewer by using the nomenclature of the field. To determine if the candidate is as good as he or she sounds, ask more probing questions. Press for details on how specific aspects of the work was accomplished; ask for verifiable numbers such as costs, productivity figures, and profits. Describe some common problem scenarios and ask what the applicant did specifically to cope with those problems in the past. Glib applicants probably have not had to deal with such specifics and will flounder in their response.

2-44   Recently I interviewed a candidate who tried to bowl me over with his "salesmanship." He started by saying, "I'm the man for this job," and went on to toot his own horn. When I tried to get details, he just bragged about his "accomplishments" in a vague way. I got rid of him as fast as I could. Was I right?

Yes. Most braggarts have little real background.

2-45   How do I handle people who evade my questions and turn them around to fit their backgrounds?

I know what you mean. Here is a typical example.

INTERVIEWER: For what type of purchases did you have authority for final decisions?

APPLICANT: I know a great deal about valves.

INTERVIEWER: Did you buy the valves for your firm?

APPLICANT: I recommended which lines to buy.

INTERVIEWER: Who actually negotiated the deal?

APPLICANT: My boss.

By probing, the interviewer learned that the applicant had not actually negotiated purchases.

A similar situation arises when applicants tell you only what they want you to hear and evade the important questions.

INTERVIEWER: Tell me about your supervisory experience.

APPLICANT: I'm a top producer and always led my department.

INTERVIEWER: That's an enviable record. How many people reported to you?

APPLICANT: I was too good a producer to waste time supervising others.

By continuing to press for details, you can dig out the real facts.

2-46   Some applicants try to turn the interview around and interview me instead of letting me interview them. If I ask them a question about their experience, they ask me a question about the job. What's the solution?

It is not a good idea to give applicants too many details about a job before you learn about their backgrounds. If an applicant persists in this type of behavior, say: "I appreciate your interest in the details of the position, but first I would like to learn more about you. If you come close to our needs, we can discuss the job."

2-47   Many of the résumés I get are from out of town. It is very expensive to invite people to come to see us, so I usually conduct my first interview on the telephone. How can I get the most from a telephone interview?

A telephone interview can be very effective. However, unlike a personal interview, it does not give you a chance to observe the applicant's reactions and body language. Here are some suggestions for getting the most from the telephone interview.

Give advance notice, since many applicants are currently employed and cannot speak freely at their place of work and since you cannot be sure when people will be home. Call the applicant's daytime number and set up an appointment at a convenient time for both of you. The phone interview will often be in the evening, when the applicant is freer to talk.

Plan the phone interview as carefully as you would an in-person interview. Read the application and/or résumé carefully and note the areas which require elaboration. Don't be afraid to ask hard questions, such as reasons for desiring to leave a job, causes of unemployment, relations with superiors, and details on work background.

Study the job spec carefully. The résumé may give an indication of meeting the job spec, but often a candidate will meet some essential requirements and not others, or have superficial experience which is blown up in the résumé. Probe to determine if the applicant's experience and skills are close to what you are seeking.

Note the answers to your questions. Note taking is even more important in a telephone interview than in a personal interview. Also, it is not a distraction to the interviewee, as it would be in person. Interviewers tend to remember an applicant they see (and what was said) more readily than an applicant they interview by phone—so be thorough.

Since you cannot see reactions on the phone, you must listen for them. A voice can reveal confidence or lack of it. Hesitance, equivocation, and long pauses between thoughts often reflect weaknesses. Nervous laughter, frequent digressions, evasions, and nonresponsive replies are danger signals.

As in the personal interview, some applicants may be nervous over the telephone. Take time to build rapport and the tension will be eased. Give the applicant adequate time to answer each question and *listen* carefully to the answers. Follow through when you need more detail.

If the applicant seems to be all that you desire, set up a time for a personal interview to gain a more thorough view of the person. It is not a good idea to hire somebody solely on the basis of a telephone interview. Personal characteristics and other intangibles that cannot be determined on the telephone must also be considered in the hiring decision.

Remembering the Applicant

2-48   Is it a good idea to take notes during an interview so I can remember each applicant?

When you interview a number of applicants for the same job, it is not easy to remember everybody. Indeed, you may mix people up in your mind. One way to remember is to take notes. Do not make stenographic transcriptions. If you take too many notes, you will be so busy writing that you cannot listen properly to the applicant's answers. You may not obtain important information and opportunities to follow up with added questions. Also, taking detailed notes inhibits applicants. They become so concerned with what you are writing that they curtail their responses. Some applicants become very nervous, thinking: "Everything I say will be held against me." Just write brief phrases to help you remember salient points.

Make any notations about personality or other intangibles *after* the applicant has left. Some people may read comments which you would not want them to see. Take a few minutes before seeing another candidate to make your comments and to summarize your impressions.

2-49   How about taping interviews?

Audiotaping or videotaping interviews would certainly help you remember candidates and enable you to review the interviews in privacy and at your leisure. However, it is very time-consuming to view or listen to interviews. Taping is generally not feasible, except in cases of very important jobs where several executives may want to review the interview in depth.

2-50   What kinds of notes should I keep during the interview so that I will remember each applicant?

Begin with job factors. Using the job specification as a guide, note the background of the candidate on each item. For example:

Job spec	Applicant bkgrd
Knows COBOL	3 yrs working COBOL
Speaks Spanish	Knows conversational Spanish
Supervise min. 6 people	Supervised 10 people

Intangibles are more difficult to note. Examples are better than just vague comments. Instead of observing that an applicant is creative, note examples of creative work. Appearance is often a factor in making a hiring decision. In commenting on appearance, don't use vague terms like "rumpled" and "sloppy." Note: "Clothes unpressed, shoes not shined."

Often personality factors are decisive in choosing among candidates. Be sure to keep clear notes. Do not just observe: "Applicant appeared to lack self-confidence." Note: "Applicant was hesitant in answering questions." Or "Applicant looked down at the floor during entire interview."

2-51   Is there some form I can use to summarize an applicant's background?

An interview summary sheet is presented in Figure 2-3. You can use it as a guideline, but it is better to tailor the categories to meet your specific needs.

Making the Hiring Decision

2-52   The toughest part for me in the selection process is making the hiring decision. I often have people who look very good but do not meet all the specifications. Should I stick to the job spec or trust my gut feelings?

Look at the whole picture, not just parts of it. For example, the job spec may call for a degree in computer science. Your candidate has completed 3 years in the computer science program but has not attained the degree. However, he has excellent work experience. This could often compensate for lack of a degree. Or the job calls for sales experience. The applicant has none, but her personality and other factors have given you the feeling that she would be a good salesperson. Unless the specification is a "knockout factor"—that is, it is essential in order to do the job— your educated judgment is a critical factor in making the decision. If this were not the case, you could feed the data into a computer and let the decision be made purely by facts.

2-53   Is there any one facet of an applicant's background that you consider most important in making a hiring decision?

Probably the most significant evaluative factors are the accomplishments of the candidate. "What is past is prologue." People who have succeeded in the past are more likely to suc-

Interview Summary Sheet

Applicant _____ Date _____

Position applied for_____Interviewer_____

| | Applicant's | Qualification |
| Job Factors[1] | background[2]_____ | rating[3] _____ |

Duties_____

_____

_____

_____

Responsibilities ____ ._____

_____

_____

_____

Skills required _____

_____

_____

_____

Education required:[4] (level)_____

    Specific types_____

    _____

    Educ. achievement _____

    _____

Other job factors _____

_____

_____

_____

1. Job factors should be listed from job specification for position applicant applies for.

2. Interviewer should note aspects of applicant's background that apply to each factor.

3. Rate applicant on a 1-to-5 scale on how closely background fits job specification.

4. Level of education = how much schooling completed; type represents subjects related to job taken; achievement represents grades or standing.

Figure 2-3

Figure 2-3 (Continued)

Personal Factors	Comments
Growth in career	
Accomplishments	
Intangibles	
Appearance	
Motivation	
Resourcefulness	
Stability	
Leadership	
Creativity	
Mental alertness	
Energy level	
Communication skill	
Self-confidence	

Comments

☐ Applicant's strengths _____

_____

_____

_____

   Applicant's limitations _____

_____

_____

_____

☐ Applicant should be hired. _____

   Recommendations for additional training _____

(Continued)

Figure 2-3 (Continued)

☐ Applicant should not be hired _____

    Reasons_____

    _____

    Additional comments _____

    _____

ceed in the future. In addition, the accomplishments of which the applicant is most proud gives insight into his or her thinking about the nature of the work. If the applicant is particularly proud of an accomplishment that to you appears routine, you may have a narrow-thinking applicant with limited growth potential.

An applicant for an office manager position states that her major achievements were "keeping the work flowing, putting out fires, and assuring that the work was done correctly." The description indicates that she is a "maintenance" type person. This is good if that is what your job calls for. However, if the job requires innovation and creativity, it would be better to choose somebody whose accomplishments included introducing new systems or eliminating time-wasting programs.

2-54 There are some jobs in our company for which applicants are hard to come by. Is it wise to fill the job with an available candidate—even if he or she is not fully qualified—when it is unlikely that a better candidate will come along in the immediate future?

Whenever you hire, you take a big risk. No matter how good you may think you are when it comes to selecting people, you still do not really know if a person can do the job until he or she is actually at work. Since hiring (and then firing) is not only expensive but can also lead to legal problems, you should make every effort to pick somebody who has a reasonable chance of success. If the deficiencies of a less-than-ideal candidate can be corrected on the job by training, coaching, and support, take the risk. However, if the "dubious factors" are not correctible in a tolerable period of time, pass the candidate by and wait for a better one.

2-55 Often candidates make a big impression on me because of appearance or personality. Am I being unduly influenced?

Appearance and personality are important in some jobs. However, these factors are often overemphasized. The best word processor may be bypassed in favor of a more attractive competitor. The sales manager who hires only handsome men and beautiful women may lose the hardest-driving salespeople who do not depend on their charm alone to make sales.

"Charming" people may make great impressions because of their glib talk or outgoing style, but this should not be the sole basis for hiring—even if charm is an asset for the job. Look at the whole person, the full background, the record of success or failure, the closeness to the job spec.

2-56   Recently I hired a man whom I thought I could relate to easily. We came from the same part of town and even went to the same high school. But we couldn't get along at all. Where did I go wrong?

It is an advantage to work with people you can get along with, but this is not necessarily tied into having similar backgrounds. Many people are unconsciously biased toward people who are like themselves. They may come from the same neighborhood, have the same ethnic heritage, be graduates of the same college. Conversely, people may be biased against those who have different backgrounds. A case in point is the supervisor from the University of Michigan who would never hire a graduate of its archrival, Michigan State. Silly, but people do this consciously or subconsciously all the time. To overcome your biases—both pro and con—identify them clearly. When you are faced with an applicant who fits into one of your "molds," make a concerted effort to put that factor in its proper perspective.

2-57   I hired a woman who was the fastest typist I'd ever seen. I was sure I had a winner. Typing is an important part of the job, but it also called for doing many other tasks, which she couldn't handle. How could I have foreseen this?

You fell victim to the "halo effect." When an applicant is so good in one aspect of the work, we put a halo around her head. "If she's such a fast typist, she must be good in everything else." The halo effect is even more common with intangibles. "He's so intelligent, he can handle anything." Then we find that as bright as he is, he can't get along with other people. The opposite phenomenon is the "pitchfork effect." We project a single weakness to the entire background and eliminate an excellent candidate who might overcome that weakness with our help.

2-58   Sometimes I take an immediate dislike to an applicant. I don't know why, but I know I hate him or her. Am I being unreasonable?

Your reaction is not unusual. Perhaps you unconsciously associate the person with somebody with whom you had an unpleasant experience in the past. If you feel this way about an otherwise qualified candidate, ask someone else in the company to interview the person. A second opinion may prevent rejection of a potentially valuable addition to the staff. However, if you have to work closely with this person, it may not be fair to either of you to hire the candidate—unless you are willing to overlook your "feeling" and make a sincere attempt to get along.

2-59   We often have several candidates—all of whom meet the basic requirements. How can I make a fair comparison among them?

List the job factors on a chart such as the one below so you can compare the candidates side by side. If it is possible, put weights on each factor.

Job factor	Weight	Appl. 1	Appl. 2	Appl. 3
Typing skills	10	8	6	9
Computer operations	20	18	15	15
Telephone voice	10	10	6	4

Do the same for education, intangibles, and other personal factors. If it is not feasible to put numerical weights on factors, refer to your notes on a candidate and make narrative comments on each factor. Then you can systematically evaluate each person and make a sound decision.

2-60   Is it a good idea to have several people interview an applicant for a job?

In larger companies, a representative of the personnel or human resources department interviews applicants and refers only satisfactory ones to the supervisor. In such cases, there are at least two interviews. If you are the only person who has interviewed an applicant, it is a good idea to get another person's opinion. You may have missed important facts. You may have been overly influenced by one or another factor.

The other interviewer can compensate for your bias. Who should the other interviewer be? If the new employee will relate to supervisors other than yourself, ask one of your peers to hold the second interview. If not, your boss should conduct it.

Always seek opinions of others. Even though you may have to be the final arbiter of who gets the job, their input can be invaluable.

2-61   We work in teams. It is our practice to have all members of the team interview applicants. This is very time-consuming. Is it worth it?

The team concept involves every member of the team, and selecting new members should be a group activity. It need not be time-consuming if team members are properly oriented on what they should be interviewing for. It isn't necessary for each member to conduct a full interview. The team leader should structure the interview so that each member is assigned appropriate facets of background to discuss. Team members can then concentrate on that part of the applicant's background in which they have the greatest knowledge. They will also have an opportunity to size up the applicant and to share their evaluations with the rest of the team.

Testing Applicants

2-62   Our personnel department uses tests to help screen applicants. I am not really sure what the test results mean. I've asked the personnel people, but their answers are often too technical. What do the tests test?

If your company uses any testing, you should know just what the tests are supposed to indicate. It is the responsibility of the personnel or human resources people to give all supervisors a thorough and understandable explanation of those tests. Several types of tests are used in screening applicants.

1. *Intelligence tests.*   Like the IQ tests used in school, intelligence tests measure ability to learn. Among the most popular are the Wonderlich tests, which are brief and simple and can be administered by people with a minimum of training. Although such tests distinguish between very high or very low intelligence, they do not differentiate significant differences in the middle ranges. For example, if a candidate scores 10 out of a

possible 50, he or she is probably not as bright as a person scoring 40. But if one candidate scores 32 and the other 34, there is little to indicate that the person with the higher score is really brighter. More complex tests like the Wechsler-Bellevue, which must be administered by trained psychologists, give deeper insight not only into basic intelligence but into types of intelligence.

2. *Aptitude tests.*   Many tests are designed to determine aptitude for specific skills, such as mechanical ability, clerical skill, and sales potential. Such tests are helpful in screening inexperienced people to determine if they have the aptitude to succeed in the type of work for which they will be trained. Some aptitude tests can be administered and interpreted by people with little training in testing. For example, an office manager can give a clerical aptitude test to an applicant, score it, and interpret it by referring to a simple instruction sheet.

3. *Performance tests.*   Performance tests are most helpful because they measure how well candidates can actually do the job for which they apply. A lathe operator can be tested by performing real lathe work; a typist or data entry clerk can be tested for speed and accuracy by performing a typical task; a truck driver can be given a road test. When job performance cannot be tested directly, written tests on job knowledge may be used. Responses to questions on various aspects of the job are scored against a master answer list. The employer can then ascertain whether a candidate knows enough about the job to do it. Oral tests may also be used. For example, an auto mechanic may be asked to give the firing order of a V-8 engine. The major problem with this type of test, as with any verbal test, is that some people may be able to "talk a good job" but not really do it well.

4. *Personality tests.*   Tests designed to identify personality characteristics vary from *Reader's Digest*-type quickie questionnaires, to highly sophisticated personality evaluations such as the MMPI (Minnesota Multiphasic Personality Inventory), to in-depth evaluations by a psychologist. This is a controversial area. Supervisors should never make decisions on the basis of personality test results unless the full implications are made clear to them by experts.

2-63   We don't have a personnel department. Are there any tests I can use myself?

Supervisors can administer performance tests and some aptitude tests with a minimum of training. You can design your own performance tests by asking an applicant to perform a common phase of the job. For example, have an applicant for a secretarial job set up and type a typical letter. Ask an applicant for a customer service job to role-play a customer complaint. However, to avoid charges of discrimination, you must use the same test for every applicant and measure it by the same criteria. (More on the equal employment ramifications of testing in Chapter 3.)

2-64   Our company doesn't hire enough people to warrant setting up a testing program. Are outside sources available to do the testing? How costly are they? Is it worth it?

For most jobs, professional testing is not necessary. It may be helpful in selecting management, sales, and specialized personnel. Many organizations offer personnel-testing services. They range from highly respected firms to charlatans with a magic formula for separating winners from losers. Costs vary considerably.

If your company believes it can benefit from testing, retain an industrial psychologist to study the types of jobs, current screening methods, and other factors that may be identified by testing. (You can locate industrial psychologists through your local university or the American Psychological Association.) If a testing program is recommended, do not necessarily have the person who made the recommendation administer it. Obtain a list of approved psychological-testing groups (again from the American Psychological Association). Contact those that seem appropriate. Costs vary, and only your management can determine if it is worth it.

2-65   Doesn't the government provide free testing for some jobs?

State employment services offer free skill and aptitude testing for many types of jobs. Contact your local job service and find out what tests are offered and how they may help your company. The service will conduct the tests before referring candidates to you, so you know that the applicants have the basic skills you are seeking.

2-66   Do private employment agencies test applicants?

Some agencies give skill tests, particularly in clerical jobs such as data processing and secretarial work. Always ask the agency what types of tests are used and how they are interpreted.

2-67   My company sends applicants to a testing organization, but I never see the reports. I have to make the final decision on hiring. Does this make sense?

Because tests often uncover private matters that have no bearing on job performance, psychological reports should be kept confidential. However, any facet of an applicant's background which is related to job performance should be passed on to the supervisor.

2-68   How much weight should be given to test results in making the hiring decision?

The test is one of several tools in the selection process. It should be considered along with the review of work history, the personal evaluation of interviewers, and the verification of the candidate's background. One should not overbalance another. Some people give more weight to tests than they should. Because of a test's alleged objectivity, they feel it has more significance than other tools. If they hire someone whose test score is low and that person fails on the job, they may be later criticized for ignoring the scores. On the other hand, if they hire someone with high test scores and the person still fails, the blame will be put on the test rather than on their own judgment. Don't fall into that trap.

Checking References

2-69   Applicants can say anything about their experience. How can I verify what they have told me?

Checking references is one of the oldest approaches to verifying background. The assumption is that a former employer will tell a potential employer the whole truth about a candidate. However, we know that this is not always the case. Employers are often reluctant to make negative statements, either because they don't want to prevent the person from working—so long as it is not for them—or because they fear litigation (see questions 2-81 and 2-82). Still, the reference check is virtually your only source of verification.

2-70   Whom should I call to get the best information about a candidate?

Contact the immediate supervisor for whom the applicant worked. Get that person's name from the application form or at the interview. If you can, avoid talking to personnel or human resources staff. These people only have information that is on file. The immediate supervisor will be able to give you details on exactly how that person worked along with personality factors and other traits that may be important.

2-71   What's the best way to get the supervisor to give me useful information?

When you phone the supervisor, greet him or her by name to establish immediate rapport. Start the conversation this way: "Mr. Robinson, I'm Henrietta Good, office manager of Intercounty Marketers. How are you today? (Wait for response.) We are considering a former employee of yours, Valerie Wilson, for a position in our office. I would appreciate it if you could *verify* some of the information given to us."

Note the verb *verify*. This is an important word to use, since it is nonthreatening. Most people do not mind verifying data. Then ask a few verification questions on dates of employment, job title, and other obvious items from the application, such as "Valerie said she reported directly to you."

Once Robinson has verified a few facts, shift to a question that requires a substantive answer, but not one that calls for an opinion. For example: "What were Valerie's specific duties relating to customer relations?" *Important:* When Robinson responds, make a comment. Do not go on to the next question immediately.

ROBINSON: She had frequent contact with customers.

YOU: That would be very important in the job she is seeking, since it calls for a good deal of telephone contact.

The reason for commenting is to make the interchange a conversation—not an interrogation. Continue in this manner for the next five or six questions. Once you and Robinson are telephone friends, he will be more likely to give you opinions about Valerie's work. Now you can ask about performance, attitudes, or work problems and obtain meaningful information.

2-72   What if an employer is reluctant to answer an opinion question?

If the employer refuses outright to answer a question, don't push. Point out that you understand the reluctance but that it would be helpful if you knew a little more than just a candidate's duties. Comment: "I'm sure you would like to have as much knowledge about a candidate if you were considering somebody." Then ask another opinion question. Do not repeat the same question. Once the responses start coming more freely, you can return to the first question, preferably using different words.

2-73   When I telephone for a reference, I sometimes get the feeling that the employer is holding something back. What should I do?

You can often tell by a person's voice, the hesitation in his or her answers, or the vagueness in the responses that you are not getting the full story. One way to handle this is to say: "Mr. Controller, I appreciate your taking this time to talk to me about Alice Accountant. The job we have is of great importance to our department. We cannot afford to make a mistake. Now are there any special problems we might face if we hire Alice that we should know about?"

Another approach: "Amal will need some training for the position we have in mind. Can you point out any areas in his background or mode of working that we should give particular attention to?" The respondent may then tell you of some of Amal's weaknesses that you would have to work on to make him productive.

2-74   Sometimes an employer who dislikes a former employee—possibly because of a personality conflict or because the employee quit—may give a poor reference. How can I tell?

If you received good references from the applicant's other jobs, it's likely that the poor reference was based on a personality conflict or some other factor unrelated to the work. If possible, find out the names of other people in the company who are familiar with the applicant's work and contact them.

2-75   An employer's response to an inquiry may point up a negative characteristic. How can I tell if it will affect the way the applicant performs my job?

Get specifics. For example, if a supervisor responds that the applicant couldn't take direction, ask: "What type of direction didn't Carmen follow?" You might find it involved work above the level of the job for which you are considering Carmen; or you might decide it was the supervisor, not the applicant, who was at fault.

Double-check by speaking to other people in the company or by bringing up specific questions on taking direction in reference checks with other companies.

2-76   When should reference checks be made?

Check references once you feel that the applicant has a reasonable chance of being hired. If you have more than one finalist, check each one before the final decision is made. The reference checks may turn up information that suggests a need for futher inquiry. Probe into any deficiencies which are mentioned to determine if they do exist and if they can be overcome by training on the job.

If reference checks turn up information that you feel needs to be explored further, arrange another interview with the applicant to go over these new areas. You will also have a chance to get to know the applicant better.

Never tell an applicant: "You are hired subject to reference checks." If the references are all good but you ultimately choose another candidate, the applicant may develop unjustified negative feelings toward a former employer. It is also not wise to tell an applicant that he or she was rejected because of a reference. Information received from references should be considered confidential.

2-77   My boss told me that the key question to ask in a reference check is "Would you rehire this person?" Do you agree?

This is a good question, but the answer may be tricky or evasive. For example: "It's against company policy to rehire." Instead, you might ask: "If you were hiring for another company for this type of position, would you hire Clara?" If the answer is no, probe for details as to why. Again, the reason may be personal rather than job-related.

2-78   How carefully should I plan my telephone reference checks? Is there some guide to follow?

A prestructured telephone reference guide not only helps you keep the interview on track but also provides a form for making a written record of the results. A reference check guide is presented in Figure 2-4.

Telephone Reference Check Guide

To be effective, a telephone reference check should be pre-planned. The unique feature of this guide is that it encourages the checker to formulate special questions which apply to the specific job rather than be restricted by a close-ended format. The guide begins with general questions that apply to most applicants, followed by several categories of special questions. Before making the check, the checker can fill in those questions that should be asked.

COMPANY CALLED _____ PHONE _____

PERSON CONTACTED _____ POSITION _____

PERSON MAKING REFERENCE CHECK _____DATE _____

"This is _____ of _____. We are interested in _____ and would appreciate it if you could tell us what you can about him (her)."

1. How long have you known applicant? (Dates?) In what relationship? _____

2. What was applicant's position? To whom did applicant report? _____

3. I would appreciate your comments on applicant's progress.

   _____

   _____

   _____

4. How did applicant get along with superiors? associates? subordinates? _____

5. Was applicant a creative person? Can you give examples?

   _____

   _____

6. Is applicant a healthy, energetic, hard worker? _____

   _____

7. What were the applicant's strong points?_____

   _____

   _____

Figure 2-4

Figure 2-4 (Continued)

8. In what areas did applicant need help or added training?

   _____

9. We are considering applicant for a position as _____

   Do you feel he (she) is suited for this? _____

   Why? (Why not?)_____

   _____

10. What personal attributes strengthened or weakened applicant's personal effectiveness? _____

    _____

    _____

11. Are you aware of any personal difficulties such as drinking, or emotional problems?_____

    _____

12. How was applicant's attendance, punctuality, etc.? _____

    _____

13. Applicant indicated earnings of $_____ per _____ Is this correct? Any incentive pay?_____

    _____

Specific questions re work background (to be formulated for each applicant individually)

Questions	Answers
14. *Job skills* (e.g., How were applicant's office skills? Was applicant fluent in Spanish? How was applicant's sales record?)	

(Continued)

Figure 2-4 (Continued)

Questions	Answers
15. *Responsibilities:* (e.g., Describe applicant's supervisory	
16. *Accomplishments:* (e.g., What did applicant do that made him (her) stand out above others in the same type of work?)	
17. *Intangibles:* (Each job has certain intangible factors incumbent to it. For applicants who meet the public, a question to ask: How did applicant relate to customers? For supervisors: How did applicant get along with minority employees?	
18. *Special comments:* (List questions that arise out of information developed from the reference's responses.)	

19. Why did applicant leave job?_____

20. Would you rehire? (If not, why not?)_____

Comments of person making the reference call: (If pertinent, note any problems, doubts, or areas of uncertainty or concern that have arisen from the call.)

2-79   Our company prefers writing for references. Isn't this better than a telephone check, since we will have a written record?

No. Most written references are inadequate. They give very little information. Companies are often reluctant to put negative factors in writing. However, you may use a written reference form to get basic information and follow it up with a telephone call.

2-80   Our company uses an outside investigation bureau to check references on applicants. Is this a good idea?

There are some excellent reference-checking organizations, but they are expensive and should be reserved for high-salaried personnel, especially those with sensitive positions. Trained investigators interview people who know the applicant—both on and off the job. They check credit bureaus and other sources to pick up additional information. The main drawback to outside investigators is that they often know little about the job the person is seeking and cannot get meaningful information on job factors. You will have to do this on your own anyway.

The Fair Credit Act requires that any company using outside investigators advise applicants in writing that such an investigation may be made and tell them (if requested) what company made the investigation. Applicants have the right to get a copy of the report from the investigating firm.

2-81   Can a company be sued by a former employee if he or she gets a poor reference?

In the United States anybody can sue anybody else for any reason at all. That doesn't mean that the plaintiff will win the suit, but defending any legal action is expensive. The legal concept involved here is called *defamation.* If an employer "defames the character" of a former employee causing damages (i.e., loss of a potential job), that employer may be held liable for those damages and have to pay for loss of income and perhaps emotional distress.

Even if the employer gives you accurate information it could still be interpreted by some jury as defamation. For example, you ask about attendance and the employer responds accurately: "She was absent 13 days in the last 2 months." As a result, you reject the applicant. She sues the employer and wins because the jury feels that her reason for absence, the illness of her mother, was justifiable. The employer didn't disclose that fact. Theoretically, had you known it, you might have probed further and found that the mother has since died; thus this type of absenteeism would not recur. You, the inquirer, are not liable, but the respondent, the former employer, may be.

The risk of legal action has made many employers unwilling to give any information other than verification of dates of employment. As a result, reference checking has become extremely difficult. Yes, keep trying to "sell" the employer on telling you more, but some companies absolutely prohibit any staff member from giving out information.

One solution is to have applicants sign an authorization permitting former employers to give information to you. You may then tell the references that you have this release. If they ask for a copy before talking to you, you will have to delay conducting the reference interview until they get it.

2-82   When I am asked for a reference about a former employee, how much can I tell without risking litigation?

To be absolutely safe, limit your response to purely factual data such as verifying dates of employment, reason for leaving, and salary.

Making the Offer

2-83   One of my toughest problems in hiring is negotiating salary. We hire technical people and they often bargain. How should I respond?

In most jobs, the company sets the salary and there is no place for negotiation. It's take it or leave it. In jobs where good applicants are hard to find, the company may have to negotiate with applicants.

General discussions about salary should take place well before an offer is made. Most people are offered a moderate increase over current salary when hired for a new job. Occasionally, a higher increment is warranted for improved credentials, an advanced degree, or a professional license that the candidate has received since starting his or her last job .

Sometimes applicants are unrealistic about what they can obtain. It is advisable to let the applicant know the salary range early in the interviewing process. If the candidate is totally out of line, he or she will withdraw or be eliminated before additional interviewing time is wasted. If the candidate is within range and is being seriously considered, the negotiation should take place before a final job offer is made.

During the interview, find out what is most important to the candidate: type of work, opportunity to accomplish specific goals, and so on. Show how those things can be attained on the prospective job. Emphasize not just the salary but the benefits package, the frequency of salary reviews, and opportunities for advancement. Few good applicants will reject an offer on salary alone.

2-84   I have a really good candidate, but he's the first person I've seen. Should I hire him or wait until I've had a chance to see others?

If people with the skills you seek are scarce, don't wait. If you believe the candidate meets your specs, make an offer. He will probably have a choice of several offers. On the other hand, if you have several candidates who look good on paper but have not yet been seen, try to stall this candidate for a reasonable time. Say: "You certainly have many of the qualities we seek and we are definitely interested in you. However, we are committed to interviewing several other candidates. We should have an answer by_____." If the candidate indicates that he has other offers, suggest that he contact you before making a final decision.

2-85   Our company requires all people we hire to take a medical examination. About 99 percent pass, so I usually hire someone, set a starting date, and have the person take the exam on that day. Is this legal? Is it a good practice?

Requiring a medical exam for employment is legal, but you cannot reject an applicant on the basis of this exam unless you can show that the reason for the rejection is job-related. For example, you learn that the applicant has a heart condition that might be aggravated by heavy lifting, and the job calls for such lifting. Rejection will probably be upheld. On the other hand, rejecting the same applicant, not because of the work, but because your health insurance won't cover the preexisting condition is not legal.

The Americans with Disabilities Act (ADA) prohibits preemployment physicals *before* a job offer is made. However, once that offer has been made, the employer may require a medical examination before the applicant begins work and may condition the job offer on the exam results, with the following provisos:

- All entering employees in the same job category must be given the exam—not just those with obvious disabilities or above a certain age.

- Information resulting from the exam must be kept in a separate file, not in the employee's general personnel file.

- The information must be kept confidential. Only information about necessary work restrictions and accommodations may be given to appropriate supervisors.

Because the job offer is conditioned on passing the medical examination, you should caution applicants who are currently employed not to give notice or leave their present jobs until your company informs them that they have passed the exam and the job offer is validated.

2-86   I read about a company that was sued by a former employee who claimed that when he was hired he was told the job was permanent: 6 years later he was laid off. Isn't 6 years permanent enough? Nobody should expect lifetime employment guarantees.

Permanent means "lasting indefinitely." Many companies refer to "permanent employees" to distinguish them from "temporary" or "probationary" employees. Most lawyers recommend that companies eliminate the use of this term. Instead, differentiate "regular employees" from temps or people hired on trial.

2-87   When I hire workers, I tell them there will be a review in 6 months. Some of my people assume this guarantees a raise. The raise depends on performance. How can I make this clear without antagonizing and perhaps losing the applicant?

Most people know that a review is just what it sounds like. However, to make sure that you don't run into problems, explain what the review will cover. Point out (if true) that most people do get a raise, but occasionally an employee needs additional time to become productive and earn that raise.

2-88   Should a job offer be in writing, or is an oral offer just as good?

Most firms do not put job offers in writing, except with higher-level positions. An oral offer is just as binding as a written offer. However, some companies make oral offers and supplement them with a letter confirming the terms. The confirmation ensures that both parties fully understand the terms and eliminates later claims of unkept promises, which may have been assumed by the new employee.

2-89   What should a job-offer letter contain?

All job-offer letters should contain:

- Title of job
- Job description (may be attached)
- Starting date
- Salary
- Benefits (may be in attached brochure)
- Work hours

Salary should be stated by pay period rather than on an annual basis. Instead of "$24,000 per year," say: "$1000 per half month." The reason is to avoid claims that, when salary is listed in annual terms, the employee is guaranteed a minimum of a year's employment. Have the applicant sign a copy of the letter to acknowledge acceptance of the job.

Since a job-offer letter is a contract, it should be carefully reviewed and approved by your company's attorney.

2-90   Our company has an "employment at will" policy. All application forms include this statement: "All employees are hired at the will of management and may be terminated with or without reason at any time." Is this legal?

Employment at will is covered fully in Chapter 14. This disclaimer on an application form is legal and is recommended to protect companies from potential unlawful-discharge suits.

2-91   Our company has a number of "secret" procedures, and all employees are required to sign a statement that they will not work for a competitor if they leave. Is this enforceable?

"Restrictive covenant" contracts are common in companies that operate in sensitive areas, where a former employee may provide competitors with information that will give them an advantage. The enforceability of such contracts varies from state to state. Usually they are enforceable if limited in scope. For example, prohibiting a person from working for a competitor for a few years is more likely to be accepted than prohibiting the employee from working for a rival forever. Such a contract should be prepared by an attorney to make sure it complies with appropriate laws.

2-92   One of the most frustrating things that happens in hiring is having a candidate accept a job offer, get a counteroffer from his or her present employer, and then take it. Not only do I lose a good applicant, but I have to start all over again. What can I do to prevent this from happening?

Assume that any applicant who is currently employed will get a counteroffer and prepare that person to reject it. Make the following points:

1. "You've done a great job at your present company. When you announce that you plan to leave, your boss will undoubtedly make you a counteroffer. Why will the boss do this? Because the company needs you now."

2. "If the company really appreciated your work, it would not have waited until you got another job to give you that raise. You would have had it long ago."

3. "Many people who have taken counteroffers find that once the pressure is off, the company trains or hires somebody else and lets them go."

4. "You will always be looked upon as the disloyal person who threatened to leave just to get more money."

5. "When raises come around again, guess who gets overlooked? You've already had yours!"

These arguments are highly effective counters to company counteroffers.

2-93   When I've made my decision, should I notify all the rejected applicants that the job is filled? When and how?

Some companies tell applicants that if they do not hear from the company by a certain date to assume they did not get the job. Others prefer to write or phone applicants who have been seriously considered. Do not notify other candidates until shortly after a new employee starts. If for some reason the chosen candidate changes her or his mind and doesn't start, you can go back to some of the others without having them feel they were second choices.

It is not necessary to give a reason for rejection. The most diplomatic approach is to write or say: "One of the other candidates was closer to our current needs." If you are asked to explain in what way, do not cite any specific reason. Simply say, for example, that because of the successful candidate's background, you feel he or she can be productive more rapidly.

3

Complying with Equal Employment Laws

In every aspect of his or her job, the supervisor must always be aware of the laws which govern dealing with employees. Knowing and understanding federal, state, and sometimes local laws on equal employment practices are integral parts of the supervisor's responsibility. The supervisor is the one person who has direct contact with the rank and file, and ensuring adherence to these laws is a principal part of the job .

Although state laws differ somewhat from the federal law, this chapter will deal primarily with federal legislation. Information about any special provisions that your state or local government may have added to federal law can be obtained from the human resources department, legal counsel, or general management of your company.

There are five major federal laws concerning equal employment.

■ The Civil Rights Act of 1964, Title VII, as amended, prohibits discrimination in employment on the basis of race, color, sex, religion, and national origin.

- The Age Discrimination in Employment Act (ADEA) of 1967, as amended, prohibits discrimination in employment against individuals 40 years or older. (Some states prohibit discrimination against individuals at any age over the legal maturity age of 18.)
- The Americans with Disabilities Act (ADA) of 1990 prohibits discrimination against people with disabilities.
- The Equal Pay Act of 1963 requires equal pay for employees of different sexes for equal work.
- Executive Order 11246 (1965), as amended by Executive Order 11375 (1967), applies only to companies having federal government contracts of $50,000 or more and more than 50 employees. In addition to complying with the above laws, such companies must have written affirmative action programs for women and minorities.

These laws apply not only to making hiring decisions, but to every aspect of dealing with people on the job. They cover how you assign work and how you pay, train, discipline, and terminate employees. They include rulings on dealing with pregnant employees, sexual harassment, and religious issues.

Interpretation of these laws comes from both administrative rulings and court decisions. Answers to the questions posed by supervisors in this chapter draw upon these rulings and decisions. However, because interpretations of legal matters may be very tricky, it is strongly recommended that an attorney be consulted whenever any problems—particularly formal charges—arise.

The EEO quiz in Figure 3-1 will give you some idea of what you know (and don't know) about the equal employment laws.

Overview of Equal Employment Opportunity Laws

3-1   My main concern in interviewing people is that I might ask an illegal question and not even know it is illegal. Where can I find a list of what I can and cannot ask?

The simplest way to determine if a question is permissible is to ask yourself if knowing the answer to this question is necessary in determining if the person can do the job for which he or she applied. Steer clear of personal or curiosity questions and any

What Do You Know About EEO?

To be a better employment interviewer—in fact, to do your job properly—you must be thoroughly familiar with the various state and federal laws concerning equal employment opportunity. To help you measure your knowledge of these laws, take the following quiz. It covers only a few of the key factors in the laws but should give you some insight into understanding this very important area.

Questions

On an application form or in an interview, you may ask: YES   NO

1. What is the name of your nearest of kin?   _____   _____

2. Do you own a car?   _____   _____

3. Do you have a permanent immigration visa?   _____   _____

4. What foreign languages do you speak?   _____   _____

5. Have you ever been arrested?   _____   _____

Indicate if each of these help-wanted ads is legal.

6. "Receptionist—if you're a cutie, you'll like this duty"   _____   _____

7. "Management trainees—college degree—top 10 percent of class only"   _____   _____

8. "Accountant—part time—opportunity for retiree"   _____   _____

9. "Personnel—experienced recruiting at black colleges"   _____   _____

10. "Sales—recent college graduate preferred"   _____   _____

Indicate if each of these practices is legal.

11. A company may test applicants to measure intelligence or personality providing the publisher of the test vouches that it is nondiscriminatory.   _____   _____

12. A company may refuse to hire applicants because they are homosexual.   _____   _____

13. A company may refuse to employ applicants because they are over 70.   _____   _____

Figure 3-1

Figure 3-1 (Continued)

14. A company may refuse to employ an applicant
    if she is pregnant.   _____   _____

15. A company may ask if a woman has small
    children at home.   _____   _____

A company may indicate an age preference

16. if it is for a training program.   _____   _____

17. if older people cannot qualify for the company
    pension program in that firm.   _____   _____

18. if the job calls for someone at least 21.   _____   _____

19. if the job calls for considerable travel.   _____   _____

Miscellaneous and affirmative action questions

20. A company may specify that it requires a man
    for a job if the job calls for considerable travel   _____   _____

21. A company may specify that it requires an
    attractive woman to greet customers and visitors.   _____   _____

22. To implement an affirmative action plan, it
    is enough for a company to advertise in all
    ads that it is an "equal employment oppor-
    tunity employer M/F."   _____   _____

23. Affirmative action plans must include both
    numerical goals and timetables for each
    department and job classification.   _____   _____

24. Companies hiring more women than men
    need not have affirmative action plans to
    recruit more women.   _____   _____

25. A minority employee must be given first
    consideration for promotion even though
    he or she is less qualified than other candidates.   _____   _____

ANSWERS

The answers given below are based on federal law. Some states have interpreted the laws somewhat differently. In addition, new laws, administrative
rulings, and judicial interpretations are promulgated from time to time.
These may change the base on which the answers have been constructed.

(Continued)

Figure 3-1 (Continued)

Keep in mind that the job-relatedness of a question and whether asking it has a disparate effect on minorities are key factors in determining a question's legitimacy.

1. No   Since family names may show national origin if they differ from the applicant's, you may not even ask whom to notify in case of emergency until after an applicant is employed.

2. No   Unless a car is needed to perform the job itself (e.g., sales or service), you may not ask. Requiring ownership of a car discriminates against minorities, who are more likely to be poor. You may ask if they can get to work without any problems.

3. Yes   Immigration laws require that aliens working in this country have a permanent immigration visa (green card).

4. Yes   However, you may not ask how the applicant learned the language, as it may identify his or her national origin.

5. No   Government agencies and courts have ruled that inasmuch as ghetto residents and minorities in general are arrested for slight causes, asking about arrests is discriminatory. You may ask, "Have you ever been convicted of a felony?" However, this may be asked only when it has a direct bearing on the job (e.g., jobs where employees have access to money or stealable goods). The Equal Employment Opportunity Commission (EEOC) has ruled that it is unlawful to refuse to hire a minority applicant because of a conviction unless the circumstances make employment "manifestly inconsistent with the safe and efficient operation of that job."

6. No   "Cutie" signifies female.

7. No   You need to substantiate that students from the top 10 percent of the class have performed significantly better than students with lower grades.

8. No   The Age Discrimination Act protects people over 40 against discrimination due to age. Since most retirees are over 60, specifying "retiree" implies that people between 40 and 60 are not welcome.

9. Yes   You may ask, as long as it doesn't specify that the applicant must be black.

10. No   "Recent college grad" implies youth.

11. No   The Supreme Court, in *Griggs v. Duke Power Co.,* upheld the EEOC's requirement that tests have a direct relationship to

Figure 3-1 (Continued)

effectiveness on the job for each specific job in each company using the tests. The publisher cannot vouch for job-relatedness. It must be validated against each company's experience.

12. Yes Homosexuals are not covered by the federal law or by most state laws. However, some state or local laws prohibit discrimination on the basis of sexual preference.

13. No Federal law covers *all* people age 40 and over.

14. No Pregnant women may not be refused employment unless the work may endanger their health (e.g., heavy physical work or exposure to dangerous substances).

15. No Since men are not usually asked this question, it has been interpreted as a means of discriminating against women.

16. No Training programs may not be limited to young people.

17. No This is not an acceptable reason for age discrimination.

18. Yes Federal law prohibits discrimination only after age 40. There is no maximum age. (State laws differ in this. For example, some state laws begin coverage at 18 or 21.)

19. No Ability to travel is not related to age.

20. No Ability to travel is not related to sex.

21. No A company's desire to have an attractive woman as a receptionist does not make it a bona fide occupational qualification.

22. No The company must take several positive steps to recruit or promote minorities and women. Just advertising that it is an "equal employment opportunity employer M/F" is not enough.

23. Yes Executive Orders 11246 and 11375 and Revised Order 4 all call for numerical goals and timetables in implementing affirmative action plans.

24. No Until the women are represented in proportions related to their presence in the work force of an area, and in each job category and department, affirmative actions plans are required.

25. No Minority personnel should be given preference for promotion only when the qualifications of all candidates are about equal.

Ideally, every employment interviewer should score 100 percent. Failure to comply with any one of these rules can result in complaints, investigations, hearings, and penalties.

(Continued)

question which even hints at the person's race, religion, national origin, age, sex, or disability. Some guidelines on legitimate and unacceptable questions appear in Figure 3-2.

3-2   We operate in several states and state laws vary. How can we have a consistent EEO policy?

Of course, your policies must comply with federal laws. Some state laws are stricter than federal law. In those states you will have to conform to the stricter rules. However, to assure consistency throughout the company, use as a guideline the rules of the strictest state in which you operate.

3-3   I have a job opening for a fork-lift truck operator. This person not only drives the truck but has to stack materials which are often very heavy. Can't I insist on a man for this job?

The law allows a company to restrict the gender of the applicant if a *bona fide occupational qualification (BFOQ)* exists. But this is narrowly interpreted. (e.g., You can require a woman to model women's clothes or a man to model men's clothes.) The assumption that only a man can do heavy lifting is not true. It is permissible to require tests to determine if an applicant can lift weights of the poundage required for the job, but such tests must be given to both men and women. Other considerations are the amount of lifting involved. If the the fork-lift operator only occasionally has to do lifting, this would not be considered a significant job factor. Even if she couldn't pass the lifting test, she would be eligible for employment if she could do the greatest portion of the job (operating the truck), since others could be assigned to do the limited amount of lifting needed.

3-4   We sell construction materials to builders—most of whom are tough old-timers who don't believe a woman could know anything about construction. A woman applied for a sales job with us. These guys would never buy from a woman. Can I reject her on this ground?

The government does not consider acceptance by customers as a BFOQ. Over the past 20 years, many women have broken into jobs that men never thought they could succeed in and have done very well. Don't let your preconceived notions influence your decisions.

Legal and Illegal Preemployment Questions

Here is a series of questions that the New York State Division of Human Rights has compiled as being lawful and unlawful preemployment inquires. Since New York appears to be stricter than most states and the federal government, by following these recommendations, a company may be less likely to find itself in difficulty with the authorities because of preemployment inquiries.

Subject	Lawful*	Unlawful
Race or color		Complexion or color of skin. Coloring.
Religion or creed		Inquiry into applicant's religious denomination, religious affiliations, church, parish, pastor, or religious holidays observed. Applicant may not be told, "This is a (Catholic, Protestant, or Jewish) organization."
National origin		Inquiry into applicant's lineage, ancestry, national origin, descent, parentage, or nationality. Nationality of applicant's parents or spouse. What is your mother tongue?
Sex		Inquiry as to sex. Do you wish to be addressed as Mr.? Mrs.? Miss? or Ms.?
Marital status		Are you married? Are you single? Divorced? Separated? Name or other information about spouse. Where does your spouse work? What are the ages of your children, if any?
Birth control		Inquiry as to capacity to reproduce; advocacy of any form of birth control or family planning.

*Inquiries that would otherwise be deemed lawful may, in certain circumstances, be deemed as evidence of unlawful discrimination when the inquiry seeks to elicit information about a selection criterion that is not job-related and that has a disproportionately burdensome effect upon the members of a minority group and cannot be justified by business necessity.

Figure 3-2

(Continued)

Figure 3-2 (Continued)

Subject	Lawful*	Unlawful
Age	Are you over 18? If not, state your age.	How old are you? What is your date of birth?
Disability	Do you have any impairment—physical, mental, or medical—that would interfere with your ability to perform the job for which you have applied? If there are any positions or types of positions for which you should not be considered, or job duties you cannot perform because of physical, mental, or medical disability, please describe.	Do you have a disability? Have you ever been treated for any of the following diseases...?
Arrest record	Have you ever been convicted of a crime? (Give details.)	Have you ever been arrested?
Name	Have you ever worked for this company under a different name? Is any additional information relative to a change of name, use of an assumed name, or nickname necessary to enable a check on your work record? If yes, explain.	Original name of an applicant whose name has been changed by court order or otherwise. Maiden name of a married woman. If you have ever worked under another name, state name and dates.
Address or duration of residence	Applicant's place of residence. How long a resident of this state or city?	
Birthplace		Birthplace of applicant. Birthplace of applicant's parents, spouse, or other close relatives.
Birthdate		Requirement that applicant submit birth certificate, naturalization, or baptismal record. Requirement that applicant produce proof of age in the form of a birth certificate or baptismal record.
Photograph		Requirement or option that applicant affix a photograph to employment form at any time before hiring.

Figure 3-2 (Continued)

Subject	Lawful*	Unlawful
Citizenship	Have you the legal right to work in the United States? (Applicant must show green card or other proof.)	Are you a citizen of the United States? Of what country are you a citizen? Whether an applicant is naturalized or a native-born citizen: the date when the applicant acquired citizenship. Requirement that applicant produce naturalization papers or first papers. Whether applicant's spouse or parents are naturalized or native-born citizens of the United States: the date when such spouse or parents acquired citizenship.
Language	Inquiry into languages applicant speaks and writes fluently.	What is your native language? Inquiry into how applicant acquired ability to read, write, or speak a foreign language.
Education	Inquiry into applicant's academic, vocational, or professional education, and the public and private schools attended.	
Experience	Inquiry into work experience.	
Relatives	Name of applicant's relatives, other than a spouse, already employed by this company.	Names, addresses, ages, phone numbers, or other information concerning applicant's spouse, children, or other relatives not employed by the company.
Notice in case of emergency	Request for emergency name and address *after* employee is hired.	Name and address of person to be notified in case of accident or emergency.
Military experience	Inquiry into applicant's military experience in the armed forces of the United States or in a state militia. Inquiry into applicant's service in the U.S. Army, Navy, or other military branch	Inquiry into applicant's general military experience. Type of discharge.

(Continued)

Figure 3-2 (Continued)

Subject	Lawful*	Unlawful
Organiza-tions	Inquiry into applicant's membership in organizations that the applicant considers relevant to his or her ability to perform the job.	List all clubs, societies, and lodges to which you belong.
Driver's license	Do you possess a valid driver's license?	Requirement that applicant produce a driver's license prior to employment.

3-5   The girls in my department are all young. The oldest is 26. I think it is important to have a congenial group. It is OK to hire only young people in my department? The company can place older women in other departments where they fit in better.

Your policy is in violation of the age discrimination law. Also, you are making the assumption that the young women will not accept older co-workers. This is not necessarily so. A lot depends, of course, on the individual's personality. If the applicant is outgoing, easy to talk to, and friendly, she will probably fit right in.

Incidentally, it is not wise to refer to women as "girls." Many women resent this and consider it demeaning and an indicator of discrimination.

Similarly, even though your department has historically been all-female, a male should not be disqualified provided he has the skills and desire to do the work.

3-6   We have a young, dynamic group in our department. I want to encourage the institution of new ideas, the latest technologies. Is this justification for a BFOQ to hire only younger applicants?

The main thrust of the Age Discrimination in Employment Act is to overcome this type of thinking. You cannot assume that old people have only old ideas. It is a stereotype that must be eliminated. Creative thinking, study of new technologies, and innovation are not governed by age. Hiring decisions should be based on the total individual, not on stereotypes about age, sex, race, or ideology.

3-7 During our busy season we often work weekends. I have had applicants tell me that they can never work on a Saturday or a Sunday because of their religious beliefs. It is important that we have people who can work those days. What can I do?

The law requires you to make reasonable accommodation for a person's religious beliefs unless it results in undue hardship for the company. If an employee can never work Saturdays but can work Sundays, you can schedule that person accordingly. If you are not open for business on Sundays and need people only on Saturdays, and there are other employees who can cover the Saturdays, you must hire that person and excuse him or her from Saturday work. However, if you are a small organization and there are not enough people qualified in that work to cover the Saturday shift, it may be considered an "undue hardship" and you can refuse to employ that individual.

Sustaining "undue hardship" is not easy. For example, a hospital had only three operating-room nurses on staff. Two had to be on duty at all times. That meant that all had to be available 7 days. To hire a nurse who could never work on her Sabbath would be an undue hardship for the hospital.

A retail store open 7 days with 10 clerks required that 6 of the clerks work every Sunday. Each was scheduled to work two Sundays a month and was given a weekday off to compensate. An applicant was rejected when she told the boss that she could never work on Sunday, since the members of her family were strict churchgoers and attended both morning and afternoon services every Sunday. The EEOC ruled that it was not an undue hardship to have the other clerks cover the Sundays. Although the ruling may be considered unfair to the others, who would have to work more Sundays than before, the unfairness to other employees is not "undue hardship."

Americans with Disabilities Act

3-8 I am concerned about the new disability law, which talks about accommodation. What sort of accommodation must be made for disabled people?

Accommodation varies from very simple, inexpensive acts to reconstructing a facility by building ramps, elevators, and special lavatories for the disabled.

Some easy accommodations: The job calls for standing at a workplace. The applicant cannot stand for long periods of time. Providing a high stool so the employee could sit and still reach the work is virtually cost-free. Or the job calls for telephone work. The applicant has a hearing deficiency. Purchasing a special amplifier for her telephone is a low-cost accommodation.

3-9   We have a wheelchaired applicant who is a great accountant. However, our accounting department is on the second floor. We do not have an elevator or ramp. To build one will be very costly. What should we do?

If the cost of building a ramp to the second floor is excessive, other types of accommodation might be considered. You could let the man work on the ground floor and have his work brought to him. This may be inconvenient, but it is not an undue hardship. Most large companies would be required to build the ramp, because the cost would be reasonable; however, the same amount of money to a smaller company may make the difference between profit and loss.

3-10   What is a "disability" under the law? I have an employee who is constantly out sick. Does this make her disabled?

A disability is defined as a physical or mental characteristic which the employee cannot change (e.g., blindness, inability to use limbs, mental retardation) and which impairs the person's ability to perform major life activities. Included in this definition are people who have a record of such impairment or are regarded to have such an impairment. Courts have expanded the definition to include such "impairments" as obesity, shortness of stature, and AIDS.

With that in mind, many people who are not obviously disabled may be covered. However, just being out sick is not a disability. The type of ailment is what is considered. If the person's malady significantly impairs her ability to perform major life activities, she may claim coverage.

3-11   Are drug addicts and alcoholics protected by this law?

If a person can perform the job satisfactorily, a previous record of alcoholism or drug addiction is not reason enough to refuse hiring. However, if the person is still addicted and it is manifested in a recent history of poor attendance or poor performance, you can reject the applicant—not because of the addiction but because of the poor work record.

3-12   One of my friends is the chief mechanic of a large factory. He has four mechanics working for him. Last year he hired a disabled worker. The guy is terrific with tools. He can fix anything. But he is limited to working in the repair shop. About one-third of the work has to be done at the site of the problem. A machine breaks down and the mechanic goes to it; people can't bring heavy equipment to the shop. This repair work often requires crouching and crawling. The disabled worker can't do this. Before the new man was hired, all the mechanics took turns repairing heavy equipment. Now the other mechanics have to do more of the harder, dirtier, more fatiguing work. The result has been poor morale and lots of griping. My people work in a similar way. In light of this, can I refuse to hire a disabled worker?

If the applicant can do the mechanical work, you would have to make accommodation by assigning her or him—just as your friend did—more of the benchwork. To avoid resentment, before the new employee starts, discuss the issue with the others, sell them on the idea that the disabled applicant is a good worker and deserves a chance to work. How would they feel if they had an accident and became disabled? Most people are willing to make sacrifices if they think they are justified.

3-13   My people are worried about exposure to AIDS. Can I refuse to hire somebody who is afflicted with this disease?

No. The courts have ruled that AIDS is a covered disability. All medical reports show that AIDS isn't spread by casual contact. Explain this to your people. To overcome unjustified fears, many companies have instituted AIDS awareness programs. Using videos, pamphlets, articles in the company house organ, and talks by doctors, they teach their employees the facts about how AIDS is spread and allay their fears. If fear of AIDS becomes a problem in your department, suggest to your management that the company adopt such a program.

3-14   With all the concern about medical conditions that might cause problems on the job, can we require applicants to take a physical exam before we hire them?

Yes, but you cannot refuse to hire people on the basis of the physical unless the reason is job-related (see question 85 in Chapter 2).

Criminal Records

3-15   Is it true that we cannot inquire if an applicant has an arrest record? In this crime-ridden society, I want to avoid hiring criminals. Anyway, what does having an arrest record have to do with equal employment?

The reason asking about arrests falls under the EEO laws is that police are often tougher and more likely to make arrests in minority areas than in more affluent neighborhoods. Thus, asking about arrests has an adverse impact on minority people. More important, just because a person has been arrested does not mean he or she is guilty of a crime. Our criminal justice system is based on a person being innocent until proven guilty. An arrest is not proof of guilt.

3-16   I understand that a person is innocent until proven guilty. Can I ask applicants about convictions for crimes?

Yes, but you cannot refuse to hire a person because of a conviction unless it is job-related. For example, a woman applies for a job as a cashier in a store. She has been convicted for driving while intoxicated. This has no bearing on the job for which she has applied and cannot be used as a reason for rejection. On the other hand, if her conviction were for shoplifting, it would be a legitimate reason not to hire her.

3-17   What about a person who has served time for murder, assault, or rape? I wouldn't want that kind of person working near me.

I can understand that. The courts have not established clear guidelines in this area. I would take into consideration how long ago the crime was committed. If it was many years ago, it should not be a factor. Check with your attorney on the relevant laws in your state.

3-18   Our employees handle cash and we are very concerned about their honesty. We used to give polygraph tests to applicants, but now they are illegal. Suppose we suspect

an employee of theft. Can we then use a lie detector test in our investigation?

Because of the controversy about lie detector tests, polygraphs and similar tests were banned by federal law except in relation to government employees, defense contractors, and a few other organizations. For example, companies providing armed security personnel and companies that manufacture controlled substances can also use them.

You can use lie detector tests as part of an ongoing investigation involving theft, embezzlement, industrial espionage, sabotage, and similar offenses. However, if a test is requested, the employer must:

- Give the employee advanced written notice of the date, time, and conditions of the test
- Provide the employee with a statement summarizing the incident that is under investigation and why the employee is under suspicion
- Advise the employee in writing that he or she has the right to refuse to take the test and that anything said during the test may be used as evidence against the employee
- Allow the employee to review the questions to be asked
- Inform the employee that he or she may terminate the test at any time
- Give the employee a copy of the test results, along with any opinion or conclusion resulting from the test

An employer cannot discharge or discipline an employee solely on the basis of the test results or refusal to take the test. This law does not apply to written or oral questionnaires designed to test honesty. There are several types of "honesty tests" on the market, but their effectiveness is unclear.

Sex Discrimination

3-19   Most of my concerns about the EEO laws relate to women. When I hire a woman, I want to be sure she can come to work on a regular basis, yet my boss says I cannot ask her about any arrangement she's made for child care. This is important. Why can't I ask about it?

The most common sex discrimination complaints involve questions about child care. We don't usually ask men about child care, so we shouldn't ask women. It still is more usual for the mother—not the father—to stay home when a child is sick; however, many parents are now sharing this responsibility. We should not ask questions of one sex that we do not ask of the other.

3-20   If I ask all applicants—male and female—about child care, will I be in compliance with the law?

Your approach might be considered a subterfuge. Don't ask either sex. You can address the issue by making it quite clear before you hire anybody—male or female—that the company is very strict about attendance. Specify the penalty for absenteeism. When people know you are serious about it and know they do have problems in this area, they are likely to withdraw from the job. Remember, you must do this with both men and women.

Many companies have more liberal policies on family-related absenteeism and arrange for time off when an employee needs it. The Family and Medical Leave Act of 1993 requires companies with more than 50 employees to give unpaid leave to employees who need this time for child care or other family problems.

3-21   Can I ask any questions about children, marital status, and other personal data? We need this information for our benefits program.

Not before hiring. Preemployment inquiries should be limited to matters that can help you evaluate the qualifications of the applicant. After the new employee is on board, have him or her fill out an employee record form in which all these questions may be asked.

Unfortunately, most questions about family have an adverse impact on women. You ask a man how many children he has and he answers "Five." You think: "Great. With that size family, he has to work hard and won't quit too easily." But if a woman gives the same response, you think: "Five kids. She'll always be taking time off to care for one of them."

3-22   Our company requires people to work overtime at short notice. Women who have to pick up their kids from day care or sitters can't do this. Can I make inquires on the subject before I hire anybody?

Don't assume that because some women have to pick up their children they cannot work overtime. Many women (and men) can call on friends or relatives to do this with little notice. Of course, tell the applicants about the need to work overtime at short notice before you hire them.

3-23 I feel that a stable family life is important. How can I explore a person's family background during the interview?

Many inquiries that once were considered essential to good hiring decisions are no longer legal. For example, because employers felt that churchgoers were responsible people, questions concerning church were often asked. Such inquiries are now illegal under the EEO prohibition of discrimination on religious grounds.

By asking general questions about activities outside of work, you can pick up information about a person's character. For example: "How do you spend your leisure time?" This may elicit a response like "We go on family excursions." However, just because the applicant said the word "family" does not open the door for you to ask questions about the family. If the answer indicates "church work," it doesn't allow you now to ask, "What church?"

3-24 I know the equal pay law requires that we pay men and women at the same rate for doing the same kind of work. But now some women are claiming equal pay for work of "comparable worth." What does that mean?

As we all know, women have often been paid lower salaries than men doing the same work. This ranged from the lowest to the highest echelons in many companies. A male clerk started at a higher salary than a woman; the female office manager was paid less than her male counterpart. Unequal salaries were made illegal under the Equal Pay Act of 1963.

Even when the wages of men and women with the same job title were equal, variations in titles were used to pay women less. The male porters were paid more than the female maids in a hotel; male attendants in a hospital were paid more than nurse's aides. The law has made these distinctions more difficult to sustain.

Over the years some job categories were predominantly male or female. Secretaries, typists, nurses, elementary school teachers, and retail salesclerks were chiefly female jobs, although some men also did those kinds of work. Carpenters, electricians, outside salespersonnel, and most management and professional jobs were male-dominated. Jobs that were traditionally female were usually paid at lower rates than so-called male jobs.

The "comparable worth" concept aims to correct these inequities. Some jobs that are classified at lower levels because they have been traditionally female require as much skill as some higher-paid male jobs, even though they are totally different. The hospital electrician is paid more than a nurse. Is his job more skilled? Or is the differential based on sex? Comparable worth would break jobs into components that could be measured by objective job analyses and priced accordingly. This approach is being used with some government jobs now, but has not as yet been adopted to any extent in the private sector. Comparable worth has received support in some court cases, but its legal future is still far from clear.

3-25   I know it is illegal to refuse to hire a pregnant woman just because she is pregnant. Some of our jobs require heavy physical labor, which may endanger the woman or the baby. Not only are we concerned from a humanitarian point of view, but we also fear litigation. What can we do?

Exceptions can be made for bona fide occupational reasons. This must be examined case by case, and you should consult both your medical and legal advisers.

3-26   At what period of the pregnancy can we require a woman to take a leave of absence?

The decision to leave is not the company's. Unless there are compelling job-related medical reasons, the decision to leave is left to the woman and her (not your) doctor.

3-27   One of my employees left to have her baby 6 weeks before she delivered and then took 6 more weeks before returning to work. Her sick leave covered 10 days (2 work-weeks). She filed a disability insurance claim for the balance of the time. Pregnancy is not a disability. Must we pay it?

Pregnancy *is* considered a disability and your company must pay her the same as if she had broken a leg and been out the same period of time. The same rules hold for women who are out for pregnancy as for any other covered reason.

3-28   We had a case recently where a woman decided to stay home to take care of her new baby for 6 months. Can she claim disability pay?

No. Disability is defined as inability to work because of physical or mental illness. The woman's coverage for disability ends when she is medically able to return to work. After that, if your company has 50 or more employees and is covered under the Family and Medical Leave Act of 1993, she is entitled to unpaid leave of absence for a maximum of 12 weeks. Benefits must be continued, but salary need not be paid.

If your company is not covered by this law, the new mother has no legal protection in most states. Some state laws require that she be guaranteed reemployment in the same job or one of similar status if she returns to work within a specified period of time. Check with your local authorities. Of course, companies can do more than the law requires, and many do give some paid or unpaid leave to mothers who want more time to care for new babies.

3-29   Even before the family leave law was passed, our company allowed women unpaid time off to take care of their babies. Last year one of our male employees, a new father, demanded the same privilege. We gave it to him, but did we have to?

Yes, even without the new law, any special treatment given to one sex must be given to the other.

3-30   Much has been reported recently about sexual harassment on the job. It's gotten to the point where some of my male colleagues are afraid even to talk to the women they supervise. What exactly is sexual harassment?

Sexual harassment is defined as any unwelcome sexual advances or requests for sexual favors or any conduct of a sexual nature when:

- Submission is made explicitly or implicitly a term or condition of initial or continued employment
- Submission or rejection is used as a basis of working conditions including promotion, salary adjustments, assignment of work, and termination
- Such conduct has the purpose or effect of substantially interfering with the individual's work environment or creates an intimidating, hostile or offensive work environment

Each of these issues is examined in detail in the following questions.

3-31   I can understand what is meant by explicit sexual advances, but how can one determine "implicit"?

Any implicit action is subject to interpretation. What appears to be harmless flirting to a supervisor may be interpreted by the applicant or employee as an advance. To eliminate any possible misunderstandings, avoid even casual flirtatious remarks in dealing with members of the opposite sex.

3-32   In most of the harassment cases I read about, it is a male supervisor who is accused by a female worker. Can men claim to be harassed by a female boss?

Yes. There have been several such cases. The law applies to all people regardless of gender.

3-33   What about homosexual advances?

Federal and most state laws do not deal specifically with discrimination on the basis of sexual preference. However, any demand for sexual favors—even if it is from a member of the same sex—would be harassment under the law.

Some state and local laws do prohibit inquiry into sexual preference and discrimination on this basis. Check with your attorney on whether there are such laws in your area.

3-34   Demanding sexual favors from an employee is relatively easy to understand, but I'm confused about creating "an intimidating, hostile, or offensive working environment." What does this mean?

Let's say that a department has been all-male and now women are being hired. The old-time employees may resent the women and may even feel threatened. They make life unpleasant for the women by making snide remarks, failing to provide them with the information or training they need, giving them the wrong tools, and doing the countless other things that people can do to make newcomers feel unwelcome. This is one example of a hostile environment.

If you are the supervisor of this department, you have an obligation to prevent such hostility. If it should develop, correct it immediately or your company can be charged with sexual harassment.

3-35   I told one of the women who works for me that she looked nice. My boss chastised me, saying that my remark

could be interpreted as sexual harassment. Is he being overly zealous?

It is not considered harassment if a man comments that a woman is dressed nicely or looks pretty. But if he should make comments about the size of her bosom or her other physical characteristics, it could be interpreted as creating a hostile environment. Sure, a woman may be flattered by such remarks, but generally they are not welcome and are considered harassing.

3-36   I would never make sexually inappropriate remarks, but I have men working for me who are constantly making such comments. Am I responsible for what they do?

Yes. The law does not apply only to supervisors. Note that the language used is "working environment." Anything going on in the workplace is the responsibility of the company. You, the supervisor, represent the company. It is your job to make sure that all your people behave in a businesslike manner on the job. If you don't stop these kinds of remarks, the company can be charged with sexual harassment, and you, the supervisor, will be held accountable.

If you hear one of your men making sexually inappropriate comments, speak to him privately. If several are doing so, bring them together and point out that it is a violation of the law and that the company takes the matter seriously. If the behavior is repeated, progressive discipline should be applied, just as it would be for violations of any other company rule.

3-37   I am offended by people who use street language in my presence. I've heard my share of four-letter words, but it doesn't mean I accept people speaking this way. In some of the departments in my company, these words are in constant use. Some of the women have complained to me about it, even though the users are not in my department. I have spoken to the supervisors of these men and they say: "They always speak that way. They did it before we had women here and they are not going to change. It's their natural way of expressing themselves." What should I do?

If the pattern continues, the company may be charged with sexual harassment for not taking action to stop the offensive language. First, explain to the immediate supervisors of these people the legal ramifications of not stopping it. Discuss it with the human resources department or the person in the company responsible for EEO compliance. It may appear to be a petty matter, but if no action is taken, trouble can result.

3-38   One of the sales representatives who comes into our office makes a point of telling off-color jokes to the women in my department. Some of them think he is hilarious, but I see the look of disgust on the faces of others. Nobody has complained. He doesn't work for our company. Is there anything I can do about it?

The law states that an employer is responsible for the offensive behavior of non employees when the employer and its agents—in this case, you—know about it or should have known about it.

Speak to the person on whom this sales representative calls and tell him or her to discuss the matter with the sales rep. If the undesirable behavior continues, the company has an obligation to tell the sales rep that it cannot continue to do business with him.

3-39   In answering the previous question, you said something that disturbs me. You said the company is responsible if the supervisor knows or "should have known" about it. I can understand knowing, but how can it be determined if he or she "should have known?"

This is a very delicate point. One interpretation is that a diligent supervisor knows what is going on in his or her department. For example, a male supervisor may claim that he never heard men in his department make sexually oriented comments to women. The Equal Employment Opportunity Commission has ruled that this is not an acceptable excuse; a conscientious supervisor should know what is happening in the department.

Companies can protect themselves to some degree from such charges by establishing and publicizing a procedure for dealing with complaints of sexual harassment. A responsible executive (not a junior clerk) should be in charge of the program. All employees should be informed about what is considered sexual harassment and what procedure they should follow if they feel they have been harassed. The procedure should always include a meeting with the executive, who should investigate the complaint and, if true, correct it; if not true, the executive should explain the reason to the complainant.

If a complaint is then made to federal or state authorities, the action your company has taken will be a major part of your defense. If the complainant did not follow the procedure, a charge that you "should have known" will be less likely to be upheld.

3-40   When men and women work together, romances may develop and flirtations are common. Can this be considered harassment?

The key language in the law's definition of harassment is "unwelcome sexual advances." Nothing is wrong when both parties are happy about an encounter. However, the danger of the office romance is that if one person wants to end it and the other persists, it can develop into harassment.

3-41   Here's a situation I had to face last year. One of my clerks, Lisa, went out a couple of times with Tony, a guy from another department. It never developed into a romance, but Tony kept bugging Lisa to go out with him again. He would come into our office several times a day to talk to her. I told her this was interfering with her work. Lisa assured me she did not want to see him, and it was becoming an annoyance. Next time Tony came in, I called him aside and told him that he was not welcome in my department and that I didn't want to see him here again. He didn't come back, but he continued to harass Lisa by telephoning her after work. I told her I couldn't do anything about that. Did I handle the situation right?

Speaking to Tony was the right thing to do. It kept him out of the department and enabled Lisa to work uninterrupted. However, it did not stop the harassment. Even though he now called her at home after work, they were both employees of the company and the company could be held in violation of the law. Your next move should be to take the matter up with your company's EEO officer or personnel department. The officer should speak to Tony about his behavior and, if it persists, take disciplinary action. Both you and others in the company should document everything that you do.

Hiring and Working with People from Other Cultures

3-42   We are getting lots of people from other countries applying for jobs. I know some are here illegally. Is it a problem if we hire them?

The immigration laws prohibit an employer from hiring undocumented aliens. All new employees must present documents proving that they are legally in this country. This usually is the "green card," although there are other acceptable documents in certain cases. Personnel departments are usually knowledgeable about the paperwork involved. If your company is not fully cognizant of what should be done, get in touch with the local office of the Immigration and Naturalization Service to obtain the necessary forms.

3-43   Wouldn't it be safe, then, just not to hire people who are not U.S. citizens?

No. Discrimination on the basis of national origin is a violation of the law. All people legally in this country are protected, whether they are citizens or not. You cannot even inquire if a person is a citizen unless he or she is being considered for a position in which government clearance is needed. Even then, you cannot ask for proof of citizenship until after you have made the job offer.

3-44   I have a group of Hispanic workers in my department who usually talk to one another in Spanish. My other people feel uncomfortable because they don't know what the group is saying and think that the remarks are being directed at them. All of the Hispanic workers speak English. Can I order them to speak only English on the job?

No, unless the need to speak only English is job-related. For example, if an employee discusses matters related to a customer's order with another employee in a language the customer does not understand, you can require that the employee always speak English in the presence of customers.

3-45   Some of the people applying for work in my company speak no English at all. Must I hire them? If I do, how can I train and communicate with them?

If they are legal residents or citizens and the job is one in which speaking English is not essential (e.g., if no customers are involved), ability to speak English is not a bona fide occupational qualification.

This is not a new phenomenon in America. From the beginning, we have been a nation of immigrants. Except for those people who came from the British Commonwealth, all had to learn English after they came to these shores. Employers have dealt with language barriers in many ways. Even among "new immigrants," there are people who have enough knowledge of English to act as unofficial interpreters. Also, many jobs for which immigrants are hired are manual and can be taught and supervised nonverbally. Many companies encourage their immigrant employees to take English-as-a-second-language (ESL) courses in local schools. Some large organizations provide such courses in house.

3-46   Some of our people come from remote societies on other continents and from cultures very different from ours. How can I help them adjust to doing things our way?

People learn best by imitating their peers. Try to integrate the new employees with Americans or other immigrants who have adjusted to American ways. Provide an American mentor to guide each newcomer. If someone does have serious problems in adjusting, recommend counseling. Most of the communities where various cultural groups live have people trained in this area.

3-47   Management is very high on working with a "diverse" work force, but my old-time employees resent the "pampering" of immigrants and other minorities. How can I get them to go along with our policy?

People have to be trained to accept differences in the way things are now as against how they used to be. For example, Digital Equipment Corporation set up a program in which small groups of employees met for at least 4 hours a month to explore assumptions and sterotypes about their own culture and those of others. The program had the following goals:

- Identify and eliminate preconceptions and myths about the new ethnic groups in the company.
- Encourage workers to develop relationships with people in other cultural groups and thereby broaden understanding of cultural differences.
- Listen for assumptions that cause differences in the perception and perspectives of other cultures.
- Help people overcome the limits they impose on themselves, both individually and as members of the group.
- Explore and identify group differences.

You can call upon consultants in the field of cultural diversity to develop programs that meet the specific needs of your organization.

Applying EEO on the Job

3-48   One way I recruit people is to ask my present employees to recommend friends or relatives. I was told this is illegal. Is that right?

If this is your only source of recruiting, you will perpetuate the same racial and ethnic population you now have. Most people still primarily associate with "their own kind." You can ask for referrals from your own people, but you should use other sources as well and not give referred people preference over applicants from other sources.

3-49   We have the opposite practice. We will not hire friends or relatives of our employees. Is this legal?

This is not a violation of the EEO laws so long as it is administered in a nondiscriminatory manner. For example, if exceptions are made occasionally, but always seem to be for white employees, the policy is discriminatory.

3-50   If one of our employees marries another, one has to quit. Is this legal? Is it a good policy?

It is legal in most jurisdictions so long as the person who has to quit is not always the woman. Some companies require the lower-ranking spouse to leave, but since this is most often the woman, the policy is not acceptable. The best approach is to allow the couple to decide between themselves which one will leave.

Is this good policy? It is not a good idea to allow one spouse to supervise the other, but why lose a good worker just because of the marriage? A smarter policy would be to transfer one of them to another department.

Although discrimination on the basis of marital status is not expressly prohibited in the federal laws, it is barred by administrative interpretation of the sex discrimination prohibitions. Some states do have specific laws prohibiting discrimination on the basis of marital status. The policy of requiring an employee to leave if he or she marries another employee is being challenged in cases pending in some of these states.

3-51   Some of the young people in my department come to work dressed in clothes more appropriate to leisure activities. The women wear shorts and tank tops; the men, shirts open to their navels. Can I require them to dress in more suitable clothes?

Dress codes are legal provided they do not discriminate. For example, if you prohibited the woman from wearing shorts, but did nothing about the men's open shirts, it would not be equal treatment under the law. Another form of dress code discrimination is to prohibit a Muslim woman from dressing as prescribed by her religion or an orthodox Jew from wearing a yarmulke. Other than these types of situations, dress codes do not violate the EEO laws.

It is best to have companywide dress codes rather than let each department set up individual requirements. Of course, there may be different dress rules for people who work in an office or who have contact with the public as against those working in a factory or warehouse. But departments in which people do similar work should follow the same dress codes.

3-52   I can understand requiring security guards, nurses, and people in similar jobs to wear uniforms, but our company requires all employees to dress in the company uniform. Factory workers have standard workshirts or smocks with the company logo. Male office workers must wear company blazers and slacks; females, blouses and skirts that resemble the uniforms in parochial schools. Is this legal? Also, we have to buy our own uniforms. Is this right?

It is legal. This is a common practice in Japan and in many other countries. When foreign companies open U.S. facilities, they often follow the same rules. Provision must be made for exceptions arising from physical disabilities or religious tenets that require people to wear special clothes. Having employees pay for their uniforms is also legal. Although many companies do provide the uniforms, others do not. Nurses and security guards usually pay for their uniforms. This is not an imposition, since they will save money by not having to wear their own clothes.

3-53   Our company recently prohibited smoking on the job. Doesn't this invade the rights of smokers and, indeed, discriminate against them?

There is no law prohibiting discrimination against smokers. If a policy does not concern race, religion, national origin, sex, age, or disability, or cannot be construed to be related to one of these, no law applies.

3-54   In our state, companies must prohibit smoking except in designated areas. Now some of our people take several smoke breaks a day, leading to reduced productivity. Can I discipline people for this?

It is not illegal to discipline people who violate any company rule. Excessive time away from the workplace is usually against company rules. The issue should be covered in the company policy manual. It is best to have a heart-to-heart chat with smokers when their smoke breaks begin to interfere with productivity. Point out that if the practice continues, disciplinary action will have to be taken.

3-55   Can I ask people whether or not they smoke before I hire them?

Under federal law, it is not illegal to ask this question. However, some states have recently passed laws prohibiting employers from refusing to hire people because they smoke *off* the job. It is OK to prohibit employees from smoking on the job. Smokers should be told before they are employed about company rules regarding smoking on the premises.

3-56   Is it true that the government has banned testing in the selection of applicants because tests discriminate against some minorities?

No. Tests can be used so long as they meet the EEO guidelines. Employers must validate any tests that they use. That means the employer must show that there is some relationship between what the test measures and performance on the job. For example, if you insist that a person for a clerical job pass an intelligence test with a score of 80 out of 100, you have to show that people who have achieved this level actually perform better than those who do not. Validation studies must be conducted by professionals. It must also be shown that the tests do not have adverse impact on minorities. Many test suppliers can help you determine if their tests meet your requirements.

Age Discrimination

3-57   I understand that the age discrimination law applies only to people over 40. Does that mean that I can refuse to hire a 35-year-old person and not violate the law?

It is the federal law that prohibits discrimination against people over 40. Several states have set the age at 18, so if you work in one of those states, you violate state law.

I would not suggest that in any state you reject an applicant because of age unless there is a bona fide occupational qualification for age in the job. One 35-year-old woman who was turned down for a job complained to the Equal Employment Opportunity Commission (EEOC). She was told that she could not file a charge because she was under 40. However, the next day the EEOC asked the state job service to refer a 45-year-old woman for the same job and when this woman was rejected, took appropriate action.

3-58   Our application form asks for date of birth. Are we violating the Age Discrimination in Employment Act (ADEA)?

The EEOC has allowed this question provided the application form includes a statement that discrimination because of age is illegal. However, most experts in EEO law suggest that age or date of birth *not* be asked on the application, since it could be used as evidence against an employer if a person claims he or she was not hired because of age. After employment, you can obtain the information for benefits purposes and personnel records.

3-59   The law requires that we get proof that an applicant is over 18 or, if not, that the applicant has working papers. If I can't ask age, how can I know if such papers are needed?

You can ask: "Are you over 18?" If proof of age is needed, the new employee should bring it along on starting day. If there is any doubt about age, do not put the person on the payroll until such proof is furnished.

3-60   One of my people will be 65 next year. He's been a marginal worker for years and I've been looking forward to his retiring so I can get a real producer in his job. Now I hear he isn't planning to retire. What can I do?

The Age Discrimination in Employment Act prohibits forced retirement at any age. The only way you can terminate the employee is for inability to meet performance standards. However, because you have accepted his marginal work for a long while, you cannot now demand higher standards. It would be considered a subterfuge for age discrimination. Some companies have persuaded older people to take retirement by offering financial incentives. However, if you put this in the form of an ultimatum—directly or subtly—you would be in violation of ADEA.

3-61   People over 65 often either cannot be covered by our health and life insurance programs or will cost us a lot more for coverage. If we hire older people, can we exclude them from these benefits programs?

No. The law requires that all workers (and their spouses) regardless of age be covered by your health insurance policies, and the extent of such coverage for older workers must be equal to that provided for employees under 65. However, for all other types of benefits, an employer may provide reduced coverage so long as the actual cost of those benefits is the same as for younger workers. For example, you may provide a lesser amount of life insurance for older workers so long as the premiums are the same as those paid for younger workers.

3-62   To reduce costs, our company encouraged older workers to take early retirement by giving them a bonus and continuing their benefits. We did this in good faith, but some people have filed suit for age discrimination. What can we do to prevent such suits?

You may ask people who accept such offers to sign a waiver of their rights under ADEA. Several steps must be taken to make such a waiver legal:

- The waiver should be in ordinary English, not in legalese.
- It should specifically refer to rights and claims under ADEA and related laws and rulings.
- It must exclude claims arising after the waiver is signed.

- It must provide something of value beyond which the employee would have been entitled to anyway (e.g., severance pay the employee would have received if just laid off).

- It must be in writing and advise the employee to consult an attorney.

- It must allow a 7-day period after signing in which the employee can revoke the waiver.

Such documents should be prepared by an attorney.

Affirmative Action

3-63 Are we required to give women and minorities preferential treatment in hiring and promoting?

Under the civil rights laws, no preferential treatment is required. People should be hired for their abilities regardless of race, religion, national origin, age, sex, or disability. However, companies with government contracts may fall under one of the laws that do require affirmative action.

Under Executive Orders 11246 and 11375, any company with government contracts in excess of $50,000 and more than 50 employees must have a written affirmative action plan committed to hiring women and minorities in proportion to their representation in the community in which the firm is located. Determination of such goals is very complicated and requires the assistance of specialists.

As a supervisor, all you need to know is what your company's goals are for various minority groups and for women, so you can make every effort to comply with them. If your department is not in line with the affirmative action goals of the company, you should make an effort to hire or promote a person in the group in which the deficiency exists. This does not mean you must hire unqualified people just because of their minority status. But if you have two candidates of relatively equal qualifications, you should give preference to the minority candidate even if he or she needs more training or support to become productive.

3-64 Can a white man who has been bypassed for promotion so that the company could hire or promote a minority candidate or a woman claim that he has been discriminated against?

"Reverse discrimination" has been a bone of contention since the institution of affirmative action. Various court rulings have come down in these cases. Generally, minority/female promotion or hiring over white males will not be considered reverse discrimination if the company has not met its affirmative action goals. On the other hand, if the goals have been met or the company does not have an affirmative action plan, the white man's claim may be upheld.

3-65   In our town, which is predominantly white Anglo-Saxon, we have large populations of blacks, Poles, Chinese, Italians, and Jews. Must we set goals for hiring them in proportion to their number in the community?

The minority groups that are specified as "protected classes" are African-Americans, Hispanics, Asians, Native Americans, and women. You would have to set goals only for the blacks, Chinese, and of course women.

3-66   What about Vietnam veterans? I was told to seek out and hire them.

Under the Vietnam era's Veterans Readjustment Act (1974), government contractors must have affirmative action plans for veterans of that conflict. This applies only to the first 4 years after discharge, so by now most Vietnam veterans are no longer eligible for preferential treatment. However, disabled veterans are covered for life.

Dealing with Complaints

3-67   What do I do to prevent our people from filing charges with the EEOC or state commission on civil rights?

There is no way to completely stop people from filing charges against you. If all supervisors are aware of the laws and their ramifications, you are less likely to violate them. Periodic seminars, conducted by your EEO officer or an outside consultant, should be held to reinforce this knowledge.

Be sure to avoid asking applicants questions which are not necessary to determine their qualifications. Be particularly careful to avoid asking women questions about marriage, family, and children. Never imply that a job is better suited to a man, a younger person, or someone "who will be accepted by our customers."

To avoid charges from your own employees, establish a system so that complaints can be adjudicated without outside interference. All employees should be given full information (through printed materials, films, meetings, and other channels) about their rights and how to handle violations. A senior officer of the company should be given the responsibility of monitoring this program. In large organizations, a full-time EEO administrator may be appointed; in smaller firms, the personnel director or another executive should administer the program.

All complaints should be investigated immediately and thoroughly. The complainant should be kept informed of progress, and if the complaint is sustained, action should be taken to correct it. Such action should be congruent with the offense and may range from warnings on a first offense to disciplinary action for repeat violations.

Figure 3-3 presents 12 ways to keep alert to your EEO responsibilities.

3-68   What do we do if a complaint is lodged?

Your first indication of a complaint may be a letter from the EEOC or state authority asking you for information concerning the situation. If you receive such a letter, consult your attorney immediately. Every complaint has serious legal ramifications, and you should not try to deal with it without legal aid.

Sometimes you do not get a letter. An investigator shows up at your office and requests certain information. You are not obligated to give any information without proper notice (unless a court order has been issued). Politely indicate that you need time to assemble the material and will be happy to provide it at a later date. Then contact your attorney.

If you do not have the opportunity to consult a lawyer, call in your boss or another executive. *No supervisor should ever deal with an investigator alone. Higher-level management must become involved immediately.* If you are required to answer questions, give only the information asked for. Do not volunteer more than what was asked and do not add your own opinions.

Keep a record of the questions and answers. The investigator will undoubtedly be taking notes, so you take notes as well. If the case does reach the hearing stage, you will know just what the investigator has written in his or her notes and your can refer to yours to correct misunderstandings.

12 Ways to Keep Alert to Your EEO Responsibility

G o along with the spirit as well as the letter of the law.

O ffer women and minorities opportunities that were previously denied to them.

O pen training programs to minorities, women, and the disabled and encourage them to complete these program by offering counseling and support.

D iscipline your people equitably and carefully document what you do.

B e aware of your own biases and work to overcome any influence they may have on your job decisions.

U se all your people's capabilities optimally. Do not base your views about a person's capabilities on age, sex, or race. Judge disabled people not on what they cannot do but on what they *can* do.

S et realistic performance standards based on what the job really calls for. For example, do not specify that a job calls for heavy lifting when most of the lifting is done mechanically.

I gnore stereotypes and judge people by their individual capabilities, strengths, and weaknesses.

N ever use racial epithets or slurs—even in jest.

E ncourage all your people to deal with their co-workers as human beings, whether they be black or white, Hispanic or Anglo, male or female, disabled or able-bodied. Mold them into a team.

S eparate sex life from job life.

S upport your company's equal employment and affirmative action program fully in every aspect of your job.

Follow these suggestions. They add up to **GOOD BUSINESS.**

Figure 3-3

Usually the EEO representative will try to resolve the case on the spot. If it is easily settled, do so. However, hiring a rejected applicant or rehiring a discharged one may not end the case. You may be required to furnish back pay from the time the applicant applied or the former-employee was discharged. You may be ordered to institute an affirmative action program. That's another reason you need a lawyer.

If the issue goes beyond this, a formal hearing will be held. It is like a court case without a jury. The EEO (or state equivalent) is both prosecutor and judge. The rules of evidence that are part of the judicial system do not apply. You are considered guilty until you prove yourself innocent.

If the ruling goes against you, you can appeal to the courts. The process is expensive and time-consuming—another reason it is best to do all you can to avoid such cases.

3-69   What are the usual penalties for violation of EEO laws?

Penalties range from requiring you to hire, rehire, promote, or adjust the pay of the complainant (usually with back pay) to financial settlements with those who cannot or do not want to be hired or rehired. You can be required to institute an affirmative action program to compensate for your discrimination. You will probably be monitored more closely by the agency.

Some complainants may sue you in the courts under various other laws rather than go through the EEOC. Here settlements may include not only back pay (compensatory damages) but additional penalties for emotional suffering (punitive damages). The process can be very expensive.

3-70   One of my employees thinks that he is being discriminated against because of his race. He is a poor performer but doesn't see that his work is substandard. How do I handle the situation?

Make sure that all your people know the performance standards you expect from them. There should be a clear understanding of what is and is not acceptable performance. If employees do not meet the standards, work with them to help them acquire the skills and techniques that will enable them to perform satisfactorily. Be patient, since some people take longer to become productive than others. Be sure to document what you have done.

If you have made every effort to help a worker become effective but he or she still does not meet the standards, termination may be appropriate. It is unlikely that charges of discrimination will be sustained.

3-71   How long must we keep application forms and other records in case complaints are issued against us?

Each law has its own time limits. The maximum time required by any law on applications and personnel records relating to discipline, promotions, terminations, and so on, is 1 year. Many lawyers recommend that records be kept longer for added protection.

4

Training

To ensure the success of our people, we must train them to perform their jobs in the most effective manner. Even people who have had previous experience in the work they were hired to do must be trained to perform their jobs according to the standards established in the organization.

Unfortunately, training tends to be haphazard in many companies. New employees are thrown into the work—in the hope that they will pick up the tricks of the trade by osmosis. This approach may work—some of the time. However, unless supervisors take the time to train their people carefully and systematically, the result will be poor productivity, unsatisfactory quality, high turnover, and low morale.

For many supervisors, training is time-consuming and a distraction from what they consider to be their primary function: getting the work out. But unless serious consideration is given to training, the supervisor, the department, and the company will suffer in the long run.

Systematic Training

4-1　I remember when I was being trained for my first job. All my boss did was demonstrate the job and say, "Watch what I do and do it." It took me quite a while to figure out

for myself all the things I eventually had to learn. Isn't there a better way?

Of course there is. There is a systematic approach to training which has been used effectively for many years. Known as job instruction training (JIT), it is designed to teach people to perform a task by breaking it down into four steps:

- Preparation
- Presentation
- Performance
- Follow-up

Most jobs can be broken into steps: performing clerical work, operating a computer, working on a machine, even handling customer complaints. This simple four-step method makes training far more effective. You will find a summary of JIT in Figure 4-1 and more details in answer to the next few questions.

4-2   What must I do to prepare the trainee for the training?

Preparation is both physical and psychological. Physically, all training equipment and facilities should be in place before you start. If you are training somebody to operate a computer, you should have the computer, software, training manual, data, and other materials arranged before the training session so you will not be interrupted looking for things that you need once you start.

Psychologically, the trainee should be told what is going to be taught, why it is performed, and how it fits into the overall picture. If you are training a machine operator, you might say: "You will be trained to drill two holes in a series of metal sheets. I will show you how to be sure that the holes are always in exactly the same place, so that the sheets will fit in the next operation—bolting them to the chassis of the snowmobiles our company makes. Now the trainee knows that he or she is not just drilling holes that must be accurate, but is making snowmobiles.

4-3   Is this the time to demonstrate how to do the job?

Yes, but it is not just "watch me." It's "tell and show." First you tell the trainee what you are going to do and then you do it. Explain the reason for each step so the trainee fully understands what you are doing. When people know why they do something, they usually learn it and retain it better. Whenever possible, rely on the appropriate senses. If people can feel the pressure of a mechanical movement, smell an odor in a chemical process, take a sip in cooking a recipe, they are more likely to learn and remember what has been taught.

4-4   The only way I really can tell if a trainee can perform the job is to let him or her do it. When do I let the trainee do the job?

Once you feel that the trainee has a good idea of what to do, say: "OK, now you try it. But before you do anything, tell me what you are going to do." Then have the trainee tell and show you. Ask questions about each step to make sure that the trainee knows why it is being performed. In this way you will get immediate feedback and can correct errors and misunderstandings. Once you are satisfied that your trainees can do the job, you can let them work on their own.

They are not yet totally on their own, of course. You must periodically check to make sure that they are doing things correctly. As you become more and more convinced that a trainee is performing satisfactorily, you can spread out the time between each of your visits until you are not giving that trainee any more supervision than other people doing the same work.

4-5   Is this the end of the training?

No. There is one more step: follow-up. The follow-up is very important, because people tend to change what they have been taught. Careless people skip some steps. In a 20-step procedure, they pass over 2 steps somewhere in the middle and then can't figure out what has gone wrong. Smart people may think they have found a better way. The follow-up enables the supervisor to see if such changes have been made and to correct them.

Initiate the follow-up 3 or 4 weeks after the presentation. Tell the trainee, "You have been on the job for 4 weeks. Let's review what you are doing." Then the trainee tells and shows you. If any changes have been made, they can be identified and corrected.

4-6   You used as an example a 20-step procedure. If we had such a procedure, would we train just one step at a time?

That would take forever. The human mind can absorb many steps at one time, optimally 6 to 8. If you have 20 steps, break the procedure into three sets of steps: two sets of 7 steps and one of 6. Train each set separately and then bring all three together.

Four Steps That Guarantee Learning

1. Preparation
   - Make a job analysis so you know exactly what has to be taught.
   - Break the job down into specific tasks. Set a timetable for each task.
   - Provide the proper equipment and materials.
   - Arrange the workplace in the manner that the worker will be expected to keep it.
   - Describe the job to the worker. Learn what he or she already knows about it.
   - Explain the purpose of the job and how it fits into the overall objectives of the department and the organization.

2. Presentation
   - Tell the worker how to perform the operation. Stress the key points.
   - Demonstrate how to perform—verbalize what you are doing.
   - Instruct clearly, completely, and patiently, but give no more at any time than the trainee can master.
   - Encourage questions and answer them fully.

3. Performance
   - Have the trainee do the job. Correct errors as they are made and explain what you are doing.
   - Have the trainee explain each point as he or she does it.
   - Be sure the trainee understands.
   - Develop confidence by giving praise.
   - Continue until you know that the trainee can do the job.

4. Follow-up
   - Let the trainee do the job alone.
   - Designate to whom the trainee can go for help.
   - Check frequently in the beginning and then taper off.
   - About 3 to 4 weeks after the presentation step, review the entire operation. Have the trainee tell and show you what he or she has been doing. Correct any changes made in the procedure.
   - Use positive reinforcement. People learn much better when you praise their accomplishments than when you criticize their failures.

Figure 4-1

4-7   Is the job instruction training (JIT) approach all I need to train people?

It depends on the job. For the routine jobs found in many companies, particularly in the lower echelons, this four-step method will do the trick.

For many other jobs, the basic steps can be mastered using the JIT method, but the more complex aspects must be taught through additional training techniques. For example, in training a customer service representative, you teach the basic steps in handling a complaint through JIT, but use role-plays, case studies, and other training methods to convey the more subtle, individualized aspects of customer service.

4-8   I was just transferred to another department and I have to train some new people. Since I'm not 100 percent sure what they will have to do, I looked over their job descriptions. To my shock, I found that the descriptions were several years old and in many cases no longer accurate. Is this common? What should I do?

Unfortunately, outdated job descriptions are commonplace. Jobs are constantly changing, but the descriptions do not always follow. If the company makes a radical change, such as bringing in new equipment or significantly different methods, it will usually initiate a new job analysis. Even if no major changes occur, all jobs change slowly and often imperceptibly over time. Look at your own job. If you are working in the same position today that you held 2 years ago, it's likely that you are not doing the same things you did then. Duties you once performed are now being done differently or not at all; new tasks have been added. Does the job description reflect the changes? Review all job descriptions carefully at least once every 2 years to ensure their accuracy.

When you discover outdated job descriptions, you will have to make a new analysis of each of the jobs involved (see Chapter 2). If there is no time for a complete analysis, carefully observe the workplace and talk to employees currently performing the work. You will pick up at least enough information to start the training process.

4-9   I'm training a woman who keeps interrupting me with questions. How can I finish the training at this rate?

Let her ask those questions. It indicates that she is eager to learn and wants to do the work properly. Sure, it takes time, but encouraging questions during training may save much more time down the line in correcting errors and redoing work.

4-10   One of my new people seems to take forever to learn the work. Is this a sign that he is stupid and I'd be best off letting him go before his trial period is over?

Slow learners are not necessarily stupid. Often they develop into superior employees. Be patient. If one approach does not work, try teaching the employee in a different manner. Make a sincere effort to help. If the employee still cannot do the work, it may be best either to transfer him to a job within his capability or to let him go.

4-11   In my own training I found that I move along rapidly for a while and then hit a period when nothing penetrates. I just feel I can never learn it—and then everything falls into place and I move ahead again. Is this usual?

You are following the learning curve. It is a normal phenomenon. The mind can absorb only a certain amount of information at any one time and then stops to assimilate it. A plateau is reached at which no new information can be processed. Once the processing is completed, the mind opens up again for new learning. As you begin to train others, remember the learning curve. It may appear that a trainee is unable to grasp what you are teaching. He or she may be at a plateau. The best thing to do is stop for a while—a few hours or even a few days—before introducing new material. In due course the plateau will be overcome.

4-12   Is it better to train a person off or on the job?

Off-the-job training has many advantages over on-the-job training. Training off the job is intensive; the trainee does nothing but learn and therefore learns a lot faster than in being trained on the job. Off-the-job training is usually conducted by professionals, who not only have all the know-how but have no other duties to distract them from the training. Off-the-job training does not interfere with production.

Despite these impressive advantages, there is one overwhelming limitation to off-the-job training: it is not cost-effective unless you train several people at the same time. Most supervisors train only one worker at a time, so it must be done on the job.

4-13   The jobs in my department do not require a lot of training. New workers can learn in a few hours and with a few days' experience can become fully productive. Training them on the job slows down the assembly line, but the boss wants the line to be moving at regular speed immediately. What do I do if I have several new employees coming in on the same day?

Training of this type is best done off the job. Some companies have what is called "vestibule" training, in which a simulated workplace serves as the training facility. Workers are taught the job before they are assigned to their regular stations. This eliminates the slowdowns and errors of training on the job itself.

Of course, not every company can afford to set up such a facility, and it isn't really cost-effective unless a great number of people can be trained. An alternative is to bring people in before or after hours on the first few days to train them in the basics of the job. Even though they will have to build their speed and accuracy on the job, it will reduce downtime on the line.

Setting the Training Schedule

4-14   All the training I do is on the job—and that brings up a tough problem. I'm so busy with regular work, I have difficulty finding the time to do it. How can I realistically schedule training for my new people?

It's a difficult problem for most busy supervisors, but since training new people is an essential part of your work, you must make it a high priority. In setting a training schedule, you have to make time. Ask yourself: "What part of my work can I delegate?" Often we spend time doing things that really should be done by others (see Chapter 5). Next ask yourself: "What can I skip altogether?" Here is the chance to streamline your job. Perhaps you are spending too much time on nonproductive tasks. Last and most unpleasant, ask: "What will I have to do after everybody goes home, so I have time during the workday for training?"

4-15   Setting schedules for off-the-job training is easy, but not for on-the-job training. I may plan to devote Tuesday from 2 to 4 to training and an urgent matter comes up at 2:15. There goes my schedule. How can I draw up a realistic training schedule when I never know when a crisis will develop?

You can accommodate for crises and other interruptions by building flexibility into your schedule. Unless there is a training plan, training becomes haphazard—and haphazard just doesn't work.

4-16   How do I start developing a training schedule?

You have already started. When you made or reviewed the job description, you determined the areas, or phases, in which you have to train that person. You should know from experience how long it will take to train a person in each phase and the total estimated training time.

Let's say that it will take you 3 weeks to train your new worker. It is not feasible to set up a training program three weeks in advance. There are too many imponderables. At the time you make the job analysis, you can determine what phases should be taught in each week—and even here you must be flexible. Then plan a week at a time. Use the prototype plan in Figure 4-2 as a guide. In the first column list the time scheduled; in the second column, the phase or subject matter to be trained; in the third column, training methods; and in the fourth column, training aids. Place a checkmark in the final column when training is completed.

4-17   I have a list of all the areas (phases) in which I want to train a new employee. Does it make any difference in what order I do the training?

One of the basic principles of all training, whether it be in school, on the athletic field, or on the job, is that you start with the simple and work up to the complex—not the other way around. Many supervisors don't even think about this in sequencing their training. A common error is to train people in that phase of the work you happen to be doing at the time you schedule the training. For example, you are working on a Project 3, so you decide to train the new person in how to handle a Project 3. Even though she may be able to learn a Project 3 before she learns a Project 1 and a Project 2, it would be better from a training viewpoint to start with 1 then go to 2 and eventually get to 3.

4-18   What do I list under "training methods" and "training aids" on my scheduling plan?

If you are using the four-step JIT method, indicate which steps you are using. If you are using any other methods, list them as well. (Other training methods are discussed later in this chap-

On-the-Job Training Schedule

Job _____

Equipment needed for training _____

Time (day/hour)	Phase	Training methods	Training aids	Completed

Figure 4-2

ter.) Training aids include audiovisuals, charts, models, and actual equipment used on the job.

4-19   Isn't practice an important part of training? My people learn to operate word processors and the real learning takes place in practice sessions. Practice makes perfect.

Yes. Practice is important in any repetitive type of work, and provision should be made for it. However, practice does *not* make perfect. Practice makes permanent. If trainees practice wrong things, they will become perfect doing things wrong. When your trainees are practicing, check them from time to time. If they are doing it wrong, correct the problem immediately before it become ingrained as a bad habit.

4-20   I'm a busy person. When I'm busy with other things, I tell my trainees to practice. However, often there is not that much to practice, particularly in the early part of the training program. What can I do to make this time worthwhile for the trainees and for the department?

You must build constructive tasks into the early stages of your training so that when trainees are not being taught new things, they can be productively engaged. For example, in one customer services department, job analysis showed that about 80 percent of the time the customer service representative was on the telephone dealing with customers. The rep would listen to an inquiry, key it into the computer, obtain the answer, and relay it to the customer. In the remaining 20 percent of the time, when information was not that easily available, the rep had to research and get back to the customer. The company correctly believed that it was not a good idea to allow a semitrained person to deal with a real, live customer—and it took 4 weeks before a trainee acquired this knowhow. So the first thing the trainee was taught was the research. For the balance of the training period, when the new worker was not being trained or practicing on the computer, he or she could help the other reps with their research, thus doing useful work and at the same time augmenting the on-the-job training.

Using Other Employees As Trainers

4-21   I'm much too busy to train my new workers, so I delegate the job to one of my experienced people. Is this OK?

Generally, it is not a good idea to let another person be the primary trainer, particularly if the training period is longer than a week. Participation in training gives the supervisor the chance to build a rapport with new employees—one that may shape their relationship for the long term. It also enables the supervisor to make early assessments of areas in which new workers may need added training or special coaching, and/or even to determine whether certain workers should be retained after the trial period. As supervisor, you should be the prime trainer, but you may use other employees as backup trainers. You can't always be there, and trainees should be able to go to others for help.

4-22   I picked my best worker to train new people, but he was a terrible trainer. He had no patience with people who were not as fast as he was. How do I choose a training assistant?

This happens very often. Good workers are not necessarily good trainers. Just because the person knows how to do a job doesn't mean she or he can train others. Many of us learned this when we attempted to teach a friend or relative how to drive a car.

In addition to thorough knowledge of the job, the person you choose as a training assistant must have:

- *The personal characteristics needed for training.*   Effective trainers have patience, empathy, flexibility, and good communication skills.

- *An ability to teach.*   Even people who have the personal characteristics needed, should be given training in how to train. If your company has a "train the trainer" program, your backup people should take it; if not, it is your responsibility to train them in how to train. Your company's training department (if you have one) can be of help.

- *A strong, positive attitude toward the job and the company.*   If you allow a disgruntled employee to help in the training, that person will inject the trainee with the virus of discontent.

From time to time, observe how your backup people are performing as trainers just as you check their other work. You may find they need some refresher training in this aspect of their work.

4-23   One woman in my department has all the attributes of being a good trainer, but she doesn't want to do it. She feels that unless she is paid to train others, it is an imposition to ask her to do it. Is she right?

Employees should never feel that the scope of their work is limited to the details of the job description. All job descriptions should specify that related assignments may be assigned. Training is one of these related assignments, and in most companies training assistants do not receive added compensation. The exception is when the thrust of the work becomes training others. Now the job has changed in its nature and should be reclassified.

4-24   How should you persuade such a person to take on training assignments?

Perhaps you shouldn't. If that person is really unwilling to train others, she will be a poor trainer. However, if you feel that she just needs added incentive, find out what she seeks from her job. If she is seeking growth opportunity, show her how the experience of training others will prepare her for advancement to a supervisor's job. If she is seeking interesting work, show how training can utilize her creativity. If it is more money that she seeks, point out how this additional activity will be considered in her performance evaluation.

4-25   Our company uses mentors rather than depending on one or two people to aid in training. Is this a good idea?

Mentors are experienced workers who are chosen to act as trainers, counselors, and friends to new employees. Some companies call them "big brothers" or "big sisters." Mentoring is a valuable tool in getting new people to feel comfortable on the job. The mentors should meet the qualifications discussed in question 4-22 above and should be given training in how to handle the mentoring role.

Training Methods

4-26   My workers have to interact with people in other departments, as well as with customers and vendors. To help them hone their skill, I have been using role-plays. However, the exercises often degenerate into farce. We have fun, but my people aren't being trained. How can I make the role-plays more realistic and have my people take them seriously?

To be effective role-play, must be carefully structured. The participants should be briefed on what the goals of the exercise are, and each participant should be given a specific part that he or she will play. Improvisation, of course, makes the exercise more spontaneous and allows for flexibility, but the degree of improvisation allowed should be carefully established. For example, the script for a role-play on dealing with an employee's gripe would establish just what the gripe is, the types of personalities of the "supervisor" and "griper," the relationships between them, and so on. The players can add or subtract from the script so long as they stay within these guidelines. In that way the role-play will be realistic and not run off into unrelated areas. The trainer should break into the role-play at any time to curtail digressions. The exercise must be carefully planned. Supervisors should seek special training in how to develop and use role-plays before adopting them as training tools.

4-27   The trouble I find with role-plays is that the people assigned to the roles get the benefits. The others are just onlookers. How can I get everybody in the group involved?

One way is to give the roles to groups. Each group studies and discusses its role and decides how it should be played. Then one member of the group comes forward to perform the role. In some instances, the others may step in to supplement the primary player. For example, if the person playing the supervisor misses an important point, others in the supervisor's group may step in and ask a question or make a comment to augment the point.

4-28   Case studies of realistic situations can be good training aids. How can I find cases to use in training my people?

A case study is a description of a real or a simulated situation and is usually presented in some detail. It may be presented in print, on film, or on video. Here are some major sources:

1. *Harvard Business School.*   Harvard has been the chief advocate of case study learning and has developed many highly complex cases. Its annual bibliography describes in summary form the cases and how you can purchase them. Most Harvard cases are designed for management training rather than for the training most supervisors perform.

2. *Book publishers.*   Many publishers of business books also publish casebooks and texts in specialized areas such as personnel, production, and marketing. Check the business section of your library for the names of these books.

3. *Film and video producers.*   Check the catalogs of the major producers for current titles. Films and videos can also be

found in libraries or through the audiovisual department of any college of business administration.

It is best, of course, to develop your own cases to meet the types of situations your people are most likely to face. Use the published cases as guidelines and adapt them to your needs. Also, training departments often develop internal cases for their companies. Companies that do not have training departments may find it advantageous to hire a consultant in training to help them develop meaningful cases.

4-29 We have video equipment for screening the video cases you mentioned. How else can we use the equipment for training purposes?

The use of video is probably the most dramatic innovation in training in recent years. You can purchase video training tapes in most fields. *One word of caution:* Never purchase a video training tape unless you preview it. Most companies that sell these tapes charge for the preview, but it's worth it. Catalog descriptions give only a limited amount of information. Previewing allows you to determine if the tape will really serve your purposes.

4-30 What about customizing tapes?

Customizing tapes to fit your own training needs is even more valuable—but it can be expensive. Here are some of the ways to use video to enhance the effectiveness of training.

1. *Taping demonstrations.* A good demonstration is an important component of training. Who does the demonstrating? Either the supervisor or one of the best people in his or her department. No matter how good a live demonstration is it can be done only in real time. If the demonstration is videotaped, it can be shown in real time to show the pace—and then in slow motion to show the steps. Once you have a good video of the demonstration, you can use it to show all the people being trained in that type of work.

2. *Taping job performance.* Suppose you are training a mechanic to disassemble, clean, and lubricate a piece of equipment. In a live situation, you say: "You are not doing what I told you to do." The mechanic responds: "Yes I am. I'm doing exactly what you told me." You have to convince the employee to do it your way. If you tape this mechanic performing the job and play it

back, the employee will see, accept, and readily correct the mistakes.

3. *Taping role-plays.* The effect of a role-play is greatly enhanced if the participants can review the tapes after their performance and critique and discuss what occurred.

4. *Taping presentations.* For people who must make presentations at internal meetings or at outside functions, there is no better way of training than studying videos of one's own of practice presentations.

It is not a good idea to try to produce any video that you will use over and over again—such as a demonstration—without professional help and equipment. Production can be expensive. On the other hand, performance, role-play, and presentation tapes are not ones you will be showing over and over, since they are geared primarily to helping the person who is being taped. In these situations, you can use a camcorder or other inexpensive equipment.

4-31 We train telemarketers. It's not important how they look. It's how they sound that we are concerned with. Would audiotape do the job?

Audiotape is an excellent training tool for people who use the telephone. Audiotaping equipment is inexpensive and available in most offices. If you do a great deal of telephone work, ask the various telephone companies to suggest appropriate equipment. If your needs are not extensive, simply purchase a telephone tap from a consumer electronics store. The tap is a miniature microphone embedded in a suction cup. You put the cup on the outside of the telephone instrument (you don't have to take anything apart) and plug it into your tape recorder. Use a voice-activated recorder to enhance spontaneity. Some voice mail systems also have this capability.

Begin the training by taping role-play situations between the trainer and the trainee and then play them back and critique them. Once you feel the trainee is ready for dealing with customers, tape all conversations for the first several days, play them back with the trainee, and critique their actual performance. Repeat the process periodically to monitor progress.

A note of caution: There are legal implications when you tape calls with people outside the company. Check your state laws. Usually, there will be no problems so long as the conversations are kept confidential and are used only for training. You cannot use the tapes as evidence in any litigation that might ensue.

4-32   I supervise customer service reps, who spend all their time on the telephone. How can I critique their work without having to listen in on every call?

Listening in on calls is not only time-consuming but frustrating. You may hear a rep say things which are so horrendous that you want to shout into the phone, "Stop!" It is far better to tape the calls, as suggested in question 4-31. From time to time have the rep tape several calls. Then listen to them together and have the rep critique his or her own calls. Ask: "What could you have done to make this call more effective?" Raise specific issues: "Notice that the customer became very upset when you said.... How could you have handled the situation so the customer would not have blown up?"

Be positive. Even if the customer service rep has handled a situation very badly, be constructive in your criticism. By stressing the good points and suggesting ways to improve weaker areas, you are more likely to build the employee's skills.

4-33   Our company doesn't have a budget for videos or fancy visual aids. Are there less expensive ways to add visual impact to our training?

Visual impact is important. People tend to remember more of what they see than of what they hear and still more of what they see and hear together. But visual aids need not be expensive. A simple chalkboard or flipchart can be used to draw diagrams, present charts, or display phrases that highlight the material.

The claims manager of an insurance company had a difficult time getting her new claims clerks to understand exactly what happened to a claim from the moment it was received by the company until it was finally disposed of. She solved this by displaying a flowchart on an easel. When the trainees could see how the claim flowed from department to department, they learned, understood, and remembered the process much more easily.

When you are training people in an activity that can be demonstrated, such as operating a piece of equipment, the visual aid is the equipment itself. If it is not feasible to use the real thing, a model of the equipment is an excellent substitute.

One of the least expensive pieces of visual-aid equipment is an overhead projector. Transparencies can be made inexpensively and can be used in many types of training.

Continuing Training

4-34   Our company believes that training never ends—that supervisors must be constantly training and retraining people to keep them on the cutting edge of their jobs. I agree, but what can I do to keep continuing training from becoming boring to my people?

Seek new approaches. From time to time, you do have to go back to the basics with all your people—including yourself. When you develop new approaches, you make training more exciting and productive. If you have not used cases or role-plays, try them. Take seminars on training; read books on training methods to pick up new ideas. Attend meetings of trade associations. Make friends with supervisors in other companies—not just in your field—and learn what they are doing to train their people.

4-35   The best trainer I ever had was the coach of my high school basketball team. We weren't the best players in the league, but the coach always had patience with us, taught us how to act and react on the court, and kept us motivated and excited. Should I try to emulate him when I work with my people?

Definitely. The supervisor is—and should behave like—a COACH:

C hange. The coach must keep people alert to new technologies, new methods, and new approaches.

O bserve. The coach must keep observing people to identify what additional training is needed.

A ssess. The coach must assess what has been accomplished and measure it against the desired goals.

C ounsel. An important part of the coach's job is to counsel people individually, commend them for their strengths, and encourage them to improve where needed.

H elp. The coach should help people hone their skills and improve their work by providing training and by recommending courses, seminars, readings, and other sources of learning. The coach should help the group and each member of the group succeed by motivating people to do their very best.

4-36 I'm so busy training my people that I don't have the time to train myself in the new things developing in my

field. If I fall behind, my people and my company will fall behind. How can I keep up?

It is very important to keep up with the state of the art in your field. Not only is this valuable in your present job, but it will prepare you for advancement in your career. Here are a few things you can do.

Set aside a *minimum* of a half-hour a day for study. Do it on your lunch hour, before or after work, or if you commute by train or bus, during commuting time. If you drive to and from work, listen to tapes on management or other business, professional, or technical matters on the way. Subscribe to trade and professional journals. Buy books and tapes.

Join a professional society in your field and go to meetings. You will learn a great deal not only from the formal programs at the meetings but also (and perhaps more so) from the informal chats with other members.

Network. Get to know people in your field. You may meet them at association meetings. Keep a file of people who are knowledgeable about equipment, methods, or other developments in the field. Contact them when you need information or advice about problems on the job. Even if you do not know a person, don't be afraid to write or phone. Most people are happy to help. A very successful executive commented that he owed much of his success to clipping articles from trade publications. When he needed information on a subject, he'd refer to the article and telephone the author. He said most people not only were willing to help but were flattered that he had called.

4-37   I would like all my people to be able to do all the work in my department, but how can I train everybody to do everything?

Cross-training—that is, teaching people to do the work that other people in the group are doing—adds flexibility to a department. If extra help is needed in one area, other people who are already trained can be transferred to it. Cross-training enables departments to function when emergencies, absences, or downsizing occurs.

Both the supervisor and the workers must take time from their regular work to learn other skills. When jobs are not too complicated, cross-training is relatively easy. A clerk-typist can learn to use a word processor or operate a switchboard. A drill-press operator can learn to run another machine with minimum time and effort. However, with more skilled or technical jobs, it is not always easy to cross-train.

The most common form of cross-training is to let people work with others when they are not busy. For example, Manny, the stock clerk, has completed making an inventory. Instead of giving him another assignment in his usual work, have him help Betty at the checkout counter. Next week, Betty may help Manny enter stock records. In time, each will be able to do the other's job.

4-38   Some people resent cross-training. They feel that they were hired to do one kind of work. When the subject of cross-training comes up, they argue that the work is beneath them; or if the work is of a higher level, they feel they should be paid the same as people working at that level. How can I get them to accept cross-training?

At the time they are hired, all employees should be told what their primary job will be and should be given a job description. They should also be told that they will be required to do any other related job that is assigned, and that includes cross-training.

When you assign new work or the training for it, point out to your workers that cross-training will enhance their skills, make them more valuable to the company, and be an asset in their own career development. Emphasize the importance of working in a team. A good team player will do everything necessary to help the team achieve its goals.

The complaint may be about remuneration: "Sandra gets 50 cents an hour more than I for doing this work. I should get the same if I do it." Respond: "Sandra earned the additional wage by learning and performing this work over time. By acquiring new skills, you will be in a position to command more money or attain a promotion. The more you can do, the better it is for the department, for the company, and especially for you."

4-39   What type of on-the-job training and formal education do you suggest for those interested in management positions?

Some large companies provide in-house training programs to groom employees for management. In most companies, however, those interested in moving up the ladder have to take the initiative themselves.

In today's society, most managers have college degrees, so the first step is to encourage those who have not completed college to do so. An MBA or other advanced degree is not essential, but it can be an asset. Also, many potential managers have degrees in liberal arts or other areas, but are lacking in formal knowledge of management. They too can benefit from further education. Here are the major sources:

■ The continuing education divisions of most colleges and universities offer courses and academic programs in various business subjects that can help people cope with managerial positions.

■ Countless seminars are offered in the subjects needed to be a successful manager—general management, computer skills, supervisory techniques, basic accounting, human resources development—as well as in special areas that fit the needs of special jobs. These programs range from one-day intensive sessions to minicourses that last up to several weeks.

■ Trade and professional associations and some schools offer correspondence courses.

In recommending which courses, seminars, or correspondence programs an interested employee should take, review the needs of the company and the background of the person. Suggest programs which will not only help the employee augment his or her present skills but also fill a valuable need in your organization. Most education-oriented companies provide tuition-refund programs or other assistance to employees who desire to further their education.

4-40   Our company is putting all its clerical operations into the computer. Some of our old-timers are afraid to learn the new ways of doing the work. They say they are too old to learn: "You can't teach an old dog new tricks." Are they right?

Wrong. Unless the work requires extensive education or training, anybody with basic intelligence and the willingness to learn can be taught most of the "new jobs" performed in today's business world, including computer operations. These old-timers undoubtedly have the basic intelligence. Your job is to motivate them to want to learn the new work.

The first step is to overcome their concern about being too old to learn. Maybe old *dogs* can't learn new tricks, but humans are not dogs and age is not a barrier to learning. Many men and women have taken on new challenges and learned new ways well into their advanced years. Tell them about other older people you know who have learned the computer; if an older employee in any part of the organization has made the change successfully, have him or her speak to your people—a living example.

Work with these people one at a time. Patiently teach each one the work and keep offering encouragement. Once a worker masters the job, the others will see that it can be done and they will make the added effort to learn.

4-41   I have been transferred to a department that is below production standards. My predecessor did not keep up with things. My job is to retrain the workers. One of them is a woman who has been with the company for several years and who feels she knows everything about the job. She challenges everything I tell her. Without resorting to "Do it my way or else," how can I get her to accept retraining?

In dealing with retraining, you must first overcome resistance. Tell your people that the new training is not a threat to them, but a means of helping them do their job more effectively. Assure them that your goal is to work with them and not against them and that once they learn the new methods, work will be easier for them. They are being taught to work smarter, not harder.

People resist change because it takes them out of their comfort zone. They are at ease doing things in the same way and don't want to become uncomfortable. Point out that until they learn the new ways, it may be difficult, but once the techniques are mastered, discomfort will be overcome.

As for the "know it all" woman who challenges you, be especially sensitive to her needs. Let her know that you recognize the contribution she's made to the department and that you depend on her to be a leader in getting the new methods under way. Turn the challenges to you into challenges to her. Say: "Sure, the old way did the job, but let's try this. I bet that with your skills you can get more production with less effort. Let's see what you can do."

4-42   Our human resources people give new employees a 2-hour orientation on the company, the benefits, and the rules and regulations. Then I have to orient them to my department. Is this important if they already have the company orientation? Can you give me some tips on doing this?

Even though new employees are given a general orientation, they also need to be oriented to the department. This may be even more important than orienting them to the company. To most employees, the company is some nebulous entity. The rank-and-file worker identifies with the department.

When you interviewed your people before hiring, you probably told them about the work they would do. Now expand on that and answer any questions they may bring up. Introduce them to the other workers in your department and to the people in other units with whom they will interact. Discuss the function of the department, how it relates to other departments, the kinds of work performed by each of the members, and the importance of the department's work to the goals of the company.

A good way to describe what each person in the department does is to draw a chart showing where each one works; list the names and positions. Since new employees are introduced to so many people on the first day and are often confused as to who is whom in the department, the chart will help them remember.

Describe the type of training new workers will be getting, when it will be done, and what is expected from them. If training assistants or mentors are used, describe their function.

If the job requires interaction with other departments, take new workers around to those departments and introduce them to the people they will deal with. Point out the lunchroom, rest rooms, and other facilities. If the company is small enough, you (or a personnel officer) may also schedule a tour of the entire operation.

4-43   I have a tendency to cram as much as I can into my trainees at each session. I seem to lose them after a while. How long should a training session last?

People differ. Some learn a lot faster than others; some can absorb more information at any one time than others. You have to go by experience. If you pick up signals that a trainee is tiring or that what you are teaching is not being absorbed, stop the session. After a while you will learn just how much any one person can be taught at a session and schedule training accordingly.

4-44   We use an instruction manual for every job. The manual tells trainees what to do and how to do it. If they forget what to do or face a problem they can't handle, all they have to do is refer to the manual. Doesn't this eliminate the need for other training?

Instruction manuals are excellent training aids, but they do not obviate the need for other training. For most jobs, the supervisor must take an active role in the training process. Even if the trainee is required to read the manual, the supervisor must help translate what is on paper to what is done on the job.

Many jobs do not lend themselves to "training by manual." The work is too diversified and involves activities and problems that cannot be put into a standard form. Manuals serve best in highly routinized types of work.

4-45   The problem I find with training manuals is that people tend to refer to them whenever there is a problem and never use their own initiative. There are times when we have to do things not exactly by the book. How can I encourage my people to act independently without making the manual appear to be irrelevant?

True, the manual is the first source to refer to when something is unclear. It is designed to cover most of the problems that will arise on the job. However, it is not possible to anticipate every conceivable variation. People should be trained to recognize situations in which the manual is unlikely to resolve their problems. In such cases, they should be encouraged to base decisions on their own experience, knowledge, and creativity.

4-46   My son is being taught a variety of school subjects using interactive computer programs. They are very effective because they enable him to learn at his own pace. Why aren't companies using such programs to train people on the job?

Interactive computer programs work this way: The student sits down at the computer; a question appears on the screen. The student keys in a response. If it's correct, the computer jumps to a more difficult question; if it's incorrect, the computer asks simpler questions until the error is identified and corrected. People who have previous background in a field or who learn rapidly can breeze through what they already know and move on to new material; slower people can take their time.

Because most companies have their own way of doing things, generic programs (such as those available to schools) have limited value. Customizing these programs is very expensive. However, some generic programs such as basic accounting skills can be valuable to any organization. If your company does not use basic programs, look into them on your own. Check any computer software catalog to determine what programs might be of interest.

4-47   As a department manager, I have two subordinate supervisors who direct the work of the staff. One of them is a very efficient technician, but he has some very strong ideas on work methods which differ from mine. In training people, he will not follow my instructions, but insists on doing it his way. This is causing confusion and dissension in the ranks. What can I do?

It is important that the work in a department be done in a consistent manner. If your assistant supervisor trains his people in a different way, it will be detrimental to the operation. Make every effort to show him the importance of consistency. Point out that this is a team effort and that everybody must work toward the same goal. If all else fails, you may have to order the supervisor to do things your way.

4-48   I supervise a department in which people have many different specialties. I do not know enough about some of the jobs to train new employees in that field. What can I do?

Many supervisors supervise people in specialties outside of their own. Usually, they have enough background to determine if the work is being done, but cannot perform the jobs themselves, since they lack the technical skills required. They cannot train a new person, so they must depend on people who do have the skills to do the training. Sometimes other employees of the company can be called upon to train. At other times the only choice is to hire an outsider who has the requisite skills and needs minimum training.

Arthur is a top-level administrator and supervises a group of people engaged in a computer-oriented project. Although Arthur is computer literate, he is not skilled in programming. When his key programmer left, there was nobody in the company who could train a successor. To meet this critical need, Arthur promoted a less skilled programmer and sent her to an intensive training program given by the manufacturer of the computer equipment. He also contacted a programmer he had met at a professional society meeting and arranged for her to be used as an ad hoc consultant when special problems arose.

4-49   Training meetings are our way of continuing training. How can I make a training meeting more valuable?

The trouble with most training meetings is that they are poorly conceived and even more poorly conducted. A training meeting should be carefully planned. As supervisor, you should determine the objectives of that meeting: to teach the participants a new method, to perfect a technique, to develop certain skills. The meeting should concentrate only on that objective and not become an open-ended discussion.

Once you have set clear objectives, select the method to be used. Is it to be a demonstration followed by practice? A lecture followed by questions? A participative workshop? Choose a battery of training aids: handouts, videos, cases, role-plays, and so on. Then assemble the needed equipment: chalkboard, overhead projector and transparencies, slide projector and slides, VCR and TV monitor, computers and peripherals.

Handouts or other reading materials should be distributed long enough before the meeting so that people can study them in advance. Then, the meeting can concentrate on expanding, demonstrating, and clarifying the information. Brand-new material, particularly technical or complex matters, should not be introduced.

If you do not have adequate background yourself in the material, bring in an expert to conduct the meeting or at least to assist you. When training people about a new piece of equipment or a computer program, use a representative from the manufacturer or supplier to lead the training meeting. If the meeting relates to dealing with customers, bring in a good customer; if it relates to matters in which other departments are involved, hold a joint meeting with the people in the other department.

In meetings devoted to retraining or sharpening skills, let one or two of the people in the group who are particularly adept in those skills either conduct the meeting or play a major part in it. Try to get as much group participation as possible. Meetings which center on lectures from the supervisor are rarely as effective as ones in which the participants really participate.

4-50   I have been asked to conduct a training meeting in my company. Do you have any special tips on how I can make this a success?

Here are ten tips for conducting better training meetings:

1. Don't talk down to trainees. You are dealing with adults, not children. Many are experts in their specialties.

2. Don't do all the talking. Listening to the same voice all the time is difficult. Let the participants truly participate.

3. Let trainees express themselves. Training should be a shared experience between trainer and trainee.

4. Don't teach by the book. If you do not use material beyond that available in a book or training manual, there is no reason to have the meeting.

5. Prepare for each session. You should know 10 times more about the subject than what you present in the session.

6. Include people who have approximately the same background on the subject. If very advanced students are mixed with beginners, neither group will profit from the experience.

7. Keep the sessions short, but not so short that participants do not have time to absorb the material.

8. Ham it up a little. The trainer should be a performer to some extent. Make the material as interesting as possible.

9. Be visual. Seeing is believing. Visual aids make presentations easier to understand.

10. Summarize at the end. Set aside the last 5 minutes of each session for a summary to clear up any misunderstandings.

4-51   Does it pay to tape training meetings?

Usually it is not feasible to tape routine meetings. However, if you have an outside expert making the presentation or you are covering a complex subject that can benefit from subsequent review, tape the session in either audio or video.

Audiotapes are advantageous when the message can easily be reinforced just by listening. People can review the tapes while driving home, while jogging, and so on. If the matter can best be learned by observation, videotaping is more effective. Make the tapes available for people to view at your facility or to take home to watch on their VCRs.

4-52   Lara is the only person in the department who can do the work that she does. She keeps this information to herself and has refused to train others for fear of losing her job if others know how to do it. How can I get her to share this knowledge?

The situation cannot be allowed to continue. Suppose Lara becomes ill, goes on personal leave, or quits. Assure Lara that she is a valuable employee and that in sharing her knowledge, she will enhance her importance by taking on more responsibilities. If she still refuses, find another way to learn the work or to teach others (see question 4-48).

4-53   We are a small company and just do not have the time to train people. We hire experienced personnel and hope it will work out.

Even experienced personnel should be trained in the way your company performs the work. You must make time for training even though it may cost money in overtime pay or tuition for courses or seminars. The time and money spent on training will be returned with dividends by better and faster work. If your company does not have qualified trainers, retain consultants to do it for you. Use local schools and colleges for training in generic areas related to the job, such as computers, math, and science. Contact equipment manufacturers to see if they provide training in operating their computers or machines. Train all your current managers in how to train and make it an area in which they will be rated in their performance reviews. Top management must give full support to the training commitment if it is to be effective.

4-54   I try to cross-train my people so that each one can do any of the jobs. However, people rarely have the chance to "cross over," and when they finally get to do so, they've forgotten the training.

Immediate training so that everyone in the department can do everyone else's job is rarely effective—for the very reason stated in your question. It is better to train people as the need arises and to direct cross-training to deal with specific situations. Once trained, people can immediately practice what they have learned and will retain it much better. When the need arises, they will be able to perform the job with little or no added training.

4-55   Do all jobs lend themselves to cross-training?

Generally, cross-training is most effective when the job does not require extensive training or education. Clerical jobs and many service jobs are easily cross-trained. However, it is not feasible to try to cross-train a carpenter to do an electrician's work.

4-56   We cross-trained several employees last year and they asked for salary increases on the ground that they were now more valuable to the company. How should the situation be handled?

Perhaps they are more valuable to the company and are worth more money. They may be able to command a higher salary in another company now that they have added skills. One way to avoid losing people (or creating resentment) is to limit cross-training to very specific aspects of the work. Then your people will be more useful to you but will not attain such a higher level of skill that they are in a position to bargain for salary increases.

5

Delegation

Most managers have more work to do than they can ever expect to accomplish in the course of a normal workday. In order to get their work done, they must delegate part of that workload to subordinates.

To delegate means to assign a subordinate duties or tasks *and* the power and authority to get them done. It is not just assigning the least challenging or most unpleasant parts of the job to subordinates. Effective delegation requires that significant aspects of the work be delegated so that the subordinate will not just be relieving the supervisor of some work, but will gain from the experience of doing it.

Many supervisors have difficulty delegating. In this chapter we explore these problems and examine questions on how supervisors can improve their delegation techniques and utilize their people's talents and skills more effectively.

Importance of Delegation

5-1 I'd like to delegate more to my people, but I just can't take the chance. If they mess it up, work piles up and my boss holds me responsible. If I do it myself, I know it will be done right. Why delegate?

Of course, you are responsible for getting the work done correctly. But if you try to do everything yourself, you'll never succeed. You'll be putting in 10- and 12-hour days, while some of your people are sitting around with little to do. This can lead to burnout, ulcers, heart attacks, and nervous breakdowns.

Supervisors who do not delegate are not doing their job. Remember, too, that people learn from delegation. If you don't give them complex assignments, how do you expect them to grow?

5-2   One of my friends delegated everything and just spent his time overseeing the department. His people became so independent, the company felt it could do without him and eliminated his job. Is there such a thing as too much delegation?

The mistake that manager made was not seeking more challenges for himself. Most companies encourage their managers to delegate and reward good delegators by promotion. Your friend should have used the time saved to become even more valuable to the organization.

5-3   What parts of the work should I delegate?

The purpose of delegation is to free you to do work of a higher level. The delegated work is of a lower level to you, but may be of a higher level to the subordinate.

Define total projects that you can delegate. It may be handling all of the matters related to a specific problem or dealing with everything concerning a customer. In this way the subordinate has meaningful work that can lead to increased value to the company.

5-4   What should I not delegate?

Don't delegate work just because you don't like to do it. Often it may be important for you to do something yourself. Base the decision not on liking or disliking the work, but on its importance.

Sometimes the pressures of a job dictate what should be delegated. A crisis develops and you must handle it, so you delegate whatever you are doing at that time to somebody else so you can take charge. Although delegation is necessary at the time, it should not be limited to assisting you in crisis situations.

5-5   I've been a "doer" for so long, I find it very tough to delegate. I know that I should delegate tasks even though I

can do them better and faster on my own. I find myself looking over my people's shoulder as they work. Will I ever be comfortable delegating?

You've taken the first step by acknowledging the need to delegate. Now you have to implement it by choosing a specific assignment to give to one of your people. Communicate what has to be done, set control points, and check the work only at those points. Make sure the worker has the tools and authority to do the job and be available if help is needed. Suppress the urge to look over an employee's shoulder.

After a few successful delegations, you will develop more confidence in your people's ability and feel more comfortable in delegating. Sure, it may take the subordinate longer to do it than if you did it yourself, but the employee will improve with experience. You should use your time and energies for more important aspects of the work.

5-6   How do I delegate without worrying all the time that the work will get messed up?

By following the five elements of good delegation:

- Select capable people
- Communicate
- Set control points
- Provide tools and authority
- Make help available

These elements are discussed in the answers to the following questions.

5-7   What do you mean by "capable"?

The person to whom you delegate must be capable of doing the assigned work. You should know the capabilities of each of your people. Assign them projects in which they can succeed. They may have to be given some added training or develop deeper knowledge of the job on their own, but if they have the basic skills they will succeed. Tell your people that you have confidence in them and that you will be available to help them if they have any problems.

5-8   On many occasions I should have delegated work, but nobody in my department was able to do it. There was no

time to train people, so I had to do the work myself. Is there a better way?

This is not unusual. The work must be done, so you do it. To avoid this type of situation in the future, make it a high priority to train one or more people in that area so next time you can delegate the work.

Communicating What You Delegate

5-9   When I delegate, I give my people detailed instructions. They tell me they understand and then get everything wrong. How can I be sure they really do understand?

Typically after a supervisor gives an assignment, he or she asks the subordinate: "Do you understand?" Inevitably the answer is yes. Perhaps your assistant Maria, for example, really does understand; or perhaps she thinks she understands, but really doesn't and in good faith says that she does. Or maybe Maria doesn't understand at all, but is too embarrassed to tell you. She says yes and now will try to figure it out for herself.

Instead of asking, "Do you understand?" ask: "What are you going to do?" Now Maria will tell you what she is going to do. If what she tells you is wrong, you can correct it before she does it wrong and creates a problem.

Rather than ask a general question on what the subordinate plans to do, some supervisors direct specific questions to various aspects of the assignment (e.g., "How are you going to transfer that file?") so they can obtain feedback on key parts of the work.

5-10   When I give my people an assignment, I always ask if they have any questions. Won't this provide the feedback?

Asking for questions is good, but only *after* you learn whether your people have a basic understanding of the assignment. If they think they understand the basics and don't, or if they do not understand at all, they won't ask the right questions. Once you know that they understand the essentials, their questions will enable you to expand, elaborate, and clarify.

5-11   Is it a good idea to ask the subordinate to put into writing what he or she plans to do?

If an assignment is complex or long term, it is a good idea to have subordinates develop a plan of action before they start the work. The plan should include the steps to be taken in doing the work and the resources needed: computer time, personnel, equipment, and so on. If special funds must be allocated, a budget should be prepared. It is important to set a timetable so that both you and your subordinates know just when each phase of the work will be completed. The plan will also serve as a means of reference and control.

For short-term assignments, a detailed plan is not necessary. However, some supervisors find it helpful to get a brief statement in writing on such assignments.

5-12   I know that for any communication to succeed—particularly when assigning work—it must be not only understood but accepted by subordinates. If they don't "buy what you are selling," the work just isn't going to done. How can I gain this acceptance?

Unless the subordinate accepts what is communicated, he or she will not be committed to it. Here's an example:

Early on Tuesday morning, Janet, the supervisor, assigns the preparation of a report with a deadline of 3 p.m. Ian looks at the amount of work involved and says to himself: "No way can this be done by 3." Do you think he'll meet the deadline? Of course, not. To gain acceptance, let the subordinate know the importance of the work and then get him or her into the act.

Janet might say: "Ian, this report must be on the boss's desk when she comes in tomorrow morning. She needs it for an early morning meeting with the executive committee. When do you think I can have it?"

Now Ian thinks: "This is important. If I skip my break and don't call my sister, I can have it by 5."

Remember that originally, Janet had indicated that she wanted the report by 3 p.m. Why 3 when she really doesn't need it until the next morning? Maybe Janet is one of those people who believes that if she says 3 Ian will knock himself out and have it by the time the office closes at 5. No overtime work would be needed. However, most people don't react that way. When faced with what they consider an unreasonable schedule, they don't even try. So give your people reasonable time frames to complete their work. Even better, have them set their own schedules within acceptable limits.

5-13 What if the work really is needed by 3 o'clock—because after Ian finishes his part, the report must be proofread, photocopied, collated, and bound?

As supervisors, we must recognize that it is not always possible to meet all the conditions we would like to meet. We may have to make compromises—and hope that our boss is willing to accept them. If the total assignment cannot be finished by 5, Janet may have to allow some overtime or get additional help so the boss can have the report when she needs it.

Maintaining Control

5-14 Even with good communication, once a project is under way, all kinds of problems may develop. What can I do to keep it on track?

Set control points. This is the third element of good delegation (see question 5-6) and it can be the most important in keeping the project on target. A control point is a place at which you stop, examine what has been accomplished, and—if errors have been made—correct them. If major errors are not discovered until the last minute, the problem will get out of hand.

A control point is not a surprise inspection. The subordinate knows exactly when each control point is established and what should be accomplished by then.

On Monday morning Gary, the supervisor, gives a project to Kim. The deadline is the following Friday at 3 p.m. The first control point is Tuesday at 4 p.m., at which time Kim should have completed parts A and B of the assignment. Note that Kim knows exactly what is expected. They meet on Tuesday at 4 p.m. and find that there are several errors in part B. That's not good; but it's not terrible, because those errors can be corrected before the work continues. If there had been no control point, the errors would have been perpetuated throughout the entire project.

5-15 If problems develop between control points, does the subordinate have to wait until the meeting to discuss them?

No. Supervisors should be available to handle problems any time they arise. Say that at 11 a.m. on Tuesday, Kim realizes that she won't be able to complete part B by the 4 p.m. deadline. She doesn't have to wait until the meeting to tell Gary that she is behind schedule. Supervisors should be informed as soon as possible about problems and delays so they can take appropriate action.

5-16   Won't my people think that I don't have confidence in them if I keep such close tabs? It's annoying to have the supervisor looking over your shoulder and checking everything you do.

Let your people know at the outset that you do have confidence in them, and emphasize that the control points are designed to help them—not check them. Control points are most important the first few times a person tackles a new assignment. As the employee becomes more experienced in that work, the control points can be reduced to a very few to ensure that there are no misunderstandings.

5-17   I find it best to give my people interim and final deadlines on projects I delegate. In this way I can keep control over how things are progressing. Should I set the deadlines or let the subordinates set their own?

Setting timetables is an excellent way of ensuring that a job will be done on time, and the interim deadlines serve as control points. In situations where completion time is critical, you must tell your people exactly when the job is to be finished. Together, determine the time each *phase* of the project should be done. This gives employees some control over the work.

If exact time is not a major issue, the entire time schedule should be set participatively. Experienced workers know how long it should take to accomplish the work. Your job is to ensure that the time schedule is reasonable and will meet the overall goals of the department.

5-18   My company encourages us to let our people think for themselves and to be individually responsible for the quality of their work. Of course, as their supervisor, I'm the one held accountable if the work I delegate does not meet quality standards. To make sure it does, I have to keep after people by constantly checking their work. This is not what's supposed to happen. How can I get my employees to be truly concerned about quality without acting as a baby-sitter?

Start by making sure that your workers know exactly what is expected of them. The standards by which quality is measured should be deeply entrenched in their minds. Reinforce these standards from time to time through meetings and one-to-one counseling sessions. When your people consistently do high-quality work, recognize and reward them tangibly and intangibly. Once you instill pride in work, you will not need to look over people's shoulders.

5-19   You mentioned "tools and authority" as key elements of effective delegation. It's obvious that supervisors must provide the right tools, but how much authority should we delegate without giving up our own power?

Give subordinates enough authority to get the job done. If they need the authority to purchase supplies or materials or to lease or rent equipment, give them a maximum amount they can spend without your approval. If a job may call for overtime, give them the authority to automatically order it so the work does not get bogged down because you or another executive is not around to make the decision.

5-20   I know that another key element of delegation is being available to help subordinates. I always let my people know that I am there to help and that they can bring me any problems they have. As a result, however, I am constantly being interrupted with problems—many of which people should be solving themselves. What should I do?

Make it a rule that when a person brings you a problem, she or he should also bring a suggested solution. Now your people will have to think things out first. Once they do, they may be able to solve their own problems and leave you alone. Even if they do come to discuss their solutions with you, it is far better to review their concepts than to solve their problems for them.

5-21   When I delegate, my people keep coming back with so many problems and questions that I wind up doing most of the work myself. How can I overcome this?

As suggested in response to question 5-20, when your people bring you a question or problem, ask them to bring with it a possible solution. In addition, except in the case of a real crisis, limit the time you will deal with these matters to the end of the workday. If people know they cannot barge in on you at their convenience, but have to wait until you have time for them, they will get into the habit of trying to solve their own problems.

Day-to-Day Problems in Delegation

5-22   When I am busy, I often throw a new assignment at my people and let them sink or swim. Even if they have never performed this type of assignment before, they are skilled people and can research what has been done in the past. Is this OK, or should I take the time to go over the assignment with them personally?

It depends on two things: the complexity of the assignment and the experience and skills of the subordinates. For jobs that are intricate and complicated, it pays to take some time to go over the chief phases of the project and be available to clarify matters which develop later. You can give more leeway to people who have done related work in the past and to those who are more skilled than to people who are novices and less skilled.

5-23   My people are overworked as it is. How can I delegate more to them? I have to do all of it myself.

There is a limit to how much any person can do in a normal workday. If your people are working up to their capacity, you cannot delegate more. However, many people can do more than they are now doing by better organization of the work. The goal is to have people work smarter—not harder.

Remember, you are delegating work not because you are lazy and don't want to do it, but because you need the time for more productive and profitable activities. Talk to your key people about what they are now doing. Perhaps some of it can be eliminated (is it really needed?), done more efficiently, or delegated to one of their subordinates.

Give workers the chance to make suggestions themselves on how greater efficiency can be accomplished. The people who work day to day on a job often have better insights into methods than do their supervisors.

5-24   One of my workers resents it every time I delegate something to him. He makes me feel that I am imposing by giving him work that he feels I should do myself. How can I get him to accept delegation?

When they start on the job, all employees should be told that from time to time you will be delegating work to them in addition to their regular assignments. In this way, they will not be surprised or annoyed when you do so.

When delegating a new assignment to this particular employee, take the time to explain why you are giving the work to him. Let him know the importance of the work and how it will help meet the department's goals. You need not be apologetic. You are not asking a favor or requesting the employee to do work you should be doing. As a supervisor, you alone will have to handle certain phases of the work—but this is not one of them.

5-25   How can I delegate work without making the employee responsible for the outcome?

The employee *should* be responsible. Delegation includes responsibility for the outcome. This gives the person the feeling that he or she is part of the process, not just a tool used by you to do a task.

5-26   In delegating work, I prefer to break a project into parts and assign the parts to various people. It's been suggested to me that I present the entire project to the group and ask people which part they would like to take. Delegating in this way would take more time. Also, dissension might result if more than one person wants to work on the same part. Which is the better way?

When people have a say in what they are going to do, they are more likely to approach the assignment with the enthusiasm and commitment needed to make it succeed. The little extra time it takes to plan the project as a group pays off in better and often faster results.

When you get a complex project, instead of you breaking it into parts, present the entire assignment to the group and discuss how it should be designed. Who handles what phase will follow easily. Most people will pick the area in which they have the most expertise. If two people want the same area, have them iron it out between them. If the issue becomes sticky, step in and diplomatically resolve it. "Ari, you did the research on our last project. Let's give Barbara a chance to do this one."

As for the tough or unpleasant aspects of the project that nobody wants, you will have to make the choices. Make sure that you spread this type of work among all your people. If one or two people must do all the tough jobs because of the nature of the assignment, assure them that on the next project they will be given more pleasant tasks.

5-27   Is it better to delegate assignments at a staff meeting or privately?

If the work involves only one person or a small group, assign it privately. If the work will involve most of the department, or if their understanding of the project is important to its accomplishment, describe the project to the entire staff at a meeting and then make the specific assignments. In this way, everyone will know which people are directly concerned and what type of support they expect from the rest of the group.

5-28   I have subordinates who in turn supervise other people. How can I encourage them to delegate to their staffs?

Set a good example. If you delegate significant work to subordinate supervisors and follow the principles of good delegation discussed in this chapter, they are likely to emulate you and delegate work to their people. Give them training in how to delegate and offer personal counseling and advice to help them with their concerns.

In your meetings and in one-to-one discussions with these supervisors, point out the importance and benefits of delegating. Let them know that delegating is an important aspect of supervision and that when you appraise their performance, their success in delegating will be a significant factor.

5-29   One of my people keeps asking me to delegate more work to her. She's capable of doing the work, but when I do assign her these special projects, she antagonizes the other staff members by acting superior. She doesn't exactly say: "The boss knows I'm better than you. That's why he delegated this project to me." But it is expressed by her demeanor. What should I do?

"Eager beavers" who want to take on more work can be major assets to a department. They not only help you get the work done, but groom themselves for advancement in the process. However, no matter how well a person does the work, if he or she has negative personality traits, the value of the effort is negated.

Your "eager beaver" most likely does not realize the effect of her posturing. You should have a heart-to-heart talk with her. Let her know how much you value her work and point out how important it is to obtain and maintain the support of the other people on the staff. She will probably deny that she is flaunting her assignments, so be prepared for arguments, rebuttals, and excuses.

Try this approach: "Karen, I'm sure you would never say to anybody 'I'm better than you are.' But sometimes we act in ways that others may interpret as showing off or acting superior. (Give Karen some examples of what she did or said.) When people act that way, they may not realize it or notice how others react. I gave you this assignment because I know you can do a good job. However, if others resent you, not only that job but the entire work of the department will suffer."

If the heart-to-heart talk does not help, consider personal counseling or even special training in interpersonal relations. Programs such as the Dale Carnegie course have helped many people become more effective in interacting with others.

5-30   How can I get my boss to delegate more work to me?

Ask for it. Most executives have more work than they can handle and would like nothing better than to give it away. But they may have the same fears that others have about delegating. They worry that the work may not be done right, that it may not be finished on time, or that they may be imposing on their subordinates.

Brian was about to leave the office and noted that his boss, Shareen, was still absorbed in her work.

BRIAN: Still not done with the project?

SHAREEN: After I finished the calculations, I found additional data and have to redo them.

BRIAN: Let me help.

SHAREEN: It would be great if you could, but you haven't been trained in this work, so I have to do it myself.

BRIAN: I don't know how to analyze the data, but I can enter it into the computer and save you the time that would take.

After Brian proves to Shareen that he has capabilities she can depend upon and is willing to learn, her reservations about delegating work to him will be lessened. By volunteering to help, Brian started a relationship with his boss that will pay off down the line with more and more challenging assignments.

5-31   What are the major reasons that delegation fails?

Supervisors fail as delegators for many reasons. Here are some of the most common.

- *Delegating only dirty or boring work.*   It is normal to want to get rid of work that is unpleasant—and some of it should be delegated. As a supervisor, you can use that time more productively. But, if the dirty work is all you delegate, your subordinates will resent it. Delegated work should challenge subordinates and give them an opportunity to develop their skills.

- *Overloading the staff.*   Do not give people more work than they can handle. Except in emergency situations, make sure that your staff is working to optimum capacity but not overburdened.

- *Failing to delegate authority.*   People need authority to do what must be done to achieve a goal. Someone defined hell as "responsibility without authority."

- *Failing to communicate.*   Let your people know exactly what is being delegated. Ask for feedback to make sure that it is understood and accepted.

- *Exercising too little (or too much) control.*   The supervisor who delegates an assignment and just assumes the subordinate will do it correctly and on time is just as bad as the supervisor who watches every move and requires constant progress reports. You must make sure that the subordinate knows exactly what is expected and how it will be measured (quality, quantity, and other factors). Set control points to check on what has been done. These should give you adequate control—not too much or too little.

5-32   How can I be sure to delegate in the best manner?

The Delegation Worksheet in Figure 5-1 will help you follow the steps of good delegation.

Delegation Worksheet

Delegated to _____

_____

Date of assignment _____ Deadline _____

Brief description of assignment _____

_____

_____

_____

_____

COMMUNICATION

Delegate's description of assignment_____

_____

_____

_____

_____

Areas that must be clarified_____

_____

_____

_____

_____

_____

Comments_____

_____

_____

_____

_____

_____

Figure 5-1

Figure 5-1 (Continued)

CONTROL POINTS

1. Date _____ Phase to be completed _____

_____

Performance standards: _____

_____

Date this phase completed _____

2. Date _____

Phase to be completed: _____

_____

Performance standards_____

_____

Date this phase completed _____

3. Date: _____

Phase to be completed: _____

_____

Performance standards_____

_____

Date this phase completed _____

4. Date _____

Phase to be completed_____

_____

Performance standards _____

_____

Date this phase completed _____

TOOLS NEEDED

_____

_____

_____

(Continued)

Figure 5-1 (Continued)

AUTHORITY PROVIDED _____

_____

_____

Date assignment completed _____

Comments_____

_____

_____

_____

_____

_____

_____

_____

_____

What I can do to make this person even more effective in the next delegated assignment? _____

_____

_____

_____

_____

_____

_____

_____

6

Communicating with Your People

One of your most important responsibilities as a manager is to be able to give subordinates instructions, directions, ideas, and suggestions. Downward communication is the subject of this chapter. Equally important is obtaining ideas, suggestions, and comments from your people. We will examine upward communication in Chapter 7.

However, upward and downward communication cannot really be separated. Communication is like a two-way radio. The sender sends a message; the receiver receives it and then immediately responds. With that response, the receiver becomes the sender; the sender, the receiver. The roles of sender and receiver are always in flux. In order to be an effective communicator, you must never forget this. You may send orders or other "messages" to your people, but unless you know how what you sent was received, you are not truly communicating.

Often what is sent is not what is received. Somewhere between the sender's radio and the receiver's radio, static has intervened to distort the message. The static may emanate from the sender, the receiver, or the communication channel itself. Some of the causes of static are shown in Figure 6-1. Because the roles of sender and receiver constantly shift, the items listed in each column could emanate from either side.

In between sender and receiver are the channels of communication. If José in Dept. A wants to communicate with Vera in Dept. B, he must channel his message through his boss, who relays it to Vera's boss, who gives it to Vera. Going through channels adds opportunities for misinterpretations and misunderstandings that often distort the original message. Communications can be expedited and distortions minimized by allowing direct contacts for most routine matters.

To be good communicators, we must also take into consideration psychological factors. Both senders and receivers come to the communication table with their own agendas—with preconceptions, biases, and attitudes about themselves, the other party, and the situation. These factors influence the way people present the message and the way it is received. In addition, the emotional state of the parties at the time is an important part of the communication process. One may be happy or resentful; another, hurried or at ease. All this affects how messages are sent and received.

The Words We Choose

6-1 I'm a technically trained manager and in most of my work I deal with other technical people. Specialized terminology is essential to our communication. However, I often have to share my ideas with nontechnical managers in the company. I feel frustrated when they can't follow my line of thought. As managers in a technically oriented company, shouldn't they take the trouble to learn the technical language?

It would be helpful if they had a knowledge of the vocabulary you use, but since they do not, it is *your* job to translate the technical terminology into plain English. If that is not feasible because of the nature of the work, take the time to explain the meanings of the terms that other managers should know so they can understand the project.

6-2 My people have much less education than I do. I try not to talk over their heads, but I don't want to sound condescending. Any ideas?

Communication: A Two-Way Process		
Sender	In Between	Receiver

Verbal
    Vocabulary
    Jargon
    Semantics
	Channels of communications	Listening
		Prejudice
		Nonverbal clues
		Emotional set

Vocal
    Articulation
    Tone
    Tempo
    Volume		

Visual
    Body language
    Visual aids		

Attitude
    Lack of sensitivity
    Emotional bias
    Cultural differences		

Figure 6-1

In speaking to your people, it is essential that you choose vocabulary they will understand. This does not mean that you should talk down to them. Do not assume that you must use only two-syllable words. People's "listening vocabulary" is a great deal larger than their speaking vocabulary. Listen to the vocabulary of TV newscasters and commentators. It is a good model to follow.

6-3   Sometimes when I am talking with my people, I notice a blank expression on some of their faces. I wonder whether they have understood me. How can I make sure without embarrassing them?

A blank expression is an indicator of not understanding. Repeat the instruction quietly in simpler words without commenting that you are restating it.

6-4   In recent years we have hired a large number of people who speak very little English. How can I communicate with them?

As discussed in Chapter 3, question 3–45, if you have other employees who speak the language, use them as unofficial interpreters. If not, nonverbal communication often can get the message accross.

6-5   I'm so accustomed to using jargon in my work that I find myself using it in nonwork situations as well. Often I am not understood. Is this common? How can I overcome the habit?

Most occupations and professions—even companies—have their own private language or *jargon*. This terminology enables people in a particular field to speak to one another in shortcuts. It also conveys a feeling of "being on the inside." If you are making a presentation to people outside your field, it is not only distracting but impolite to use terminology they do not understand. In preparing your talk, delete all jargon. Review or rehearse the talk with someone who is not in your field to make sure that you did not miss anything. In informal conversations, try to catch yourself and if you use an unfamiliar or "inside" term, repeat the idea in different words.

6-6   Sometimes I use a word whose meaning I think I really know, but the listener thinks I means something entirely different. I know that some words have more than one meaning, and you can tell which one is intended from the context. Sometimes, however, you can't know for sure. How can I avoid ambiguity?

This is a problem of semantics, the way in which words are interpreted. The same word may have different meanings to different people, depending upon their experience with the word in the past.

Two executives of a coal-mining company were attending a convention. Each received an identical message from the home office. "Return at once; strike at mine." One executive was the chief engineer. He thought: "Terrific, we found more coal." The other was the labor relations manager.

How do you know how people will interpret your words? You don't. If you deal with the same people day after day, you learn by experience. But if you use a new word or work with a new person, you may not know. The only way to make sure that a word is understood the way you intend it is by feedback (see questions 6-31 to 6-35).

The Way We Speak

6-7 I know it is important to speak clearly and distinctly. What are some of the roadblocks to clear communication?

Many people do not realize that they are not speaking clearly. They do not hear themselves as others hear them. Here are some of the major problems in articulation.

Mumbling.   Mumblers do not enunciate words fully. Most don't even know they are mumbling. Their words are so blurred that listeners cannot figure out what is being said. And if the listeners are subordinates, it is unlikely that they will say, "Hey, boss, you're mumbling." Instead, they will guess at what the boss is saying—and probably guess wrong.

Swallowing word endings.   Not finishing a word is not quite as bad as mumbling. But if you don't finish a word, your listeners will. Again, misinterpretation can result.

Speaking too fast or too slowly.   If you speak too fast, you will be difficult to follow. If you speak too slowly, you lose the interest of your listeners. Even worse, people will anticipate what you are going to say and stop listening.

Adding word whiskers.   Many people interject extra sounds, words, or phrases into their speech: "uh," "uh-huh." "y'know," "right," "OK." Such interjections add nothing to the message and are very distracting.

6-8 Since I can't hear myself, how do I know if I am guilty of poor articulation?

In order to hear how you really sound, you have to record your voice without being aware that it is being taped. One approach is to attach a tape recorder to your telephone (see question 31 in Chapter 4). After a while you will lose self-consciousness that you are being recorded. Listen to several taped conversations to detect unwanted speech patterns.

6-9   Suppose I discover that I mumble, swallow word endings, speak too fast or too slowly, or add word whiskers. Is it tough to correct these habits?

It's easy. These types of speech problems are not serious. They are usually bad habits which can be overcome by careful attention and a sincere effort to change. Simple awareness of the problem can do the trick. If you know that you mumble, you will make a concerted effort to stop mumbling, and if you know that the fifth word out of your mouth is always "y'know," you'll stop saying "y'know."

6-10   One of my friends has a bad stammer. It has held him back in his career. Is it correctable?

Since most supervisory and management jobs call for good communication skills, a stammer or a stutter can be a major impediment to advancement. Fortunately, much has been learned in recent years about these speech patterns. Your friend should see a speech therapist, who can evaluate the nature of the problem and in many cases help overcome it. Most universities and many private sources offer programs in speech therapy.

6-11   One of my people has a foreign accent that makes him difficult to understand. He has superior technical skills. When I suggested that he do something about his speech, he became very upset and even hinted that I was discriminating against him. What can I do?

Most people who learn English as a second language become proficient enough to make themselves easily understood. A few do retain a heavy accent which can become a serious barrier to their effectiveness. Like a speech defect, an accent can be changed through speech therapy.

Most people with heavy accents will accept and often seek out suggestions on how to improve their speech. However, some are highly sensitive about the issue. Often they understand, read, and write English fluently and assume that they also speak it well. Since your employee appears to be very sensitive, handle the matter diplomatically. Compliment him on his technical prowess and his command of the written language. Hint that by working on his oral communication he could be even more effective. Do it over a period of time so that he will begin to see your point without it becoming a major issue. If other people in your company have overcome this communication barrier by speech therapy, have them speak to the employee to reassure him that it is not a disgrace to take the program. In fact, it will benefit him in both his job and his personal life.

6-12   I don't have much formal education, but I am good at my job. Sometimes I feel that my diction is hindering me from getting ahead. What can I do?

Take a course in diction and speech at your local high school, community college, or university. Be sure that the course is in speech, not public speaking. Speech courses concentrate on diction; public speaking, on giving talks.

6-13   My job calls for me to make presentations at meetings in the company and sometimes at trade or professional associations. Although I am college educated and have been successful in my career, I freeze up when I have to speak in public. How can I overcome this?

You are not alone. Surveys show that more people are afraid to speak in public than to perform any other activity in their lives. Taking public-speaking courses can help. One very successful program for overcoming fear of speaking is the Dale Carnegie course. Another approach is to join Toastmasters. These informal groups meet on a regular basis and each member gives a short talk. The sessions are an excellent way to gain experience in a nonthreatening environment.

6-14   Some of my people speak ungrammatically and have poor diction. This conflicts with the image my company wants to project. What can I do?

If poor diction is widespread in your department, it would pay to conduct in-house courses in grammar and speech. Many business schools and some public school systems offer such programs to companies in their community at reasonable cost. You could also suggest that those who need it take courses in local schools on their own. A company tuition-refund policy would encourage them.

6-15   I tend to speak softly. My people don't take me seriously. How can I sound more assertive?

Some people have naturally soft voices and cannot speak more loudly without strain. It is not necessary to speak loudly to be assertive. By stressing key words, pausing before and after them, and using a rising inflection, you will sound more forceful. Practice with a tape recorder. You will find that these techniques can be acquired readily and will make your communications more assertive.

6-16   One of my subordinates is a known big mouth. She doesn't mean to hurt people by what she says, but her tone of voice is often offensive. How can I get her to change?

Most loud mouths do not realize that they are antagonizing people. When confronted, they will deny it. Your first step should be to let your subordinate hear herself. If the problem arises mainly in one-to-one conversations, diplomatically tell her that she is coming across in a manner you are sure she does not want to. Suggest that she work on her tone of voice. Have her ask friends (either on or off the job) to call any offensive remark to her attention when it happens. If the problem occurs at meetings, tape an entire session and play back her comments (privately). Then discuss the issue with her.

Nonverbal Communication

6-17   People communicate not only with words but with their body language. How can I learn to read a person's body language?

Wouldn't it be great if we could buy a dictionary of body language? Then any time a person made a gesture, a facial expression, or a movement, we could look it up and read the person like a book. The reason we can't buy such a dictionary is that body language differs from one person to another. Sure, some gestures—a handshake, a smile—may seem universal. But when dealing with specific people, we cannot be sure that they are using their body as we have come to expect.

For example, when people nod, we usually assume they are agreeing with us. However, some people nod just to acknowledge that they are listening. Some people fold their arms when they subconsciously disagree with us; others fold their arms just because they are cold.

When you work with the same people over time, you can learn their body language. Through astute observation, you discover that when John smiles in one way it has one meaning, but a slightly different twist of his lips means something else. People do give messages nonverbally, and you must be prepared to look for such messages when communicating with them. Many successful salespeople make a conscious effort to study and remember the body language of their prospects.

6-18 Is it true that sometimes we communicate totally non-verbally and may not even realize it?

Many nonverbal actions subconsciously convey messages. You bring one of your people into your office for a "shape up or ship out" conference. Where do you place him? Across the desk. The desk itself is a power symbol; placing him face to face is an indicator that you mean business.

Now you bring another person into your office to persuade her to cooperate in a joint activity. Where do you place her? You angle your chair so you are sitting side by side. Face to face = confrontation; angled = rapport. The mood is set and you still haven't opened your mouth.

6-19 Could I be contradicting myself or projecting images I don't want to project with my body language and not know it?

Communications experts say that most people do not contradict themselves by their body language, because body language flows naturally from what they are saying. But as noted in question 6-17, some people may interpret certain types of gestures in a different way than you intended. There is little you can do about this unless you get feedback on how you are being perceived.

6-20 I deal with people from other countries and they seem to interpret my body language differently than Americans do. Is body language "culture-biased"?

Yes. People from different cultures use their nonverbal language in many ways. For example, in certain cultures, people stand almost nose to nose when talking. If an American, who normally stands about a foot away in conversation, should take a step back in talking to a person from that culture, it might be considered an insult. In dealing with people from other cultures, you must make the effort to learn their communication habits.

6-21 When I talk to somebody, I expect that person to look at me. If a person keeps evading my eyes, I feel that it indicates lack of cooperation, lack of interest, or insincerity. Am I right?

Eye contact is important. When you speak to others, you should look right at them, just as you expect them to look at you. But don't take the term "eye contact" literally. Don't stare straight into somebody's eyes. It is very distracting. Look at the whole person.

If people do not look at you when you speak to them, it *may* mean that they are uninterested, insincere, or uncooperative. It could also mean that they are shy, are in awe of you or your position, or are simply expressing a cultural trait. For example, in some Latin American cultures young women are taught that it is impolite to look straight into the face of a person in a superior position—such as you, the boss. The are told to look demurely at the ground.

6-22 Is it true that people remember much more of what they see than of what they hear?

Yes, and people remember even more of what they see and hear together. If we could augment what we say with what our listeners can see, we would be much better communicators. Charts, diagrams, illustrations, photographs, models—anything that can be shown to listeners—should be used as much as possible. Remember Ross Perot's use of charts and graphs in his TV talks during the 1992 presidential campaign?

Television programming has made the simultaneous use of seeing and hearing into an art. One of the finest and most enduring examples is *Sesame Street*. This is audio/video simulcasting at its best. Children learn to read and increase their vocabularies easily. At a more sophisticated level, all good TV programs and commercials make the most of integrating sound and sight.

Whether you are making a presentation to a group or speaking to just one person, try to back up what you say with something that can be seen. Prepare slides, flowcharts, and handouts in advance. Use a chalkboard or blank-paper flipchart to write or draw additional visual material as you present the information.

Listening

6-23 When people speak to me for any length of time, I find it difficult to keep listening. My mind wanders and I may miss important parts of what is being said. How can I become a better listener?

Listening is not easy. Most of us cannot sustain our attention for long periods of time. Even when what we are hearing is very interesting, from time to time our minds will wander. To understand this phenomenon, let us look at the anatomy of listening.

The average American speaks at the rate of 130 to 140 words per minute. The human mind can absorb ideas at the rate of 600 to 800 words per minute, perhaps even faster. If the mind can absorb ideas four to five times faster than anyone is likely to speak, what happens to that mind when that s-l-o-w speech hits it? It wanders. We think of other things and stop listening. The speaker keeps talking. Out of her mouth are coming words, but into our ears comes just the droning of a voice. Suddenly out of the droning we hear an attention grabber—"... and that's why Lisa is quitting"—and we didn't know Lisa was planning to quit. We ask some questions and get back on track. But how often do we not get an attention grabber and miss a good deal of what has been said?

It is not possible to totally listen to anybody; the droning effect is always there. It can be minimized, however, if we make a conscious effort. We must train the mind to prepare for distraction. When the words begin to fade and the droning takes over, it's time to STOP! LISTEN! Training and discipline are needed, but it can be done.

6-24   I try to give full attention to my people when we talk, but I'm constantly interrupted with phone calls. I don't have a secretary, so I pick up the calls. It's just as disturbing if I let the phone ring. How can I avoid interruptions?

Today many companies use voice mail, which can be set so the phone will not ring when you do not want to be interrupted. If your company has not installed such a system, you must take other steps to prevent interruptions. If you know you are going to have a lengthy conversation with one of your people—say, a discussion of a new assignment or a performance review—instead of holding it in your own office, go to a conference room. If nobody knows you are there, no phone calls will go through to you.

6-25   My desk is always covered with papers. That's the way I work. Often, when I should be listening, my eyes focus on a letter or memo on my desk and I read it instead of paying attention to the speaker. I try to clear my desk of papers

when I have a meeting, but it's not always possible. Any suggestions?

Many people are compulsive readers. They leap at anything they see in print. They read the cereal box on the breakfast table every morning—even though they read it yesterday. The only way for you to avoid the problem at work is to put all the papers that are on your desk in a drawer when you know you are going to have a long discussion. Even better, if you can, go to a conference room—and leave the papers behind.

6-26   Usually when I interview people, I sit in my comfortable executive chair, my hands folded behind my head, maybe I rock a little. One day I was interviewing a man who had one of those dull, dreary voices, and all of a sudden out of the droning I hear, "Mr. Valdez, you are not listening to me." He was absolutely right. I was so embarrassed I did not know what to do. How can I prevent this from happening again?

People with uninteresting voices often turn listeners off. But they may have much of value to say. To remain alert, don't get too comfortable. Instead of leaning back with your hands behind your head, lean forward into the other person. By being physically closer, you make yourself psychologically closer. You hear better and have better eye contact. Also, because you are not so comfortable, you will be less likely to daydream.

6-27   How can I let people know I am really listening?

Be an active listener. Ask questions about what people have said. Paraphrase what they said. For example, after a comment is made, say: "So the way I understand it is . . . ." Then repeat in your own words what was said. In this way, the other party knows you are listening.

6-28   When I talk to people, I sometimes feel that they are not listening. How can I get them back on track?

Ask questions from time to time during the discussion. Don't ask quiz questions to test people's knowledge; ask questions that stimulate their thinking. For example: "What ideas do you have on how rerouting might be accomplished?" "What reaction can we expect from the XYZ people?" Your questions will not only keep people alert but will encourage them to participate in implementing the work.

6-29   I try hard to listen to my people, but I've heard their problems over and over again. I anticipate what they are going to say and that turns them off. What can I do?

The longer you work on a job, the more likely you are going to hear the same problems. However, you still should listen fully because although the problem is old hat to you, it is new to the person facing it. He or she deserves all your attention. In addition, even if the problem appears to be the same as others, certain nuances may make the solution somewhat different. Since you can never be sure that the problem is exactly the same as others, you must listen to the entire matter that is presented.

6-30   It is important to show empathy when listening to an employee's problems. How can I do this without appearing to be sentimental or overly concerned?

Don't confuse empathy with sympathy. Empathy is putting yourself in the other person's shoes, so you know how he or she feels. Sympathy is feeling sorry for the situation a person faces. For example, if one of your people has been bypassed for promotion:

EMPATHY: I understand that you are disappointed. It is normal to feel that way when you don't get something you had hoped for.

SYMPATHY: It's too bad you didn't get the promotion. I'm sorry it didn't work out for you.

Feedback

6-31   I give my people instructions and when I ask if they understand, they always say they do, but then they do it wrong. Why does this happen?

Sometimes people think they understand something but interpret it differently from what you intended. Others do not understand but are too embarrassed to admit it. They nod in agreement and then try to figure it out for themselves. Do not ask if what you say is understood. Instead use the feedback loop described below to learn if what you said has been communicated.

As pointed out, communication is a two-way process. The sender sends a message to the receiver; the receiver responds. When you, the sender, receive that response, you become the receiver. To determine if what you said was received as you intended, you should filter the response through that extraordinary computer between your ears. It has been programmed to seek out clues as to whether what you said is what was received.

Perhaps you were mumbling; perhaps the other person was not listening; perhaps there was a semantic misinterpretation or some other form of static that distorted the message. Now you can correct it. By continuing to use this loop, you filter each response in succession. If, from the clues, you find that the receiver has misinterpreted or did not fully understand the message, you can clarify it in your next message.

It is not easy to pick up every communication clue, so you will have to augment the process by asking a question after every three or four interchanges. From the answers you can pick up more clues and make necessary adjustments.

6-32   How can I frame a feedback question so I won't sound condescending or nitpicking?

To ask someone to tell you what you said in his or her own words is condescending. Ask general questions about key parts of the assignment: "What are some of your ideas on computerizing inventory?" "What problems do you anticipate we will face when installing the new machines?" Such questions give you the benefit of the other person's input and at the same time enable you to learn how well you are being understood. Intersperse the general questions with specific queries on areas where you feel the person may need added information, clarification, or training.

To avoid being a nitpicker, rely on the judgment of your experienced people. Do not ask them to report on how every facet of the work will be done. Concentrate on the major aspects; the minor ones will fall into place.

6-33   Some of my people give me good feedback and I am confident they know just what to do. But then they ignore what was agreed on and do it in their own way. When I confront them about this, they deny that they are doing it. How can I get them to follow instructions?

Supervisors whose people express understanding and agreement and then go their own way need another tool to make sure that what is agreed to will be done. One effective instrument is the *plan of action*. After you and your people discuss an assignment, ask them to develop a written plan of action based on what was said. Once it is approved, this document becomes both a guideline as to what will be done and a point of reference in case of a disagreement. It is the benchmark by which both you and your people can determine how the assignment is progressing.

6-34   Often my people do not understand my instructions, but are reluctant to tell me. What can I do to make sure that they let me know if what I say is not clear to them?

Good feedback practices should minimize this problem, but there will still be occasions when people hold back from asking questions—either because they are shy or reticent or because they fear that you will consider them stupid for not catching on faster.

If the reason is fear, look to yourself first. Are your actions or reactions sending signals to your people that you think their questions are stupid? You may not realize how your verbal and non-verbal reactions to questions appear. Lack of patience, sarcastic comments, and even certain gestures may be interpreted as demeaning by your people.

6-35   How can I build my own feedback loop when communicating with my boss?

Ask questions. Don't wait until the end of the discussion when your boss asks, "Do you have any questions?" From time to time during the discussion, raise a pertinent point. It may be in the form of a paraphrase: "So the way I understand this is…." Or it may be a specific question on a specific point: "Do you want projected figures or actuals?" When the discussion is over, not only will you have a clearer idea of what is expected of you, but your boss will know what you intend to do.

Attitudes, Biases, and Emotions

6-36   I work in a technical environment. One man in my group is very guarded in our discussions. He has great technical skills, but seems reluctant to share them. Since we work as a team, his input is essential to our progress. How can I get him to open up?

Often people who are reluctant to share information are afraid that others will get credit for their ideas. This may stem from deep-seated insecurity or from past experience. People who have long-term psychological problems cannot be easily changed. However, if the reason is unfair treatment in the past, give the man recognition both publicly and in private. Praise his ideas in front of the other members of the team. When you report to your boss on the team's progress, give credit to him (as well as to others whose ideas are used). It will not take the employee long to accept that his work is appreciated and to become a more willing contributor to the team.

6-37   Some of my people are "selective listeners." They believe that they are always right and hear only what they want to hear. They tune out when others—including me—do not completely agree with them. How can I get them to at least listen to others?

In dealing with such people, try to find out why they feel that they are always right. In some cases, they may have superior knowledge of the work, but even experts are not always right. In other cases, they may have such strong feelings about a subject— and a resistance to anything that may make them change those feelings—that they block out opposing views.

In the former case, patient exposition of the logical reasons for an opposing opinion may help you win your point. In the latter case, even the most cogent arguments will not work. When people have strong attitudes about something, it is almost impossible to penetrate their minds with contrary ideas. A good example is the political controversy over gun control. Most people have very strong ideas for or against gun control—and will not even accept the fact that their opponents have any standing at all. Neither side will open up to the arguments of the other. If "ideology" is the reason that some of your people tune others out, there is little you can do to overcome it. However, most people are not that deeply involved in the issues that arise on the job. You may be able to ferret out their real objections to your views and perhaps sell them on at least opening their minds to discussion.

6-38   Some of my people are very sensitive and when I have to speak with them about their mistakes, they are quick to take offense and often overreact. How can I be more gentle with them and still get them to do their work right?

It is not necessary to be tough with people when correcting them. True, some people may not take you seriously unless you sound stern, but most people respond better to gentleness. When criticizing, focus on the work—not on the person. Never say "You are _____ (dumb, slow, careless, lazy, etc.)." Instead say: "This report had errors in it" and then point out the errors. Or "The deadline was yesterday. Let's discuss how we can work together so the next project will be done on time."

6-39   My assistant is a very bright person, but she does not know as much about the work as I do. When I make suggestions or give her advice about a project, she agrees that my ideas are good, but then ignores me and does it her own way. Her approach sometimes leads to serious errors and requires reworking. What makes a person act this way and what can I do about it?

There could be many reasons for your assistant's behavior. First look at yourself. How do you give the advice? Some managers project negative images when giving suggestions to their subordinates. By their manner of speaking or even their nonverbal language, they make the subordinate feel inferior. Some people react to this image negatively and consciously or subconsciously reject it and act on their own.

Since you cannot see or hear yourself as others do, you may not be aware of how you come across. Ask a friend or business associate to listen to you and to point out any negatives in your manner of delivery. Work on your own communication skills. Practice giving instructions or suggestions. Use a tape recorder or videocamera. With awareness and practice, you will see a significant improvement.

On the other hand, the problem may be with your assistant. She may resist suggestions because she looks upon them as a negative reflection on her work. "If the boss has to give me advice, she must think I'm inadequate." You can overcome her resistance by first pointing out the good points in her approach to an assignment. Add that by following your suggestions, it could be done even better. Follow up by giving her positive reinforcement when she accomplishes the assignment and point out that her ideas were the basis of the success—your suggestions just refined it.

6-40   I have an employee who not only won't take advice but gives me an argument in the process. He thinks he is

always right and tries to persuade me that I am wrong. I'm willing to listen and even accept his ideas sometimes, but he never accepts mine and won't even compromise. My only recourse is to order him to do something. This is not really satisfactory. How can get him to cooperate?

It is impossible to communicate with somebody who thinks he or she is always right. Good communicators must be receptive at all times. There is no easy way to change a stubborn person. Even when your employee knows he is wrong, he will probably claim to be right. Yes, you may have to order him to do the job the way you want. To soften the effect, give the orders in a positive manner. Instead of saying "Do it my way or else," try: "Last time we did this the way you suggested, we had problems with it and it took too long. I went along with you then; now it's your turn to go along with me." If you can inject a little humor do so, as long as it is not sarcastic.

6-41   One of my people has a negative attitude toward authority. He is always defensive. How can I communicate with him?

People are antiauthority for many reasons. They may have come from a home or job environment in which the "them versus us" concept prevailed (see Chapter 9). In communicating with such people, be aware of this attitude and point out where possible how what you are communicating will be of advantage to them.

6-42   Sometimes I just don't trust people. Even though I know they are experts in their field, I don't accept what they say. Is this normal?

Yes. We set up barriers against people we don't like or trust and look upon anything they say as negative. We turn them off because of our attitude. This works the other way as well. If we are particularly impressed with or fond of people, we are more likely to listen to them and accept their opinions, even if they lack the expertise of people we don't like. This is human nature. However, if we are aware of these prejudices, we can make an effort to compensate for them so we can be more objective in communicating with others.

6-43   When I criticize people, I try to be constructive. I start by praising some of the good things they have accomplished

and then discuss what they have done wrong. Somehow it doesn't work. They know that when I finish the praise criticism is likely to follow, so they are tense from the beginning. How can I overcome their resistance?

If supervisors praise their people only as a prelude to reproach, their people will know what to expect and will block it all out. Most supervisors give praise first, follow it with "but," and then bring out the bad part. During the entire discussion, the subordinate is sitting there waiting for the "but," so even the praise is not listened to. To keep the subordinate's attention, stop using "but." Instead use "and": "I appreciate the good work you did, *and* next time you do it if you do such and such, it will be better."

Praise should not be just a prologue to criticism. It should be given at various times for outstanding work. Also, there are other good ways to present your criticism without cushioning it in praise. Constructive criticism involves telling or showing how the work could be done better. You can do this directly. Of course, always be tactful. You don't say: "Your work is terrible. Here's the right way to do it." You may say: "Let's review the methods we use to do this job." Then do just that. Point out where the employee made errors by giving examples of the right and wrong ways.

6-44   My boss has an abrasive personality and is disliked by my people. Whenever he becomes involved with the work we do, my people resent his ideas—most of which are very good—just because they came from him. How can I get them to accept his input?

People do resist communication from people they do not like. They build up barriers that block out or distort the message without considering its merits. You will have no success in getting them to like an abrasive person. Instead, concentrate on helping them distinguish between the message and the medium. It will take hard work and patience on your part. Don't lecture your people on separating their personal feelings about the boss from the work involved. Instead, take each case as it comes up. The boss makes a good suggestion or presents a viable plan. Get your workers to focus on the idea or plan instead of on the person who presented it. Change will not happen overnight, but by your continuing effort, you will make strides in overcoming the resistance.

6-45   We recently hired a few bright college grads as staff people in our company. They bring to us new thinking and

new techniques that have developed in our field. The old-timers pooh-pooh these ideas. They say, "What can these book learners know? They've never even sat at a work-bench." How can I get my older workers to at least listen to new ideas?

Part of the problem may be the way the young staffers are presenting their ideas. Often people just out of school with little work experience are impatient and want to change things rapidly. Even if their ideas are excellent, they have to be sold to the workers, who obviously resent changing the old ways of doing the job. Speak to the person to whom these staffers report. Suggest that they be trained in better communication skills.

As far as your people are concerned, talk to them. Point out that we all can learn from anybody. Also, even though the workplace is an excellent source of job knowledge, much can be learned from other sources. New techniques and new approaches to work are being developed in research labs and colleges. To keep up with the competition, we must be open to ideas from any source. As suggested in answer to the previous question, work on the problem case by case rather than trying to deal with it in broad, general terms.

Communication Problems on the Job

6-46   In our company all communication has to go through channels. If I want to talk to my counterpart in another department, I have to go through my boss to the worker's boss and then to the worker. Not only does this slow things up, but often the message gets distorted as it passes through the channels. The company says that going through channels is essential for control. What can I do?

One way to alleviate the distortion is to use written communication. Writing is more difficult to distort, though interpretation of what is written may vary from station to station in the channels of communication. The drawbacks are that writing is time-consuming and that many matters cannot and should not be communicated in writing. For matters of transient concern, written communication is unnecessary. (More on improving written communications later in this chapter.)

A more effective approach is to shorten the channels of communication or to bypass some if feasible. The fewer the stations along the route, the faster the communication will be. Thus, the chances of distortion are reduced. People should be given direct access to those with whom they work on a regular basis. Safeguards can be built in to ensure that higher management is kept aware of significant developments.

6-47   We have formal communication channels, but much of our day-to-day communication is done informally. We accomplish more this way than following the channels. What is the value of formal communication?

The purpose of formal communication is to maintain control so that responsible managers will not be surprised by events. Inasmuch as most routine work will not cause catastrophic problems if something goes wrong, using informal communication networks facilitates the flow of work. We telephone a colleague in another department, meet the boss in the corridors or the lunchroom, attend a meeting on one matter and bring up some other topics. Informal channels may not be official, but without them many projects would get bogged down waiting for formal action.

6-48   Two of my employees are reluctant to come to me with problems. They go to each other for help, and often neither has the background to solve the problem. I have told them over and over again to bring those problems to me, but they still rely on each other. How can I overcome their reluctance?

They may be afraid of you. It's hard for most supervisors to believe that their people fear them. They think of themselves as nice people who are open to others and willing to help. Of course, some bosses do instill fear consciously or subconsciously by their manner of supervising. But sometimes your position per se as supervisor can cause subordinates to fear you. They feel that if they ask questions or seek help, you will look upon it as a sign of weakness or inability.

One way to overcome your employees' interdependence— and reluctance to come to you—is to work with them as a team. When you become aware that they are consulting each other, intervene. Tell them that even though you encourage your people to work out their own problems, there are times when your years of experience and expertise might be tapped to reach better solutions. Offer to sit with both of them and work together to solve a problem. By making yourself one of the group, you add your know-how to the discussion rather than superimposing a solution. Your effort should encourage them to bring you into the picture earlier, instead of depending entirely on each other.

6-49   When I disagree with others, how do I get them to understand that it is not a personal attack?

Some people are very sensitive and take any disagreement as a personal affront. Even when participants in a disagreement are not particularly sensitive, they should focus on the issues—not the people—involved. If you know someone is touchy, be very careful about how you word your arguments and carefully watch that person's body language as you talk. If signs of agitation develop, calm the person down before going on. Sometimes it is wise to postpone the discussion until he or she calms down.

Some people do not manifest their sensitivity overtly, but keep it deep inside. You may not realize that they feel wounded and are quietly but definitely resisting you. Reassure these people that you are not displeased with them and that the disagreement is specific to the issues involved, not personal. Sensitive people need frequent reassurance.

6-50   I supervise people in several remote locations so most of my communication is by telephone. I can't observe their body language and they can't see mine. I can't use visual aids. How can I make this communication more effective?

People who depend on telephone communication must become more sensitive to both their own voice and the voices of those they deal with. Manner, tone, tempo, inflection, modulation, and volume are important. All can add to, detract from, modify, emphasize, or minimize the message. As you work with each of your people over time, you can learn to interpret how each of them uses voice variations and what they mean. You will also need to ask more feedback questions in telephone communication than in face-to-face conversation.

If you are planning to make a presentation to your people by individual or conference calls, practice it first in front of a mirror. Check your gestures and facial expressions. Keep in mind that your listeners will never see these nonverbal cues. Then change the way in which you say the message to reflect what the nonverbal actions added. Tape the revised message. When you listen to it, is it as effective now without the gestures? Work on the presentation until you are satisfied.

To add a visual element to telephone conversations, tie in your phone call with fax messages. Send charts, illustrations, and other visual material via fax enough in advance of the phone call that your party can study them and be ready to discuss them with you.

Another way of adding visual impact is to draw word pictures. A word picture enables the listener to visualize in the mind's eye the image you are drawing verbally. Suppose somebody telephones you for directions to your building. You say: "Take I-80 to Exit 17, that's Mulberry Street. Make a right off the ramp to the fourth light, Elm Street. Make a left on Elm and drive two and a half miles to Oak Avenue. Make a right on Oak. We are number 11 Oak Avenue."

That's pretty clear, but you could make it even clearer by drawing word pictures: "Take I-80 to Exit 17, that's Mulberry Street. Make a right off the ramp to the fourth light. There's a McDonald's on the right side and a Texaco station on the left. That's Elm. Make a left on Elm and drive until you get to the firehouse. One block past the firehouse is Oak. Make a right on Oak. We're the yellow building on the left side." Now the listener does not have to look for street names, mileage, or house numbers. All that is necessary is to look for landmarks.

6-51 I have no trouble getting my ideas across at meetings, but when it comes to one-to-one conversations, this is a problem. How can I improve my skills?

Yours is not the usual case. Most people have more trouble with presentations at meetings (see Chapter 7). You should prepare in advance for a scheduled one-to-one conference, just as if you were going to present your ideas at a meeting with several attendees. Do your research, make notes, rehearse your message, prepare for the types of questions you anticipate. Practice with a friend or colleague. Such preparation will make you more at ease in this type of situation.

6-52 Sometimes my people do not take me seriously when I give them orders. How can I be more assertive in dealing with them?

Some managers feel that if they come across too strongly to their people, they will incur resentment. They compensate by being too soft. It is not necessary to raise your voice or sound dogmatic to be assertive. Speak with authority and be sure that your body language is congruent with the message. Don't smile when you give bad news or convey a serious message. Tell people the importance of a particular assignment and let them know that you intend to follow up to ensure that it is completed on schedule—and in the manner you have presented. Be sure to follow up, or next time people will revert to the attitude of not taking you seriously.

6-53   One of my people asks me questions and then argues with me about my response. He comments that last time he did a similar job he did it differently—or that someone else who faced a similar problem handled it differently. If he thinks he knows better than I do, why does he bother to ask me?

Some people just want assurance from their supervisor that their approach to a job is right. When you do not confirm that they are right, they argue with you. They will find all kinds of justification for doing it their own way. If your worker's approach will accomplish the job even though it is different from yours, let him do it. But if it will lead to failure, you have to show him why his way won't work. Often a past approach to a similar problem worked for that problem, but it won't work now because of even a minor variation in the situation. Patiently explain why this is the case.

6-54   How do you supervise a person who always demands a reason for the things she must do? In our loosely structured organization, we don't always know the reasons management has for asking us to do certain things. I don't like to tell her to do something "because I said so."

When people know why work is done a specified way, they can understand and remember it better. Unfortunately, it is not always possible to give reasons. If this is a common occurrence in your organization, when you orient new people tell them that at times they will be given direction without explanation. Point out that you will make every effort to learn the background and reasoning behind the work, but that policy or circumstances may make this impossible. In such a case, you and your workers must do what you are directed to do. Remind your subordinate of this when specific cases develop.

6-55   How can I communicate to my people that they must improve their productivity?

Every job should have performance standards. It is your task as supervisor to communicate to each employee what those standards are for his or her job. You can provide a written statement of the standards at the time of employment or assignment to the job. Review the standards periodically and give reinforcement to workers who are falling behind. If special assignments arise that have no established benchmarks, determine what quantity, quality, and other standards are expected. Work with your people to ensure that they are met. When standards are changed—for example, when higher levels of productivity are mandated—make sure all your workers know what the new levels are and "sell" them on the importance of meeting them.

6-56   My people get very upset when they are ordered to do something which they believe is unfair—such as meeting higher quotas on production. I agree with them. I want to say, "Look, you're right, but that's the way management wants it, so let's get it done." What should I do?

As a supervisor, you represent management and you should not disagree with or criticize management decisions when conveying them to your people. If you feel that a decision is unfair, take it up with your boss and try to get it changed.

6-57   To get my job done, I often need cooperation from other departments—requiring them to change priorities. They resent this interference with their schedules. How can I get their cooperation?

In communicating with peers, you do not have the clout that you have in communicating with subordinates. You can never order them to do something; you have to sell them. If possible, show them how what you request will be of benefit to them. If it really will not benefit them but has to be done to benefit the company as a whole, play up their loyalty to the company as being above that of any one department. You may have to make trade-offs. "You help me now and I'll help you on your next project."

Giving Orders

6-58   My boss believes in telling his people what to do in no uncertain terms. To emphasize the importance, he often raises his voice. Isn't this a turnoff for most people?

Direct orders are best reserved for emergency situations or cases where special emphasis is needed. Direct orders should be enunciated in a slow and deliberate manner in a voice no louder than necessary for the subordinate to hear. Shouting or bellowing orders is unnecessary and disturbing.

6-59   I like to request rather than order my people to do the assignments. It works for me, but some of my colleagues say I'm too soft. Who is right?

Asking politely, with an occasional "please" and "thank you," usually results in cooperative compliance. Most people react more favorably to requests than to orders. It's probably the best way to get things done.

6-60   Chris is one of my best people. She does her work with little supervision and can be depended upon to do it right and on schedule. However, she doesn't like being asked to do something. Even if I ask her politely, she blows up. "I know what I have to do, you don't have to ask me." Sometimes it is necessary to request or even order a change. How do I approach an employee like this?

With people like Chris, suggest rather than request. Suggestions imply that you are bringing her into the picture. Instead of saying, "Please get this report out before lunch," try: "The boss would like this report by early afternoon; it would be helpful if you could give it high priority." You are appealing to Chris's team spirit and company loyalty. Another way is to ask for her input. After presenting the situation, ask: "What can you do to help us get this to the boss?"

6-61   Can you give me some hints on the best ways of giving orders?

To make certain that your instructions are clear and concise:

- Be sure *you* know exactly what you want to be done.
- Be sure the person to whom you assign the job has the know-how, training, and experience to do it.

- Request rather than order.

- When giving instructions orally, speak clearly and distinctly.

- Give enough detail for the person to know just what should be done, but don't micromanage the job. Allow enough leeway to encourage the use of initiative, creativity, and brain power, according to the person's experience and skill.

- Get feedback from your subordinate so you know how the message has been received and interpreted.

- Do not confuse the issue by giving too many instructions at the same time.

- Set timetables so people know just what must be done and when it is expected by you.

- Follow up to make sure that what should be done is done.

Improving Written Communication

6-62   My boss hates to read details. How can I write a report for her that will be meaningful?

In writing a report for a specific person, always take into consideration what that person finds useful. Some people want details; others just want highlights and will ask for more information if it is needed. Some reports will be read by several people, each with his or her own approach to processing information.

One way to please most readers is to provide a brief summary of results at the beginning of the report and back it up with specifics. The reader can then study the summary and select the backup pages desired. Use graphs, charts, and diagrams where appropriate. Many people prefer to study a visual than peruse text or tables.

6-63   I know that planning the report is an essential part of writing one. Any ideas on how to do this?

When planning a report, always think in terms of problem/objectives, facts, and analysis.

1. *Define the problem.*   Ask: "What is the objective of the report?" "How is this report to be used?" "Who will be reading and using the information in the report?" With these facts in mind, you will know what information to seek and how to adapt it for the purpose of the report.

2. *Get the facts.*   Once the objectives are clear, obtain all the information needed. Research the files to uncover what is already known about the matters involved and what experience the company has had with similar situations in the past.

If the report requires more comprehensive study, use the library to obtain general information on the topic and to look up relevant articles that have been reported in the trade press. Speak to people inside and outside of the company who can give you information. If the report concerns equipment, contact manufacturers of that equipment and companies which use that equipment; if it concerns marketing, speak to customers; if it concerns finance, speak to people in financial institutions. Use every resource available to you.

Assemble the facts in a format that will be easy to access when you write the report. A simple way is to keep all items related to each phase in a folder. When writing the report, you will not have to search for papers: all those related to the phase on which you are writing will be in one place.

3. *Analyze the facts.*   Once the information is accumulated, all the facts should be assembled, correlated, and analyzed. If pertinent, list the advantages and limitations of the various alternatives that have been developed from the research.

6-64   Once the research is done, what steps should I take to actually write the report?

An effective business report should be easy to read. The vocabulary should be familiar to the people who will read it. An engineer writing a report for nontechnical managers should try to couch the report in as nontechnical language as the subject permits.

As noted in answer to question 6-62, keep in mind what your reader likes to read. If graphic material is preferred over statistical tables, use graphics. If exact figures are needed, provide them in backup documents.

Although there is no ideal report style, the following format has proved to be effective:

1. *Brief statement of the problem.*   Describe the problem succinctly: "As you requested in your memo dated January 20, 1994, here is the information on the brands and models of the fork-lift trucks needed in our warehouse."

2. *Summary and recommendations.*   Present the summary and recommendations at the beginning of the report. In this way,

the executives who read it can get the key information at once. They will not have to wade through reams of detail to find out what is recommended.

3. *Detailed backup.*   This is the meat of the report. In it present all the details that support the summary and recommendations. Charts, graphs, and statistical tables may make the report more easily understood. Photographs, where appropriate, can be very helpful.

Keep the language of the report clear and concise. There is no need to use an elaborate, pedantic style. Relate the language used to the interests and backgrounds of the readers. Avoid jargon unless it is understood by all readers. Give color to your report by using a variety of sentence structures, a wide vocabulary, good analogies, and timely examples. Avoid clichés.

6-65   How long should a report be?

Long enough to tell the whole story and not one word longer. Avoid repetition. A common fault in writing reports is repeating the same idea over and over in different words. People appreciate conciseness. There is so much paper to read in the business environment today that the brief but concise report is a blessing to its readers.

6-66   Is there anything else I should do before submitting the report?

Check your grammar and spelling. A good report can be considered less credible if grammatical and spelling errors are evident. Have the report proofread by somebody in the company who is competent in writing skills.

Check your figures. An arithmetic error can cause serious problems. One company based a major decision on a report, only to find later that because of a misplaced decimal point, the entire premise on which the decision was made was incorrect.

Make sure the pages are numbered correctly and the index or table of contents is accurate. Long reports should be collated and bound. Check to make sure the pages are in the proper order. Careful attention to little details may take a little more time, but it pays off in the professional appearance of the document.

6-67   When I talk to somebody in person or on the telephone, I have no trouble in making myself understood, but when I write a letter or memo I sound stilted. What can I do to overcome this?

Like many people, you probably feel that written words should be more formal than spoken words. This is not necessarily true. Written language cannot be quite as informal as spoken language—because we cannot use the nuances of voice inflection and body language to augment our message—but it does not have to be stilted.

If you are writing a letter, start with what is of immediate importance to the correspondent. Avoid the "formula" beginning: "We are in receipt of your letter requesting information about our new computer." Instead, be direct: "Yes, our new computer will solve your problem." Then tell how.

Keep the three C's in mind: *complete, concise, clear.* Ask yourself:

- What are the key matters to be discussed?
- How can I present these matters in the most concise form?
- How can I make what I say clear to the person reading the letter?

After you write your first draft, reread each sentence and ask if that sentence fits the three C's. If not, rewrite it. If it repeats something already said, delete it.

Use short, punchy sentences. You may be impressed by your own excellent rhetoric, but your letter will be much more understandable if you avoid complex, multiphrase sentences like this one: "In the light of the research in this field, it is our opinion that the program we are offering will facilitate the writing skills of your employees who undertake this training." Just say: "This program will teach your people to write better."

End the letter on a positive note. Instead of the typical "Thank you for your inquiry," end with: "We look forward to receiving your order." Such a statement indicates a direct, dynamic response to the inquiry and precipitates immediate, positive action.

6-68 We use idioms, contractions, and many other informal expressions in conversation. Can we use such words and phrases in a letter?

Why not? They would make the letter sound like you—not some information automaton. Talk to your reader. Pretend that the person reading it is sitting across from you, or that you are on the telephone. Write in your ordinary voice. Use the expressions, vocabulary, and idioms you use in conversation.

You wouldn't normally say: "Please be advised that because of the fire in our plant, there will be a 10-day delay in shipping your order." Instead, get right into the message: "Because of the fire in our plant, there will be a 10-day delay in shipping your order."

Don't be afraid to use contractions. In conversing, you rarely say: "I do not want this." "I will not be able to go." You say: "I don't." "I won't." Use these common contractions in writing. It will sound more natural. Of course, avoid "ain't" and other slangy contractions—words that shouldn't be used in conversing either.

Use personal pronouns. When speaking, you say "I," "we," and "you" all the time. But like most people, you probably cling to the passive voice in writing. Instead of "We recommend," you write: "It is recommended." This leads to awkward sentences like "An investigation will be conducted and upon its completion, a report will be made to your organization." Why not be direct? Clearly state: "We're investigating the matter and when we obtain the information, we'll let you know."

Usually when you are writing for a company, you have little opportunity to use "I" because you represent the organization. Instead you rely on the plural "we." But if you are expressing thoughts that are your own, it is better to say "I'm sorry" than to say "We're sorry."

Another way of personalizing a letter is to use the addressee's name within it. Unless you are friends or have established a first-name relationship, use the last name. Instead of saying, "By utilizing our services, your company will save time," say: "So you can see, Ms. Jones, that by utilizing our services you will have more time to do the really important aspects of your job."

6-69   I write reports and memos to others in the company. Some parts of the material are more important than others. How can I make sure people concentrate on these rather than skim over them?

Highlight them. Use a highlighter pen—one of those luminescent colored markers—to make important points stand out on the page. *Caution:* if you highlight too many lines, the technique loses its effectiveness.

If you prepare the report on a word processor, there are many other ways to make words, sentences, or even whole sections stand out. Borders, changes in fonts (bold or italics), different typefaces, various type sizes, and graphics can all do the job. Again be judicious. Too many typographic variations can make the document look too gimmicky.

6-70   I write letters responding to customer inquiries. Since most of the letters relate to a relatively few types of situations, is it a good idea to use a form letter and just check off the appropriate response?

It depends on the type of image you wish to portray to your customers. If you want to impress them with your professionalism, form letters of this type are a poor choice. You come across as cheap, uncaring, and bureaucratic. Today, with computers and word processors as part of almost every business, there is no need to use a check-off form. You can program form letters for your most usual situations and generate an individualized letter to each correspondent without it appearing to be a routine form.

6-71   It is important for me to get written reports from my people on the progress of their work. I have designed a simple format for them to use and expect their reports on my desk on the Tuesday following the end of the previous week. My people don't comply. They get the reports in later—and sometimes not at all. How can I improve the situation?

First find out why this is happening. If only one or two people fail to file the reports, the problem may lie with them. If the whole department is not complying, the problem may be in the report itself or in you.

At a group meeting, bring up the subject. Instead of haranguing people on their failure to write the report, find out why it is happening. The report may be too time-consuming or too complicated. If so, perhaps the format could be revised to make it easier to complete. Ask people for their ideas. Perhaps they do not view the report as an important part of their job. You may have to sell them on this. Perhaps the information could be obtained without the report—by computer entry or verbal message. One sales manager solved the report problem by allowing his field staff to send in audiotaped reports instead of taking the time to write them.

Look to yourself. Do you read the reports when you get them, or do you let them accumulate for days or even weeks? Maybe you don't need weekly reports. Biweekly or monthly reporting might be enough and would save work for your people as well as for you. If you do need the material weekly, you may have to spend more time selling the idea to your staff and following up when the reports are not submitted on schedule.

6-72   When I communicate orally with my people, I can get instant feedback, but when I send them written instructions I don't get feedback. How can I find out if they understand?

Conduct feedback sessions after a written communication is issued. On complex matters, you may call a meeting to discuss the instructions. In less complex matters or when only one or two of your people are involved, hold private feedback sessions. Carefully prepare the questions you will ask. Make sure you cover salient points and remain open to comments and questions from your people.

6-73   Our company has a policy that everything must be in writing. We have pads that are preprinted with the headline "Put It in Writing." Many things we do are trivial, transient, or limited in scope. Writing it down takes time—time that could be better used. Why does the company insist on this policy?

One advantage of putting everything in writing is that you have a permanent record of what is being done. It's great for the JIC (just-in-case) file. It can, however, result in much paper clutter and confusion. It is better to limit written orders and communication to more weighty matters.

6-74   Our SOP (standard operating procedure) is like a bible. Everything we are likely to face is covered there. It includes not only administrative matters but duties and instructions for all the jobs that we perform. When we have a problem, all we have to do is look it up in the SOP. Are there any drawbacks to relying on the SOP?

SOPs are very valuable tools. They serve as a permanent reference so that everybody can check on whether things are going the way they should. The negative side is that they may become rigid and inhibit new ideas from being introduced. If your SOP is used judiciously and can be revised when appropriate, it can be a significant asset.

6-75   Our CEO likes to send little notes to his people. They range from a thank you for something we did especially well to suggestions for new projects. We don't know whether he expects an answer, and he rarely follows up. Should we respond, or just put the notes in our files?

You don't have to respond to casual notes, but a brief thank-you note or card for a compliment is appropriate. If the CEO suggests a project or makes a comment about the work, you should respond—commenting on the suggestion, asking for more details, or requesting a meeting with the CEO to discuss the matter. His failure to follow up may mean he is too busy. Or he may be making the suggestion only for future reference, expecting you to draw upon it at the opportune time. If any action is taken on suggestions from the CEO, be sure to keep your immediate supervisor informed, because in the long run the supervisor will have to be involved.

7

Upward
Communication

Getting information from people is as important as giving information to them. Not only do we need feedback on how they
understand and accept our directions, but we must seek to tap
into the tremendous resources of their brain power, experience,
and creativity.

In this chapter we examine problems in upward communication, from problems that emanate in the day-to-day job environment to those that arise with more formal programs such as suggestion systems and meetings. We also look at methods of developing more creativity in ourselves and in our people.

Upward Communication
from Individuals

**7-1 I try to encourage my people to contribute ideas, but
they seem reluctant to do so. They just wait for me to make
the decisions. How can I motivate them to participate?**

People often need to be prodded to speak up. Their reticence
may stem from the fear that they will be scoffed at or rejected, or
will just appear to be inadequate if their ideas are not good. Some
people are just shy. You have to be a patient, willing listener.

When asking your people for ideas, don't express your own first. Often a supervisor will start: "Here's how I think we should go. Any other ideas?" Such an approach intimidates subordinates, who think: "How can I disagree with what the boss just said?" "She's the boss so she must know better than I." As a result, people remain silent. Instead, present the problem and ask for their ideas before you make a single comment on your own concepts.

Let your people know that you respect them and that their ideas can contribute to the work being done. When you express your confidence, people will begin to feel more sure of themselves and be more willing to participate.

7-2   Some of my people come up with ideas and suggestions that just are not good. How can I reject their suggestions without causing resentment?

Many people feel hurt when their suggestions are rejected. They conclude that you do not really care about what they have to contribute. After two or three rejections, they think: "Why bother contributing? Nobody is interested in anything I have to say." Some people will never make another suggestion again. But just because the first one or two were not good does not mean that future ideas may not be winners.

Instead of rejecting poor suggestions, use the Socratic approach. Socrates never told one of his students that he was wrong. If a student answered a question incorrectly, Socrates asked another question and continued to ask questions until the student, by working through the questions, came up with the right answer.

When one of your people makes a suggestion or comment that is not acceptable, instead of rejecting it ask a question about it. You should know what questions to ask—it's your field. Under good questioning, a person will come to reject his or her own idea without you making one negative comment. In addition, the questions will encourage the person to continue thinking and perhaps come up with better ideas.

7-3   I manage a large department. I have several section managers who in turn supervise the workers. I am sure many of their workers have ideas, that I should know about, but they can't bring them to me directly. They must go through channels. So a lot of ideas become lost or distorted before they get to me. Can I let the workers come directly to me when they have suggestions?

Bypassing section heads is not usually a good idea. It destroys their credibility with their people. You should encourage the section heads to bring suggestions made by their people to you. To minimize distortion, you may request that the worker who made the suggestion accompany the section head when the idea is presented to you.

In situations where workers are reluctant to go through their immediate supervisor, a formal suggestion program (discussed later in this chapter) would give them a direct channel to you.

7-4   I have an open-door policy. Anybody in the department can come in to see me with suggestions at any time. Is this a good idea?

The problem with open-door policies is that the door is really not always open.

Joe has a suggestion or a complaint and wants to bring it to the executive vice president, who boasts of an open-door policy. Joe takes the elevator to the executive floor. The door opens to a mahogany-paneled suite. Immediately he feels out of place. He then must go through a receptionist and secretary, who probe him about the reasons for his visit. Joe is told that the VP is at a meeting and that he will have to return at another time. Do you think he'll return?

Even if the boss involved is a lower-echelon supervisor, just going into that office may be intimidating. Only if you are truly committed to encouraging people to bring you their ideas, feelings, complaints, or other information—and you give them time and attention when they do come in—can an open-door policy work.

7-5   My boss believes in MBWA (managing by walking around). He pops into my department every once in a while and chats with my people. He says this gives him an idea of what's going on in the plant. Is this a good way to develop upward communication?

It could be if done properly. If these visits are haphazard and all the boss does is informally chat with the people, they could be a waste of time and effort. MBWA, to be effective, must be planned.

The president of a company boasted that her people were "one big happy family." Was she shocked when they petitioned for a union! She said, "I walk around and speak to the people. They have never even hinted that there were problems."

Sure, she walked around, but her "conversations" centered on small talk about their families. She never asked a job-related question. The president was getting no real information. Had she taken the trouble just to read the graffiti on the walls, she would have realized there was discontent.

In addition to making small talk with your people, you should be prepared to ask meaningful questions about their work. Ask about the progress of special projects, their opinions on material or equipment that has recently been introduced, their feelings about various company policies. Listen, perhaps take notes, and follow through by taking action on what you have learned.

7-6   I am a supervisor of other supervisors. My subordinate managers rarely talk about their people. They feel that as long as their unit's work is OK, I shouldn't be concerned with individuals. How can I get them to keep me advised of the progress of their employees?

Their silence may be due to their own insecurity. They may feel that you are interested in their people as potential replacements for themselves. Let these managers know that you have confidence in them and that in order for you to meet your responsibilities, you need to know how all people in the department are progressing.

Explain that an important facet of any supervisor's job is the development of people. In order for you to know how your subordinate managers are performing that aspect of their work, you must have input on how their workers are progressing. You should include their success in developing people in their performance review.

7-7   My people are experienced and have a good deal of knowledge about their work. However, they tend to be secretive and are reluctant to share this knowledge with others, particularly new hires. How can I get them to show these people the tricks of the trade?

Keeping one's special know-how to oneself is a way of building job security. The reasoning is: "If I'm the only one who can do this, I can't be laid off." It is important that all those doing a certain type of work be fully trained in every aspect of that work. There should be no secrets among people in the department. The first step is developing a team spirit and a feeling of interdependence in the department. Speak to those people who are reluctant to share their know-how. Assure them that their expertise is appreciated and that sharing it will enhance—not diminish—their value to the company, because they are helping build the team.

7-8   The service people I supervise are sent out on jobs both within and outside of our facility. It is essential that I get a report from them when the work is finished. Many of these people are good at the work, but don't turn in their reports. The result is delays in meeting our schedules and sometimes more serious problems. Should I enforce the report policy by disciplining the offenders?

Disciplining offenders might be necessary if the rules are not followed, but it should be used only as a last resort. By public campaigns and private counseling, make your people aware of the importance of the reports. Some companies have tackled this problem with slogans such as "The job is not done until the paperwork's done."

Make it easy to complete the paperwork. For people who are not too comfortable writing details, simple checklists often can replace narratives. Forms can be designed to be read and filled out easily. Offer rewards for accurate and on-time reports. They need not be elaborate or expensive. Some suggestions for getting all reports in on time over a 30-day (or longer) period: dinner for two at a local restaurant; tickets to a movie theater or sports event; points that can be accumulated toward selecting merchandise from a catalog.

7-9   In our hospital—as in most hospitals—physicians and surgeons are not employees but independent doctors who contract with us to use our facilities. Government regulations as well as our own rules require that patients' medical records be kept current. Many of these doctors are so busy that they neglect getting information to us until some time after the procedures have been done. The delay can be dangerous for the patient and can cause legal problems for the hospital. How can we get the doctors to give us those reports immediately?

Many hospitals face this problem. One hospital holds back any monies due doctors until all their reports are in. Another hospital has a clerk from the medical records section personally contact the delinquent doctors and dun them for the reports.

In one very successful program, "report booths" were installed at various locations throughout the hospital. Each booth had a telephone which was hooked up to a recorder in the medical records section. The doctor simply stopped at the booth and dictated the report immediately following a procedure. A variation is to have computer terminals in the report booths so the doctor can input the data directly into the computer. In the future, when information can be spoken into a computer rather than typed, the procedure will become much easier.

7-10   When I ask my people for their ideas on projects we are about to undertake, all I get is agreement with my proposal. I'm sure they must have some ideas of their own. Why don't they bring them up?

Perhaps you have intimidated them. Most managers are not martinets who brook no disagreement with their decisions. They do not sense that they intimidate subordinates, but they may subconsciously discourage contradiction. Subtle disapproval by nonverbal language, sarcastic remarks, failure to acknowledge or comment on other's ideas—all can inhibit workers from participating.

One of my consulting clients, the president of a small company, had the same problem. He asked me to find out why his people were silent. In my discussions with his people, I found that any time one of them disagreed with a decision, the president would argue his case, lobbying for why he was right. After all, he was the boss, so they didn't push too hard to make their point. After a while, they just agreed immediately rather than go through the hassle of arguments.

The solution is clear: never make your decision known until after you get your people's ideas. Be sensitive to the reactions of your people and make an effort to show that you welcome ideas and even disagreements. You may modify your concept once other ideas have been presented. Acknowledge each contribution and when the decision is made, mention how everyone's input helped you in coming to the decision.

Suggestion Systems

7-11   We have suggestion boxes all over the place, but the only comments we generally get in them are gripes. Are suggestion systems really any good?

Suggestion systems can be as good as you want them to be. All it takes is a sincere commitment and a real effort to make them work. In Japan many companies obtain an average of 20 suggestions per employee per year and up to 90 percent are implemented, resulting in millions of dollars in savings, new products or processes, and improved service. The Japanese Human Relations Association reported that in just one year these savings amounted to over $2 billion.

7-12   What do we have to do to make a suggestion system work?

It starts with total commitment to the program by top management as well as by all middle managers and first-line supervisors. All employees should be encouraged to seek ways of improving or changing things that they believe are wrong, to come up with innovative ideas, and to recognize that senior management does not have all the answers.

All suggestions should be acknowledged. If an idea is not accepted, the reason for the rejection should be explained to the suggester. If an idea is accepted, the reward should be appropriate to the value of the suggestion. All suggestion awards should be publicized and a big fuss made over the winners.

7-13   I've read that some companies give very large amounts—sometimes thousands of dollars—for suggestions. We can't afford to do that. Are large awards essential for success?

The amount of the award should be commensurate with the value of the suggestion. Probably the best formula is a percentage of the money saved or made during the first year as a result of the suggestion. The amount can be estimated and paid immediately or can be paid at the end of the year on the basis of actual savings. If the company does make or save money as a result of the suggestion, it really costs nothing to share that saving with the suggester.

7-14   Is sharing in the savings the only equitable reward?

For significant savings it probably is the best. However, all suggestions do not necessarily result in measurable savings. Other types of awards should be used. Some companies give token payments ($25 to $100) for all accepted awards and increase the amount for each subsequent award which is accepted during the year. So, for example, if a person has three suggestions accepted, the first award will be $25, the second $50, the third $75. This encourages people to keep coming up with suggestions. Some companies give points for each award, basing the number of points on the value of the suggestion. These points can be traded in for merchandise from a catalog. Employees with the highest number of points at the end of the year are given additional rewards and recognition.

7-15   How should awards for suggestions be made?

As publicly as possible. Some companies have periodic award dinners to which all award winners and their families are invited. Senior executives present the award with an appropriate citation. Photos are taken and published in the company newspaper.

Another approach is to make the awards as part of a regular meeting. Set aside a few minutes during the meeting for the presentations. When other employees see the type of recognition and awards that are given, they will be encouraged to submit their own suggestions.

7-16   We work in teams and often the entire team comes up with a suggestion. Should we reward the entire team?

If it is a group proposal, then the entire group should share in the reward. Many companies encourage group participation in suggestion programs and give special recognition to the group along with cash awards.

7-17   One of my people is loaded with ideas and suggestions—all bad. Our suggestion committee must spend hours just dealing with rejecting them. Can we discourage people from submitting poorly thought out suggestions?

To avoid frivolous suggestions, require that the suggester back up each idea with the specifics of what the situation is at present, what changes are recommended, and in what way the changes will make the situation better. If pertinent, ask for current costs, amount of savings anticipated, and other expense factors. Serious suggestion makers will have no problem coming up with these figures. People with off-the-cuff ideas will be required to either think them out or not submit them. A well-designed suggestion form such as the one presented in Figure 7-1 will help.

7-18   As a supervisor of a technical department, I expect my people to keep coming up with suggestions. This is part of their job. Why should these people be included in a suggestion program?

Employee Suggestion Form

Employee _____

Department_____

Supervisor_____

Date of submission _____

Description of present condition

_____

_____

_____

_____

_____

Your suggestions (Use additional pages if needed)

_____

_____

_____

_____

_____

Estimate of first year's savings_____

Other benefits that will be derived _____

_____

_____

If you wish to add comments from your manager, technical personnel, or others, please attach them to this form. You will receive acknowledgment and comments from the suggestion committee within 10 working days. Thank you for your suggestion.

Figure 7-1

Most companies exclude technical, professional, and managerial staff from suggestion programs. The programs are really designed to tap the creativity of people who normally are not part of the creative process. However, such people should not be prevented from offering suggestions in areas outside of their normal work. For example, an engineer who makes a suggestion on some administrative problem might be included in the program.

7-19   Should we require that suggestions be channeled through department heads?

Most companies do not require that people consult their department heads about their ideas. To do so might inhibit them from making suggestions. Some people feel intimidated; others fear that the supervisor will belittle the idea and become discouraged from submitting it. If the suggester voluntarily seeks out the supervisor for information, technical advice, or just an opinion, the supervisor should be encouraged to cooperate.

7-20   Who should be the final arbiter of whether a suggestion is accepted or rejected and what the award will be?

The decision should be made by a suggestion committee consisting of a permanent chair, who usually is a member of the personnel department, and a panel of members—all middle management or higher—from various departments. At least one person with the technical or specialized knowledge to judge a decision should be on the panel, as chosen by the chair.

Meetings

7-21   Although a meeting is geared primarily to downward communication—giving information to my people—I find it a great source of getting them to give me information. My problem is that some of my people dominate the meeting. How can I give others a chance to express their ideas?

Ask questions. Typically the more aggressive people raise their hands and demand immediate attention. When the hands go up, pick the less assertive people first so they can express their ideas before the more dominating people have their turn. If one or two people are constant offenders, take them aside and speak to them. Tell them that you appreciate their contributions but it would be nice if they gave some of the other people a chance to express their ideas.

7-22   What can I do to get shy people to speak up at meetings? They may have some great ideas, but I never hear them.

When soliciting opinions or asking for suggestions on a project, ask all participants in the meeting to write their thoughts on a pad. Then after everybody has written something, ask several people in turn to read what they wrote. Since the ideas are already on paper, they do not have to fumble around trying to think of something to say. Make it a point to ask some of the shy ones to read. Another approach is to collect the papers. You read the suggestions and then ask the writer to elaborate.

7-23   Awards are given for ideas that are submitted in suggestion systems. Should I reward people who come up with good ideas at a meeting?

Any incentive that develops productive suggestions is worthwhile. The manager of a publishing company increased the number of good suggestions obtained from his meetings by handing out $5 or $10 dollar bills on the spot to contributors of good suggestions. Sometimes he would tear a bill in half and give it to the suggester with the promise of supplying the other half when the idea was implemented. Not only did this add excitement to the meetings, but it encouraged people to think about the agenda in advance so they could develop suggestions related to the subjects being discussed.

7-24   Is it a good idea to require people to bring ideas to a meeting? Won't this result in lots of time-wasting discussions of trivial matters?

Not if it's done right. Announce the subjects in advance and request that each person who attends the meeting have at least one suggestion on each of the subjects. Because suggestions are a focal point of the meeting, people understand their importance and will generally avoid just making a suggestion for the sake of complying. They don't want to look foolish to their boss and their peers. Companies that follow this approach find that the number of good suggestions increases significantly.

7-25   Some people in my department have great expertise in some specialized areas, but they seem reluctant to share their ideas at meetings. They'll answer direct questions, but that's all. How do I get them to open up?

One approach is to give them an assignment before the meeting: "Sandra, at the next meeting, I'd like you to discuss...." Then at the appropriate time during the meeting, let Sandra take the floor and make her presentation.

Another approach is to let Sandra chair the entire meeting. By sharing the chair occasionally with your people, you encourage them to offer ideas and to participate more fully in all meetings.

7-26   Should we invite other supervisors to attend our meetings when the agenda includes items in which they are interested?

Generally it is a good idea to invite people who do not usually attend your meetings to attend when subjects of concern to them are to be discussed. This approach benefits not only the outsiders but your regular attendees as well, since they can hear the viewpoints of people with whom they do not usually have contact. These views may stimulate them to come up with new ideas.

7-27   Our meetings tend to get repetitious. We follow the same pattern each time. What can I do to make the meetings more exciting for participants?

Add excitement by using visual aids. Rent or purchase a videotape on a pertinent subject. Bring in guest speakers. Invite a customer to speak so those people whose work eventually goes to that customer can hear how it is being used and what problems the customer faces. This input often brings out suggestions on helping the customer.

7-28   What can I do to get more out of the meetings I attend?

When you attend meetings, whether in your own organization or outside, follow these steps to get the most from them:

- *Plan and prepare.*   Study the agenda and do some homework. Learn as much about the subjects as you can so you can understand what is being discussed and be ready to ask pertinent questions.
- *Don't sit with your colleagues.*   Try to meet new people. It is likely that there are people at that meeting whom you know only slightly or even not at all. By sitting with them, you can obtain new ideas and make contacts for networking.

- *Open your mind.* Get rid of preconceptions. You may think you know all about an area, but there is always something new to learn. Don't block out concepts that differ from yours.

- *Accommodate to the speaker.* Sometimes people turn away from a speaker because of the way he or she dresses or speaks or because of his or her background. ("What can a man know about child care?") If you feel uncomfortable or prejudiced about a speaker, make a concerted effort to overcome it. The speaker may have many good things to share with you.

- *Take notes.* Note taking helps you organize what you hear at the meeting and helps you remember it, since the notes are available for future reference. Set aside a page of your notebook to jot down good ideas you pick up from the speaker or from other participants. Often just one idea from that page may be the most valuable result of attending the meeting.

- *Ask questions.* Think out your questions. Restrict them to pertinent matters. Don't use the question time at a meeting as a forum for your pet projects.

- *Contribute ideas.* Relevant comments on your part not only contribute to the meeting but may stimulate ideas from others that could be of value to you.

- *Summarize.* After the meeting, review your notes while the ideas are fresh in your mind. Write or dictate a report for your permanent files. When attending outside meetings, obtain the names and addresses of the speakers. You may want to contact them for additional information at some future time.

Developing Creativity in Your People

7-29 My boss doesn't want us to be creative. She says we're doing OK now. "If it ain't broke, why fix it?"

Today's world is tough and competitive. We can no longer wait for things to break before we fix them. If we don't come up with better ideas, better ways to do things, our competitors will overwhelm us. We must always be constructively discontent— always seeking a better way to do things. We should look at everything we do with a questioning eye. "If it's working now, it will soon be obsolete." All of us must become proactive, not reactive.

7-30   Why do people resist new ideas?

When people get into the habit of doing something in the same way over and over again, they fall into a "comfort zone." It's difficult to leave that comfort zone and move into an unknown zone. It hurts. If we change the way we do a physical act, our muscles hurt until they become accustomed to the new way. If we change a mental process, we get real headaches. We don't want to hurt, so we resist new ideas.

7-31   How can I get my people to open their minds so they will at the minimum listen to new ideas, and at the optimum come up with fresh ideas of their own?

It takes time and patience. You need to persuade people that moving out of their comfort zone will pay off for them. Convince them that the unknown zone is not as scary as they think. It will not hurt that badly, and even that slight hurt will not last for long. Show, by your own example and that of others in the company, how creative ideas have helped in solving problems and in increasing productivity, enjoyment of the work, and often income. Once they accept the value of new ideas, they can work on developing their own creativity.

7-32   Most people do not consider themselves creative. They assume that only a chosen few—inventors, artists, writers—have that talent. Why is this?

From the time we are little children, our creativity is stifled. We are forced to follow rigid rules from kindergarten on. We learn to color drawings within the lines, and that habit carries over to other activities. Often to be creative we have to push that crayon outside the lines—look at things from different angles.

A fourth-grade teacher gives the class an assignment. A little girl comes up with an answer. It's correct, but it's innovative; it's not what's in the book. The teacher says: "That's not what I'm looking for." It doesn't take that child long to figure things out: study the book, parrot what's in it, and you'll get good grades. We've put up a red light to her creativity. We have to turn on the green light and encourage children to use their brain power, to look at things from several perspectives.

From the earliest days on the job, workers are taught to follow the rules. Until relatively recently workers were called "hands," and that's all they used on the job. They left their brains home. Even today, some supervisors tell people that their job is to work and not to think. However, most companies are making the effort to encourage creativity in their people.

7-33   Some companies use brainstorming to get ideas from their people. Just what is that?

Brainstorming is a technique for obtaining as many ideas on a subject as possible. The difference between the usual kind of meeting and brainstorming is that the objective is simply to generate ideas—not to critique, analyze, and reject or accept, them. Any idea, no matter how ridiculous or valueless it may seem, is welcome.

The psychological principle behind brainstorming is called triggering. Any idea can trigger another idea in the mind of a listener. A dumb idea from one person leads to a good idea from another. By allowing the participants to think freely and not concern themselves over how the idea will be received, brainstorming frees people to stretch their minds and make suggestions that, although worthless in themselves, pave the way for an idea that will have value.

In a typical brainstorming session the group tackles a single subject, announced in advance of the meeting. Once the chair introduces the subject, he or she steps back and becomes just another member of the group. One person is appointed to list the ideas on a flipchart. Ideas are called out and recorded. No comments pro or con are made. Freewheeling is encouraged. The wilder the idea, the better. Success is measured by the number of ideas that are generated. Members are encouraged to hitchhike onto ideas as they are presented. After the session, a committee selects the best ideas and investigates and analyzes them.

Brainstorming is not appropriate for all types of problems, but it can be very helpful in many situations. It works best in solving specific problems rather than in determining long-term goals or general policies. Some examples of successful brainstorming are naming a new product, finding a better way to package a product, opening new channels of distribution, making jobs less boring, and developing nontraditional approaches to marketing a product or service.

7-34   If I were more creative, my people would be more creative. What can I do to become more creative myself?

Change your way of looking at things. Learn to think laterally. Instead of being analytical and logical, look at your problems from a different angle. Color outside the lines. In one company, the most boring job was collating brochures for distribution to dealers. Turnover of personnel doing this work was excessive. There was no reasonably priced equipment on the market that could automate the job. When the supervisor complained to personnel about the high turnover, the employment manager commented: "Of course, no one will take that job. Only a mentally challenged person could sustain that work." The supervisor quickly responded: "So hire mentally challenged people."

The result: the work was subcontracted to a sheltered workshop for mentally challenged people, who performed the job in an excellent manner.

7-35   Sometimes I get some of my best ideas in the middle of the night when I can't sleep. Things that I have been pondering at work clear up in my mind. Could I program myself to make this happen at will instead of by chance?

This is not unusual. Our mind keeps working long after we have stopped consciously thinking about a matter. Psychologists call this a period of incubation in which the subconscious keeps processing information, combining it with other information that already has been stored. When we are relaxed, the results of this processing become manifest in the conscious mind.

Some people report that solutions to their problems often come in dreams. Others wake up in the middle of the night with the solution clearly in their minds. Still others get their most creative ideas in the half-asleep, half-awake period that occurs just before deep sleep or just before waking up.

Creative people often keep a pad and pencil next to the bed so they can jot down the ideas as soon as they awaken. They may even wake up during the night and make such notes. Some have reported that they did not even remember awakening, but found the notes on their pads in the morning.

It is not easy to program yourself to consciously utilize this technique, but it can be done. Using biofeedback, meditation, or self-hypnosis, you can condition your subconscious to concentrate on a subject. Seek help from professionals in this field.

7-36   Much study has been given to creativity. What do the experts recommend?

There are dozens of ways to become more creative. Here are three which should start you on the right track:

1. *Observation and adaptation.*   Every day as we live our normal
   lives we observe things happening around us. Sometimes by
   adapting what we observe in one context of our lives we can
   solve a problem we face in another aspect of our lives.

   While Sandro was waiting at a Jiffylube for his car to be lubri-
   cated, he reflected on his company. He wrote down his thoughts:
   "Our company has a fleet of delivery vans. Every time one of
   those vans needs servicing, the driver takes it to the dealer's service center and leaves it there for the day. Another driver follows
   along to take the first driver back to the shop, where other work
   is assigned. In the late afternoon the process is repeated to
   retrieve the vehicle. It takes half an hour to get from our shop to
   the service center. Therefore, we lose four person-hours just for
   transportation every time a van is serviced—plus the van is out of
   commission for the entire day, plus the driver is working on less
   productive work at the regular rate, of pay, plus we incur the cost
   of the lubrication and other incidentals. If these vans could be
   serviced at a Jiffylube, we could save a considerable part of that
   expense." Sandro checked out the situation and found it could be
   done. He made the suggestion, saving his company tens of thousands of dollars and earning for himself a substantial suggestion
   award.

2. *Modification.*   By modifying something we have, we might
   come up with something new, different, or better.

   Victor Kiam, CEO of the Remington Electric Shaver Company,
   tells this story:
   A woman in his office returned to work after undergoing
   surgery. When he welcomed her back, she said: "Mr. Kiam, when
   I was in the hospital, I thought of you. When people have an
   operation, their body hair must be shaved in the area where the
   operation will be performed—in my case, the abdomen. The
   nurse used a double-edged razor and she nicked me three times. I
   said, "You should use a Lady Remington." Kiam gave that idea to
   his research people. In a short time they developed a modified
   version of the Lady Remington as a surgical shaver. It is doing
   quite well in the marketplace.

3. *Elimination.*   Most people think that to be creative you have
   to invent something new. You can be just as creative by getting
   rid of things. Most companies are bogged down with paper-

work. A truly creative approach to the paper hassle would save companies considerable time and money.

7-37   Some people are afraid that if they come up with a cost-saving idea on the job, it will result in a cutback that affects their job or those of their friends. I know this has happened in some companies. How can we assure our people that their ideas will not hurt them?

Unfortunately, it has happened. A good idea may result in the need for fewer employees—and if the suggester has low seniority, it may cost her or him the job. In most nonunion situations, seniority is not a main factor in layoffs and the suggester is not likely to be hurt. There is no way we can completely ensure job security. However, if past company practices treated these situations positively, people will be less likely to hold back from contributing suggestions for improvement. Successful suggestions should not just be rewarded through the formal suggestion system. They should also be a factor in employee appraisals and considerations for bonuses, raises, or promotions.

7-38   Some of my people are overly creative. They approach every problem as if it never occurred in the past. They think they have to reinvent the wheel. How can I convince them that some of the old ways are still the best?

We are doing lots of things right and it isn't necessary to scrap them just because they have been used before. People should work on improvements where appropriate. However, they should also be encouraged to take advantage of past successes— to remain open to what has worked before. The old way could still be the best and could save them a good deal of the time and effort involved in creating something new.

7-39   Generating ideas is only one part of being creative. How can I creatively analyze ideas to determine their feasibility?

It's easy to reject a new concept with "We tried it before and it didn't work." Clear your mind of preconceptions and take a fresh look. Perhaps the situation in which the idea was tried was not as close to the current problem as it appears, and what didn't work then might work now. Perhaps changes in technology, capabilities of staff, or other factors will mean success this time around.

Make your analysis systematically. Don't rely on intuition. Set up criteria against which the idea can be measured. Then evaluate the new concept against each criterion. In this way, you will be using objective and pertinent guidelines to determine the value of the suggestion.

7-40 Some criteria may be more important than others. Is there a system by which I can weigh their importance?

First, divide the criteria into two categories:

- Nonnegotiable factors—those that must be met to solve the problem
- Preferential factors—those that do not have to be met to solve the problem, but that will provide a better solution if they are addressed

For an idea even to be considered, it must meet all the nonnegotiable factors. If it meets several of the preferential factors, that's a plus. To refine this even more, assign weights to each factor so that less important ones will not overly influence the decision.

7-41 My people are frustrated because some of their best ideas have been vetoed by staff specialists even before the suggestions were submitted to upper management. How can we sell these specialists when the ideas seem to infringe on their turf?

Most large organizations retain staff experts in various fields—marketing, quality assurance, human resources, and so on. Suggestions related to a particular specialty are usually sent to these experts first for an opinion. Sometimes the specialists will pooh-pooh ideas that come from employees who lack their expertise. To minimize the possible negative thinking of experts, bring them into the act before you make a formal submission. Invite them to meetings in which ideas relating to their fields are discussed. Have them inform the group about the background of the situation. Ask for their assistance in helping your people come up with new ideas. Participation will remove their feeling that they are being bypassed or made to appear superfluous.

In total quality management (TQM), a movement that has taken hold in many organizations in recent years, staff and line people are encouraged to work together to develop new ideas and approaches in reaching their quality goals.

8

Motivation and Morale

One of the supervisor's most important responsibilities is to motivate people so they will perform at their highest level. Performance can be improved only if the supervisor recognizes that people differ, and that what motivates one may not motivate another. Although there are some sound basic principles of motivation, they serve only as a foundation or set of guidelines. In applying these principles to motivating an employee, you must always take into consideration that person's individuality.

The first step in motivation is to get to know each of your people. Learn what really interests them, what goals they have, what aspects of the job they really enjoy, and what aspects they do not like. As noted in Chapter 1, the more you know about the people you supervise, the more effective you will be in dealing with them.

Motivational Principles and Techniques

8-1 I've heard about motivational principles. Aren't they just theories that have little practical value?

Don't put down theories. All concepts are based on theory, whether it is in science (Newton and Einstein), psychology (Freud and Jung), politics (Madison and Hamilton), or economics (Smith and Keynes). The behavioral scientists (psychologists, sociologists, anthropologists) have developed some cogent principles that can help us understand human behavior and interpersonal relationships. But they are theories, and all theories have to be tested in the real world. They give us a foundation on which to base our actions, making our approach more likely to succeed than hit-and-miss, trial-and-error efforts to solve motivational problems. The theories are basically sound, but in applying them in the real world, we must always adapt the principles to people's individualities.

8-2   Most books and seminars on motivation start with a look at Maslow's work. What did he contribute to these theories?

Abraham Maslow was the first of the modern behavioral scientists to make a significant contribution to our thinking about motivation. He pointed out that human beings have certain needs that extend along a continuum. Starting with the lowest-level need, they are:

- *Physical.*   People have basic needs for food, clothing, and shelter. In the working environment, these needs are usually met if workers are paid enough so that they need not be concerned about life's essentials. Most people with steady, full-time jobs satisfy their basic physical needs.

- *Security.*   People need to feel that they have some stability in their lives, that the job will be there for them over a reasonable period of time and that working conditions are safe. That is why companies with a high turnover history have difficulty in motivating their people. The feeling of security just isn't there.

- *Social.*   People need to identify with a group, to be associated with others—to belong. To this is added the desire for approval by others in the group, to feel we are liked and respected.

- *Ego.*   People want to be recognized for what they do. We all need praise and the feeling that our boss and our company appreciate our work.

- *Self-actualization.*   The highest need is also the most difficult to fulfill. Self-actualization is getting a peak experience from what we are doing. In the workplace, it can be manifested in knowing that our job is helping us achieve our goals, that the work is not only satisfactory, but satisfying.

According to Maslow, these needs are hierarchical. Once a lower-level need is satisfied, it no longer is a motivator and people must go to the next level for motivation. For example, you offer a good meal to a hungry person if he will work. He does the job and eats the meal. Now you say, "I'll give you another meal for more work." It won't help, because the hunger has been satisfied and is no longer a motivator. Reversing this: you go to a hungry person and pat her on the back and say, "You're a great person." It won't do any good unless you feed her first.

As you proceed in this chapter, you will see how the hierarchy of needs can be applied in specific situations on the job.

8-3   I've heard my boss referred to as a Theory X type. What does that mean?

Theory X is a style of management described by Douglas McGregor, a professor at the Massachusetts Institute of Technology, in an article written in the mid-1950s entitled "The Human Side of Enterprise." McGregor asserts that most management thinking is mistakenly based on the concept that people do not want to work and that leaders can get work from them only by promise of reward or threat of punishment. According to Theory X:

1. Management is responsible for organizing the work and directing the efforts of the workers, motivating them and controlling their actions and behavior to fit the needs of the organization.

2. Unless management intervenes, people will not cooperate and may even resist organizational needs. Supervisors must get the work done by being constantly on top of their people. Turn around and they will goof off.

3. Average workers will do as little work as they can get away with. To motivate them to do more, the supervisor must either threaten them with the stick: ("Do your job or you will be reprimanded and eventually fired") or promise them the carrot: ("Do a good job and you will get a raise, a bonus, or a promotion").

4. Workers lack ambition, dislike responsibility, and prefer to have the boss think for them.

5. Workers lack creativity. Without specific direction, they will not be able to accomplish what must be done.

McGregor proposes that this approach is not valid. It is based on false assumptions.

8-4   What does McGregor suggest is a true description of how workers are?

McGregor counterposes Theory X with Theory Y, which is based on four premises:

1. People are not by nature passive or resistant to organizational needs. They have become so only because of their experience in the business world.

2. All people have within themselves the motivation, the potential for development, the capacity to assume responsibility, and the ability and willingness to direct their behavior toward organizational goals. Management does not create these traits but it can and should make it possible for people to recognize and develop them themselves.

3. The essential task of management is to create a climate in which people can actualize their own goals best by directing their efforts toward organizational objectives.

4. People do not need sticks or carrots to be motivated. They will work because they want to work, and they will work better if they have a say in how they are to meet their objectives. Satisfaction from doing work that they enjoy doing is motivation enough.

8-5   I think McGregor is all wrong. I've been a supervisor for many years and have worked with all kinds of people. Believe me, workers do have to be watched every minute or they'll take advantage of you. Why hasn't McGregor been discredited?

Many managers feel this way. McGregor was deluged with letters after his article appeared. Supervisors from all types of organizations wrote to him stating the same feelings you just expressed.

McGregor answered them in a now-famous book* published a few years after the article. He wrote that he didn't disagree with the supervisors. They were basing their feelings on their experience, which did lead them to accept the tenets of Theory X.

*Douglas McGregor, *The Human Side of Enterprise* (New York: McGraw-Hill, 1960).

People behave the way they do in Theory X–dominated organizations because the climate lends itself to that type of attitude. It is a self-fulfilling prophecy. Management expects people to behave that way so they do.

McGregor asserted that if companies would change their approach to *Theory Y,* they would see the difference. Committed workers would increase productivity and quality—not because they were pushed by their supervisors to do it, but because they really wanted to do it. The book cited several examples of companies that shifted to Theory Y after the publication of his article. McGregor described just how these companies did it and how it worked out.

8-6   My boss is a Theory X manager. I try to use Theory Y in working with my people. He thinks I'm too soft. What do I do?

It is very difficult to change a person's style of management. First the boss has to be willing to change, and few people are. Your objective should not be to change his thinking, but to make your own section work effectively by using the approach that is best for you and your people. Once the boss sees the results, although he may not change his own management style, he is unlikely to interfere with yours because it is succeeding in doing the job. Some more open-minded people may recognize that they could get even more out of their people by emulating your style than by sticking to their old methods.

8-7   We've all heard a great deal about Japanese managers. Do they use McGregor's ideas?

Yes, but the approach to management in Japan is more complex. William Ouchi, who studied and wrote about Japanese management, called it Theory Z.*

Theory Z is Theory Y plus. The plus is the identification of the Japanese worker with the company. If you were to ask the average American worker to list the 10 most important things in his or her life, it is unlikely that the company would appear high on the list, if it appeared at all. A Japanese worker would probably list the company near the top.

8-8   Why do Japanese workers feel so strongly about their employers?

*William Ouchi, *Theory Z* (Reading, MA: Addison-Wesley, 1981).

The tie is due in part to Japanese culture, but it is also a result of the way Japanese employers treat their people. The major Japanese employers guarantee their people lifetime employment. They never lay people off and fire workers only under the most dire circumstances. They also provide employee benefits that make American companies look pale by comparison. Chief among these are fully paid health care for the entire family, reasonable-cost housing, and a variety of social activities.

8-9   How does this pay off?

The Japanese worker is willing to stretch for the company, as evidenced by the effectiveness of quality circles in Japan. A quality circle is a group of workers who voluntarily meet on a regular basis to discuss how they can improve the quality of the company's products or services. The high caliber of Japanese products has been attributed in large measure to these quality circles.

Quality circles did not originate in Japan. They began right here in the United States in the early 1950s, but did not succeed. Back then, when the American worker was asked to serve on a quality circle, the typical response was: "It's not my job. I'm a production worker; somebody else is responsible for quality." Of course, now we do have successful quality circles, in part because we have seen how effective they are in Japan.

8-10   The motivational theory that disturbs me is the one that says money is not a motivator. I've always been motivated by money and my people keep asking for money in the form of bonuses, overtime pay, and raises. Is this theory just a subterfuge to get people to work cheap?

The theory you refer to was promulgated by Frederick Herzberg and his associates,* who divided what people seek from their work into two categories: satisfiers (or maintenance factors) and motivators.

A satisfier is something that a person must get from the job in order to expend even the minimum effort. Once that person is satisfied, adding more of the same factor will no longer motivate him or her to work any harder. Among the satisfiers are working conditions, money, and benefits. For example, it is essential that people be satisfied with their working conditions or they will not

---

*F. Herzberg, B. Mausner, and B. Snyderman, *The Motivation to Work* (New York: Wiley, 1959).

give more than minimum effort to their jobs; once they are satisfied, giving them even better working conditions may make them
happy, but it will not motivate them.

Money is in the same category. Conventional wisdom
assumes that offering more money will generate higher productivity—and it does just that in some people, but not in others. Each
of us sets a standard at which we will be satisfied and until we
reach that standard, money does motivate us. However, there is a
point after which the opportunity to make more money no longer
spurs us on; other things become more important. For example,
when a worker is making low wages, he or she may be ready and
willing to work overtime and on weekends. Once base pay reach-
es a level at which the worker is satisfied, requests to work overtime will be turned down. The need for money is satisfied and
now other things dominate, such as the desire to be with the family after working hours. Therefore, money has limited value as a
motivator. It will motivate people until they reach the level that
they feel satisfied—and after that no more.

**8-11 I'm a salesperson. Most sales jobs are based on an
incentive program. It makes us want to sell more so we can
earn more. The program must work, or why else would the
company continue paying this way?**

Incentive programs are based on the concept that people can
make as much money as they want to make by working harder or
smarter. If this concept really worked, all salespeople would be
very rich—but you know that is not true. The key word in the
first sentence is "want." The assumption is that everybody wants
to make as much money as possible. Indeed, some people—not
just salespeople—do want to earn a large sum of money and will
work hard for it. However, most people have consciously or subconsciously established a standard at which they will be satisfied.
Until they reach that standard, money is a motivator. Once the
standard is reached, people will carefully think out whether the
extra effort, energy, or emotion that must be committed to make
that money is worthwhile.

**8-12 Who says benefits are not motivators? One of the
main reasons we get and keep our people is the benefits we
offer.**

Good benefits do attract and keep people, but they do not
stimulate people to work harder. That is exactly the definition of a

satisfier. Do you know of anybody who worked harder because the company introduced a dental insurance program? Benefits make people happy; it keeps them from quitting. More often than not, the people you wish would quit don't.

8-13 Some companies have a simple motivator: "Do your job or get fired." Does this work?

What these companies are doing is threatening to remove job security to get their people to work. Will such a threat make people work? Sometimes. If jobs are scarce and people know that they will have no job at all if they don't work, they will work. But how much work will they do? Just enough to keep from getting fired and not one bit more. This is not real motivation. Real motivation spurs people to produce more than what is needed to survive.

8-14 I know that recognition is a great motivator. Our company does not have any formal recognition program. What can I do to recognize my people?

It is not necessary to have formal programs to recognize people. Recognition starts with letting people know you see them as individuals, not just as cogs in the department's machine. Every human being has a name, yet some managers never call their people by name. They call all the men "Mac" and all the women "Dear" or "Sweetie." Dale Carnegie said that the sweetest sound to the human ear is the sound of one's own name. If you deal with fewer than 25 people regularly, there is no excuse not to learn their names and call them by name when speaking to them. If you have 100 people, it may be a problem to remember everyone's name, but with training and effort it can be done.

That's only the beginning. People crave to be recognized for their achievements, accomplishments, and successes. They want to be praised. Some supervisors never praise their people. One manager boasted that her people knew they were doing OK if she never spoke to them. "If I have to speak to them, they're in trouble." Praise—appreciation—is the lubricant that keeps interpersonal relations running smoothly.

8-15 I feel very awkward when I praise people. I'm afraid I seem phony. How can I sound sincere?

You can't sound sincere unless you are sincere—and praise must be sincere. One way is to incorporate what you are praising the person for into the praise itself. Instead of saying, "Good job,

Lee," say: "Lee, what you did—and specify what Lee has done to merit the praise—is a fine example of the professionalism we like to see in this department."

8-16   Is it a good idea to put praise in writing?

Yes. Some companies provide their supervisors with packets of thank-you cards. Every time a worker does something special, the supervisor sends a handwritten note on one of those cards to that person's home. People show the cards to everybody; they keep them forever. It's an inexpensive way to express appreciation.

8-17   My boss discourages making a fuss over people. She says it will spoil them. "They're getting paid for the job. What more do they want?"

People want a lot more than just their paychecks. It's human nature to want to know that effort is appreciated. This does not mean that you must constantly pat your people on the back, but you should be aware of what your people do and show that you appreciate those extra efforts and those great results. Let them know that you are not taking them for granted.

8-18   I'm so busy trying to build up my low-production workers, I haven't the time for those who are doing good work. They know they are doing well. Do they really need my approval?

Employees, no matter how good their work may be, still want to be noticed. Otherwise they get the feeling that they are being taken advantage of. The result can be resentment toward the job, the company, and the supervisor. Take a few minutes every day to at least chat with your good workers. Ask about what they are doing, comment on their achievements, and let them know they are appreciated.

8-19   What sort of formal recognition programs do companies use?

Probably the most commonly used is the "employee of the month," or some variation. The employee may be chosen by management, by peers, or by a combination of both. The awards may be merchandise or cash, a badge or certificate, a reserved parking space, or the employee's name engraved on a permanent plaque in a prominent place in the facility. Special recognition may also be given for special projects—for example, dinner for a team that exceeds a quota or contributes something unique to the company.

Imaginative awards for recognition add even more excitement and fun to the process. Stew Leonard owns a very successful food store in Norwalk, Connecticut. During the pre-Thanksgiving rush, some of his office staff noticed that the lines at the checkout counter were unusually long. Without any prompting from management, several clerks left their regular work to help the cashiers bag the groceries and accelerate the movement of the lines.

When Leonard became aware of this, he resolved to do something special for these people. He gave each one a beautifully knitted sports shirt embroidered with the inscription "Stew Leonard ABCD Award." When they asked what those letters meant, he told them: "Above and Beyond the Call of Duty." How proud his people were to wear those shirts.

8-20   I have always assumed that opportunity was a great motivator. I worked hard to get promoted. Yet I find that many of my people are not interested in advancement. Why is this so?

Many people do want to get ahead and, like you, will work hard if they know they will be rewarded by advancement. However, there are also many people who do not desire to get ahead. They are perfectly happy just to have a job. They do what they have to do and no more. Their real interests are in other areas. To offer people like that opportunity for advancement is wasting your breath.

Still other people say they want advancement, but expect it by just being there. They think that seniority, longevity, and satisfactory work will guarantee advancement. These people can be motivated to some degree by opportunity, but they need constant prodding and reminding. By really knowing your people, you can determine whether or not opportunity for advancement is a viable motivator for them.

8-21   My company uses contests to motivate salespeople. The theory is that offering people challenges will stimulate them to get out and make more sales. The prizes are fabulous, such as a vacation for two at a luxury hotel. Yet I note that about 20 percent of the people don't even try. With such a great award, why aren't they motivated?

Maybe they don't like vacations. More likely, no matter what the award, they still wouldn't try. Some people are afraid of challenges. They lack self-esteem and fear that by failing to win the contest or beat the challenge, they will look bad. Not only will the boss think less of them, but they will think less of themselves. These people are more likely to be motivated by other means, such as increased recognition for the good things that they do.

8-22   How can I get my people more excited about their jobs?

Most behavioral scientists agree that the best motivator is the work itself. If the job is so interesting and exciting that the people who do it are totally absorbed by it, nothing else will be needed to motivate them.

8-23   What can I do to enrich the jobs I supervise, so that my people will really enjoy them and want to stretch to do outstanding work?

Whenever possible, involve your people in every aspect of the job—from planning it through ensuring that the work is done properly.

A good example is the Ford Motor Company's experience with the Taurus. Instead of following the usual industry practice of having a group of specialists design the car and keeping all plans secret until the start of production, Ford brought in workers who represented every type of job that would be involved in building the car. These representatives worked with the designers and engineers in the planning stage, and all their suggestions were given careful consideration. Many workers—relating the plans to their experience on the production line—brought forth ideas that never would have occurred to the specialists.

When the Taurus was brought to the factory floor, the workers looked upon it as *their* car. The result: the Taurus became the most trouble-free and profitable car Ford has put out in recent years. The people were involved.

8-24   Is the hard-line supervisor gone for good?

Like the people they direct, supervisors have their own concepts of their jobs and of their relationships with others. For many supervisors, the only role models have been their own autocratic mentors, whose style they tend to imitate. If such supervisors are to change, they must recognize that they will get better results using more participatory techniques.

Hard-liners need not feel they have to go soft. Good supervisory practice does not involve coddling people. It is based on the concept that workers are adults and need not be treated as children. Adults can make decisions on the basis of facts and good judgment. They do not have to have things spelled out for them and can take responsibility for their actions.

8-25   To motivate people, a supervisor must be perceived as being fair and neither too hard nor too soft. Any suggestions?

Good supervisors are not wishy-washy, hail-fellow-well-met characters; nor are they tyrants. They are neither ignored nor feared by their subordinates. Capable supervisors have inner confidence plus the respect of their people. A simple comparison:

The ineffective leader	*The effective leader*
Drives people	Guides people
Instills fear	Inspires enthusiasm
Says "do"	Says "Let's do"
Makes work drudgery	Makes work interesting
Relies upon authority	Relies upon cooperation
Says "I," "I," "I"	Says "we"

8-26   Our company brings in motivational speakers and shows motivational videos to our salespeople. These often feature famous sports figures. Is this a good way to motivate people?

Fran Tarkington, a football great, has given many of these talks. When asked about their effectiveness, he commented that motivational speech creates an immediate excitement, but does not have any real long-term effect. Real motivation must come from within, and that starts with setting goals and committing oneself to reaching them.

Goals

8-27   Why is it important for me to set goals for myself, my department, and my people? What does goal setting have to do with motivation?

Unless you know what you want to achieve, there is no way of measuring how close you are to achieving it. Goals give you a standard against which to measure your progress.

The goals you set for yourself must be in line with what your company wants you to do. If what you want from the job and the department is not coordinated with the goals of your organization, you will be wasting time and energy.

Goals are the foundation of motivational programs. It is by reaching toward your goals that you are motivated, and it is by knowing and helping your people reach their goals that you will motivate them.

8-28   How can I motivate people who do not have any career goals?

Helping people meet their own career goals is one of the best ways to motivate people. Unfortunately, not everybody has career goals. Some people work just because they have to eat; others are not sure what their goals really are. Still others have reached their goals and are just coasting along until retirement.

However, all people want something out of a job. Some of your people may have goals that cannot be satisfied by the job itself. Find out what it is they are seeking in life. Perhaps they are going to school at night; perhaps they are writing a novel or painting or sculpting. Perhaps their prime interest is their children. Motivation for these people may be in the form of additional time off, tuition reimbursement, and of course increased recognition and praise where appropriate.

8-29   My people seem to think in short-term goals. They become confused when I try to get them to look down the road. How can I help them relate to larger objectives?

It isn't always necessary to get all your people to see the long-term goals. However, it does make motivation easier if people know what they wish to achieve. Break long-term goals into bite-sized pieces. Then as each part is accomplished, congratulate your people and show them how what they did fits into the next step. Continue in this way throughout the project. When the next project comes up, it will be easier for people to relate to long-term planning.

8-30   How do I get my people to buy into the "big picture" concept? They are so absorbed in their individual phase that they cannot grasp how each person's part fits into the over-all success of the operation.

At the earliest stages of planning, bring all the participants together, including those from other departments. Using a carefully thought out agenda, have each person describe how he or she will fit into the plan. Give people the opportunity to question or comment on each stage of the project. Set interim goals for these stages. Arrange for direct interchanges, so that participants can communicate without having to go through channels. Set periodic control points to monitor progress. If people should get out of phase, bring them back on line rapidly by showing them how what they are doing affects the work of others and the entire project. When people are aware of the contributions of other parties, they are more likely to understand and accept your direction.

8-31   How can I mesh the goals of my people with those of the department and the company?

In order for job goals to be meaningful, they must be congruent with those of the department and company. Take the time to learn the goals of each of your people. Hold meetings periodically to discuss each worker's goals and help make them congruent with departmental and company objectives. Devote part of the annual performance review to this area. Work with your subordinate to develop job goals for the ensuing year.

8-32   I have an employee who has a lot more potential than she is using. She has very limited career goals and is not interested in taking on assignments other than the routine aspects of her job. What can I do to help her (and the department) utilize her capabilities?

Not everyone is job-oriented. Instead of trying to reach her via goal achievement, find out how else her assets could be used. For example, if she is creative, give her assignments that tap her creativity. If she is very detail-oriented, assign her work that requires this skill and increase the level of detail so she can expand her contributions to the department.

8-33   I am fortunate to have several highly talented people in my department. They are all goal-oriented and are anxious to advance in both position and salary. However, the opportunities just aren't there. How can I keep these people motivated?

When people are frustrated by lack of career advancement, it is tough to keep them motivated. Most likely, they will either quit or request transfer to a department that offers better opportunities. If the opportunities are there in your department, but are temporarily blocked because of economic or internal reasons, maintain people's motivation by drawing on their hopes for future advancement. If it is unlikely that advancement will occur in a reasonable period of time, you have to expect turnover. Still, work with these people to get the most from them while they are with you. Bright people often respond to challenges. Give them special assignments that will make them stretch their minds. Get them involved in planning work for themselves and others. If possible, set up a compensation system that rewards them financially by salary increases or bonuses without promotion.

Getting More from Your People

8-34   How can I get people to volunteer to do things during slow periods instead of wasting time socializing or making personal phone calls?

Most jobs go through slow periods. Hardworking people look upon them as breaks—and we all need breaks from time to time. A bit of socializing or relaxing pays off in more and better work when it is needed. However, there is a limit to how much time people can cool their heels. Try planning special projects for extensive slow periods. Do not depend on people volunteering. Special activities might include engaging in creative-thinking sessions, working on background for future projects, and reviewing job descriptions and performance standards. When things slow down, get your people involved in these projects.

8-35   One man on my staff is a fast worker, but when he finishes his assignment, he picks up a newspaper or magazine and reads. When I ask him to help the others with their work, he responds: "I'm paid to do my work and I do it. They're paid to do theirs, so they should do it." How can I persuade him to help the slower workers?

From the minute they start a job, all employees should be told that they are expected to help one another. Nobody should feel that the work is limited to a specific assignment. By indoctrinating your people with the importance of cooperation, you will eliminate a proprietary attitude toward work. If someone still argues that "my job" is done, respond by reiterating that the goals of the department can be met only if people work together. Give your fast worker assignments that will utilize his capabilities and require him to use all his time constructively. If this is not feasible, at least prohibit him from reading material unrelated to work on the job. Rather than just sit there doing nothing, he may (no guarantee of this) volunteer to help others.

8-36   How do you get people to take more responsibility for their jobs, especially when they cannot receive financial reward for doing so?

As noted before, financial reward is not the only type of motivation you can use. Indeed, it may not even be the best in many cases. Sit with your people and discuss the type of accountability each will have for the work. Make sure all understand and accept their responsibility. Encourage them to check their own work and come to you only if problems arise that keep them from achieving what is expected. Workers become responsible for what they are doing when they—not you—are monitoring the work. Offer help when it is requested and intervene only if absolutely necessary to prevent major errors. It's tough to let people learn from mistakes, but you must do so. That is the only way people can grow. They will experience the satisfaction of doing a good job and having accomplished it truly on their own. There is no greater motivation than feeling proud about your work.

8-37   My people do very boring work. They fool around a lot and waste time—not enough to require discipline. Still, I know they could put out more work if they concentrated on the job. How can I motivate them to cut out the play and get down to work?

Are you sure that the playtime is really resulting in less work? Sometimes playtime leads to reduction of boredom and in the long run even more productivity.

In my very first job, as a personnel manager, I worked for a company in which a high percentage of the employees—all women—did low-paying, boring assembly work. As I walked through the plant I noticed that these women seemed to be gabbing, singing, and fooling around most of the time. I asked their supervisor how she managed to get any work done when her people were always playing instead of working. She told me that this informal chit-chat held the department together. "The work is so boring," she commented, "that if they couldn't play, they would quit—causing very high and expensive turnover—or else build up resentment and anticompany feelings." She added: "Watch their hands. They keep working all the time despite the chatter."

8-38   I have an employee who is very smart and creative. No one comes close to his performance. But when he has to do work which is routine, he's very lazy. Sometimes I have to lean on him even to get it started. There are not that many creative projects to assign to him, and the routine work has to be done. How can I keep him productive?

Most jobs are routine and the work must be done. If possible, give him more say in how he will do the routine assignments. His creative mind might come up with more efficient ways of completing the work.

One supervisor faced the same problem. She had an employee who was great at special projects but rebelled at doing the so-called regular work. She noted that some of her other people were uncomfortable with special projects and preferred doing the same routine over and over. By reorganizing the distribution of work, she took away all but the routine assignments from those who didn't like them and gave the special projects to the creative person. She promised to continue doing so if he made an effort to improve his routine tasks.

Another approach is to stress to creative people that doing routine work is a way of paying their dues in order to become eligible for promotion to higher positions. If they know this is only a temporary step which will lead to better work, they are more likely to perform satisfactorily.

8-39   How do you motivate an employee who knows that she has security on the job and does just enough to get by?

Most companies have people like this. They are called coasters. They know that a company is unlikely to fire old-time employees who meet performance standards even at a minimum—and sometimes slightly below minimum. It is difficult to motivate such people, and many supervisors don't even try. They consider it one of the crosses they have to bear.

Sometimes coasters can be motivated with special assignments. Making them mentors of new employees may stimulate them. Talk to them; learn what might really interest them. Try to give them work that fits those interests.

8-40   One of my subordinate managers, a lead person (someone who spends most of the time doing production work, but who has some supervisory duties), supervises a group of skilled workers. He's in his fifties, has been with us for 30 years, but has failed to keep up with thc tcchnology. His people come to me with their problems because he does not always have the technical know-how to help them. I have suggested he go to school and learn these new techniques, but he says he doesn't want to. What can I do?

Some older people are afraid to learn (see question 40 in Chapter 4). Others just do not want to make the effort. Because it is essential that people do keep up with the technologies of their work, you should insist—not suggest—that he take the necessary training. If it requires going to outside classes, make the arrangements and tell him how happy you are that he is going. After each class, spend some time with him. Discuss what he learned and show how it fits into the specific work he is doing. If the technology can be taught on the job, insist that he work with a person who knows the techniques and offer all the support you can. If he still refuses, you have no choice but to remove him from his current position and place him in a job he can handle with the know-how he possesses.

8-41   We have excellent advancement opportunities for people who have the capability and desire to move ahead. Some of my people have the capability, but are perfectly content to work from 9 to 5 doing what they have to do and no more. How can I get these people to use their talents and grow into the better positions?

As noted in answer to question 8-20, many people lack ambition on the job. They satisfy their needs outside of work. To motivate them to seek higher positions, you must answer a need that is not being met elsewhere. It could be financial. Although money is not always a motivator, it does help people meet other needs in their life. The person who enjoys skiing or surfing needs money to pursue those sports; the person who gets satisfaction from being with family needs money to give the family the best of things.

Some people seek status or prestige; others, an opportunity to express their creativity. Learn what it is that your people really want—not from the job necessarily, but from life. If you can show them how job advancement will give them more of what they want, you have taken the first step toward motivating them to work for promotional opportunities.

8-42 Josh could be one of my most capable people. When he's in the mood he produces more and better work than anybody, but most of the time he just cruises along at a below-average pace. How can I motivate him into maintaining acceptable production without being a watchdog?

Next time Josh does a superb job, compliment him on his performance. Do not say: "Josh, why can't you always do this great a job?" You will put him on the defensive, and he may even hold back from doing good work at all. Instead, tell Josh how pleased you are. Suggest that you would appreciate it if he shared some of his know-how with other workers. You might even inspire him to keep working up to his own capacity. Keep giving positive reinforcement.

8-43 I have an older employee with 3 years to go before he retires. He has, in fact, already retired on the job. He looks upon himself as the "elder statesman" to whom people can come for advice—a full-time mentor. This is fine, except that he is still expected to do his regular work, which he now looks upon as demeaning for a person of his age and stature. How can I get him to face the reality of the situation?

Have a heart-to-heart talk with him. Tell him that you admire his commitment to help the younger people, but that his regular work cannot be neglected. If he does not do it, it just is not being done and that puts an unfair burden on the rest of the department. The company does not provide for preretirement status. People are expected to function fully until they actually retire. If this fails, it may be necessary to take firmer steps to make sure he will do his work.

8-44 Like many companies, we are downsizing even though the workload has not declined. Our people have to work much harder and often longer hours just to keep up with the work. This is leading to stress and discontent. How can I motivate people to work under these circumstances?

Many companies are cutting back because of poor business. However, what often happens is that the work falls off by 20 percent and 30 percent of the work force is laid off. The remaining employees must make up the difference. Some companies "motivate" people to put out the extra effort by the fear that they too will be laid off. Negative motivation works up to a point. Jobs are scarce in many areas, and working harder is better than not working at all. However, a point is reached at which stress and unhappiness undermine performance. There are no easy answers to this problem.

One way is to encourage people to work smarter rather than harder—to develop more efficient methods and systems. As the cliché goes: "Necessity is the mother of invention." The hard facts of necessity have led to many new approaches that make work easier. Many clerical tasks have been eliminated because the paperwork was not as important as it seemed.

Stress reduction programs can help people cope with downsizing. As business picks up, people should be told that laid-off workers will soon be rehired so they can see the light at the end of the tunnel.

8-45   Our company has had layoffs, but my people view it as a management problem and just keep doing their regular work. When I ask them to work overtime to pick up the slack, they refuse. I wind up working 13-hour days. How can I sell them on overtime?

Unless you have a union contract that prohibits it, people can be compelled to work overtime. (Nonexempt employees must be paid time and a half for all work over 40 hours in any week.) It is always best to start by selling people on the importance of working overtime to keep the department's workload flowing. Make clear to them that this is not a management problem but a problem for everyone in the organization. They are expected to cooperate. If persuasion fails, set up an overtime schedule in which everyone is required to put in a certain number of hours. If feasible, give people the opportunity to select which hours they prefer. Failure to comply should result in disciplinary action.

8-46   I think my people are being overworked, but I have no power to decrease their workload. What can I do to give them encouragement?

Work along with them. Show them by example that you too are carrying a heavy workload. Give them added recognition and praise for their achievements. Encourage them to find better ways to alleviate the burden. If you are certain there is an end in sight, let them know that "this too will pass" and they will soon be getting back to a more reasonable workload.

8-47   My company formed a new division and filled it with castoffs from other departments. They weren't bad people— just not superstars. All are long-term employees whom it would be difficult to fire. I was brought in to head the department. We have been in operation now for several months, and my people are doing just mediocre work. I really need superstars. What can I do?

Of course they are doing mediocre work. They know that they were "selected" for the new department because their former bosses were glad to get rid of them. They know that they are considered mediocre workers, so they continue to produce mediocre work.

The very nature of the selection process batters their self-esteem. They recognize how the company perceives them and they will prove that the company is right by doing what the company expects: mediocre work.

Your job as supervisor is build up their self-esteem. Let them know that you do not accept the concept that they are inferior workers. Tell them that often people do not do well in one department or under the direction of one supervisor, but then excel in another department or under an inspiring leader. Tell them that you are confident that they have not had the opportunity to work to their optimum potential. You are going to help them by giving them the training, the tools, and the support they need. Then do what you promised.

It's hard work to remotivate demotivated people, but it has been done and you can do it by being a truly inspiring and supportive supervisor. Work with each of them. Identify strengths and help make them even stronger; recognize limitations and shore them up. Praise every improvement. Work with them as a team. Develop an esprit de corps. Mold them into a group that works together, helps one another, and is willing and eager to improve because they know that they can do it.

8-48   My people are organized by a strong union. What can I do to motivate them to exceed minimum performance standards?

Many unions interpret what you may consider minimum productivity as the maximum a member should do. They believe that any desired increase in production should be negotiated with the union. In such cases, supervisors can get very little cooperation from their people. Even indirect suggestions for more productivity may result in time-consuming grievances.

In this period of economic setbacks and tough competition, the survival of a company may depend on obtaining more productivity. Labor relations experts recommend that representatives of the company and union work together to reach agreement on what changes in work rules can be made to help the company through a difficult period.

In cases where a supervisor has a good personal relationship with the union members, informal efforts to build up production may achieve the goal, at least for short periods.

Motivating a Diversified Work Force

8-49   In our small, but growing company, we have to work hard and put in long hours to meet our goals. Our pay scale and benefits are lower than those offered by more established companies. We have assembled a good team of men who are willing to make present sacrifices for future gain. However, the women we have hired leave after a short time. They tell us the work is too hard and that there is no opportunity for advancement. The work is hard, but the effort will pay off in a few years. We want to bring in and promote women. What can we do?

Stop thinking of this as a gender-related problem. If you study the pattern of turnover among men, you will probably find that you have lost many of them for the same reason. Not everyone is willing or able to give up immediate money and benefits for possible future gain.

Start with the selection process itself. In screening applicants, be sure to ask about their ability and inclination to work under the circumstances you offer. You will find that many women as well as men are willing to do so. When people show signs of impatience or discontent on the job, work with them individually to help them over this setback. Strengthen their commitment by pointing to the progress already made and how it is leading to the goals you, they, and the company have worked so hard to achieve.

8-50   With the Americans with Disabilities Act (ADA) now in place, how can supervisors be fair in allotting work when they may have to give lighter workloads to disabled people than to those without disabilities?

The law does not require that workloads be lighter—only that the work or workplace be modified to accommodate the needs of the disabled person. For example, if a job calls for a good deal of heavy lifting, it is legitimate to refuse to hire a person who cannot do constant lifting. But if the job is primarily packing, which a disabled employee could do, with occasional heavy lifting, which the employee could not do, the company is asked to restructure the job so others do more of the heavy lifting. The workload would be evened out by having the disabled person do more packing or some other work.

Some employees may resent even this type of accommodation. (One solution is discussed in answer to question 12 in Chapter 3.)

8-51   Our younger employees are unhappy. Older employees doing the same work are paid more money because over the years they have received annual raises which by now give them a significantly higher salary than newer people. The younger ones work faster and better than some of the old-timers, and they resent the pay differential. Under our present system, it will take years (if at all), for the salaries to become even close to equal. How do I instill productivity in these young people—upon whom the future of the company depends—and even keep them from leaving the job?

Experienced employees traditionally are paid more than new people, but because of seniority many long-term employees get much more money than their position or productivity warrants. It is not wise to reduce the salaries of the higher-paid workers and it is not usually feasible to give rapid raises to the newer ones. They have to bide their time to earn more money.

In some types of jobs, the differential can be alleviated by giving incentive bonuses to fast and accurate workers. Another approach is to create new job classifications to which good workers can be promoted on the basis of merit—not seniority.

Financial reward is not the only way of motivating people. However, as pointed out in question 8-10, unless people are happy with their pay—which is a satisfier or maintenance factor—other types of motivation will not really work. If people are basically satisfied with their earnings and are discontent because they feel they are working as well as or even better than their higher-paid colleagues, other motivational approaches—recognition, appreciation, challenge, and participation—may help solve the problem.

8-52   How do you motivate the only male employee in a department that is and has always been primarily female? He feels that his viewpoints are not taken seriously.

In this day and age, gender separation of jobs has blurred significantly. Women work as carpenters, men serve as nurses, and young people of both sexes prepare for careers that their parents once assumed were not open to members of their sex. In time, the gender distinction will all but fade. For now, however, we do have to face it.

As the supervisor of a "women's department," set the stage by your own attitude toward the male employee. Take the time to listen to his ideas, to comment on them objectively, and to encourage your people to treat him in a professional manner. If any of them deprecates one of his suggestions ("What can a man know about that?"), point out that all ideas—no matter what their source— should be looked upon objectively and not judged on the basis of who proposed them. Your example will lead the staff to accept this employee and make him feel that he is part of the team.

8-53   We have a strong affirmative action program and have hired a number of minority people to work in our plant. Most of them have never held a steady job before and have not developed basic working habits. They come in late; they do not call in when they are unable to come to work; they walk off the job without telling anyone. When I discipline them, I get a blank look and lots of resentment. What can I do to motivate these people?

These problems came to prominence in the 1960s, when special efforts were first made to bring people with little work background into the mainstream. AT&T started a program designed to help such people relate to the world of work. New employees were given an intensive orientation on the basics of working, including all of the issues raised in your question. People accustomed to sleeping as long as they wanted were given alarm clocks and shown how to use them. They were presented with case discussions, games, films, and easy-to-follow guidelines to get them started on the right foot. Training was supplemented with on-the-job counseling by supervisors and human resources specialists. The first few work infractions were handled through additional counseling rather than disciplinary action. The program was successful and most of these men and women developed into productive workers.

8-54   We have a really diverse work force. In my department of 14 people, I have several from Pakistan, Russia, China, and Central America, plus white and black Americans. How can I meld them into a cooperative, coordinated working team when they come from such different cultures?

Look for their similarities rather than their differences. It is difficult for people brought up in one culture to acclimate themselves to another culture quite different from their own. The task is even harder when co-workers come from several different environments. All your people should be trained to do their work and should understand the goals of the department. Encourage them to mix with one another, to eat together rather than seek out people from their own ethnic group at lunchtime. Get them to share ideas. Counsel them individually on any problems they have in working with others.

To strengthen interpersonal relations, hold periodic meetings in which people from one country tell the others about their culture, its customs, the kinds of work they have done, and anything else that will help the others understand them better. If their English is limited, ask another worker who speaks their language to act as an interpreter. Encourage them to bring in pictures of their homeland. When people recognize that cultural differences are superficial barriers—that all people have similar joys and sorrows, desires and hopes—they will take the personal steps needed to work cooperatively. Eventually friendships will develop among co-workers from different national or ethnic groups.

8-55   Our town is heavily Slavic. For many years my employees consisted of immigrants from Yugoslavia or their descendents. As a non-Slavic person, I saw no differences among them and we had a smooth working group. Now with the dissension and bloodshed in what was Yugoslavia, the Serbs and Croats in the company have taken sides. They don't talk to one another, and some fights have occurred. Productivity is suffering. How can we get things back to normal?

You can't. There are some situations that are stronger than the job. The ethnic fighting in Yugoslavia will permeate the lives of all people from that area. The best you can do is to try to get people to concentrate on the job. Discussions and counseling with the leaders in each group might help them try to put aside their feelings during working hours.

Building Teams

8-56   The current fad word in our company is "empower-ment." Everyone talks about it but I'm not sure what it means.

Empowerment is giving power that you have over people back to those people. It is another term for participative manage-ment. Under traditional management systems, when the supervi-sor gets an assignment, he or she determines how it is to be done and then describes what each person will do and how to do it. Under empowerment, the supervisor and the workers together determine what and how a job should be done. The power shifts from the leader to the entire team. The supervisor becomes a facilitator rather than a boss.

8-57   I worked hard to become a supervisor and I have earned the right to use my power. I have the experience and I know what to do. Why should I give up this power that I have worked so hard to attain?

By sharing your power, you are not losing status. You are just changing techniques. As a facilitator, you teach, inspire, and moti-vate your people to use their best talents. You build a team and that will help you become even more successful.

Empowered teams come up with ideas that a supervisor alone might not have considered. Workers have a lot of insight into how their jobs are done, and the views of many add to a greater whole than the input of any one person, even an experi-enced supervisor.

Finally, when people participate in making a decision, they are committed to its success and will put out the extra effort needed to make it succeed (see question 8-23).

8-58   How do I get my people to buy into the concept of empowerment? They tell me that they feel more comfortable being told what to do and then doing it.

Many people feel that way. They do not want to stretch their brains. They are happy doing a routine job in a routine way. That is why participative management or empowerment does not always work. It will take a sustained effort to make empowerment succeed with your people. You will need to work on building their self-confidence. Over a period of time give them assignments for which they will have to plan. Start with small matters and gradually increase the complexity. In time, many of your people will respond and become team members; others may never change their ways. You'll just have to replace them with team-type people or learn to accept their ways and work around them.

8-59   How can I get my people to think of themselves as a team instead of a department?

It starts with you. When you act as a facilitator instead of a boss, your people will begin to feel and then act as team members instead of employees. You cannot just acknowledge the team concept—"From now on you are not employees but team associates; I am not your supervisor, but your team leader"—and then keep working in the same way you had before.

Team building requires careful planning. It just doesn't spring up by itself. The most successful team activities have been guided by specialists in the field—either staff people or outside consultants—who orient team members in (1) how they will be expected to work, (2) how it differs from what they are used to doing, (3) where they can go for help, and (4) how it will pay off for them.

Once the team is in place, meetings should be held to discuss and plan the projects. The facilitator may chair the meeting or assign somebody in the team to preside. One or more team members may be assigned to lead specific projects. The supervisor may serve on some of those teams as a team member and in other instances either lead the team or stand aside and provide support and technical advice.

8-60   How can I get my team members to search out answers for themselves rather than coming to me for answers?

Provide information resources within the department or in easy-to-reach places on company premises. Set up a minilibrary, a computer databank, or just a file cabinet. Team members should be taught how to use these resources. When they bring you a problem or question that could be handled through research, instead of answering it, refer them to a data source. If the issue requires speaking to another employee in another department, give them direct access to that person. Restrict your participation to problems which cannot be resolved in the required time frame by using other sources.

8-61 We don't have a formal team setup. How can I get my people to work and think like a team?

It is not necessary to go all out and change to team activity. All work groups should aim to operate as a cooperative, coordinated team. Use participative decision making where appropriate. Let people know that they are appreciated and that they are looked upon by both you and the company as valuable employees whose thinking and suggestions are welcome.

8-62 How can I reward the team rather than individuals without upsetting those who participate more actively than others?

Team rewards generally go to the whole team. If some people are not pulling their weight, peer pressure usually will impel the delinquents to shape up. If this does not work, counsel the offenders. Point out how important they are to the team's success and ask what you can do to help them. If all else fails, they may have to be removed from the team.

8-63 We follow the team concept. Individuals are expected to subordinate themselves to the team. I recently hired a highly qualified technician who comes from an environment in which each employee operates independently. She's having a problem adjusting to the team concept. How can I help?

There are many advantages to working in teams, but one disadvantage is that it sometimes inhibits individual initiative. People who are accustomed to working individually find it difficult to discuss an idea before they have worked it out fully—mainly because they do not want to share credit for their innovation. To help your new technician make the adjustment, get her into the team spirit by warmly welcoming her to the team. Take the time to discuss how the team operates and how all benefit by working together and sharing ideas. Give examples of the work accomplished and demonstrate how the synergism of team activity will make her an even more productive participant. Let her know that individual contributions are recognized.

8-64 What are the most important things I must do to make a team work?

The following acrostic can be a guide to successful TEAM development:

T raining.   Orient your people as to how the team setup differs from the previous way of doing business. Either bring in experts in team development or, after study on your part, conduct training sessions using role-plays and case simulations to train your people in how the team approach will be utilized.

E nthusiasm.   To make any team activity work, you must get team members not to just accept the idea but to greet it enthusiastically. Think of analogies in sports. One company had each team select a name and color.

A ssurance.   Teams should be assured that they will not be left entirely on their own. The team leader and other staff people are available to provide technical assistance when needed. The team should also be assured that its ideas and concepts will be elicited and welcomed by management.

M easurement.   Specific goals should be set for each team and performance standards should be clearly stated.

Other Motivational Problems

8-65   One of my people has been an adequate employee for many years. Now the job has become more complex and he can't do it. Additional training has not helped.

When a person cannot or will not keep up with the requirements of the job, every effort should be made to find out the reason and do all that can be done to help. If added training and motivation do not succeed in bringing this person up to par, perhaps the work can be restructured to use his abilities. If not, there may be another job in the company for which he can qualify.

Over a period of years, a manufacturer of electromechanical components shifted its line to electronic components. The service technicians were retrained to service the new line. One old-timer either couldn't or wouldn't learn how to service the electronic line. When all efforts failed, his work was restricted to servicing those electromechanical items that were still being used by long-time customers. The restructuring kept him productive for several years.

8-66   I supervise six employment interviewers in the state job service. My boss wants them to interview more clients than they are now seeing. They feel that to do so would

reduce their professionalism and cause stress and burnout. What can I do to meet my boss's demands and still keep my people satisfied?

Because of budget cuts and business necessity, many people are being asked to do more work than before. Your people could reduce the time spent on each interview and still maintain professionalism. Review their current interviewing techniques with them. Together you can probably tighten up the interviews so pertinent information can be obtained in less time. Review the paperwork. Much time may be saved in this area. Determine what can be handled without the pressure that leads to burnout. The client numbers may not be as high as your boss wants, but they will be higher than what your staff is now doing. Discuss the numbers with your boss and come to an agreement on an equitable workload.

8-67   My subordinate supervisors are not doing as much work as I think they should. When I discuss this with them, they say they are not paid enough to work more. When I point out that the company is paying them as much as it can, they say that the company should raise its prices so it will have more money for salaries.

Perhaps your people need a course in basic economics. Raising prices does not necessarily bring in more money; it may cause loss of business and less money and maybe fewer jobs.

Whether you are dealing with hourly workers or salaried supervisors, make it clear that they are expected to do what has to be done to get the work accomplished. Sit down with them and work out a plan of action that will be fair to both you and them. Point out that increased income comes only from increased productivity.

8-68   How can I encourage people to use their own initiative?

When your people bring you a problem, instead of solving it, ask them how they think it might be solved. Don't accept "I don't know." Ask them to think about it and come back with a suggested solution. Present them with real or hypothetical problems that relate to your current operations. Ask them to think about the issues and suggest possible solutions or approaches.

Never deprecate an idea from one of your people. Even if the idea is not good, use the Socratic approach (see question 2 in

Chapter 7). Encourage the originator to think things out until a better aproach evolves. If the idea is good, praise it, make a fuss about it, and let others know where it came from.

8-69   One woman in our department is a "floater." She is assigned to work wherever she may be needed. The other section heads tell me she is a good worker, but when she works for me she does a poor job. Should I ask that she not be assigned to me?

Maybe you antagonize her in some way. You may be too abrupt with her, too demanding, too stinting on praise. Or perhaps you just remind her of a past boss she disliked.

Ask some of the other section heads how they deal with her. Perhaps she needs to be given very specific instructions or prefers to receive a general concept and work out her own details. Analyze what you do and what others do. If you still do not find a reason for her behavior, a heart-to-heart talk with her may clear the matter up.

8-70   One of my people was recently passed over for a promotion. She is an excellent performer. How can I keep her motivated?

Find out why she was passed over. Often the reason is easily explained and understood. For example, the promotion involved knowledge of computers, which she did not have. Or despite her excellent performance, an equally good performer with much more seniority was chosen. If she feels there is good reason for another person getting the job, she will be less likely to be demotivated.

If the reason is less tangible, the issue becomes more difficult and harder to accept. Perhaps she lacked the necessary leadership skills or was not assertive enough. Assure her that leadership skills and assertiveness can be acquired and that you will help her learn these traits so she will be ready for the next opening.

Keep giving the employee plaudits for her good work. Get her involved in interesting projects. Be supportive. Once the initial disappointment passes, she will continue as a motivated and productive member of your staff.

8-71   One of my employees was promoted to a supervisory job. It was a mistake. He couldn't handle it and I am about to move him back to his old job. How can I motivate him to be productive after this blow to his ego?

Discuss the situation with the employee before he returns to the former job. Perhaps he was unhappy in the new job and will be glad to return to one in which he has a record of success. Let him know how good you consider him in his original type of work. Point out that everybody can't be good in every kind of work, and the new assignment was just not in his bailiwick. Let him know that you will give him your full support in making the readjustment. The employee may not be happy about it, but he will know that you thought enough of him not to fire him for the failure but instead to retain him in the organization.

8-72   How can I motivate an employee who has reached the top of her salary range and is not qualified for promotion?

Sooner or later this happens to many people. Some companies raise the maximum salaries in their ranges periodically to keep up with the cost of living. They can then give raises to people who have already reached the ceiling. Other companies "red circle" a salary adjustment: the red circle means that the raise is outside the range by special permission and not a change in the classification.

Nonfinancial incentives should also be utilized. As pointed out throughout this section, people will be motivated if you give them something they really want. They may seek praise or recognition; they may want an opportunity to use their special talents. Search out your employees' interests; learn what will turn them on.

8-73   My employees have no self-drive—only "What's in it for me?" What's the best way to motivate them?

Let them know what can be gained by the action. Show them how they will benefit. If a special effort will lead to a promotion, a raise, or a bonus, spell out what must be done to achieve that goal. If there is no direct reward, tie it in to their needs and interests.

8-74   We hire temporary help for special projects. Often they are with us for several months. They are not on our payroll, but are paid by the service company we contract with. We have no control over their wages or benefits. They have no job security with us. The job ends when the project ends. How can we motivate them?

Even though they are not your employees, treat them as if they were. Give them praise and recognition. Invite them to participate in company functions that occur during their tenure. Encourage the people who work with them to treat them as colleagues. Go to lunch with them; socialize if they so desire. Make them eligible for the same types of awards that you give your regular workers for attendance, suggestions, and other contributions. Tell the temporary workers you particularly like that if they desire, they could be considered for regular employment when openings develop.

8-75   What do you do when a more experienced employee learns that a new hire is making more money?

Sometimes in order to attract good applicants, it is necessary to pay a new employee a higher salary than people already in your company. Despite efforts to keep salaries secret, people find out. There is no way you can make current employees happy about the situation unless you bring their salaries in line—and that can be expensive.

8-76   I just learned that one of my engineers is seeking another job outside the company. What can I do to motivate him to stay with us?

First find out why he wants to leave. Arrange for a private meeting—preferably away from the facility. Discuss his work, how much you appreciate it, and how concerned you are about his decision to leave. Get him to tell you not only his overt reasons, but his underlying attitudes toward the company. If the motive is financial, perhaps you can raise his salary. If it relates to the way he feels he has been treated, discuss the situation and promise to correct it. Try to resolve any problems the employee may have with the work he is doing, and discuss any other factors that led to his decision. Try to sell him on changing his mind and staying.

8-77   What kinds of challenges can you offer a subordinate who has an advanced degree and is working on a job that is below her level of education?

A degree alone is not an indicator of readiness for doing many kinds of work; experience is needed. People who have just received a degree must still learn the job. In such cases, offering assignments that will give them the real-life experience they need is challenge enough. By explaining how an assignment can add to their skills, you will set the stage for their enthusiastic endorsement of the work.

Often because of business conditions, educated people cannot find jobs that utilize their degree. To motivate them, offer special assignments that will challenge their initiative and ability to solve problems. When you give them routine work, ask for their ideas on how it may be accomplished faster or better. Encourage them to use their intelligence and creativity.

Sometimes highly educated people just haven't made it on the job. Factors other than education and intelligence may have kept them from advancing. Identify the reasons and if possible help them overcome them. If personality traits or other intangible factors are involved, recommend professional help.

8-78   I have been assigned to replace a manager who will remain in the department in a lesser position. He is a good performer and has much expertise that I will have to rely upon. He is not happy about this change. How can I keep him motivated and productive?

The manager who made the decision for this change (probably your boss) should sit down with both of you and discuss the new setup. He or she should explain why the change was made and how each of you will be expected to function. The former supervisor should be assured that his job is secure and that his technical competence is essential for the success of the department. Make every effort to win his cooperation. Ask his advice; show appreciation for his contributions. Deal with him very diplomatically so he does not feel you are "bossing" him. It takes time to win such people over, so don't give up if he resists your attempts to do so.

Of course, some people can never be won over and you may have to resort to stronger tactics. For example, you may need to give this man specific orders to accomplish a task or have your boss talk to him and demand that he cooperate. But these are last resorts—to be used only if your persuasive powers do not succeed.

8-79   How do you motivate people who feel that they are underpaid and overworked?

If they really are underpaid and overworked, there is not much you can do to motivate them. However, many people who think they are underpaid are simply not aware of how the pay scale is determined. If there is a systematic approach to wage and salary administration, explain it to your employees. If there is no formal program, and wage and salary determination is indeed haphazard, you face a difficult task.

As far as "overworked" is concerned, this is a subjective issue. Sometimes people really are asked to do more work than is normal. Extra work is acceptable if it is not assigned too often and if the periods of overwork are short. Sell people on putting in the effort because of the immediate need. Most workers will go along. However, if the situation arises regularly, workers will resent it and feel that they are being taken advantage of. Also, overwork can lead to burnout and physical and psychological problems.

8-80   Some of our skilled people have to be used from time to time to do dull, boring work unrelated to their fields. The work has to be done and even though they are still being paid at their regular rate, they balk at the assignment. How can I motivate them to do the work without griping?

Skilled people should not be doing this work. It is cheaper for the company to hire lower-paid people to perform the tasks, allowing the specialists to do more work in their fields. Paying high wages for low-skill work is poor management. If there is not enough work to warrant hiring full-time personnel, use part-timers. Students, senior citizens, and others look for such jobs. This will alleviate the dissatisfaction of your people and enable them to perform the jobs they are paid to do.

However, if neither of these options is available and your skilled people must do the work, divide it in a way that no one person is overburdened. Spread the chores around. Ask your people to find better ways of accomplishing them. The challenge will add a little interest to the assignment.

8-81   We are in the process of restructuring, with inevitable downsizing and layoffs. How do I keep my people motivated during this period?

For some people, restructuring is a stimulus to work harder so they will not be among those laid off. For others, particularly when layoffs are likely to be based on seniority, it is an opportunity to put out as little as they can get away with. Still other employees—the majority—will feel insecure and uncertain about the future. Their work will be affected. With the first group, no motivation is needed; with the second, nothing will help. It's the third group that will respond to your efforts at motivation.

You cannot ignore the situation and work as if the Sword of Damocles was not hanging over everyone. Discuss the situation. Keep people advised on what is happening. Assure them that every effort is being made to keep as many workers as possible. Give them adequate notice if they are to be let go (see Chapter 14).

A major problem when downsizing is imminent is that some of the people you do not intend to lay off may seek (and find) other employment. To avoid this, speak privately to your best people. Assure them that their jobs are secure and that once the restructuring is completed, the company will be much stronger. The result will be long-term stability and greater opportunity for them.

8-82   Our company culture is changing. We are moving from an autocratic top-down management to a more participative style. Top management is all for the change, but many of my peers—other supervisors—are resisting it. Without their involvement, we lose the support of their subordinates, and the whole concept will collapse. How can I get my peers to buy the change?

It's top management's responsibility to sell all supervisors on the change, explain how it will affect them and their people, and point out the benefits to them and to the company. As a peer of these supervisors, you have no power to compel them to change. Your best role is to be an enthusiastic supporter. Talk to your peers about the program, answer their questions, show them how it is working in your department. Your excitement might break through their shell of resistance and help make the program succeed.

8-83   Like many companies, we use a security service to provide guards for our facilities. There is a tremendous turnover among these guards. Even though they are not our employees, we have to break them in and be sure they understand our special needs. This is time-consuming. What can we do to help the contractor reduce the turnover?

You and the contractor should tackle the turnover problem together. Some of the contractor's other clients may not have special security needs and may be willing to have different people assigned to their work. Explain to your current security staff the importance of having a consistent group of guards. Make the assignment more pleasant for them. If they must be on their feet throughout the shift, provide rest periods and places for them to relax on breaks; supply coffee and snacks. Stop and talk to them from time to time and encourage others to do so. Make the guards feel that they are part of the company—not just rent-a-cops. Invite them to company functions. With these incentives, guards will want to be assigned to your organization and will be less likely to quit.

Morale

8-84   What can I do to uplift morale in my office?

The reasons for poor morale vary considerably. Some are beyond the control of any supervisor. If working conditions—physical or psychological—are very poor or salaries are below standard, supervisors can do little to improve morale. The solution lies with higher management. On the other hand, poor morale is often caused by local matters—over which the supervisor has some control. When poor morale exists in some departments and not in others, the supervisor's approach to management could be the source.

The first step is to identify the reasons for the poor morale. Talk to workers with whom you have good rapport. Carefully listen. Observe what is going on in the department. Read the graffiti on the walls. On a more formal level, study the results of exit interviews and of employee attitude surveys conducted by personnel or outside consultants. If you discover that you are perceived as being too dogmatic, that you do not show enough appreciation to your people, or that you display any of the other negatives common to the "old-time supervisor," the first step is to look at yourself. You must make changes with the way you deal with your people, and follow the many suggestions made in this book. (See questions 23–25 in Chapter 14.)

8-85   The morale in my department is being destroyed by a couple of really negative people who try to sabotage everything I do as a supervisor. I can't fire them. How can I keep my department's morale up despite their negativity?

If it is at all possible, transfer them out of the department. If this cannot be done, and the work is so designed, isolate them so that they will have as little contact with the other employees as possible. Sit down with all your employees to determine if they have any gripes about either you or the department. Focus on any real problems that may be causing poor morale. The two gripers probably will have specific matters about which they feel strongly. Deal with these matters if they are valid, and make sure that the other workers know something is being done. If the issues are not valid, explain why they have no substance. More than likely, most of your workers resent these people as much as you do. Because you have not ignored the two gripers' complaints, you will probably win them over to your side.

8-86   How do I instill a good work ethic in my employees when the company itself does not give them respect?

When the company does not treat its people properly, it is difficult for any supervisor to keep the morale in a department high. It all stems from the top. You do your best to show that you respect your people as individuals and appreciate the work they are doing for you. Your efforts pay off: the attitudes of your people are better than those of workers in other departments. Then one bad move on the part of management wipes out all that you do. Leading by example is your only recourse in rebuilding the work ethic.

8-87   How can I change long-term negative attitudes that exist toward all management goals?

Find out why this attitude exists. If it is based on past bad experiences with the company, discuss how circumstances differ today. Persuade people to take the time to study and understand the new goals and help them see how they will benefit everyone.

If the poor attitude stems from "them versus us" thinking, you will have a much more difficult time changing people's feelings. Some people have been brought up to distrust authority—whether it be in school, in government, or on the job. Only if they experience through you, their immediate supervisor, that there is a congruence of interests between management and worker can this attitude be overcome. Change does not happen over night.

8-88   One of my people—a member of a minority group—is very disrespectful to me and others in the department. This has caused low morale in our group. I have spoken to him to no avail, and the owner of the business won't let me take disciplinary action for fear of a discrimination complaint. What can I do?

Before any disciplinary action is taken, every effort should be made to change this person's attitude. A heart-to-heart talk sometimes helps. The employee may be demonstrating his anger over past treatment in other jobs or other aspects of his life. Point out that you and the other people in the department do not deserve disrespect from him, any more than he deserves it from others. Tell him that you want him to succeed on the job—but this can happen only if there is respectful treatment on all sides.

Sometimes peer counseling can be more effective than a supervisory talk. Enlist the aid of one of the workers in your department, particularly another member of his minority group.

As far as disciplinary action is concerned, if the employee fails to cooperate and his disrespect leads to lower productivity or violations of company rules, you needn't fear treating him in the same way you would treat a nonminority employee.

8-89   One of my peers is very knowledgeable in her field. However, she has an abrasive personality and antagonizes her people. The morale in her section is so low that the work has suffered and some very good people have left. How can I help her build up the morale in her section?

Changing a management style is not easy. As noted several times in this book, the effect must come from within. It must start with a recognition that the current style doesn't work. Since you are not this supervisor's boss, you have no authority to intervene. However, if you have a good rapport with the woman, discuss how the poor morale in her department is hurting the company and, of course, her. Offer suggestions as to how she can use less abrasive approaches with her people. Point out that it would be better if she took the initiative in this matter rather than waiting for her boss to request that she change her style.

8-90   Our objective is to make our workplace "one happy family." Is this realistic?

There's no way anybody can make everybody happy. Indeed, even in TV families somebody at one time or another is not happy. There will be arguments among your people, even heated disagreements (see Chapter 9). Your job as a supervisor is to establish a climate in which things run as smoothly as possible and disagreements or disputes can be openly discussed and settled with minimum rancor.

8-91   Is there any way to make jobs that are really boring less boring?

There is an entire field devoted to this subject. It's called job enrichment. Experts in this area study jobs to see what can be done to make them less monotonous. One approach is to enlarge the job. For example, in the old system of processing insurance policies, each clerk dealt with one phase of the paperwork, turned it over to another clerk who dealt with the next phase, and so on. Each policy went through several clerks. This was very efficient—it was an an assembly line. However, because the work was so repetitive and dull, turnover and absenteeism were high, quality was below standard, and people were generally unhappy. By enlarging the job so that each clerk handled one policy from start to finish, the work became less dreary and in the long run production increased and morale was raised.

8-92   I've heard the expression "quality of work life." I know what the words mean, but what does it involve on the job?

We spend most of our waking hours on the job. If we work under adverse conditions, our lives will be unpleasant and frustrating, and often our attitude will carry over into our home lives. Numerous studies have been made on overcoming the negative aspects of the work environment and thus improving the morale of workers. The answer is not through superficial changes like painting the office a pastel shade instead of dull gray or installing Muzak. Such amenities are the icing; we first must bake a better cake. Solutions include redesigning jobs, changing the way in which work is assigned, and reevaluating compensation and benefits packages.

Such large-scale changes are difficult in established organizations, but with full commitment and real effort they can be made. With new facilities or new programs, quality of work life should be embedded in the planning process. A good example is General Motors' Saturn facility, whose planning and implementation made quality of work life a major objective.

9

Dealing with Problem Employees

This chapter focuses on the special types of situations that supervisors face when employees' attitudes and personal problems cause friction in the workplace. The next chapter examines general issues that occur in day-to-day dealings with employees.

Attitude

9-1 How do I deal with a negative employee?

Determine why the negativism exists. You may have learned about someone's negative attitude from previous discussions with your employee. Or you may have heard stories about this person from other workers. Sit down with the employee and discuss the situation. Probe. Perhaps the negativism stems from some real or perceived mistreatment in the past. Look into it. If there are justifiable reasons, try to persuade the employee that the past is past and that he or she must look to the future. If misconceptions are involved, try to clear them up.

Often negativism is rooted in long-term personality factors which are beyond the capability of any supervisor to overcome. The person may need professional help. If you have an employee assistance program, suggest that it be utilized.

9-2   What is an employee assistance program?

Employee assistance programs are company-sponsored counseling services. Many organizations have instituted such programs to help their employees deal with personal problems that are interfering with productivity. The problems include alcoholism, marital difficulties, depression, and other psychological disturbances.

Here's how such programs work: The company promotes the availability of the service to its people through its usual communications channels. Often a hot-line telephone number is provided. The employee who has a problem calls the hot line. After a brief screening, he or she is referred to the appropriate counselor. All contacts initiated by the employee are confidential.

In addition, supervisors are advised (and sometimes trained) to recognize when counseling may be needed and to suggest to employees that they take advantage of the service. In some instances supervisors may even require that the employee assistance program (EAP) be used as part of a disciplinary action (e.g., an alcoholic may be given the option of using the EAP to overcome the problem or of being terminated).

Although such programs are expensive, organizations that have had them in place for several years report that they pay off by salvaging skilled and experienced people in whom the company has made a major investment over the years.

9-3   How do I handle employees who have a negative attitude about any changes that are suggested? They resist change both overtly and subtly.

Many people resist change. They are comfortable doing things one way and cannot see why the work has to be done differently. This attitude cannot be overcome by logical, persuasive arguments. Negative people resist change just for the sake of resisting. If they cannot get their way by direct means, they will do everything they can to sabotage the situation so the new ways will not work and they can then say "I told you so."

In presenting new ideas to such people, get them to express all of their objections openly. Accept the objections as "making sense." Point out how important their ideas are to you and to the company, and ask for their cooperation. "You do have some good points in what you say, and as we move into this new program, let's carefully watch for those problems. We must give this new concept a try. Work with me on it and together we'll iron out the kinks."

9-4   What do I do with an employee whose first reaction to any assignment is always negative. He greets all new work with "I don't have the time" or "I don't think this is necessary."

Since you know you will get a negative reaction, present the assignment in as positive a manner as you can. Let the employee know that you have confidence in his abilities, that he is the best qualified person for this assignment. Get him to suggest ideas on how to do the assignment. Make him part of the solution instead of an additional problem.

9-5   How do I create an atmosphere of openness and trust in my staff when it does not exist at present?

Openness and trust take time to develop. It cannot be done by an edict or even by one or two acts. Start by having an informal discussion with your people. Ask them what you can do together to change the climate from what it is to what they and you would like it to be. Then take steps to implement change. For example, if people are seeking less secrecy about company plans, when a new policy is to be instituted, discuss it in advance. In your day-to-day relations with your people, encourage them to contribute their ideas. Avoid arbitrary decisions unless they are absolutely essential. Promise only what you know can be achieved. If circumstances make it impossible to fulfill a commitment, explain the reason for the change as soon as you can. Over time, you will increase the trust of your people and establish the climate you desire.

9-6   About a year ago, one of the women in what is now my department requested a transfer because she did not like the type of work she was doing. Unfortunately, there were no openings in the areas she wanted, so she has stayed on. She does her work well, but she is always complaining about the unfairness of her situation. Her attitude has affected the atmosphere on the job. How do I overcome her resentment?

Sit down with this woman and let her get all her gripes out of her system. Find out what specific things she doesn't like about the work she is doing. If possible, give her assignments which will be of more interest. Assure her that the failure to get her transfer is caused not by any negative feelings toward her, but by the lack of available jobs in the areas she wants. Tell her you will work with her to make her job more interesting and will also keep in touch with the proper authorities to see that she is considered for other openings in the company that may interest her— even if not in the types of work she originally requested.

Point out how her constant griping affects her co-workers and makes working in the department unpleasant for them. You will do your part to enrich her job, but she must do her part by not griping to the other people. Tell her you are always open to discussing her problems.

9-7   Roberto is a very good worker who would like to move up into management, but he has a negative attitude toward co-workers. He is harsh and sharp in interpersonal relations and sometimes impatient even with me, his supervisor, and with other higher-ranking people with whom he must interact. How can I help Roberto change his attitude?

Some people display a negative attitude without realizing that they are doing it. Speaking to them about how they come across to others may open their eyes. Some companies have sent their people to sensitivity training programs or other human development courses to help them overcome problems in interpersonal relations.

Often very efficient workers are impatient and intolerant of people whom they perceive to be slower and less efficient—even when those people are doing their jobs well. This attitude must be changed if impatient workers are to be considered for promotion. Such people do not usually make good supervisors and despite their technical capability should not be given supervisory responsibility. Since they are valuable workers, other methods of compensation such as incentive pay and bonuses should be used to reward them.

9-8   For the first time in 11 years we have a male employee among all females. He tends to be chauvinistic and does not mix well with the other employees during breaks or bother to converse with co-workers. The job description states "other duties as assigned." When other employees pitch in and answer phones, do copying, or fill in for the receptionist on breaks, he never helps out. He believes it's "women's work." The other employees are upset. Any suggestions?

When a new employee is hired, he or she should be given careful orientation and instructions on what is expected in the job. Orientation includes an indication of what is usually covered in "other duties." The employee will then know from the beginning that answering the phone, filling in for others, and performing other tasks are part of the job. There is no longer such a thing as gender-differentiated work.

Even if your male employee has had such an orientation, when he fails to follow procedures, talk to him about it. An informal conversation is a good start. If that fails to change his behavior, a counseling session is in order, followed, if necessary, by disciplinary action.

9-9　One of my people makes a point of trying to catch me in some error. I'm human and I make my share. He's right there to say, "Ah hah! Gotcha!" How do I break this habit?

People who play "gotcha" are trying to show their superiority. They often have no original ideas or constructive suggestions, but they get their kicks out of other people's errors—particularly their boss's. This employee is hoping to embarrass you and make you feel uncomfortable. Don't give him the satisfaction. Make a joke about it when he does: "That sure was a blooper." Or smile and thank him for calling an error to your attention before it caused real problems. If he doesn't rile you, he'll stop and try to get his kicks from somebody else.

9-10　I was recently promoted to the position of area supervisor. One of my employees has held the same position for over 3 years and shows no desire to be promoted or to leave that position. The problem is that she does the minimum amount of work and has an extremely negative attitude—which she inflicts on other employees. She constantly tries to undermine all positive efforts. If you can't terminate an individual for having a negative attitude, what are some possible solutions?

Various courts have ruled that you cannot terminate somebody for what he or she thinks, only for what he or she has or has not done. If you are seeking legitimate reasons to terminate this employee, you would have to show how her poor attitude manifests itself either in poor performance or in poor conduct. Since she meets performance standards—even at a minimum— and does not violate other company rules, you will have to show how her attitude affects productivity among her co-workers. This is extremely difficult to prove.

More effective is trying to improve her attitude. As indicated throughout this section, it is difficult to change attitudes. By giving her positive strokes for anything special she does, you might get her to take a more constructive approach.

If the other employees in the department are basically happy, her poor attitude will have little effect on them. Other disgruntled people may climb on her bandwagon, but most will ignore her. If you see signs of discontent arising among any of her co-workers, talk with those people immediately and resolve any problem before it festers into a serious situation.

9-11 Tai is a good employee with a very negative attitude. I have worked in the past with her. She is very knowledgeable, but when she is asked to do a project she responds negatively. She turns people off, although she does get the job done. The sales department is complaining about her. Tai is on the hit list to be fired. I would prefer to keep this employee. How do I help her or make her conscious of this problem? I'm sure she is unaware of the effect she is having.

The only way Tai will learn is if you tell her. It is amazing how often employees have no idea that they are behaving in a negative manner. They are probably the same way in their personal lives. However, supervisors are not psychotherapists or counselors. Try a heart-to-heart talk with her. Let her know that her job is in jeopardy because of the effect she has on other employees (and customers, if that is part of the problem). Suggest that she enroll in a personal improvement program.

9-12 Ted is the informal leader of a group of my people. He sets the tone for the department and everybody follows his lead. How can I instill in him the positive attitude I would like to permeate my department?

You have to win Ted over as your friend and partner. If he is antagonistic to you or to the company, it will be very difficult to do so. Use Ted as a sounding board for ideas before they are introduced. Solicit his opinions; discuss projects and even personnel problems. When supervisors get their informal leaders to be cooperative colleagues, those leaders can be their most valuable allies in achieving departmental and company goals.

9-13 The company encourages us to seek out and train people to replace us as we move up the company ladder or to

step into other higher-level jobs. One of my best workers has the potential for growth. She is intelligent, learns rapidly, and is good at her job. However, she is always bad-mouthing the company. It would be a shame for her to lose the opportunity to move ahead. How can I help her change her attitude?

Anticompany feelings often stem from bad experiences with a present or past employer. Some people are long-time rebels against any authority. If this employee's feelings are deep-seated, there is little you can do to change her. However, people do mature and often, when they are older and wiser, they recognize that their anti-company attitude is mistaken and work to rethink it. Let her know how highly you esteem her ability and work with her to overcome her attitude. If it is based on specific complaints, deal with them. If it is general in tone, show her the positive effects of company policy. Learn about her career goals and show her how they can be met by being open to the company's position.

9-14   Sydney is mad. He mistakenly feels he has been mistreated and nothing I can tell him will make him change his mind. He takes out his unhappiness on everybody he deals with—and that includes customers. I've heard him disparage the company to a customer. This cannot be tolerated. I don't want to fire Sydney. What can I do?

Let Sydney know in no uncertain terms that discourtesy, displays of noncooperation, or inappropriate comments cannot be tolerated, no matter how bad he feels about his treatment. Point out that he has had every opportunity to express his views and that you, his immediate boss, as well as others in the chain of command have heard his side of the story but ruled against him. If he feels so negatively about the company, he should resign. Nobody is compelling him to stay. However, if he opts to stay, he must forget the past and think of the future. Tell him that you will overlook his past attitude, even his rudeness, because you have confidence in his ability to perform effectively again. That being said, remind him that there is no excuse for impudence to anybody—especially customers—and that if such an incident happens again, you will have no choice but to take disciplinary action.

9-15   How can I get my people to respect my boss when he does all the wrong things in interpersonal relations?

It's tough to respect somebody who hasn't earned respect. You are not responsible for your boss's actions. If your people respect you, you can ask them to at least give your boss the respect his position merits. It is the position, not the holder of that position, which deserves our respect.

As bad as he is in interpersonal relations, your boss may have other significant accomplishments—technical skill, financial acumen, marketing know-how—that have contributed to the success of the operation. Let your people know about these accomplishments and how they have resulted in more or better business. "Even if he is a difficult person, we owe him this respect for what he has done for the organization."

Dealing with Personal Problems

9-16   One of my employees takes everything that is said in general conversation personally. For example, one day I was talking to a group of employees and somewhere in the conversation the term "breath mint" came up. Later that day this worker came to me and said that she felt I was trying to say that she had bad breath. Her co-workers constantly complain that they have to watch what they say and how they say it because she takes it personally. What should I do?

Some people are very self-conscious and seem to take everything anybody says as being personally related to them. The cause is often a deep-seated psychological insecurity. There is nothing you can do to help this employee. Change has to come from within. You might alleviate the problem somewhat by choosing your words carefully when you speak to this worker and by constantly reassuring her that you like her as a person. If others complain to you about her, remind them that all of us have faults and eccentricities. We must be tolerant of the quirks of others, just as they should be of ours.

9-17   One of my people is especially defensive. He thinks I am picking on him if I even make the slightest criticism of his work. How do I overcome his defensiveness?

There are times when direct criticism may be necessary and there is no way to avoid it, such as when an emergency arises or when work is totally wrong. In other cases, criticism can be more gentle. Start by praising something that the employee has done well and suggesting—not dictating—that another approach might be more effective. Don't limit praise to situations which will be followed by criticism. Use praise lavishly; otherwise people may assume that all praise will lead to criticism.

9-18   Ken, one of my best workers, is selfish. He takes credit for everything that goes well even if he had only a small part in it, antagonizing the other members of the group. He also keeps information to himself, often preventing others from doing their work. In this way, he can appear to be a hero when he finally comes through. How can I get Ken to be team player?

Ken is like the firefighter who sets fires so he can be a hero when he rescues victims. He is constantly seeking the limelight. Allowing him to take more credit than he deserves will only encourage him to keep it up. Next time he brags about an accomplishment of this type, thank him for his part and mention in front of the others in the group that you are pleased with the part each of them contributed to the success of the project. Point out specific accomplishments of each person so all will note that you recognize their work, not just the braggart's.

Failing to provide information when needed is far more serious. Discuss this with Ken. Assure him that his work is appreciated, but that this is a team effort and that information must be shared with the entire team as needed. If he holds back information, projects could be delayed or errors might ensue. Play up the importance of cooperation. If the problem continues, recommend counseling and, if necessary, take disciplinary action.

9-19   Lisa is afraid to make any decisions. She so fears that she will make an error that she stalls until she has every bit of backup possible, and even then she may pass the buck to me. How can I get her to make decisions?

Some doctors are so afraid of a malpractice suit that they order all kinds of extra and often unnecessary tests before making a diagnosis. Lisa is like that. You need to assure her that all people make mistakes occasionally and that she will not be fired or disciplined for honest errors in judgment. Insist that she make decisions by the specified deadlines. In the beginning, work with her to help her overcome this problem, but don't make a decision for her. If she says that she needs more facts, and you believe that she has enough information, compel her to make the decision now. If she asks you what she should do, throw it back into her lap: "This is your decision to make—make it!"

Assuming Lisa has the background and expertise to make these decisions, she will probably come up with good answers. If, however, you feel her solution is all wrong, you may have to intervene to prevent catastrophe. Most of the time, people like Lisa do have the right answers and just need your confidence-building support to convert their thinking into decisions.

9-20   One of my salespeople made a serious error a few months ago that caused the company to lose a good account. He has lost his confidence and this has affected his work. How can I help him rebuild his self-confidence?

All endeavors we undertake cannot succeed. Interspersed with the joys of success is the bitterness of failure. It is normal to brood over a failure, but we must overcome this as soon as possible so it will not dominate our lives. The loss of an account is serious, but if your employee dwells on this failure, he may never regain the confidence needed to replace it with new business.

The first step is to get your salesperson actively engaged in selling. If he mopes about his failure, negative thinking will dominate his behavior. He has to be given an opportunity to experience a success—even a small success—to prove to himself that he still is an OK person. Give him assignments which will lead to quick successes. Help him by coaching, retraining if necessary, and encouragement.

Remind him of past successes. When we experience failure, we tend to think our ourselves as "failures." All of us have had successes in the past: on the job, in school, on the athletic field, or in community activities. As a supervisor, learn about these successes among your people. When things go wrong, remind them that it is the situation—not they as individuals—which has gone wrong. They are still the same people who have had past successes. Assure them: "You did it before; you can do it again."

9-21   It's normal to feel depressed when things go wrong on the job. I'm not always around to help my people when this happens. Any suggestions on how they can help themselves?

Have each of your people (and you as well) keep a success diary. In the diary, have them list all the things accomplished that day that they are proud of. For example:

"Exceeded quota by 12 percent."

"Suggested an idea that saved one-third of the time on an assignment."

"Sold more raffles for my church than anyone else."

"Was complimented by the boss for the report I submitted."

If letters of praise or thanks come from a customer, a vendor, another person in the company, or even nonbusiness sources, keep them in an attached "success folder."

Now when things go bad and some of your people feel depressed, they can read the notes in the diary, the letters in the folder. That's proof that they are still successful. They can truly say to themselves, "I am an achiever. Here's my proof. I did it before and I will do it again."

9-22 Sal is a nice guy, but he frequently loses his temper and will holler and scream at his co-workers and even at me. I've spoken to him about this more than once, but it hasn't helped. How can I deal with his behavior?

If your informal talks and counseling have not helped, tell Sal in no uncertain terms that his behavior cannot be tolerated on the job and that if it is repeated once more, you will send him out of the room until he cools down. If it is repeated again, send him home for the balance of the day or take whatever disciplinary measures company policy dictates.

9-23 In my case, it's not one of my people but my boss who has temper tantrums. When things don't go exactly as he wants, he rants and raves. This upsets me, so that I can't work for hours after. I know I can't stop his rages. How can I handle it?

It's not easy to work in an environment where you are being subjected to this kind of treatment. When it's your boss you can't send him out of the room or take disciplinary action. Some bosses believe that raising the voice shows that they mean business.

If you have a good rapport with your boss, discuss the situation with him when he is in a good mood. Let him know how his behavior disturbs you and the others in the department. Perhaps he will make an effort to keep his cool if he realizes the negative effect it has on other people.

Unfortunately, many people do lose their tempers easily. It is a bad habit that is very difficult to break. You have to learn to live with it. Condition yourself to let these outbursts wash over you. When he rages, steel yourself not to take it as a personal matter. It's his blood pressure that is rising; his ulcer that is developing; his nerves that are stretching. Sure, it upsets you for a moment, but it will be over rapidly. If despite your resolve, his outbursts continue to affect you, seek counseling. With biofeedback and other behavioral approaches, you can be trained to overcome his rage.

9-24 What can we do about a woman in our office who has a serious body odor problem? We have suggested she do something about it, but to no avail. It has reached a crisis now because some of my other people refuse to work near her. My boss says I should fire her, but she is a good worker. What should I do?

Have a private meeting with her. Tell her that despite previous discussions on this subject, the problem still exists. Say: "You are a good worker, but people must work together and this problem is interfering with a smooth team effort. Some people who bathe daily and use a deodorant find that the odor still persists and is caused by a medical problem. This may be your situation." Give her 30 days to clear this up.

9-25 Yuri has been with the company for 2 years. His job requires minimal skills. He has a lot of personal problems and even has tried to commit suicide. He has received professional help. He asks for instructions daily both from me and from co-workers. But this interrupts all of us. He asks the same questions each day. I have asked Yuri to write the instructions down and to refer to his notes, or to hold on to problems and ask me several at one time—all to no avail. I feel his mental ability has deteriorated to the point that he cannot actually perform the job. But there is no place to transfer him. His doctor has asked that Yuri be placed in a lower-pressure job. We have sent his application to every department in the company and no job is available.

If your company has 15 or more employees, it is subject to the Americans with Disabilities Act of 1990 (ADA), which prohibits employment discrimination against a person because of physical or mental impairment. Psychological disorders such as those you described are probably covered. Check with medical and legal advisers. If Yuri is covered, you must make every effort to find a position in the organization for which he can qualify.

Arrange for part-time or modified work schedules, redesign job descriptions to create a job he can handle, or try any other means of accommodating his disability.

Since the enforcement of ADA is relatively new, judicial interpretation is limited. Related situations in states where disability laws have been in existence for some time—and rulings under the Rehabilitation Act of 1973, a similar law which applies only to federal contractors and others receiving federal funds—suggest that just sending Yuri's application to other departments is not enough. The company must take affirmative steps to find or create a job he can handle.

9-26 How can I supervise an employee who has a depressive disorder and is on medication? She manipulates through tears and through expressed feelings of low esteem. If I must correct her she becomes angry and full of rage. She knows her rights under the ADA. The end result is that she gets away with murder.

People on medication for depression usually have periods in which they function normally—the result of the medication. Recognize that when she is in one of her bad periods, there is little you can do. However during her "normal" periods, talk with her and show that you are concerned about her as a person. When she is in a depressed state, all you can do is patiently wait it out. The medication plus therapy should help her overcome the depression, but it takes time.

Despite her emotional condition, you do not have to tolerate temper tantrums or raging (see question 9-22). If her actions interfere excessively with her work, you are within your rights to transfer her to a less stressful position where her depression will not be as serious a barrier to getting the job done.

9-27 I have a husband and wife working for me. They are both good workers and have been with the company for several years. Recently they have been having personal problems that have carried over into the office. What do I do?

This is the reason that many companies will not permit members of the same family to work together. Have a counseling meeting with both of them, let them know how their behavior is affecting the work of the department, and ask them what they can do to resolve their problems at home. If the situation continues after this meeting, let them know that you will no longer allow their disputes to interfere with the department's work. Make it clear that this is a formal warning and if it reoccurs, you will have to ask one of them to transfer out of the department. If this is not feasible, one should resign. The determination of who should leave should be left to the couple. (See question 50 in Chapter 3.)

9-28   My boss's daughter reports to me. She relays everything that goes on in the department to her father, who then second-guesses every action I have taken without even hearing my side. Is there any way of dealing with this?

Supervising anybody who is close to the boss is always delicate. Many parents will give more credence to what they hear from a child than from somebody else. If the daughter seriously distorts what you have done, you have to clarify it so the boss will not be misled. This should be done diplomatically. You just can't say, "Your daughter is a liar." Present the facts in a calm manner and suggest that perhaps the daughter had misunderstood the situation. If it is a minor matter, ignore it.

9-29   I have a bad temper and blow up relatively easily. I know it is wrong and I feel stupid when the tantrum is over. It sure isn't helping me in supervising my people. Is there any way I can control my temper?

Controlling one's temper is never easy. There are times when even a usually calm person is so frustrated that he or she blows up. However, if you lose your temper very easily, you have to take steps to learn how to control it. The old adage "Count to 10 before you open your mouth" still holds true. By consciously waiting at least 10 seconds before you react, you give yourself a chance to calm your emotions and to think logically rather than emotionally about what has happened. It is not easy to hold back when you are anxious to tell someone off or to let off steam, but it can be done.

If you do not have the ability or will power to control your temper yourself, seek professional help. Psychotherapists use a variety of methods to aid people in overcoming this problem. Treatment usually consists of several months of behavior modification therapy.

Alcohol and Drugs

9-30   Drinking is a way of life for some of my people. They assume it is normal to drink several beers at lunch and even sneak out to their cars for a beer during breaks. They get their work done. Should I be concerned?

Drinking is not a normal way of life. Despite the fact that they get their work done, drinking does lower productivity and quality. Even people who appear to be under control are affected by alcohol. Although these people may not think they have a problem, anybody who depends on drink as part of a lifestyle is an alcoholic.

Companies should have strict policies prohibiting drinking during working hours and that includes lunch and breaks. People under the influence of alcohol are dangers to themselves and others.

Such policies should be in writing and should be explained to all new employees and periodically reviewed with everybody. Restrictions should specifically include beer and wine to avoid the excuse that people interpreted drinking as "hard" liquor. The punishment for violations should be clearly stated and rigidly enforced.

9-31   What do you do if you suspect an employee of being an alcoholic? I've never seen him drink and he's never actually been drunk on the job, but he always has the smell of alcohol on his breath and he has a poor attendance record.

Speaking to him about it will result in denials. He will probably say that the alcohol breath is caused by medication he is taking; the absences, illness. "Me drink? Only socially."

Have all your evidence available when you speak to him: performance statistics, attendance records, previous warnings. Let him know this behavior cannot continue.

Watch to see if his condition worsens. His absences are more frequent, especially on Mondays. He takes long lunch breaks and comes back sucking on breath mints. His work is uneven and disorganized. These are the signs of alcoholism. Accept no excuses. Suggest or even insist on counseling.

9-32   Telling people with drinking problems that they need counseling is not easy. Is there a good approach?

The U.S. Department of Health and Human Services (formerly Department of Health, Education, and Welfare) makes the following suggestions in its *Supervisor's Guide on Alcohol Abuse:*

1. Don't apologize for discussing the matter. Make it clear that job performance is involved.

2. Encourage the employee to explain why work performance, behavior, or attendance is deteriorating. This may provide an opportunity to question the use of alcohol.

3. Don't discuss a person's right to drink. Do not make a moral issue of it. Alcoholism is a disease which, if not treated, can lead to insanity, custodial care, or death.

4. Don't suggest that the employee use moderation or change drinking habits. Alcoholics cannot change.

5. Don't be distracted by excuses for drinking. The problem as far as you are concerned is the drinking itself and how it affects work, behavior, and attendance on the job.

6. Remember that the alcoholic, like any other sick person, should be given the opportunity for treatment and rehabilitation.

7. Emphasize that your main concern is the employee's work performance and that if he or she does not improve, disciplinary action such as suspension or discharge will be taken.

8. Point out that the decision to accept assistance is the employee's responsibility.

If the company has an employee assistance program, describe it and strongly recommend that it be utilized.

9-33 Can you fire somebody who is drunk on the job?

First, you must have an established company policy, made known to all employees, that drinking on the job or reporting to the job in a drunken state is punishable by immediate termination. Drinking on the job is easily proved if you or others are witnesses to the act. However, proving that a person is drunk is not easy. Even a police officer has to administer tests to determine if a driver is intoxicated. The safest approach is to send the employee home for the day. When he or she returns, have a counseling meeting and deal with it as indicated in answer to question 9-32.

However, if disciplinary action is taken, back it up by documenting the specifics of the employee's behavior. Instead of saying "Appeared to be drunk," write: "Unable to walk a straight line, smelled of alcohol, and talked incoherently."

9-34 What can I do with an employee who refuses to go to our EAP? He's a good worker, but he is absent too often and

doesn't call in. He comes to work smelling from alcohol. He denies he has a problem.

In speaking to him, concentrate on the absences. Make it clear that absences cannot be tolerated. Let him know that you believe the absences are alcohol related and that help through the EAP will reduce the absences. Be firm. Some companies will even tolerate a higher than normally allowed absentee rate if the person is undergoing rehabilitation counseling.

9-35   One of my people reported to me that another employee was shooting heroin in the men's room. When I got there, he was gone. I'm worried about this man. What should I do?

Assuming that your reporter did see what he said, how do you know it was heroin and not insulin he was injecting? Unless you actually see the heroin and have it tested, any action you take against this man could be illegal.

If you suspect he is a drug user, look for other signs. Some of the indicators of drug use are decreased productivity with steadily poorer quality, increased absences and latenesses with excuses that become more and more unrealistic, increased visits to the washroom, erratic moods, and possibly thefts of cash or other people's property.

If your observations sustain your suspicions, talk to the employee using the same approach you would with an alcoholic (see question 9-33). Make it clear that drug use on the job is not tolerated and explain the penalties that might ensue. Encourage him to seek counseling.

9-36   What should we do if we catch one of our employees selling drugs in the company parking lot?

Call the police. This is a violation of the law and you have a civic duty to report it to the authorities. Some companies do not want to become involved with the police. Instead, they fire the people who sell or buy drugs on company property. This has legal ramifications and advice of counsel should be sought if such action is considered.

9-37   Can an alcoholic or drug user claim protection under the American with Disabilities Act?

Yes. Both alcoholism and drug addiction are considered disabilities and you cannot discriminate by refusing to hire an applicant or by firing a current employee for these reasons. Past history of alcoholism or drug use is not an acceptable reason for failing to hire an applicant or to terminate an employee. However, the law does not protect alcoholics who cannot perform their job duties or people who are current users of drugs.

To determine if the requirement for accommodation must be met, consider these factors:

1. Does the person have a current problem or is the matter now under control?

2. Does impaired performance of the duties of the job present a potential hazard to customers, co-workers, or the employee?

3. Can the applicant perform the major aspects of the work?

Accommodation does not mean that you have to go along with the use or possession of alcohol or controlled substances on company property; nor do you have to put up with a worker being unfit to work.

9-38   One of my staff has just found out he has AIDS. The others are reluctant to work near him. I know AIDS cannot be transmitted by proximity. How can I convince the others?

Explain the situation to your people. To overcome unjustified fears, many companies have instituted AIDS awareness programs. Using videos, pamphlets, articles in the company house organ, and talks by doctors, they teach their employees the facts about how AIDS is spread and allay their fears. If this becomes a problem in your department, suggest to your management that such a program be instituted.

Problem People

9-39 Caroline is a busybody. Although she doesn't report to me, I am in a higher position than she is and have access to certain correspondence and other information that she does not have. She is jealous and gets very upset when she learns I know things about which she has not been told. These are not matters she needs to do her work. Her bickering has caused dissension between us and has upset the department. What should I do?

Is the information you are keeping to yourself important enough to keep secret? Often sharing information—even if it is not essential to the job—will help build a relationship that pays off in a smoother working environment and more cooperative co-workers.

However, if it is necessary to keep certain information confidential, set up a three-way discussion among Caroline, you, and the person to whom both of you report. Clearly define what information you and Caroline need to have and the areas in which both of you must cooperate.

9-40   How do I deal with people who are constantly whining and complaining—not only to me but to everybody in the department?

If the complaints are valid, of course try to resolve them. However, most constant whiners do not have specific complaints. They gripe about everything from the temperature in the workplace to the "unfairness" of every management decision.

Since co-workers probably are as annoyed as you are about the whiners, all of you should make a point of ignoring the gripes by refusing to discuss them or by telling the whiner that the griping is not going to accomplish anything and makes everybody uncomfortable. Disapproval of peers will do more to stop the complaints than anything a supervisor can do.

9-41   I think I'm doing a good job and my boss agrees. However, my peers—supervisors of other departments— are constantly criticizing my work. This is affecting my morale. What can I do?

There must be a reason for their attitude. Sometimes when one supervisor has a different management style, other supervisors are uncomfortable with it and rather than criticize the style, they criticize the person or his or her work.

Discuss the problem with one other supervisor with whom you have a good relationship. Try to determine the cause. If you are doing something your peers do not like, either conform to their pattern or explain that what you are doing works for you and you are not doing it to demonstrate that their way is wrong. If you cannot get through in this manner, try your boss. Perhaps his or her intervention can help solve the problem.

9-42   How do you handle a person who needs constant supervision?

Give the person very specific assignments with time frames that must be kept. Check to make sure that the work is on schedule and praise the smallest accomplishment. Once the employee gets into the habit of doing the assignments correctly and on time, extend the amount of work and set longer time frames. It won't happen overnight, but as the person becomes accustomed to this practice, he or she will need less and less supervision.

9-43   What is the best way to handle an employee who bad-mouths co-workers and supervisors?

Talk to him about it. Many people who gossip and bad-mouth others will deny it when confronted. "I never said that." Don't argue. Just continue as if nothing had been said. Point out that people must work together and that making offensive comments about others destroys the morale of the entire group. Indicate that if the employee has a legitimate complaint about somebody, he should bring it to you.

If this type of behavior continues, make it clear that you will not tolerate it and that disciplinary action could result.

9-44   Florence is one of my best accounting clerks. She has applied several times for supervisory jobs which have become available in our department. Because all these jobs require a degree in accounting, which she does not have, she has not even been considered. Despite her lack of a degree, she continues to ask for a promotion. Since three of the four promotions went to men, Florence is now claiming that the rejections were based, not on lack of a degree, but on sex discrimination. Does she have a case?

If Florence should pursue her complaint, your company would have to prove that the degree was an essential requirement. Often companies arbitrarily decide that a certain educational level is needed for a job without really determining its validity. Whether that alone will sustain a charge of sex discrimination can be determined only by the courts. Other factors, such as the fact that one of the people promoted was a woman, will be considered.

Even if the sex discrimination factor were not involved, your company should examine its job specs to ensure that what is required is really important. Perhaps having an accounting degree is not essential, just an added asset. You may be losing the services of a very good person for the wrong reason. Exceptions could be made for otherwise qualified applicants.

Florence might be able to handle the work by taking some courses in accounting to supplement the knowledge acquired from experience.

9-45   I have an employee who always sticks his nose in other departments' business. Other supervisors have complained to me about it and I have talked to him. It has done no good. What is the solution?

Some people are just curious and ask questions or make comments that are out of line. Often the habit is harmless, but it can be annoying. Speak to the employee about it again. Instead of criticizing him, tell him you can understand his interest in what other departments are doing and sometimes it is helpful to know. Point out that people may become annoyed if they feel that his curiosity imposes on their privacy. If the employee wants to know about matters outside your jurisdiction, suggest that he talk to you. If the issue is of concern to everyone, you will find out and let your people know.

9-46   A former supervisor, who was burned out, took a demotion to a highly technical position in my unit. (The company, not I, put her there.) She is not doing well in this job. She was a successful supervisor. How do I deal with her? She is on the retirement track but my busy unit needs all the help it can get.

If she does not have the technical skills needed, there is no way she can succeed in this job. Speak to your boss about finding her a job that she can handle. If she does have the technical know-how, but is not producing, find out why. Perhaps the burnout has not been overcome and she is really not up to the demands of the job. Perhaps she needs encouragement and motivation. Give her attention and positive reinforcement. If nothing helps, you will have to live with her until her retirement. If this creates an undue burden on your department, discuss the matter with your boss. There may be some other solutions to your problem, such as authorizing added personnel to your staff.

9-47   One of my best friends at work is "borrowing" tools and supplies and not returning them. I don't want to accuse him of stealing, but that's what it amounts to. How can I get this across to him before the company finds out and he is fired or worse?

Accusing somebody of stealing is a very delicate situation. The employee will usually deny it. "I intended to bring it back, but I still haven't got around to it."

Tell him that you know he intends to return things he "borrows," but keeping things too long may lead to misunderstanding by others who don't know him as well as you do. Suggest he return everything he has immediately.

Another approach is to comment that the company is planning to spot-check employees on what is being taken out of the building. You are letting him and others know so that, if they intend to borrow anything, they will be sure to sign out for it. This should discourage future thefts.

9-48   How do you deal with a problem employee who requested to be reclassified? (His job didn't change, but he probably is bored.) Our management will not approve of any reclassification that is not justified. His request was denied. He did not show up the next day. On the following day, he sent me a doctor's certificate indicating that he was suffering from tremendous stress. Two months have passed. He has not returned or been in touch with us. His sick leave has long since been used up and he is being compensated through our disability insurance.

Under most disability insurance policies, employees must submit to examination periodically by a doctor representing the insurance company. Check with the carrier and ask when it plans to do so. If your company is self-insured, have your benefits people look into the matter.

It is difficult to prove that stress is a continuing problem. It is a medical decision and doctors often differ.

9-49   What should I do with a "devious" employee whom I see before the job starts, at breaks, at lunch, and at the end of the day, but who disappears during work hours? No doubt she will claim she is being harassed if I check up on her directly.

You must check on her directly. People are paid to work and you are paid to see that the people you supervise are doing what they have been hired to do. People who are not where they are supposed to be during working hours should be confronted. This is not harassment. Unless a satisfactory explanation is given, disciplinary action should be taken.

There is no law prohibiting harassment unless it is because of the employee's race, religion, national origin, sex, age, or disability. In any case, asking your employee to do her job is not harassment.

9-50   Terry is one of those aggressive people who tries to dominate the department, Although he often has good ideas, he intimidates the other people and tries to intimidate me. This has resulted in disunity and strife in the department. What should I do?

Talk to Terry. Let him know how his behavior is affecting the other people. Point out that you are sure he means well. Even though he is trying to help the department reach its goals, his manner has caused the opposite to happen. Often people like Terry do not realize how they come across to others. Suggest that he make an effort to listen to other people instead of just pushing his ideas forward. Get his promise to make an effort to restrain his aggressive behavior.

Terry will not change overnight, but his awareness of your disapproval is the first step. You will have to reinforce it by calling his attention to his behavior when he begins to regress. It will take time. Of course, there are some people who can never change. Their patterns of behavior are too deeply imbedded. You either have to remove such people from the department or learn to live with them.

9-51   Ivana has mood swings. When she is happy, her work is superior and she makes a fine team member, but every once in a while she goes into a funk. Then her work becomes sloppy and she won't cooperate with others. Unfortunately, these bad periods are becoming more and more prevalent. How can I help?

Medical or psychological problems may underlie these mood swings. Since moods are often caused by hormone or other chemical imbalances, suggest that Ivana see a physician. If your company has an employee assistance program, you should strongly advise her to use it. When she is in a funk, bear with her but don't coddle her. Be considerate of her feelings, but insist that she do her job.

9-52   Larry is a conniver. He spends more time trying to get out of work than doing the job. If he used the energy he

exerts in trying to manipulate me and others to do the work he should be doing, he'd be a highly productive worker. How can I get him to channel his energies constructively?

Let Larry know in no uncertain terms that you are aware of his manipulations and that you will not tolerate them. Tell him that with his creativity, he could be a valuable member of the team. Some people who behave in this way do so because they are bored with their work. Give him assignments that will challenge him. Even in routine jobs, suggest that he develop new approaches. With your encouragement and positive reinforcement, Larry will begin to derive satisfaction from the work instead of the process of getting out of it.

9-53   One of my people believes that because of her technical expertise, she should be getting more responsibility and the pay that goes with it. The job she does requires using only a portion of her skills. Also, other aspects of the work she performs are below her skill level, but this work has to be done. At this time we cannot restructure the job to her satisfaction. I've tried to explain the situation. How can I get her to accept my arguments?

Review the job description with her. Let her know that her technical skills are important to the accomplishment of the job. However, since there is not enough work in the technical area to utilize all her time, she must also do the less skilled work. Assure her that this decision is based on the job itself and not on her as a person. If true, tell her that this is a temporary situation and as soon as the need for more technical work develops, the job could be restructured.

9-54   I'm a busy guy and get impatient when my people don't follow orders. I tell them what to do and they question why it has to be done that way. My usual answer is "because I told you to" or "it's company policy." This results in reluctant obedience and unenthusiastic effort. How can I get more cooperation?

You are using the classic boss response. Its like the parent who answers his children's objections with "because I'm the daddy and I told you to." This may work with small children, but not with adults. Your people will be more cooperative and enthusiastic if they understand the reason they are asked to do something. Be more patient. Take the time to explain, to answer their questions, and to listen to their ideas. No one person can always be right. Your people may come up with better ways of approaching the problem.

There are times when you, the supervisor, may not know the reasons for a company policy which dictates that certain practices be followed. Tell your people that you don't know why the company has established that practice and that you will try to find out and let them know. Then do it. Most company policies have sound rationales. Policies that appear to be meaningless may be needed for legal or tax reasons or may be established to meet a customer's need. Once your people understand the reason, they are more likely to endorse the policy.

9-55   Luis is a very good and knowledgeable member of my group. His problem is that he believes he is the only one who can do a task correctly. When assigned a project in which he must work with two or three others, he tends to do most of the work because he doesn't trust the others to do it right. This holds up the work and frustrates his teammates. How can I get him to overcome his distrust?

There are some things you can do to help Luis that might alleviate the problem in your department. In the short run, give him assignments in which he is the sole worker. Gradually assign him jobs in which he must depend on others for information or support. Let him know that you have confidence in these people and that he must depend on the accuracy of their work without checking everything himself. Make sure he knows that he cannot check on others and still accomplish the assignment on time. As he becomes accustomed to working this way, he should overcome his distrust of the abilities of co-workers. When assigned joint activities with these people, he will work more cooperatively.

Most likely, Luis's lack of trust is not limited to the job. He probably manifests it in all aspects of his life. You might recommend professional counseling to help him overcome his distrust.

9-56   How appropriate is it for me to discuss problem people with other supervisors?

Since other supervisors may have faced the same problems in their years of experience, they can be of great help to you. This is especially true if another supervisor has worked with one of your people in the past and has had similar problems. You should also take advantage of the expertise of human resources specialists, who can give you valuable advice on these matters. If the problem involves a very personal matter, you may not want to identify the employee so as not to infringe on his or her privacy, but the situation itself can be discussed.

9-57   My boss is so afraid of a discrimination complaint that she shrinks away from any problems involving minority employees. Some are taking advantage of this. What can I do?

All people should be required to meet the company regulations and performance standards. All violations should be documented carefully. If minority workers are treated in the same way as all others, you are not in violation of the laws. The key phrase here is "as all others." If you are stricter in enforcing rules with minorities than with nonminorities—consciously or subconsciously—you open the door to problems. For example, a white worker is 5 minutes late and you excuse him; a black worker comes in 5 minutes late and you write him up. In due time the black worker is disciplined for lateness. You have all the documentation to show that he was late and that he had been warned. His argument: This is discrimination because you wrote up only him and not white people with the same record.

Because minorities have the extra clout of the civil rights laws, managers sometimes are more lenient with them than others. This is not fair to the company or the other workers. Fair treatment and good documentation may not prevent discrimination claims totally, but they will discourage frivolous complaints.

9-58   Carrie is a perfectionist. She is not happy unless everything is 100 percent. This may be commendable in some cases, but Carrie never is satisfied and checks and rechecks her work, so it takes her forever to get it done. I tell her that this isn't necessary, but she doesn't listen. Why does she behave in this way and what can I do?

Perfectionists generally have low self-esteem. They feel compelled to do everything perfectly so nobody can criticize them and make them feel even lower. Their fear of rejection dominates their lives. They won't take risks. Often they are afraid to make a decision, because if it's wrong they will look bad. Carrie may be a compulsive perfectionist. Only professional counseling will help.

Other people who demand perfection may be able to deal with it on their own if they learn from experience that lack of perfection will not be held against them. In assigning work to such people, set parameters which must be met. Let them strive for excellence, not perfection. Be sure to reinforce their successes with praise.

Boss–Subordinate Relations

9-59   How do I handle an employee who is campaigning against my direction and attempting to engage co-workers on her side? She has never addressed the problem to me directly. Instead, she is exceptionally attentive whenever I am around.

If the other workers are not paying much attention to her, all her diatribes against you will fall on deaf ears. If your people are being influenced, then you have to do something about it. You undoubtedly have some partisans among those people who are telling you what she is doing. Speak to her about the "rumors" you have heard. Tell her you are sure that this is a misunderstanding, because you have enough confidence in her to believe that if she had any grievance she would take it up directly with you. Tell her that if she has any specific complaint you would be happy to discuss it with her. This should stop the campaign. If she persists, confront her and let her know that you will not tolerate her behavior.

9-60   I was hired from outside the company to supervise my department. One of the older employees feels that he should have been given the job and he resents me. In the year that I have been there I have won the respect of the other people, but he is still a thorn in my side. How do I win him over?

It is unlikely that you will ever make him into a fully cooperative employee. The resentment is too deep. It's been a year. You have given him enough time to accept the situation. Have a serious discussion with the employee about his future. Acknowledge that he is a proficient person in his field, but make sure he knows that *behavior* is an equally important component of the performance review. If the employee desires advancement in the company, he has to show that he can work with all kinds of managers, even those he may not like. Tell him you are asking him not to like you, but to work cooperatively with you and the entire department.

9-61 My co-supervisor and I have different approaches to management. I believe in strict adherence to the rules, but she is often too soft with people and lets them get away with things. As a result, the people ignore me and go to her whenever they need a ruling on something. I've spoken to her about this, but she ignores me. What else can I do?

Using co-supervisors is not usually a good idea because it leads to conflict of authority. Its like the child who knows that mom is easier than dad. One approach is to differentiate the areas in which each of you has authority. Matters relating to your area must be handled by you. Try to work out a method of operation on which both of you can agree and make it a point not to override the other even if you disagree.

9-62 How do you handle an employee who cannot accept positive and constructive criticism?

What appears positive to you may appear negative to the employee. Sensitive people take all criticism personally and even when it is accompanied by constructive suggestions as to how to improve, they look upon it as a blow to their ego. If you are aware of someone's sensitivity, temper all criticism with assurance of your confidence in the person. Use suggestions instead of direction. Give such people opportunity to contribute their own ideas on improvement rather than imposing your ideas on them.

9-63 What should I do when I really dislike one of my subordinates? I just don't trust him.

Try to find out why you don't like him. The reasons for likes and dislikes are often difficult to discern. Has he done something specific that caused this dislike? Is it just an intuitive dislike? If your feeling is based on tangible reasons—past behavior, something he said with which you disagree, or an antagonistic personality—you can weigh in your mind whether this is a good enough reason to maintain your attitude toward him.

If you are not sure why you don't trust him, but you truly do not, it may be that he reminds you of another person with whom you have had problems and you are "projecting." Rethink your relationship. Your antipathy may be based on shaky grounds. Try to find something you can admire in this person. Make an effort to like him.

No matter what steps you take to overcome your aversion, you may still retain that dislike. It is not necessary to like people to work effectively with them. You may have to take overt steps to keep from letting your feelings affect your work relationship so that you do not let your dislike influence your decisions.

9-64   My people are asking me about a situation in our company that I do not wish to discuss. How can I avoid this?

You are not obligated to discuss anything that you believe is not appropriate. Tell your people that at this time it would not be proper for you to discuss the situation. If pertinent, add that when the proper time comes, you will be happy to talk with them about it.

9-65   I am a woman manager of a predominantly male department. One of my people is constantly testing my ability to stay in control in front of the other employees. How can I handle this in a dignified manner?

Some men resent women as bosses and try to show the others than no woman is capable of that responsibility. By testing you, he is hoping you will blow up and maybe, if he is lucky, you will burst into tears. Keep your cool. Use humor. Make a joke about his testing you. This will show the others that you are not easily flustered.

9-66   One of the women in my department is constantly balking at my directions. How can I deal with her?

Confront her. Next time she fails to comply with a direction or in some other way expresses resistance, ask her why she is doing so. Let her know that a cooperative work team is essential and that her actions militate against a smooth working team. Ask if she has any specific complaints. Suggest that she is probably unaware that her actions are affecting the department and that you are sure she will be more cooperative in the future. If, after this discussion, she continues to act in the same way, take more formal actions in the form of counseling and, if necessary, discipline.

9-67   The woman who formerly supervised my department is now in a staff position in the company, but she continues to stick her nose into my department's activities. How can I get her out of my hair?

Because of her previous responsibility for the department, this employee obviously maintains an interest in its activities. She has a long-term relationship with your (formerly her) employees. Sometimes it takes a while to break old habits and concentrate on a new job. Tell her that you understand her interest in what is going on in the department and that you will ask her advice when her expertise can be of help. However, in order for you to meet your responsibilities, she must let you do your job and not interfere. If this approach does not succeed, discuss it with her boss, who probably is concerned with having her put all her energies into her new assignment.

9-68   I think I'm an easy-to-talk-to boss, but one of my people is so intimidated that he is afraid to ask questions about the work. The result is misunderstandings and errors. How can I get him over this?

Some people are basically afraid of authority figures. This may have developed in childhood, from fear of questioning parents or teachers, or later from reactions of previous bosses. The problem may stem from insecurity and fear of appearing to be stupid by asking a question.

You may not be able to overcome your employee's fears, but you can minimize them as they relate to you. To ensure that he does understand your instructions, ask questions of him. Build in a lot of feedback. Compliment him on his perspicacity for asking the questions. Once he sees that you do not consider him inadequate because he raises questions, he will be encouraged to take the initiative and ask more questions in future communications.

9-69   Some of my employees have complained to my manager that I "pick on them." My manager has not explained exactly what I have been doing that precipitated those complaints. All I demand is that people do their job and meet standards. Is this picking on them?

It is not what you are doing, but how you are doing it. Requiring people to meet standards is your job. You can do it in many ways. Some supervisors constantly nag employees about their work; others use sarcasm; still others yell at their people or state or imply stupidity when correcting errors. Listen to yourself when you criticize. If you are using any of these approaches, you are "picking" on people. Make an effort to be more positive. Be calm, moderate your tone, be constructive, and never, never nag.

9-70   As a supervisor who talks to his people and is open to their ideas, I am always shocked to discover that they have demands or complaints I never knew existed. What am I doing wrong?

You may believe that you are open to their ideas, but your manner in listening to them or perhaps your lack of follow-through on matters that are important to them has given them the impression that you are not sincerely interested. Check your listening habits. Do you turn off things you do not want to hear or are not interested in? Even if you believe that a gripe is not justified, tell your people you will investigate it—and do. There may be issues involved that you were not aware of. Report back and if the complaint is justified, do something about it. If not, explain what you have learned. In time you will build a real rapport with your people and not be hit with unexpected complaints.

9-71   One of my employees, an unsuccessful contender for my job, does everything she can to make me look bad. For example, she recently spent hours developing "data" to show that a major improvement I had initiated was not working. Had she devoted that time to doing the work, my improvement (which did work) would have taken off much sooner. How can I gain her cooperation?

Counsel with her. Point out that you respect her expertise in the work and welcome her ideas. Let her know that you are aware of what she is doing and that if she is concerned with the best interests of the department, instead of looking for ways to make your ideas fail, she should be helping make them succeed. Her suggestions for improvements are welcome. Make sure she knows that her future advancement depends on her cooperation with you.

9-72   Mark is a bowling buddy of my boss. It is very difficult to supervise him. He is sloppy and has poor work habits. The other employees resent him. However, when I reprimand him, my boss asks me to be easy on him. What can I do?

Have a serious discussion with your boss. Tell him how Mark's poor habits are affecting the work and morale of the department. Ask the boss what he can do to help Mark become a satisfactory worker. Sometimes senior supervisors do not realize how of their interventions for friends can affect the department's morale.

9-73   Although our company is small, we have our share of office politics. There are two cliques vying for influence with the owner, who thinks that competition between these

cliques is a good way to motivate each group to do its best. As office manager, and not part of either group, the owner expects me to be the referee. How can I meld these cliques into a cooperative team?

Not easily. Healthy competition is a good way to stimulate people to stretch, but rivalry between cliques can be unhealthy. Cliques have sabotaged the work of their rivals or have purposely misled management to gain an advantage. Breaking up established cliques is virtually impossible. The first step is to get the owner to change her attitude and make this clear to the staff. Then, by establishing teams made up of members of both groups and assigning them projects on which they must work together, you will eventually blur the lines between the cliques.

9-74   Some of my employees question every decision I make. I spend an inordinate amount of time justifying my decisions to them. Any suggestions?

Before a decision is made, bring your people together. Present the situation; obtain their input; list the proposed solutions and achieve consensus on the steps to be taken. Usually the decision will result from this consensus and there will be no further need to explain it. However, as the responsible manager, you may at times feel that a different approach should be taken and you may choose not to follow the consensus. If you do so, explain why you have made your decision and sell your people on it.

9-75   As a line supervisor, I do the same work side by side with the people I supervise. How can supervision be conducted adequately under these circumstances?

Line supervisors, or "lead people," have been used by organizations from the beginning of the industrial era. One of the better workers is chosen to lead the others in the work. This person shows by how he or she works what is expected of the others. Because the leader is a member of the group, not a person superimposed on the group, he or she is looked upon as the first among equals rather than as a boss. The relationship should lead to closer rapport, better understanding of the needs of the staff, more rapid attention to day-to-day problems, and easier liaison with higher management.

The negatives of being a lead person are that you are often so busy with your own production that you have no time to carry out the supervisory function. It takes a great deal of energy to do both jobs simultaneously. However, with proper planning and organization, you can succeed. Your own production quotas should be lower so that you can devote time to the supervisory and administrative aspects of the job.

9-76   In my first months as a supervisor, I made all the mistakes you can make in dealing with people. I antagonized some of them and now I realize how important it is to gain their support. What can I do to reset these relationships?

Speak privately to each of the people involved. Apologize for past treatment. Tell them that you realize now it was a mistake and blame it on your inexperience as a supervisor. Tell them you want to start afresh with them and ask what you can do to make the relationship more cordial and cooperative. Make every effort to change your approach and do whatever is necessary to accomplish this goal.

9-77   One of my older workers is not as strong as he used to be. How can I give him less strenuous work and not make it appear to be favoritism?

In making assignments, spread the work in such a way that more of the less strenuous work is given to this man. If anybody should object, point out that this man has paid his dues over the years by doing his share of the tough jobs. He's still carrying his load, but with less physically taxing work that utilizes his skills. Most people will accept that explanation.

9-78   How do I supervise someone who is bright and energetic but loves to give me numerous suggestions on how to do things? I feel that I would hurt her feelings if I didn't incorporate at least some of her ideas into the work. Usually I go along with her, but I am used to managing people who don't offer so many suggestions or just don't get so involved. I am not sure what to make of this employee. Will she later challenge my authority?

The real problem is not that she will challenge your authority, but that other people in the department will feel left out if she dominates discussions about the work. Encourage her, but also elicit ideas from the others. Since you are not used to managing people who contribute ideas, you must change your own attitude. The best supervisors recognize the importance of staff participation. Once all your people become involved in making suggestions, you needn't worry about any one of them being a challenge to your authority.

9-79   Sometimes the pressures of my job are so great that I feel I will panic. How can I hold this in so as not to reveal it to my subordinates?

When the pressures get too great for you, get away from the people you supervise. If you have a private office, close the door and try to relax. Do relaxation exercises such as deep breathing. If you can, get out of the building. Walk around the block or the parking lot. Some people need to do something physical like kicking the wastebasket or screaming. If that is your need, make sure you do it in a very private place. The panic will abate and you can get back to work.

9-80   How can I handle employees who call me at home during the evening with a problem?

Good managers let their staff know that they are always available. However, most supervisors do not wish to be disturbed with problems during their off-hours. Upon receiving such a call, clearly state that, unless it is an emergency, you prefer not to be called at home about business problems. If people persist in calling you, refuse to answer their questions, but tell them you will be happy to talk at work. When they realize that the calls are not producing the results they want—to gain your favorable attention to their problem—they will stop phoning at night.

9-81   One of my fellow supervisors frequently comes into my department and chats with my people. He is an amiable guy and we all like him. However, he is keeping people from doing their work. How can I handle this without hurting anybody's feelings?

Rather than order your people not to talk to him, speak to him about it. He may not realize how much time he is taking from their work.

9-82   During a heated discussion over a work-related issue, Sarah blew up and said: "I have no respect for you as a manager and do not like working for you." I am very reluctant to approach her about anything now. How do I get past this?

Sarah probably is as upset about this as you. Since her remark came out in the midst of a heated discussion, she most likely did not mean what she said. However, the incident cannot be ignored. Take the initiative. Have a private meeting. Tell her how much this has upset you. She probably will admit it was a rash remark and that she too is upset. Do not focus on her exact words: "I have no respect for you." Try to get some specifics about matters where she and you have disagreements and discuss them logically. This should set the stage for a better future relationship.

9-83   Maurice has no self-discipline. His wild ways both on and off the job are the talk of the department. He often ignores rules. For example, we don't allow food or drink at the workplace, but he often sneaks a container of coffee into his cubicle. When challenged, he protests the rule and goads the others to agree. I don't want to fire him. What can I do?

You can't teach self-discipline. Inasmuch as Maurice is getting a lot of attention from his peers for his wild behavior, he has no incentive to change. All you can do is be firm on his following company rules. When he violates a rule, take immediate action. Give him an informal warning and tell him that disagreement over a rule is not an excuse to violate it. If he tries to goad others to go along with him, explain the reason for the rule and tell them that if they feel a rule is unnecessary or wrong, they should take whatever steps the company has established to challenge it.

9-84   Two of my workers are very critical of me—not by direct comments, but by remarks they have made to other people in the company. There are no jobs within the company to which I can transfer them. What can I do?

Confront them. Let them know that if they have any complaints, they should bring them to you rather than talking to others. Tell them that you are open to their ideas and willing to resolve any misunderstandings, but that unless they bring complaints to you, there is no way change can happen. Reaffirm the importance of working together. Reiterate that only by cooperation can the goals of the department and the company be met.

9-85   Although my company has always had women supervisors of all-female departments, I was the first woman promoted to supervise a department of both sexes. I have been accused of favoring my women workers over the men. This is not true, but how can I avoid the perception?

Many supervisors subconsciously favor people with whom they relate. Some male managers may feel that other men are more capable than women to do certain tasks; women managers have similar preconceptions. Stop thinking in gender-related terms. Review the decisions you've made over the past several months. Did the gender of the people involved have anything to do with the decision? If so, perhaps the perception is justified.

In making assignments, arranging for special projects, scheduling overtime and other routine duties, make sure that both men and women are given equal consideration. At meetings, make sure that both men and women are given the opportunity to express their views.

9-86   How do you differentiate between the symptoms of a problem and what the problem really involves?

Symptoms represent the surface of the situation; the real problem is often deeply buried inside the individual. Joel is always griping about his workload. If his workload is no greater than that of others in the department, this is a symptom of some deeper problem. By probing and observation you may learn that the real problem is that Joel is not getting enough attention from you. Brenda says she cannot learn the new procedure. You know she has the intelligence to learn it; be patient and the real problem will unfold: she is afraid she will not do as well working in the new way. She needs encouragement and motivation, not added training.

In many cases the complaint may reflect the real problem, but you cannot assume this is always so. If you know your people, you should have insight into deeper aspects of these symptoms. Ask such questions as "Why do you feel this way?" "What can I do to help you?" "In what way do you think this should be done?" Probing may take some time, so be patient, but the real problem will be revealed.

9-87   One of my employees is an overbearing, domineering, macho type. He resents having a woman as his boss and tries to intimidate me—and he succeeds. I'm afraid to criticize his work or deal with problems he causes. What can I do?

It is easy for a man or a woman to be intimidated by bullies. First, ask yourself what he can really do to you. It is unlikely he will become physically violent, since he knows that would cost him his job. At the most he will make you uncomfortable. One way of dealing with bullies is humor. Turn potential confrontations into a joke. Get the other employees to see how ridiculous his behavior is. This will eliminate one of his major satisfactions in being a bully—to show his co-workers that the boss can't order him around.

Take a course or read some books on assertiveness. You can learn how other people have coped with similar situations.

9-88   Some of my people are so obstinate that they fight every attempt I make to introduce new concepts. Why do they do this and how can I overcome it?

The reasons for obstinacy differ from person to person, but one common factor is the reluctance to get out of one's comfort zone. To motivate people to accept a new idea or approach, you must show them how the advantages will outweigh the discomfort of making a change. Ask questions instead of pushing your idea. Learn what benefits they want to derive and sell them on your concept by showing how it will help them achieve those benefits.

10

Day to Day
on the Job

Many of the problems that supervisors face are routine day-to-day situations which do not clearly fit into any category, yet they take a great deal of the supervisor's time. Included here are problems related to work assignments, interpersonal relations, tardiness and absenteeism, and work habits.

Work Assignments

10-1   I have been assigned to implement a program in branches other than my own. Since I have no formal authority over these people, how do I get their cooperation? I sense that they resent an outsider interfering with their department.

Start by discussing the program with the supervisors of those branches. If it is a major project, a representative of upper management—somebody who ranks higher than you and the branch managers—should meet with all the supervisors involved and orient them about the importance of the project and what your part in the program will be.

In the beginning, the branch supervisor should be included in all matters related to that branch's activities in the program. As the people become more familiar with you and your role in the program, the need for the supervisor's direct participation will become less important.

Treat the people in the branches in the same way as those you have direct control over. Learn to know them as individuals and show them you respect them. Because of the temporary nature of your assignment and the fact that you are an outsider, be especially diplomatic and sell your ideas rather than imposing them on these people.

10-2 I am a very quick worker and become impatient with slow people. How can I get my employees to accept the need for faster work and how do I deal with those who just won't follow my lead?

You must recognize that everybody cannot work at the same pace. Some people just are slower than others. If the reason for their slower speed is physical, the only way to increase the pace is by restructuring the job so it can be done more rapidly. It is unlikely that the "slow employee" can work any faster.

Another approach is to reanalyze the job. Performance standards may be based on outdated or unrealistic data. If so, new standards should be set and sold to the people. In other cases, work can be done faster than at present, but workers will not exceed what they have been told are the standards. If you feel that performance standards are based on minimum productivity and you want your people to produce more than the minimum, develop motivational programs to encourage them to do more than they are now doing.

If the problem is laziness, poor attitude, or poor work habits, it may reflect a subtle rebellion against you or the company. Uncover any grievances and resolve them. When workers feel that they are being treated fairly, and that their concerns have been listened to and appropriate action has been taken, they are more willing to stretch and do more and better work.

10-3 I set deadlines for the projects assigned to my staff. One of my people is almost always late in completing the assignments. When I discuss the issue with him, he says the deadlines are unreasonable so he ignores them. What can I do to avoid this in the future?

Instead of you setting the deadlines, both you and the employee together should determine when projects are due. Let him come up with what he considers to be a reasonable deadline. If you do not agree, work out a schedule which you both feel is attainable.

10-4 Marjorie doesn't know the meaning of "urgent." No matter how important or "top priority" a task may be, she takes her time in getting to it. How do I get her to change?

Some people have their own concepts of what is and is not important. If you tell such people that something is urgent, they interpret it to mean "urgent to you, but not to me." Take the time to explain why it is necessary to put other things aside and do the new work. Together look at the other work Marjorie is doing and determine what can be deferred to make time for this assignment. Get agreement on what she will do, when it will be started, and when it is expected to be finished. Follow up to make sure it is done.

10-5 What do you do with a person who insists on doing things his way, even when I have demonstrated how another approach is better? I have discussed the matter with him many times, but he will not change.

People often refuse to change the way they do things. They are comfortable with a certain routine and, as they will always tell you, "It works, so why should I do it differently?" Your employee is typical of the many people who don't like to get out of their comfort zones. Such people have to be persuaded that just because a procedure works does not mean it is the best way. Point out that unless your company remains open to new and more efficient ways of doing things, your competitors will get ahead. Insist that he try the new way, at least give it a chance. Give him whatever training or coaching is needed and praise him for his improvements. It takes time to accept change, but after a while most people do.

10-6 When work schedules must be changed, how can I handle conflicts between the needs of the company and the personal needs of a worker?

It is not always possible to arrange work schedules to fit the personal requirements of your people. When schedules must be changed, every effort should be made to consider the individual's preferences. In cases where some people must be inconvenienced, most companies use seniority as the arbiter. In cases of real hardship, exceptions may be made.

Sometimes, it is a matter not of scheduling the work among several people, but of requiring people to work overtime or on weekends. Whenever possible, ask for volunteers for the extra work. Some people seek opportunities to earn overtime pay; others either cannot or do not want to do so. If this approach does not provide adequate staffing, you may have to compel people to work those hours. Try to schedule overtime in as equitable a manner as possible. Again, in cases of conflict, the least controversial approach is seniority. Other means may lead to concerns about favoritism.

10-7   Janos is ambitious and is always asking for more responsibility. Then he complains that he has too much work to do. How can I handle this problem?

Janos should know how much work the added responsibility brings with it. Make sure that this is clear to him before giving him new assignments. Often complaints about too much work are based, not on the amount of work, but on the inability to organize the work so it can be done in a reasonable time frame. Have Janos set timetables for new assignments, so both you and he know how much work actually has to be done, in what order and manner he plans to do it, and when each phase will be completed. If the assignment proves to be too much, work out other ways that it can be done or provide the necessary assistance to Janos so he can complete it.

10-8   I know that some of my people can do more than their basic tasks, but all they want to do is the minimum. How can I motivate them to seek out additional responsibilities?

Unfortunately, there are many people who are content with minimum productivity. They will do exactly what they have to do and not one bit more. It is unlikely that you can motivate them to do more. You can assign more work to them and they probably will do it, but they will never volunteer to do more.

In between these people and those who actively seek additional work are the many employees who are willing, but not necessarily anxious to take on added work. Perhaps they are shy and feel their boss will think that they are too forward, or perhaps they fear peer reprisals if they volunteer to do more than assigned. These are the people you can motivate. Seek them out. Let them know that you have confidence in their abilities. Offer them challenges. Let them know the types of added contributions they can make and encourage them to reach out. Offer them training in new areas. Send them to seminars or in-house programs that will give them the knowledge and skills they need to take on new projects.

10-9   Several of my people keep bringing me questions on matters that I have explained to them over and over again. I am very patient with them, but this constant repetition of what they have been told lowers both their productivity and mine. How can I help them retain this information?

During the training sessions, get very thorough feedback from your people to make sure that they really do understand what has been taught. Ask questions. Carefully listen to the responses. Asking, "Do you understand?" is not enough. Raise specific questions that require people to explain in detail how they understand the material. If there is a time lapse between training and actual performance of the work, have an additional feedback session when a project begins. Give people an oral quiz. The process takes awhile, but it is less time-consuming and less annoying than being interrupted to answer questions when you are doing something else.

If appropriate, develop written job instructions or work manuals. Such materials provide an easy reference to workers who need to check on a procedure or relearn something they have forgotten or do not understand.

10-10   Every once in a while I am shocked to learn that a task I had assumed was being done has not been done at all. What is the best way to react and to deal with it?

Don't panic. Find out why. When you assigned the work, was it made clear who was to do it and when it was to be completed? Perhaps there was some oversight on your part. If the assignee indicates that he or she did not know that the project was supposed to be done at this time, bawling out the person will not solve the problem. You may have to reorder priorities to get the work under way immediately, so it can be finished with minimum additional delay.

It is easy to set up a control system to prevent work slippage. Prepare a chart listing each of the assignments you make, the name of the assignee, and the dates of the control points you have established. (See question 14 in Chapter 5.) Now, at a glance, you can note the status of each assignment and take action if things are not going according to schedule.

10-11   How can I distribute work equitably? I supervise a group of social workers. No matter what I do some of my people complain that they have too heavy a caseload.

You can never make everybody happy about his or her workload. Sometimes, because of the pressures of the job, people may carry heavier workloads than they can handle, and there is little that can be done to relieve the pressure short of hiring more people. At other times, however, certain people are given more work than their peers. Typically, the boss recognizes that a worker is faster or more productive, so that person is "rewarded" with more work. It doesn't take long for the employee to recognize what is happening and to raise a legitimate objection. Rather than pour routine tasks onto such people, assign them more challenging work. They are less likely to complain if they get satisfaction from what they are doing. Many people have commented: "I never worked so hard, but I never enjoyed a job as much."

As for those marginal workers who do little and complain they are working too much, keep giving them the routine work. No matter what you do, they will still be unhappy about the work assignments.

10-12   Overtime is rare in our company, but every once in a while a job must be finished that day and we fall behind. Some of my people will stay until the job is done, but others walk out at 4:30 and leave their work unfinished. How do I get these people to understand that they just can't walk out when the closing bell rings?

New employees should be told that such situations will occur from time to time and that occasional overtime is a job requirement. Let them know how often this is likely to happen and how much time they are likely to have to put in. (For example: "Work backs up about once a month and we rarely stay later than 5 or at the most 5:30." Write this policy into the company procedures manual and reiterate it periodically at meetings. Make provisions for excusing people for exceptional reasons. Employees who have not completed the assigned work should let you know by, say, 3 p.m., that the work will not be completed by 4:30, so you can determine if overtime will be needed. Workers who will have to remain can then telephone their families or make other arrangements for staying late.

10-13   Because of the nature of our work, my people are located in various parts of the building, far from my office. I know that some of them take advantage of this and extend their lunches and coffee breaks and occasionally leave early. How can I keep better control over them without seeming nosy or distrustful?

Let people know that you expect them to follow company rules and be back from breaks and lunch on time. Spot-check with an occasional telephone call or an unannounced visit. Have a business-related reason for the call or visit so you will not appear to be spying on whether people are at their desks. If someone is away once, don't make an issue of it. Just comment: "I tried to reach you earlier today, but you weren't in." Then discuss the business matter with no further comment about the absence. The message will get across. If someone is absent more than once or twice, counsel with the offender and make it clear that rules must be followed.

10-14   Because my people have expertise that is needed by other departments, they are frequently interrupted by outsiders for advice or information. This is part of their job, but the interruptions have become so time-consuming that they impede my ability to accomplish the department's goals. What can I do?

It appears that your department has two roles: one to service other departments and the other to accomplish its own objectives. If the former is interfering with the latter, a determination must be made as to where priorities lie. Discuss the matter with top management. If the expertise provided to others is of primary importance to the company, you will have to reevaluate your department's goals. If the unit's own work is more valuable, make arrangements to limit the amount of time that your people are available to outsiders. If the two roles are of relatively equal importance, you should fix the amount of time your people devote to each aspect of the work. You might also require all requests for technical assistance to flow through you or a designated assistant, to ensure control over each aspect of the department's work.

10-15   If I treat people in different ways because of their personalities, how can I avoid others looking upon it as favoritism?

People do differ and you cannot deal with each employee in exactly the same way. Patty needs lots of pats on the back to do her work. Ignore her and she sulks. Tony doesn't like to be closely supervised. Candace constantly asks questions. Successful supervisors recognize this. They will give Patty reassurance, leave Tony alone so long as his work is OK, and answer Candace's questions. The fact that you give more pats to Patty and take more time with Candace will not make Tony feel you are favoring them. As long as you treat all people fairly, the stigma of favoritism to anyone will be obviated.

10-16   In our department we always seem to be putting out fires. We are short on personnel. Also, our goals are vague and tend to change every hour. How can I build a cohesive team?

Until your department stabilizes and has a specific set of objectives, the only way to build a team is to look upon yourself as a fire brigade. Firefighters work cohesively to meet the constantly changing problems that come up. Build up your people's ability to handle a variety of situations. Encourage flexibility and reinforce it by praising workers for their ability to roll with the punches.

10-17   I have been able to increase job satisfaction in my department by placing people into functional groups and giving them more autonomy in their jobs. However, this arrangement is being undermined by top management, with its constant demands that my people attend meetings, handle emergency problems, and work around scheduling conflicts with other departments. How can I decrease the impact of management's demands?

A discussion with top management concerning the effect of these interruptions on your people is the first step. Try to minimize the number of meetings they attend. In many cases, people need not be invited. Request that any changes in scheduling be channelled through you so you can control conflicts with other departments. Get top managers to accept the importance of your department's prime mission so they will be less likely to interfere with its accomplishment.

10-18   What is the best way for a supervisor to handle changes?

As pointed out earlier, people resist change because they do not want to leave their comfort zones. Change is uncomfortable. Prepare people well in advance for a change; sell them on its importance and on how it will help them in the long run. Except in emergency situations, institute change gradually—by evolution, not revolution.

10-19   My assistant constantly misses deadlines. He always has good excuses, but the delays appear to be deliberate. What can I do?

Next time you give your assistant an assignment, ask him to suggest a suitable deadline. If it is reasonable, go along with it. If the deadline he suggests is not reasonable, work out a satisfactory target date and assure him that you have confidence that he can meet it.

Follow-up a few days before the deadline to determine whether your assistant is on target. If not, remind him that he agreed to this deadline and ask what you can do to help him catch up on the work. Follow-through is important because it shows your subordinate that you take his deadline seriously and that you are there to help him—not criticize him—if problems arise.

10-20   Rita is really trying her best. She is always on the job and on time, but her performance is below standard. Is there any way I can help her reach at least minimum standards?

First determine whether the work is above Rita's level of ability. If she does not have the basic ability to perform, there is little you can do. Despite her good attendance record and her desire to succeed, she just won't make the grade.

However, if the job does not require special skills or aptitudes that Rita lacks, the problem may be that she is a slow learner. Through patience and experimentation with different training approaches, you may be able to help her build her productivity.

Another reason for Rita's below-standard performance may be an overwhelming fear of failure. Perhaps she did fail in the past and suffered the consequences. To help her over this hurdle, give her easy assignments that she can succeed in readily, and praise each success. By recognizing that she can do things right, she will build up her self-esteem and take on more difficult work with more confidence.

10-21   Like many supervisors, I spend a good deal of time with my less productive workers trying to help them become more effective. As a result, I often ignore my good people. How can I make sure they do not feel left out?

Like all supervisors, you have a limited amount of time. A prime concern is how to use this time most effectively. The cliché that the wheel that squeaks the most gets the grease fits your situation. Your less productive people need your help and you give it to them. However, most people want attention and recognition. Ignoring good people may make them think that you do not appreciate their work. Many a good employee has intentionally turned in unsatisfactory work just to get some attention from the boss.

No matter how busy you are, make time to talk to each of your people—if not every day, then as often as possible. Comment on their assignments, praise their accomplishments, or exchange ideas. Just a few words will do it. Know your people. Some workers need more attention than others. Whether they are good or bad producers, it is important to give them sufficient recognition to meet that need. Others prefer to be left alone. Even then, you should tell them from time to time that you are aware of their accomplishments.

10-22   How should I handle an employee who "yesses" me to death? He agrees with all my comments and criticisms and then does exactly as he pleases, paying no attention to what he just agreed to. I've talked to him about this and he responds, "I'm doing just what we said."

Some people are so absorbed in themselves that they block out any ideas they do not like. They say they agree because they hear only what they want to hear. If this is a deep-seated problem, only professional help may solve it. Other people are just inattentive and don't really listen. With such people, the work assignment should be put in writing if it involves more than just a simple instruction.

After an oral discussion of the assignment with your employee, ask him to write a memo letting you know how he will do the work. If the memo does not reflect what you said, straighten it out immediately. If it is OK, hold him to it. When the employee digresses, refer him to the memo. No matter what he may say about his concept at that point, he cannot use that as an excuse. The memo is proof of what you agreed to.

10-23   I have been a supervisor for several years. More and more my administrative duties have taken me away from hands-on operations. In some cases, I have lost touch with the details of the tasks I assign. Under these circumstances, how can I evaluate my workers' skills?

It is not uncommon for supervisors to lose touch with the nitty-gritty details of the work they supervise. Although it is essential to keep up with the state of the art in your field, it is not necessary to know every nuance of every activity. You should know the performance standards expected and how to measure them. Your evaluations—both formal and informal—should be based on these standards. Occasionally it becomes necessary to understand the specific details. You will have to make the time to acquire that information.

10-24   Sometimes our methods and procedures do not make sense to the workers, and some "bright" people decide to change them to make the work easier. Individual approaches can be expeditious, but sometimes they impinge on what others are doing and cause problems. How can I get my people to follow procedures they do not really agree with?

All employees should be indoctrinated with the importance of following procedures. If possible, let them know the reason for that policy. Advise them that the company insists that procedures be followed to ensure consistency throughout the organization. Assure them that any ideas they may have to improve the procedures are welcome and let them know how such suggestions should be made. Remind that no matter how good they believe their ideas are, they cannot put them into use without approval from management.

10-25   Over the 18 years that Stan has been with our company, he has been promoted several times. These promotions were based on his loyalty and dependability rather than on his talent. He is now in a position which is beyond

his ability to handle. How can I demote him without crushing his morale and losing his loyalty?

If possible, transfer Stan laterally to a position that he can handle. Another approach is to create a job at the same salary level that is structured to fit his abilities. If neither of these alternatives is feasible, you may have to demote him. Discuss the situation frankly. Let Stan know that you respect his abilities and his dedication, but that everybody is not suited for every type of job. This assignment simply was not right for him. If it is necessary to reduce his salary, explain why and assure him that when other openings arise within his scope of expertise, he will be considered.

10-26   I hired a new staff member a few months ago. At the interview, she impressed me with her knowledge and intelligence. Now that she is on the job, I find that she is not as flexible as she had led me to believe. How can I get her to improve?

Even the best interviewers cannot learn everything about an applicant in the few hours of the interviewing process. There is no way to tell how a person will do a job until she or he is actually on the job.

If your new staff member has all the other qualities you desire, work with her to improve her flexibility. Let her know how important this quality is to the job and how confident you are that she can become more flexible. Give her an example of her rigidity—a specific instance in which it caused difficulties. If a similar situation develops, call it to her attention immediately. Unless she is innately stubborn, she should be able to overcome the problem with your support.

10-27   Burt is a superior worker. I am more than pleased with the quality and quantity of his work. But Burt is a wanderer. He frequently leaves his cubicle and roams around the building chatting with other people. How can I get through to him that he must spend less time roaming and more time working?

If Burt's work is going as well as you say, his wandering may be due to boredom. He completed his work faster than the others, and since it is of high quality, you have no complaints about it. The only way to stop Burt from wandering is to keep him so busy he has no time to leave his workplace.

10-28   My accounts payable supervisor has been authorized to scrutinize all company charges from both external and internal sources. She has great technical skills and has saved the company money by her good work. However, she oversteps her authority by reprimanding co-workers and managers alike for minor discrepancies in their vouchers. How can I get her to stop these diatribes and still keep doing good work?

Many good workers do not realize that their skills in dealing with people need improving. Let her know that what she is doing affects the morale of the group. Suggest more diplomatic ways for her to correct discrepancies. Enroll her in a course or seminar on interpersonal relations. Once she understands the importance of getting her point across without antagonizing others, she will be an even better watchdog over company expenditures.

10-29   I supervise 32 technicians in a hospital radiology department. I am constantly barraged by people who demand special consideration for vacation schedules or who want to spread their vacation days over the whole year. What is a fair way to allow employees to request vacation time?

Some organizations have strict rules as to when vacation time may be scheduled. If your hospital allows vacations to be taken one day at a time, it is difficult to set schedules. One approach is to require all members of your staff to lay out their vacation plans by a specific date. Those who select full weeks should give you their first, second, and third choices. Determine specific schedules on the basis of seniority. For those who wish to take all or part of their vacation time in single days, establish a policy as to how far in advance of the time-off notification is required. Stick to this rule. As in all matters dealing with people, exceptions may have to be made occasionally—for example, in the case of family emergencies. Make clear to all your people just how emergencies will be handled.

10-30   One of the men in my office has been with me for 18 years and has become very jealous of another worker who has been in the department for 5 years. The senior person becomes upset if I give the junior person assignments that he wants. I base my decisions as to who does what on individual strengths, existing workloads, and other job-related

factors, not on seniority. How can I pacify the senior worker when this happens?

Make clear that all assignments are made as you have stated. If your senior worker objects, state your reason clearly. For example, because the employee is currently working on another job, you gave his junior colleague the current assignment. Always reinforce the fact that this is not a matter of favoring one over the other. When you assign the employee his next project, make sure you let him know how much confidence you have in his ability to do the job.

Interpersonal Relations

10-31   I know that good relations among my people are essential. From time to time, some of my people get into hassles. How do I handle these situations?

Talk to the parties involved. Try to determine why the conflict has occurred. If it involves a job assignment, clarify what you expect from each party. If the issue is personal, try to resolve the differences. Make every effort to get each party to understand the other's viewpoint and at least try to compromise. If they cannot work it out themselves, suggest and, if necessary, impose solutions.

10-32   How can I deal with employees who cannot put aside personal dislikes or negative feelings about others in the department?

Find out the reason for these feelings. Negative feelings may be based on real or perceived grievances. If so, bring the parties together and clear the air, so that real problems can be worked out and imagined situations can be clarified.

Sometimes a dislike is based not on specific behavior but on an intuitive sense. Employee A dislikes employee B because B reminds A of someone whom A had a conflict with in the past. Worker A projects this onto B.

Talk to workers who appear to have a grudge. Point out that it is not necessary to like people to work with them. Ask conflicting parties to find something admirable in each other. If your employees make an effort to overlook negative feelings, and to focus on positive aspects of their co-workers, the department's work will flow more easily and morale will greatly improve.

10-33   Kaiti and Sue are two key members of my unit. It is important that they work well together. On the surface they seem to be fine, but they are constantly criticizing each other to other members of the unit. When I try to discuss the matter, they deny any problem and profess to be good friends.

Employees are often reluctant to get their supervisor involved in gripes they have with other workers. They are afraid it might affect their performance reviews or other aspects of their job. They hide any problems from the boss and instead vent their feelings with co-workers. If these gripes are not seriously affecting the work, its best to ignore them and let employees talk things out themselves. However, if the squabbling and complaining do lower the unit's morale and affect productivity, you will have to step in.

Have a heart-to-heart talk with Kaiti and Sue separately. Learn what is really bothering them and encourage them to talk the conflict out between themselves. Let them know that you are available to act as a mediator to help resolve the situation. (Guidelines on resolving conflicts among workers are given in Chapter 11.)

10-34   When dealing with employees who don't get along, should I speak to each person individually or gather together all the people involved to discuss the situation?

If only two people are involved, speak to each separately first. If this does not lead to the desired result, bring them together and work it out.

If the friction among workers is widespread, hold a general meeting. Set the stage by giving a brief talk on how the discord in the department is affecting productivity. Then lead a discussion on what can be done. Generate ideas from which solutions can be developed. Meetings of this sort encourage people to settle minor interpersonal disputes. They also help identify specific situations that may require your personal intervention.

10-35   Bruce has several bad habits that annoy his co-workers. He butts into their personal affairs; he questions everything they do on the job; he makes sarcastic remarks. My

people don't want to work with him, and his behavior is keeping them from optimum performance.

People like Bruce can destroy the morale of a group. Usually annoyed co-workers will let Bruce know in no uncertain terms that what he is doing is not acceptable. Peer pressure is a powerful tool. As Bruce comes to realize that what he is doing is unwelcome, he may tone himself down.

Some people just don't acknowledge that what they are doing is wrong. Despite peer pressure, they need to be forcefully made aware that their behavior will not be tolerated. If this is the case, have a serious talk with Bruce. Point out that he may not realize how his actions are affecting the morale and productivity of the department. Make sure he knows that his cooperation will be a factor in evaluating his performance. Emphasize that if he does not heed this warning, further action will ensue.

In some organizations disciplinary action leading to termination could be imposed. Other organizations may not allow this step. Moving Bruce to another department will alleviate your problem, but will just transfer it to another supervisor.

10-36   We have six people working in our office. Three report to me; the others, to a colleague. Five of these people always place the blame for any problems on Lucy, one of my employees. She is a meek person who is afraid to protest. I don't believe she is always at fault.

Next time this happens, investigate the situation carefully. If the fault lies elsewhere, you and/or your colleague should confront the offender. Point out that what is important is not who made the error but what steps can be taken to avoid repetition. By seeking to find a scapegoat, these workers are only evading the real issue. Talk to Lucy and let her know that she was not at fault in that instance. After a few such interventions, Lucy's co-workers will no longer feel that they have to place the blame on a specific person.

In addition, Lucy needs to know that you, her boss, do not think of her as an inefficient person. She may need counseling to overcome her meekness. You might suggest that she take assertiveness training.

10-37   How can I stop employees from discovering what each other earns? Jealousies and strife inevitably result when one person learns that another is earning more.

There is no way you can keep salaries secret. Somehow, sooner or later, it becomes known. A paycheck is left on a desk; a clerk with access to the information blabs; a conversation is overheard. The only way to avoid disgruntlement over salary is to have an established wage and salary policy. When everybody is paid on a scale based on job classification with increments based on open formulas, there are no secrets.

10-38   What's a good way to control excessive amounts of general conversation among workers during work hours?

Allowing conversation on boring jobs helps improve productivity, (See question 37 in Chapter 8.) However, on jobs where work stops when people talk, conversation may have to be limited. To prohibit all conversation unrelated to work is not only impossible but undesirable. People do need periodic breaks from routine, and a few minutes' conversation with a colleague about last night's game or a TV show relieves tension and clears the mind. Talking to co-workers about families and interests helps develop a rapport that transfers into better business relations.

At what point the time spent in conversing becomes counterproductive is hard to determine. Use your best judgment. It is not a good idea, even if it were possible, to say: "You may not spend more than X minutes a day chatting." If any one person or group of people is not performing up to your expectations because of excess chatting, talk to each one. Suggest that the employee may not realize how much of his or her workday is spent in this nonproductive activity. Monitor "chatting time" and if it does not decrease, take a firmer stand.

10-39   As team facilitator, how can I encourage group members to share information more easily?

If your group is small, promote informal discussions. Let people feel free to meet frequently to share ideas. In larger groups, set up regular idea-sharing meetings. Encourage members of the group to lunch together and kick around ideas in that informal atmosphere. Make it easy to bypass channels of communication to facilitate sharing ideas within the department.

10-40   One of the supervisors in my organization is very domineering. His attempts to overpower and manipulate the rest of us has caused dissension within the supervisory group. The big boss thinks this man is great. How can I deal with him?

Often domineering people do influence the boss into think-ing that they are indispensable. The boss stands by them because he or she has been manipulated into believing that doing so is in the best interest of the organization.

It is futile to attack the dominator. Not only will you fail, but you may do your career serious and lasting damage. The only way to handle it is one situation at a time. When a matter in which you are involved is under discussion, stand up against the dominator by using logical point-by-point refutations. Never attack the person; discuss the ideas. Although there is no assur-ance that your boss will agree with you, you have a much greater chance of making your point. If the other supervisors follow your lead, the domineering manager's influence will wane and the boss's attitude toward him may change.

10-41   What is the best way of handling jealousies among my people? If I give an especially desirable assignment to one, some of the others are envious.

Your employees will be less jealous if you avoid giving desir-able assignments to the same people all the time—even if those people are the best suited for that work. There are times when it is necessary to give specific work to specific people. In such cases of apparent favoritism, let the envious ones know that the "favored" ones had the background and skills needed for that par-ticular job. Encourage them to develop similar skills so they can share in that type of work in the future.

10-42   The four people in my department depend too much on me to organize and work out their projects step by step. How can I get them to take more initiative, both individually and as a group, and to work more participatively?

People who are not accustomed to working things out for themselves will not take the initiative. They expect everything to be laid out, and then they will do just what they are told.

For the first assignment, choose a job which is relatively uncomplicated and one for which people have the necessary know-how. Sit down with the assignee(s) and elicit suggestions on how the job should be done. Answer their questions with "How do you think it should be done?" Force them to make the decisions. Praise good ideas and ask questions about weaker ideas to help people reflect and come up with better answers. Once your employees get into the habit of working participative-ly, they will take the initiative in future assignments.

Of course, some people simply do not like to participate; they prefer to have things worked out for them. Most are good workers once they are told what to do. By working patiently with them, you can help build their self-confidence so they feel more comfortable in a participative environment. If this does not succeed, you will have to go along with the way they work best: by spelling out their assignments for them.

10-43   Mavis and Mabel are constantly arguing on how work should be done. Mabel wants to keep doing things the way she has for years. Mavis is open to newer, untried ideas. How should I handle these constant conflicts?

Some people who have been doing work in a certain way for many years find it difficult to change. Others, even with a depth of experience, enjoy seeking out the new and untried. As the person in the middle, you want to keep both workers happy and productive. Let them know that you respect them and that each can contribute good ideas to the department. Sometimes doing the job the old way is just as effective as using a different technique. Change for the sake of change is not productive. In such cases, go along with Mabel. Where there would be a significant improvement by using Mavis's approach, accept that. In each case, let the other know why you made the decision and praise each one for her input.

10-44   My three colleagues and I work in a different building from our boss. Because of the separation of our facilities, ours is a relatively unsupervised unit. Since we are all experienced professionals, this should not be a problem— except for one thing. One of our colleagues does not do his fair share of the work. He spends several hours each day talking on the telephone or using the computer to take care of a personal business. Often he ignores our unit's work to the point that the rest of us cannot finish important assignments on time. We don't want to tattle to the boss, but it has gotten out of hand. What should we do?

What this man is doing is more than goofing off. He is stealing company time and equipment for his own use. This is unfair not only to you and your boss, but to the company. You should report his actions to your boss. The reason the boss leaves you alone is that she or he trusts you. Your colleague has violated that trust, and if you do not report it you are equally guilty.

If, for some reason, you do not want to go to the boss immediately, use peer pressure. Let your co-worker know that you and your associates do not appreciate what he is doing and that you will not continue to do his work for him. Your colleague may not realize your dissatisfaction and may even think that you admire his ability to beat the company, assuming that you share his "them versus us" attitude. Your warning offers him a chance to straighten himself out. If the behavior continues after your discussion, you have no alternative but to report it.

10-45   What is the best way to supervise a diverse age group? My people range in age from 25 to 75.

Ignore the age factor. Think of people as the total of their personalities. You will find that mixed age groups can be very effective. The young learn from the old; the older pick up some of the enthusiasm of the young. Specific problems between workers may develop, but treat them as conflicts of personality, not age.

10-46   Ray's constant gossiping is causing problems within my department. He always finds some "juicy tidbit" to talk about.

Gossip can be very disturbing, especially when the person gossiped about must work with the person spreading the word. Speak to Ray and let him know that you will not tolerate lies (which include half-truths) about others. Enforce your position by reprimanding him if he continues his gossiping.

One company busybody noticed a man from one department talking for a long time with a woman from another section. The gossiper immediately assumed they were a "couple" and spread the word around the company. Both of these people were married, and when the rumor that they were having a relationship reached their spouses, complications ensued. The woman involved sued the gossiper for defamation of character. A settlement was reached in which the offender publicly apologized to the man and woman.

Tell this story to Ray, your gossiper. It may deter him from spreading "juicy tidbits."

10-47   Denise is one of those overbearing people who dwells on trivial aspects of everything she does. She'll waste my time and the time of others on some insignificant detail. I've discussed this with her and at times have gruffly told her to keep quiet. It hasn't done any good. What should I do?

Denise is seeking notice. By bringing up petty details, she forces you and others to pay attention. Even reprimanding or telling her to be quiet demonstrates that you are aware of her. People like Denise need positive reinforcement for the good things they do. If they get enough attention from you in this way, their need to annoy you and others becomes less pressing.

10-48   Anthony is a religious zealot. He is dedicated to saving the souls of all of us. He plagues us with tracts and annoys my people with his proselytizing. I'm afraid that if I speak to him about it, I'll be violating his civil rights protection. What can I do?

The civil rights laws protect an employee from discrimination because of religion, but this protection does not imply that a person can use work time to preach. Tell Anthony that he must restrict his religious discussions to off-work hours. Also let him know that others have the rights to their religious beliefs, and compelling them to listen to his beliefs on the job violates their religious rights. As for the tracts, if the company does not permit distribution of nonjob-related material in the facility (e.g., advertisements, political pamphlets), the distribution of religious material can also be banned. It must be treated in the same way as any other printed matter that is not generated by the company.

Absenteeism and Tardiness

10-49   Absenteeism has plagued my company forever. Has any organization found a way to deal with this, short of firing the absentees and starting over with better people?

In every organization, people do get sick, have personal matters that must be attended to, or just feel like they need a day off. Absenteeism is one of the most chronic and expensive problems that companies face. It costs loss of productivity, breakdown of programs, failure to meet deadlines, and dissatisfaction of customers.

Companies have tried everything to deal with the problem. Most companies enforce their absentee program with some form of punishment. If employees are absent more than a certain number of days over a specified period of time, they are suspended; if absences continue, eventually they are fired. Does this policy work? At best, it deters some people from staying home for trivial reasons when they are on the verge of being fired, but as soon as the time period is over, they start again. In the long run, punishment doesn't work. When you fire somebody you may lose an otherwise good worker, and there's no guarantee that the replacement will have a better attendance record.

10-50   My company is considering a program to reward people who do not take time off. Does this work?

It helps somewhat but still does not solve the problem. Invariably, the people who win attendance awards are those who would have been there anyway. The chronic offenders are still absent.

10-51   So why bother with reward programs if they don't help?

They do help a little. Their main value is with marginal types of workers—those who, before the reward system, would get up in the morning, sneeze, and think: "I've got a cold. Better stay home." Now such people go to work anyway. Rewards reduce absenteeism somewhat, but they are not a panacea. There is no one way to curtail absenteeism because there is no one cause of it. It must be approached differently with each person. Various techniques are explored in answer to later questions in this section.

10-52   One of my people has been absent far more than I consider reasonable. She has an excellent excuse each time. How can I find out the truth?

People who have sporadic attendance records usually do have good excuses. Their car broke down; they had to appear in court; the IRS is auditing them. All logical and possible, but often not true. Companies should have specific policies on how much absenteeism will be tolerated. Guidelines as to acceptable reasons should be published, and written proof or other verification should be required.

10-53   Gary just doesn't take care of himself. His "run-down" condition leads to frequent illness and, of course, absenteeism. How can I help him?

It is unlikely that you can help Gary. Only Gary can help Gary. All you can do is provide some guidance. If your company has a wellness program, encourage him to participate. If he refuses to take basic steps to keep himself healthy, your only recourse is to take whatever disciplinary action your company dictates to curtail excessive absenteeism.

10-54   I've heard about wellness programs. What do they involve, and do they really work?

Wellness programs are formal or semiformal attempts by companies to keep their people healthy. Such programs vary considerably. Some organizations distribute pamphlets and newsletters on health matters; others provide seminars and workshops to help people stop smoking or lose weight; still others build gyms or exercise rooms for their people or pay for their membership in a health club. The most comprehensive programs include an annual or biennial medical examination, followed by a conference between the employee and a physician or a nurse. At the conference, the results of the exam are discussed and recommendations are made concerning any medical problems that were discovered.

Such programs are expensive, but companies have found them to be cost-effective. Healthy people have better attendance records and are more alert on the job than less fit employees. Since health-care insurance is one of the fastest-growing costs in America today, keeping people healthy can lower that expense.

10-55   Mike drives a fork-lift truck in our warehouse. He is a 28-year-old bachelor whose lifestyle is beginning to interfere with his work. He stays out late most nights and comes to work groggy and sometimes hung over. He's made careless errors in his work, and twice he just barely missed having serious accidents with his truck. When I suggested that he change his lifestyle, he said that what he does on his own time is none of my business. What other approach can I take?

Unless Mike is alert in a job like his, he may injure himself or other people. You must have a serious discussion with him. Let him know that what he does on his own time is his business, but when it begins to affect his work, it is your business. Tell him that you will send him home unless you feel he is physically and mentally alert. Adhere strictly to this policy. If he does not improve, let him go. You cannot take risks with the safety of your people.

10-56   Marilyn is a good worker, but she has a sick mother and is often absent because she must accompany her mother to the doctor or take care of her other needs. Is there any way I can deal with this excessive absenteeism?

In most companies, people who are absent for reasons other than their own illness are not paid for the days they take off. Some companies allow such absences to be charged to personal or vacation time. However, the loss of pay or vacation time will not reduce Marilyn's absences, because her obligation to her mother is more important to her than the lost pay.

If Marilyn's mother is seriously ill, you may suggest that Marilyn take an unpaid leave of absence for a period of time to care for her mother. Under the Family and Medical Leave Act of 1993, companies with 50 or more employees must give this option to employees for a maximum of 12 weeks.

If, however, this is a situation which may last for years, a leave of absence won't solve the problem. Suggest to Marilyn that there are services that transport chronically ill people to doctor's appointments, shop for the housebound, and perform other chores. She can locate such organizations through community services in her mother's area. Although there are times when the mother will need Marilyn's personal attention, many of the routine matters could be handled through such services.

10-57 How do I handle a staff of people who are always requesting time off? Sometimes they call in at the last minute. It seems to me that they feel everything else in their lives is more important than the job.

Establish and strictly enforce a rule that all requests for time off be made several days in advance. In this way you can set up your schedules with some knowledge of who will not be there. You are not obligated to grant time off just because it is requested. If people have taken too much time off, tell them that you cannot spare them. Discuss why people need the time off and find out if they could handle the matter on their own time or at a more convenient time for the department.

Of course, there will still be times when people call in the morning, not to ask you for permission, but to tell you that they will not be in. If this happens more than once or twice, speak to each offender. Reiterate the importance of regular attendance. Make sure that people understand the effect of their absence on the department and on their co-workers. Let them know that unless a real emergency occurs or arrangements have been made in advance, you expect them to report to work.

10-58 Most of my no-shows are on Monday or Friday. How can I reduce absenteeism on those days?

Extending the weekend is a common occurrence. The problem is exacerbated when there is a Monday holiday and people stretch the weekend into a 4- or 5-day vacation. Some companies penalize employees for such absences by creating strict rules based on points or demerits. For example, absences on Tuesday, Wednesday, or Thursday rate 1 point; Friday or Monday absences rate 2 points; absences after a holiday rate 3 points. Absences may be excused for verified medical reasons.

10-59   Absences are serious, but tardiness is annoying. In every company, some people just can't seem to get to work on time. My people work as a group. If one is late, it affects the work of all. How can I get them in on time?

On assembly-line or other activities in which the entire operation is held up by one person's lateness, it is essential that each employee be indoctrinated from the beginning with the importance of being on time. Have workers who live near new employees talk to them about the best routes for getting to work, traffic patterns, and the optimum time to leave for work to ensure promptness. Reinforce these discussions by talking with latecomers at their very first lateness. Enforce the rules if subsequent lateness occurs.

10-60   I've heard about flextime. How does it work and does it reduce tardiness?

Flexible hours have helped reduce tardiness in many organizations. Although there are many variations, a typical flextime program requires that all employees be on duty during the "core" or busy business hours. The starting time and, therefore, the quitting time varies.

Before Sandro's company went on flextime, his hours were 8 to 4. Sandro has two children in elementary school, and he felt uncomfortable leaving the house in the morning without seeing the children safely on the school bus. If the bus was on time, Sandro was on time; if it was late, he was late.

After the company went on flextime. Sandro was given the choice of working from 7:30 to 3:30; 8 to 4; 8:30 to 4:30; or 9 to 5. He chose 8:30 to 4:30. This solved Sandro's tardiness problem, because it's unlikely that the school bus would be more than half an hour late.

Flextime is not applicable to many situations. A prime example is assembly-line or group activities in which it is essential that everybody start together.

10-61 If some of my people come in early and others later, how can I supervise those who are there before or after my hours?

One of the real problems in flextime is the role of the supervisor. The supervisor is not expected to work all the hours that the department is open. You must feel confident that the early birds and late stayers can be trusted to work effectively without your presence. Controls can be designed to help you, but unless your people are truly committed to their work, flextime will not be successful.

10-62 Joanne is one of my best computer operators. She accomplishes more work than any of the others. Joanne is also a single parent with two children. The 4-year-old has to be brought to a day-care center and the baby to a sitter before Joanne can get to work. There is no way she can do this and be here at 8:30, our starting time. She has asked to be allowed to take a short lunch break instead of the full hour to make up the time. We do not work on flextime. Can I do this?

Anytime you make an exception to a rule, you set a precedent that others may want to follow. "If Joanne can come in at 9 and take half an hour for lunch, why can't I?" To avoid this complication, before you make the decision, discuss the situation with all the other people in the group. Remind them of Joanne's circumstances. Point out that Joanne is a good worker, liked by everyone. In order to accommodate to the situation, it would be nice to allow Joanne to come in later and make up the time at lunch. The change is not going to inconvenience anyone, but it must be understood that this is a special ruling for a special situation and should not be considered a precedent. Let people know that unless *they* agree, Joanne's lateness cannot continue, and she will have to resign. By making the decision a group decision, you will prevent potential problems.

10-63 When we started at 8 a.m., Ashim frequently came in about 15 minutes late. When I asked him why he was late, he usually said, "I just couldn't get up this morning." Recently we went on flextime. Ashim chose the latest starting time, 9 a.m., and I figured that would cure his lateness. It didn't. Now he comes in at 9:15. What should I do?

The reason for Ashim's lateness is not that he can't get up in the morning. That is only a symptom. To solve any problem, you first have to find the real cause; you must go beyond the symptoms. What you need to know is why Ashim can't get up. Maybe he has another job; maybe he carouses all night; maybe he hates this job; maybe he hates you. Unless you know the critical factor, you cannot solve a problem. With tardiness there is no universal critical factor; therefore, there is no universal solution. Flextime is great and works in many cases, such as with Sandro (see question 10-60). Ashim may need counseling to work out what is bothering him. Only then you can grapple with the tardiness.

10-64   I have spoken to Diane several times about her tardiness. After each discussion, she promises to be on time and keeps her promise for several months, but eventually reverts to her old habits. How can I keep this from happening over and over again?

Don't wait until Diane is late again to talk to her. Periodically congratulate her on her record of promptness. By giving her this reinforcement for being on time, she will be encouraged to keep up the good record.

10-65   My people punch the time clock when they come in or go out. The department is so set up that I do not have direct contact with all my people all the time. I know that some latecomers have friends punch them in and early leavers have friends punch them out. This is against regulations, but unless I actually see it happening, I have no proof. What can I do?

Make sure that everybody is aware of this rule, and of what the penalty is. Often when companies do not enforce a rule, people assume that either the rule is obsolete or nobody really cares. Put up posters and cartoons to remind people of the rule. To show that you mean business, periodically monitor the time clock. When the boss is standing there, nobody is going to punch somebody else's card. Give formal warnings to violators: both the worker who punched the card and the person whose card was punched.

10-66   When should I speak to an employee after a lateness or absence?

Immediately. When the employee reports in late or after an absence, hold an immediate conference. Bring the offender into a private place and discuss the matter. If it is a first or second offense, sell the employee on the importance of on-time attendance. Get a commitment to be there and/or on time in the future.

If the person has a previous record of lateness or absences, have the data with you so you can give specific dates and times. Let the person know how seriously you take the matter and what will happen if the work pattern continues.

10-67   What about excuses? All employees have excuses.

Listen to them. Sometimes people do have acceptable excuses. You and your employees must have the same understanding of what is acceptable. Even if the excuse is ridiculous, you must listen to it. Psychologists have shown that when people are preoccupied by something—this latercomer's excuse, another employee's gripe, or a customer's complaint—they will not absorb anything you say until it is out of their system. So let them talk. Once their mind is clear, they will listen and you can make the point that it is important that they be on time.

10-68   Yvonne is a very conscientious worker. She comes to work no matter how sick she feels. One day she was so sick that she had to lie down for an hour. Would I have been within my rights to have sent her home when she reported in such a condition?

It is commendable that she does not want to miss work. However, an ill person cannot perform optimally and by coming to work she may exacerbate her illness. Tell her that by going home now and taking care of herself, she might avoid missing several day's work if she becomes even sicker. Also sick people may carry contagious illness into the workplace. Let her know that you appreciate her wanting to work, but it is better for her and the company for her to take care of herself.

10-69   Our sick leave policy provides 10 sick days a year. If it is not used by the end of the year, it is lost. Many of our people look upon sick leave as an entitlement. In November and December we have a lot of people calling in sick just to use up their time. I know they are not sick. What can I do?

Sick leave is for illness. Make sure that your people know it is not an entitlement. When they return to work after a "late-year illness," and it is obvious they have made a miraculous recovery, confront them. Tell them that what they are doing is not fair to the company and to their co-workers, who must take over their work. If they protest that they were really sick, don't argue. The message has been sent, and they will think of your words next time they want to use sick days.

A better way of avoiding this type of problem is to allow sick days to accrue over the years. In this way, if employees are really sick and have to take a long absence, they will be paid for a much longer period. Some companies reward people who do not take all their sick days over a period of years by converting unused sick days to vacation time.

10-70   At my company, if a latecomer punches in even 1 minute late, the card prints the time in red ink. All lateness results in docking pay in 15-minute increments. Is this fair to people who are barely late?

If this policy has been publicized and enforced, employees should expect it. It is not feasible to adjust pay records on a minute-to-minute basis. Docking pay for lateness is one way to get people to make an effort to be there on time.

Work Habits

10-71   Housekeeping is important in the work we do. Not only does it make our workplace more attractive, but when things are neat and in order the work flows more smoothly. Despite my nagging about keeping the place tidy, some of my people just don't clean up. What can I do?

What is clean and neat to one person may be sloppy to another. Make sure that your people know just what is expected of them: putting tools or papers in the proper places, removing waste, sweeping or dusting, and so on. If you cannot be there at closing time, assign one of your people to be responsible for the housekeeping. You can rotate that assignment each week. Praise people when the place looks good. Instead of nagging when housekeeping is not satisfactory, make suggestions as to how it could be improved.

10-72   Some of my employees use poor language, including four-letter expletives. This creates a poor impression with

visitors and customers. How can I control inappropriate language?

Not only is street language not appropriate in a business setting, but it can be offensive to co-workers and cause sexual harassment complaints. (See question 37 in Chapter 3.) Explain to your people that offensive language is just not acceptable in the workplace. Caution them that they can be disciplined if it continues. Some supervisors make a game out of "cussing" by fining employees a small amount each time they use an expletive. The money collected goes toward some group activity such as a dinner, a sports event, or movie.

10-73   Some people in my department dress for work as if they were going on a picnic. Can I insist that they dress appropriately?

Dress codes are legal in the workplace. (See question 51 in Chapter 3.) You can require that your people dress in a manner appropriate to the work that they do. It is unrealistic to require workers in the factory or warehouse to wear the same type of clothes as office workers. Let your people know what is and is not acceptable. Speak to those who violate the code and send repeat offenders home to change rather than allow them to work in improper attire.

10-74   My former company had a written dress code. My current organization has nothing in writing, but expects people to dress properly. How can I enforce such a vague rule?

If your people dress in what you believe is not a businesslike manner, speak to them about it. Have an informal talk about what is and is not acceptable in the workplace. Comment on how nice a co-worker looks and use her or him as a model. *A brief caution:* Keep in mind age differences. Young people do dress differently from more mature people, so select models who are in the same age group as the offenders.

Some companies bring in fashion consultants to talk with employees on this subject. Videos, books, and articles on business dress can be used to reinforce the program.

10-75   Jan-Sin is a wonderful person, does her job really well, can be depended upon, is very knowledgeable, and will go over and beyond her responsibilities. The problem is that

she is "messy"—so messy that she irritates the other people who work in the same office with her. Her desk is in frightful disarray. Even when others try to help her, they cannot, because no one can figure out what she is doing in all that mess! Any suggestions?

There are many people like Jan-Sin. They have their own system, and what appears to be chaos to others is clear to them. Ask them for a specific file, and they'll put their hand on one of the piles of papers around the desk and pull it out. But nobody else can ever find anything, and it is unpleasant to have to work around such people.

Employees with long-established work habits find it hard to change. Because Jan-Sin is a conscientious worker, she may be willing to take some steps to alleviate the situation. Suggest that she keep only items on which she is currently working on her desk; all others must be returned to the files. Help her develop the habit of having a place for everything and keeping things in their proper place. It takes a lot of patience and effort to turn a messy person into a neat one.

10-76   Craig is my best technical employee, but he has terrible interpersonal skills. How can I best use his talents?

Many technical jobs require minimum contact with others. If you have such jobs, assign Craig to that work. He may be more valuable to the organization sitting all day at the computer or working in a laboratory than supervising others or dealing with customers.

Interpersonal skills can be acquired if a person really wants to do so. Craig may not be conscious of how he comes across to others. Many technical people are so absorbed in their work that they are unaware of their lack of interpersonal skills. The Dale Carnegie program and other courses in interpersonal relations have helped many people improve their skills.

10-77   Anne, one of my file clerks, is more concerned with her hair, fingernails, and personal life than her job. She has fallen way behind with her work. I have talked to her and made suggestions. Recently I gave her a schedule of priorities (what to do in the morning and what to do in the afternoon). She doesn't follow it. I talked to her again but it seems impossible. How can I get her to change her ways?

You have been very patient. Some people do not take their jobs seriously. They probably were the same way in school. Give Anne one more chance. Tell her that if she wants to keep her job she must meet the performance standards. You have tried to help her meet them by giving her suggestions and a schedule. Give her 30 days to improve. People like Anne need to have the consequences spelled out for them. If she fails to comply, let her go.

10-78   Clyde is a good worker and a likable fellow. However, he has to be constantly reminded to return tools and equipment when he has finished with them and to pick up from the tool room the items he needs for his next assignment. This has slowed down the work of the department and has frustrated me. Any suggestions?

In giving Clyde assignments, make up a checklist of all the items he will need. Tell him he must check each item on the list to make sure he has it before reporting to the workplace. Require him to check it again when the item is returned. Go over the list with him each day until the check system has become ingrained as a work habit. In time, it will no longer be needed.

10-79   I'd love to give more responsible work to Ramon, but he repeatedly forgets to do things that he has agreed to do. What can I do to help Ramon remember?

When you and Ramon have completed your discussion of his assignment, ask him to write out what the various phases of the work are and when he believes each phase will be completed. Check his progress from time to time to see if he is on track. By having a written reference, he is less likely to neglect a phase.

10-80   We have had several complaints from customers about one of our salesclerks. They say she is abrupt and sometimes discourteous. I've talked to her about this and she just denies that it is true. How else can I approach her?

If you had only one complaint, it could have been unjustified, but several indicate a real problem. Let her know the specifics of the complaints. Instead of saying "You were rude," tell her exactly what the customer reported. People often do not realize that they are discourteous. Under pressure to expedite an order, they do not think of the effect on the customer. This is not an excuse. The survival of a company depends on customer satisfaction.

All people who deal with customers in person or on the telephone should be thoroughly trained in customer relations. The training should be reinforced by periodic refresher programs. Whenever someone is cited for discourtesy, the supervisor should counsel the person directly. Repetition of the offense should lead to disciplinary action and, if necessary, termination.

10-81   There's a busybody in my department who eavesdrops on telephone conversations and comments on the matter being discussed, even though it does not concern her. She will stand near my desk when I am conversing with somebody and interrupt with her views. How do I make her understand that this is not acceptable?

Your busybody has taken the concept of belongingness too far. She feels that as part of the department, she should know everything that goes on and that her views should be expressed. Let her know that you appreciate her interest in the activities of the department, but that there are many aspects of the work which are not part of her job. Tell her that listening to other people's conversations not only is impolite but distracts them from their work. The next time she stands by your desk when you are talking to somebody, stop and ask her what she wants. Unless it is an emergency, suggest that she come back later to discuss the matter with you.

10-82   I supervise a former co-worker who at one time was a top performer. Now he is burned out. He is apathetic, procrastinates, and ignores direct orders. Whenever I approach him, he becomes defensive. How can I help?

Have a serious discussion with him. Let him know that although you are now his supervisor, you are still his friend. Tell him how the company appreciates all the good work he has done in the past and that you and higher management feel he has much that he can still contribute. Suggest that he seek counseling (through your employee assistance program, if you have one) to help him past his current state.

In addition, help him overcome his procrastination and other immediate problems by working with him to get him started and to redevelop work habits that had previously made him a valuable employee. Be patient. Work with him to help him reestablish himself. If all your efforts fail, you will have to either terminate his employment or live with his attitude until he retires.

11

The Supervisor As a Counselor

Effective supervisors spend a good deal of their time in counseling their people. When a problem develops with one or several employees, it is the responsibility of the supervisor to straighten it out with minimum loss of productivity and with maximum satisfaction of the people involved.

In this chapter we will look at several aspects of the counseling function:

- Conflict resolution among employees
- Formal grievances
- Gripes and gripers
- Techniques of counseling

Conflict Resolution

11-1 I am a believer in participation. When I give my people an assignment, I expect them to work out the manner in which it will be accomplished. What do I do when they disagree on how to proceed?

You can either mediate or arbitrate. In mediation, the manager listens to both parties and tries to help them reach a meeting of the minds. In arbitration, the manager makes the decision as to what course to follow.

11-2   Which is better?

Both approaches have their advantages and limitations. Arbitration takes less time—and time may be important. But the third-party decision may not please either side. The manager probably has the experience and expertise to make the decision, but unless both parties accept it, they will not be committed to its achievement.

Mediation is time-consuming, but if done properly it results in both sides agreeing and committing themselves to a course of action.

11-3   How does one go about mediating a dispute?

The first step is for the mediator, who is usually the supervisor over both of the disputants, to explain the rules that will be followed. Unless these rules are understood, the process will not work. Let's look in on a mediation session to see what transpires. The supervisor, Mike, is mediating a dispute between Gary and Diane.

> MIKE: OK. As I understand it, we all agree that the new system is good. The disagreement is on how to start it. Gary, what is your opinion?
>
> GARY: This is too complicated for our people to master in one fell swoop. I think we should phase the system in gradually over the next 3 months. We can train one segment at a time and when that part is mastered, start implementing it right away. By the end of the 90 days, everyone will be fully trained and using the new system.
>
> MIKE: Now, Diane, tell me what Gary's plan is as you see it.

Note that Mike did not ask Diane to rebut Gary's plan, but to restate it. This is the first rule of conflict resolution: Have each person restate what the other has said to be sure both parties are talking about the same thing. Because Diane is aware this will be asked of her, she must listen carefully to Gary. Typically, people who have strong feelings about something do not listen. They are so busy planning a rebuttal that they don't give full attention to what the other side is saying.

DIANE: Gary wants to phase the project in over 3 months and train along the way. He doesn't think our people are smart enough to learn the process any faster.

GARY: That's not what I said. The people are smart; the new system has many complicated procedures which need to be mastered in smaller segments, then applied on the job before the next segment is taught.

MIKE: Before discussing this point, let's hear what Diane's idea is.

DIANE: I think we should set a date—say, 60 days from today—and institute the system then. We can train our people during the 60 days so they can all step into the new system at the same time.

GARY: Diane wants to train our people while they are using the current system, then change to the new system before any of the work has been actually tried on the job.

MIKE: Diane?

DIANE: That's more or less what I said, but there's more to it. For one, some of the work is not too different from what we are doing now.

Now both parties can discuss the arguments for an against each plan. After they do so, Mike summarizes:

MIKE: OK. Now lets list the areas where you both agree so we won't waste time rehashing them. Both of you agree that the training plan is basically satisfactory?

BOTH: Right.

MIKE: Both of you agree that phases 1 through 5 can be taught while the people are still using the current system?

BOTH: Yes.

MIKE: Now let's examine the areas where you don't agree.

In most disputes, there are more areas of agreement than disagreement. By listing these items on a flipchart or pad, the mediator can rapidly dispose of areas of agreement and focus the parties on those matters which must be resolved. Mike will guide Gary and Diane through these points and they will iron them out and reach agreement.

11-4 Mediation can take forever. Is it a good idea to set time limits?

Yes. If all points are not settled by the end of the first meeting, call another session. Encourage the parties to discuss the issues between themselves. They may resolve key items before the next meeting. The amount of time devoted to mediating any one disagreement depends on the urgency of the situation and the time demands of the manager and each of the participants. After every effort is made to mediate in the scheduled time frame, there may still be items on which agreement has not been reached. In this case, the mediator will have to arbitrate and make the decision alone.

11-5   What is the best way to arbitrate?

Here are five steps to follow in arbitrating a conflict:

1. Get the facts—all the facts. Listen to both sides carefully. Make sure you understand each point of view. Investigate on your own to get additional information. Don't limit yourself to the "hard facts." Learn about underlying feelings and emotions: how the situation affects the morale of the people, their perceptions of fairness, and the long-term effects.

2. Evaluate the facts. Make a careful analysis of all aspects of the problem. Weigh them. What are the ramifications of the decision—on other people, other projects, other departments?

3. Study the alternatives. Are the solutions suggested by the disputants the only possible choices? Can compromises be made? Is a totally different resolution possible?

4. Make the decision that you believe is best.

5. Communicate the decision to the disputants. Make sure they fully understand it. If necessary, "sell" it to them so they will agree and be committed to implementing it.

Do not let arbitration deteriorate into a win-lose situation. The person whose idea you accepted may gloat; the other person may feel he or she is a loser. Point out that both positions were well thought out. Give the reasons you made the decision. Try to get full agreement and commitment from both sides. If the decision is a compromise, neither party may be happy. Demonstrate how this decision will benefit both sides. Use the worksheet in Figure 11-1 as a guide.

11-6   When I am the one having a conflict with another person—say, the manager of another department—what can I do to prepare for the mediation or arbitration session?

Conflict Resolution Worksheet

THE PROBLEM

_____

_____

_____

_____

Employee 1 _____

His/her view _____

_____

_____

Employee 2 _____

His/her view _____

_____

_____

Areas of agreement _____

_____

_____

_____

Areas of disagreement _____

_____

_____

_____

RESULTS OF INVESTIGATION

The facts _____

_____

_____

Figure 11-1

Figure 11-1 (Continued)

Do you have all the pertinent records? _____

Have you made a personal investigation? _____

Do you understand the implications for: _____

    both parties to the dispute? _____

    other people? _____

    the organization? _____

Your analysis of the facts _____

_____

_____

_____

Possible solutions _____

_____

_____

_____

_____

_____

_____

Have you stretched to seek the nonobvious solutions? _____

Possible compromises _____

_____

_____

_____

_____

Have you considered all sides of the situation? _____

Have you considered the ramifications of your
decision on all concerned? _____

(Continued)

Figure 11-1 (Continued)

YOUR DECISION

_____

_____

_____

_____

_____

_____

_____

_____

Have you communicated the decision to
the disputants?   _____

Do they fully understand it?   _____

Do they accept it?   _____

Have you explained how both parties
gain by your decision?   _____

Have you obtained their commitment
to comply?   _____

Assemble all the facts that pertain to the case. Determine what both you and your opponent want to accomplish. Try to anticipate how he or she sees the situation and how that viewpoint differs from yours. Where do you agree? Disagree? What compromises are you willing to make? What compromises do you think will be amenable to your opponent? Arm yourself with facts, ideas, and positive suggestions. Avoid accusations, complaints, and recriminations.

11-7 Sometimes conflicts arise within my department that are not based on logical disagreements. People just don't get along with one another. How do I deal with "feelings"?

Determine why people don't get along. Is the conflict due to a specific situation or to an unspecified dislike? If it is specific, try to resolve it. If it stems from some previous real or perceived misunderstanding, seek out the root of the problem. Often this is not possible, since the dislike is based on intangibles. (See question 32 in Chapter 10.)

There are no magic formulas which will solve this type of problem. When two people dislike each other, it is difficult to get them to suddenly become friends. Insist that they put their personal feelings aside and get the work done.

11-8   Does it ever pay to force a confrontation? Sometimes I just want to say: "Either you two folks work together or I'll fire you both."

If all efforts fail, a dogmatic approach may be in order: "I will no longer tolerate this kind of behavior." However, such a dictum is not easy to enforce—particularly when dealing with long-time employees or union members. Use every other means of resolving conflicts before resorting to confrontation.

11-9   We have no team spirit in my department. There is constant bickering. How do I prevent flare-ups among my people?

This is not uncommon. Sometimes bickering is caused by hidden dislikes. One approach is to conduct a meeting on the importance of teamwork. Start with a brief warm-up and then ask everyone to write the name of each person in the group on a pad. Next to the name, each employee should state what he or she likes best about that person. Give the group plenty of time to write. Everybody must think of something nice about each of the others. Then have each person look right at the person described and read what he or she has written.

Maria might say: "Tom, when I ask you for help, no matter how busy you are, you stop and give me what I need." Since Maria has never once thanked Tom or acknowledged that his help is appreciated, Tom has looked upon her as an ungrateful pest. Now he'll feel more positive about her.

Ron might say: "Lil, when I come in in the morning, I'm grumpy. You always make me feel better by greeting me with a cheery 'good morning.'" Lil knows Ron is a grump and has never liked him. This acknowledgment makes her feel better about him.

People leave the meeting feeling good about one another, and these positive feelings carry over into the work. It's hard to dislike somebody who has just said something nice about you.

11-10   Making lists of compliments sounds fine. But suppose nobody can say anything nice about an employee?

First make sure everybody has something written down next to each name on the pad. Then pick as your first presenter an upbeat person who you know will have good things to say. His or her lead will set the stage for the rest. Often a person who has not yet found something nice to say will hitchhike on the remarks of a previous presenter.

Under no circumstances should you allow people to say what they dislike about others. This leads only to more friction.

11-11   I can see how complimenting co-workers will help immediately after the meeting. Does this exercise have any long-term value?

Like any one-time activity, it can have a lasting effect only if it is followed up. Supervisors must keep alert to the interactions of their people. When one member of the group makes a nasty remark about another, the supervisor should remind the offender of the compliment given to that person at the meeting. The reminder reinforces the effect of the meeting and clears the air, reestablishing the good will that was created.

11-12   One of my staff came to me and complained about the manner in which two other employees handled a situation. I did not witness it and have only this person's report. How should I respond?

Since the information may or may not be correct, you have to investigate it before you take any action. It could be based on incorrect information or a personal vendetta. Thank the person who gave you the information and tell him or her that you will investigate. Then check it out. If the information is correct, take action. If it is baseless, diplomatically let the reporter know what you have learned.

Gripes and Grievances

11-13   There are rarely any grievances in our company. Since we have over 1000 employees, isn't this unusual?

A low grievance rate may not be as good an indicator of morale as it appears on the surface. In any large organization there cannot help but be misunderstandings, dissatisfactions, and just plain gripes. The fact that no grievances are called to management's attention does not necessarily mean that there are none. It may mean that it is difficult for an employee to bring grievances to the attention of management.

11-14   Should companies establish a formal procedure to handle grievances?

Grievances and gripes which cannot be uncovered and treated fester in the minds of the aggrieved. This may manifest itself in poor work, purposeful slowing down on the job, absenteeism, and high turnover. It could lead to unionization and organized employee antagonism. Some means should be provided for employees to bring grievances to the attention of the person in the organization who has the authority to correct them.

11-15   Grievance procedures are usually set forth in a union contract. The ones I have studied seem so complicated and legalistic. Can you suggest a simple, systematic grievance procedure for a nonunionized organization?

Here is a simple four-step procedure:

1. The aggrieved individual discusses the problem with the immediate supervisor. Every attempt should be made to resolve the problem at this level. Most grievances have a basis in fact and can be resolved either by correcting an inequitable situation or by logically explaining to the complainant why the problem exists and what can or cannot be done to correct it.

2. If no settlement is reached, the individual should be given the opportunity to bring the problem to the next level of management without fear of reprisal.

3. The unresolved problem is submitted to the human resources manager, the general manager, or another highly placed executive. Usually agreement is reached at this point.

4. The aggrieved party and management may submit the grievance to a mutually acceptable third party for arbitration. This step is unusual in nonunion organizations, but management may wish to have the arbitration option available when it is in the best interests of all to solve the problem. If failure to resolve a grievance could lead to litigation or the intervention of a government agency, arbitration is a better alternative than legal action.

A useful form for dealing with grievances is presented in Figure 11-2.

11-16   I have had complaints from some of my people for which there was absolutely no basis. Can I just tell them that and get the matter out of the way?

Even if there is no basis for a complaint, it should be given adequate attention and investigated to uncover all the facts. There may be facets of which you were not aware. Tell the complainant that you will investigate it—and do so. Then discuss your findings with the employee. Remember that the issue is very important to the complainant, even if it appears trivial to you. Do not ignore it or glibly pass it over by saying, "I'll take care of everything," and then forget about the incident. A broken promise is the surest way to break down the entire program of sound employee relations.

11-17   What about grievances against supervisors? Few people will bring up a complaint about their immediate supervisor if they first have to discuss it with him or her. How can this be avoided?

Every employee should have the opportunity to express such a grievance without having to discuss it with the supervisor first. If this were not possible, many important grievances might never come out in the open. In recent years there have been a number of cases in which companies did not even know about sexual harassment complaints against supervisors until they were notified by government authorities that charges had been filed. The reason: the first step required that the employee talk to the supervisor—the very person who committed the alleged offense.

When the grievance involves the immediate supervisor, the employee should be able to bring the matter to the attention of the human resources department or a designated management representative. A complete investigation should be made, and if the complaint proves to be justified, steps should be taken to correct it at once. The procedure must be carried out diplomatically, and the complainant should be protected from reprisals.

11-18   How do I handle complaints from another manager's employee about that manager?

If the complaint concerns sexual harassment, dishonesty, or some other serious matter, discuss it at once with a higher-level

Grievance Worksheet

Grievance presented by _____

Date _____

Grievance

_____

_____

_____

Report of investigation

_____   _____

_____

_____

Grievance was justified   Yes ☐   No ☐

If justified; action taken

_____

_____

_____

_____

Date reported to employee _____

Did this resolve the situation? _____

_____

_____

If not justified

Date reported to employee _____

Was employee satisfied with report? _____

Comments _____

_____

_____

Figure 11-2   *(Continued)*

Figure 11-2 (Continued)

Did you handle the matter promptly? _____

Did you report your findings promptly
to the employee involved? _____

Did you follow up to ensure that what you
said would be done was accomplished? _____

Did this action help the department? _____

What can you do to be even more effective next time a grievance is presented?

_____

_____

_____

_____

_____

_____

_____

Other Comments

_____

_____

_____

_____

manager. The situation should be investigated by somebody who is in a position to do something about it. Even if you believe it is not true, you cannot take risks that may put the company in jeopardy.

Most of the complaints you will hear about other managers are not that serious. They usually relate to "unfair" treatment by a supervisor, excessive workloads, or alleged favoritism toward others. Tell the employee that he or she should discuss the matter with the supervisor. If the employee is reluctant to do so, he or she can bring the complaint to the human resources department. Make it clear that you have no jurisdiction in this matter and there is really nothing you can do. However, if you have a good rapport with the other supervisor, you may informally alert your colleague to problems in the department, without identifying specific complainants.

11-19   How do I address salary complaints from my subordinates when salary decisions are out of my hands?

Everybody should know how salary adjustments are determined. If salary increments are limited to annual reviews, employees should not expect raises at other times. If raises are restricted to a specific percentage above current salary, this should be explained. If there is a freeze on salaries because of the economy or the company's financial condition, explain that to your people. Salary complaints and other issues involved in employee evaluations are discussed in Chapter 12.

11-20   Alberta was passed over twice for promotion by her previous supervisor. She was recently transferred (laterally) to my department. From the first day she has been griping to me and her co-workers about her "unfair treatment." What can I do to make her a productive employee?

You have to convince Alberta that she is starting with a clean slate. Tell her that what is past is over and the reasons for her failure to be promoted will not be considered by you. Any future opportunities will depend on her performance in your department. Give her added attention to get her on the right track. Praise every improvement. When she realizes that you are dealing fairly with her, she will quit griping about past "injustices" and begin to live in the present.

11-21   What can I do when an employee gets me so upset that I am afraid I will blow up and say something out of line? Is it a good idea to wait until the next day to address the problem?

Count slowly to at least 10. If this does not cool you off, walk away and when you are calm—even if it is the next day—speak to the offender.

Sometimes a problem must be addressed immediately. In such a case, restrict your comments to the problem, not the person. Discuss the repercussions of what has happened rather than demanding an explanation of why it happened.

Listen to the other person's side of the story; then concentrate on resolving the problem rather than placing blame. Get the other employee to suggest how the problem can be solved or the situation salvaged.

11-22   What if I do blow up? How can I minimize the damage?

If you do blow up, give yourself some time to recover. Go over to the employee and say something like this: "What you did yesterday upset me and I'm sorry I lost my temper. The important thing is that we both work to correct the situation and make sure that it will not recur."

11-23   One of my people holds grudges. It's been weeks since a problem he caused was solved, but he is still sulking and griping to everybody about me. What's the answer?

If this person feels that you put him down in addressing the problem, he will look upon it a personal defeat. Griping is a manifestation of this attitude.

In solving any problem, try to let the person involved feel part of the solution, not the problem. Everybody should win. It is not a case of "I win, therefore you lose." However, this man does feel that he lost and you won. To overcome his sense of defeat, show your confidence by giving him an assignment he is sure to succeed in; offer all the support you can. In time his successes will reinforce his self-esteem and he'll stop griping about you.

11-24   Trudy called me at home at 10:30 p.m. and started griping about the "unfair treatment" she was getting from me and the other bosses. I suggested this was not the proper time for a discussion and she banged down her telephone. I feel guilty about putting her off. What should I have done?

Obviously Trudy was very upset when she called and it was not a good time for a rational discussion. Had you hung up on her, it would have been wrong. Despite the hour, you might have let her talk for a while until she calmed down and then suggested you discuss it during business hours the next day. But it was she who hung up, so there is no reason for you to feel guilty. When you see her again (her own guilt may cause her to stay home the next day), have a calm, personal chat with her. Let her air her gripes and deal with them systematically. Figure 11-3 lists some guidelines.

How to Handle a Problem

1. Determine objectives. What are the company's or department's goals?

2. Get all the facts. Review the record. What specific rule has been broken? What previous offenses have been committed? What is the employee's performance record.

3. Talk with the employee. What is his or her story? Are there extenuating circumstances? Was there a logical reason for the action taken? If so, is the offense correctable? If not, what can be done to correct future offenses? Uncover opinions and feelings. Facts alone do not always give the whole picture. Often, opinions and emotional attitudes play an important role. It is not uncommon for an attitude based on incomplete information to be more influential than one based on the truth.

4. Weigh and decide.
   - Fit the facts together.
   - Consider their bearing on one another.
   - What possible actions can be taken? Try to have several alternatives to consider.
   - Check company policies and precedents.
   - Consider the objectives. Does the decision help accomplish them? What is the effect on employees? On other members of the department? On the company?

5. Take action. Company policy may specify what types of problems can be handled by the immediate supervisor, or at which point other levels of management must be consulted. If the decision is yours to make, choose the alternative that will best suit the objectives of the company and resolve the situation. Then put it into effect immediately. If other levels of management must be consulted, do it fast and try to bring the situation under control as soon as possible. Poor timing can negate the entire effect. Take action while the incident is current.

6. Check results. Follow up as soon as results can be checked. It may be necessary to check on the action several times, depending upon its complexity. Watch especially for changes in the attitudes and relationships of the employees who are affected by the decision as well as in others who work closely with them. Finally, ask yourself: "Did this action help the company and my department?"

Figure 11-3

11-25   Sonny is at best an average worker. He just about meets the performance standards for his job. Yet every time somebody gets a promotion or a transfer to a more desirable job, he gripes about favoritism and unfair treatment. He's just not good enough for promotion and not bad enough to fire. Any suggestions?

If Sonny complains about favoritism to others, review his own poor record with him. Tell him that just meeting performance standards is not sufficient grounds for promotion. Suggest that he do something about his performance to warrant a promotion in the future. Offer to help him by coaching him or training him in skills he does not have. Marginal workers like Sonny probably will not take you up on your offer. There is no way you can prevent his gripes, but because most of his co-workers know the real reason for his lack of advancement, they will pay little attention.

11-26   Thelma questions everything going on in the department—mostly behind my back. I hear about her gripes from my boss or other supervisors. Nine out of ten of the complaints are unjustified or have been taken care of. What can I do?

Your boss and co-supervisors are probably just as tired of Thelma's complaints as you are. They have learned over time that these gripes are usually not worth their time. Suggest that if Thelma comes to them with any complaint, they should refuse to listen and tell her to bring it directly to you. She probably never will go to you, since her satisfaction comes from telling other supervisors how terrible you are. If they do not listen, there is no point in making the complaints.

11-27   What do I do about a chronic complainer? This guy is always griping about something. Nothing satisfies him. He's getting on my nerves.

You'll find people like this in every company. They complain not only about their own problems but about general matters that are of no concern to them. Since they sometimes have legitimate complaints, you cannot just ignore them. You have to at least listen, and it can be annoying and time-consuming.

One way to minimize griping is to give people more attention. Some gripers are just seeking more recognition. They want to be the center of attention. By talking to your employee, asking his opinions, and praising his good work, you will give him attention and therefore less reason to gripe.

11-28 Ali looks upon himself as an "advocate." We don't have a union and Ali feels that because some of his co-workers are afraid to bring their complaints to my attention, it is his duty to do so. Although occasionally he does tell me things that I should know about, most of these gripes are trivial. How can I get him to mind his own business?

Win Ali over to your side. When he does help you straighten out a serious problem, let him know that you appreciate his calling it to your attention. Help him differentiate between time-wasting gripes and real problems. Most important, talk directly to the people who are afraid to come to you with problems. It could be that they lack trust in you. This is a signal to build up their confidence so that they will come to you with their own complaints and not have to rely on Ali. Make the need for an "advocate" unnecessary.

11-29 Leroy is the "advocate" in my department. He speaks for his "less articulate" co-workers. He may tell me that Larry is upset because he didn't get as much of a raise as he expected or that Carmen feels she is not getting a promotion because of her sex. Often this is not true. How can I tell Leroy to mind his own business?

Tell him you appreciate his calling your attention to these situations, but that you expect your people to speak for themselves. However, if you know that Larry or Carmen is really shy, his bringing their feelings to your attention can be a benefit. It will enable you to take the initiative in dealing with them before their discontent becomes more serious. People like Leroy often state their own gripes by suggesting the problem is somebody else's.

11-30 We have a union. When an employee has a complaint, what should I do to avoid having to go through the time-consuming grievance procedure?

It depends on the militancy of the union. In some situations, the union has indoctrinated its members to bring even the most trivial matters to the attention of the union steward, who then determines if it should be filed as a grievance. In other situations, the worker and supervisor may try to work it out privately before filing a grievance.

If you have a good relationship with your people, encourage them to let you know what bothers them so both they and you can resolve problems without bringing in the union. Since many workers are just as anxious as you are not to have to go through the red tape of a grievance procedure, rapid and satisfactory solutions can result. Follow the same rules that a supervisor in a nonunion environment would use to resolve the matter. (See Figure 11-3.)

11-31   What do I do when an employee has filed a grievance and I have to meet with the shop steward about it?

You should not be taken by surprise when a grievance is filed. In most cases the employee involved has let you know that he or she is going to bring a situation to the union, so you have time to prepare for it. In most companies your first contact will be the union steward, usually a worker in the department, who will try to settle the matter informally. If that does not succeed, a grievance meeting is arranged.

In preparing for such a meeting, review the union contract. All grievances must be tied into a specific contract clause. A formal grievance is defined as a contract violation. Ask yourself in what way what you are accused of doing has violated the contract. You may wish to discuss the matter beforehand with your labor relations people. In some organizations, a representative of the labor relations department accompanies the supervisor to the meeting. Make notes so you will have all statistics, work records, performance standards, and other pertinent matters at hand to respond to questions.

Let the employee or the steward state the union case fully. Don't interrupt. Answer only questions that are asked. Don't volunteer any information. Under no circumstances should you get emotional. Keep cool and don't fall prey to intimidation. At this stage the issue is a matter of negotiation, so try to resolve it in the best interests of all.

If you cannot reach agreement, the next phases will probably involve meetings between the union representative and your boss or other higher-ranking managers. At these meetings you will be a witness, not a negotiator. Follow the lead of management. It is now in company hands.

11-32   Our contract contains work rules which are keeping us from making changes that can really improve our productivity. Is there any way I can persuade the union to let us make changes?

If these work rules are written into the contract, nothing can be done without changing the contract. You will probably have to wait until a new contract is negotiated. You might make suggestions to management that such changes be brought up when the negotiations take place.

Some work rules are not in the contract, but have been agreed upon by union and management as part of their ongoing relations. Such rules may be discussed with the steward or other union representative and, if the union agrees, may be instituted immediately.

Most union contracts have a "management prerogative" clause which gives management the right to decide on any matters not specifically prohibited by the contract. In such cases, changes in methods may be instituted unilaterally. However, it is a good idea to sell the changes to the workers and the union before instituting them.

11-33   What is the best way to handle informal complaints?

Follow these four steps:

1. *Listen.*   Remember that even if the gripe appears unfounded to you, it is serious in the mind of the complainant.
2. *Investigate.*   Take nothing for granted. Look at the record. Talk to others.
3. *Report back.*   If the gripe is unfounded, explain it to the complainant. If it is substantiated, go to step 4.
4. *Take action.*   Do what must be done to correct the situation.

11-34   When I explain a decision, how specific should I be?

Mature adults like to know the basis on which decisions are made. To say "I'm the boss and this is what I decided" is equivalent to telling a child—"because I said so." Let your people know and understand the logic behind your decisions and clarify any misunderstandings before the decision is implemented.

11-35   Sometimes I am so bogged down with other matters that I can't even think about a complaint at the time it is made. After I am presented with a complaint, how fast should I make a decision?

If it is a matter on which immediate work depends, you must make the decision immediately. If the complaint is of a more general nature, you can defer decision making until you have time to give it proper attention. But don't procrastinate unnecessarily. Putting off decisions you are reluctant to make will not help the situation and may even exacerbate it.

11-36   What is the best way of preventing grievances from arising?

Generally, fair treatment and open-minded listening will prevent most problems from developing into grievances. For example:

- Let employees know how they are doing on their jobs on a regular basis. People want feedback not only on their failures but on their successes.
- Listen to suggestions and encourage employees to give them.
- Do not make promises unless you can keep them, and keep the promises you make.
- Eliminate minor irritations and trivial problems as they arise. Don't let them fester into serious dissatisfactions.
- Make a decision as soon as possible after receiving a complaint.

11-37   How do I get employees to solve their own problems?

As supervisors, we often make our people feel that we have all the answers. This leads them to believe that if they should bring their problems to us, we will handle everything. The first step in getting our people to think for themselves is to change this perception. Yes, we may have a lot of knowledge in our field, but our people also have more understanding than they give themselves credit for.

If your people bring you a problem, instead of giving them an answer (unless it is a matter that requires immediate action), throw the question back: "How do you think this should be done?" Insist that they work it out for themselves. If the problem requires background that they do not have, suggest sources that will give them the knowledge they need. If they come up with an answer to their problem with which you do not agree, do not veto it immediately. Listen to their side and question any weak points. Help them correct the course themselves. As you build up their skills, they will develop the confidence needed to make their own decisions.

11-38   How do I deal with complaints about the red tape in our organization? We are a government agency and there is nothing I can do about it.

In most highly structured organizations there are volumes of regulations that govern the way things are done. Often they are archaic and hamper efficiency. There is little you can do officially. Smart managers learn to circumvent obstructing regulations. They find ways around the red tape so the job can be accomplished. As this depends a great deal on the type of setup and the people with whom managers must interrelate, there are no guidelines to follow. Just as kids in the inner cities learn "street smarts," bureaucrats learn "organizational smarts" to help them survive and achieve their goals.

11-39   When I can do something about a gripe, I do it. But I do not have the power to resolve many of the gripes my people bring to me. I pass them on to higher management, which often either ignores or dismisses the complaints after cursory consideration. How do I keep the respect of my people when this happens?

Let the people responsible know how important it is to your people to have their complaints listened to and seriously considered. Tell them that you deal with every problem for which you have the authority, but other complaints must be dealt with elsewhere. Point out that you screen all gripes and do not pass on complaints that are not justified or do not warrant consideration. Follow up on every complaint which you channel to them and keep your people informed of the progress. If a complaint is rejected, learn the reason and pass it on to your people. They will realize that even if they do not get everything they want, at least you are taking their complaints seriously and are doing all you can within your power to see that the proper authorities are informed.

11-40   My people often gripe about company policies that I dislike as well. I can't change the policies. Is it OK to tell them, "Look I don't like it either, but it has to be done that way"?

This attitude may make you popular with your people, but not with your bosses. Supervisors are part of management and must represent management to the employees. Even if you disagree with policy, try to find out why the policy was made and explain it to your people. There may be legal or pragmatic reasons for a policy that you and your people do not clearly understand. Even if you disagree, make no comment about the subject and encourage your people to do their best under the circumstances.

Counseling

11-41   What's the difference between counseling and just talking out problems with your people?

Counseling is a means of helping troubled employees overcome the barriers to good performance on the job. Supervisors should talk with their people regularly about job-related matters. Counseling carries this one step further, as supervisors try to help workers understand and perhaps overcome personal problems.

11-42   I'm not a trained psychologist. How can I counsel my people?

A supervisor should not try to deal with people suffering from serious neuroses or psychoses. Such people need professional help. From time to time, one or more of your people may be faced with such overwhelming personal or business problems that they cannot focus on their jobs. What you are doing in your counseling role is offering them the chance to talk out their problems and perhaps decide for themselves what should be done.

11-43   What do I do if I want to help one of my people overcome serious problems?

Be an empathetic listener. Your role as a counselor is to let the employee unburden his or her problems. Encourage this by asking questions. Never criticize, argue a point, or make judgmental comments. Your job is to act as a sounding board to help release the pressures that are causing a problem. Help the employee clarify the situation so the solution will be easier for him or her to reach.

11-44   Can you provide some guidelines on how to counsel?

Listen carefully and patiently. Make no comments while the employee is talking. Use only noncommittal indicators to show that you are listening, such as nodding your head or saying "yes" and "uh-huh." Don't indicate agreement or disagreement with the employee until you have the entire story.

Never argue with the employee, no matter how unrealistic the story may sound to you. Saying something like "That's silly" may raise a barrier that destroys rapport. Listen to what is *not* being said. Often troubled people mask the real problem by talking about superficial matters. Do not suggest solutions. Help the employee clarify the situation and come to his or her own conclusions.

11-45   How do you start talking about someone's personal problems without appearing to be nosy or invading privacy?

If you and the employee have a good personal relationship, he or she will not consider you nosy. You have always shown interest in that employee as a person. All you have to do is carry this further by commenting about his or her obvious change in attitude or behavior. If you do not have this type of relationship, talk about job-related matters without being critical. For example, "This new program hasn't been as easy to implement as we expected. Has this caused any special complications for you?" Out of this discussion the personal problems may emerge. "The program is OK, but I just haven't been up to par lately."

11-46   How long should a counseling session last?

If you really get deeply into a problem, you should not have a time limit. You must be prepared to spend at least an hour with the employee. Don't just walk over to the employee and start a conversation that you know might evolve into a counseling session. You have to schedule a block of time. If the meeting must be curtailed, set a date as soon as possible for a second session. Too long a lapse between meetings may cause a loss of momentum.

11-47   To help me understand counseling better, can you demonstrate how it works?

Here is a short version of a counseling session: Joan, the supervisor, is counseling Mae, usually one of her best people, whose work has fallen off significantly. Instead of working, Mae often sits glumly at her computer gazing off into space.

> JOAN: Mae, you and I have worked together for a long time. I feel I know you very well, so it is clear to me that something is bothering you. Is there anything I can do?

Note that Joan did not comment that Mae's work was poor or that she was daydreaming on the job. Mae knows that Joan is aware of that. Joan's objective is to show concern and empathy.

MAE: No, Joan. I'm just so worried lately that I can't think straight.

JOAN: Would you like to tell me about it?

MAE: I really don't want to bother you with my personal troubles. You have enough problems running this department without having to listen to mine.

JOAN: But I really want to help you. I can't unless I know what is bothering you.

MAE: It's my mother. She has Alzheimer's disease and it has progressed to the point where she needs constant attention. My sister and I give her as much time as we can, but the doctor thinks she should be put into a nursing home. We've looked into several homes and found one that seems fine, but I feel so guilty about abandoning her.

JOAN: I can understand that. Mothers are special to all of us and we do feel an obligation to them, but sometimes we have to do what is best for them even if we don't like it. Aren't there alternatives to nursing homes?

MAE: Yes. We've looked into home care, but her need for night and day attendants and other medical assistance makes a nursing home more desirable.

JOAN: Is the nursing home you chose close by?

MAE: Yes, and there are visiting hours in the evening so I could see her after work and on weekends.

JOAN: Then you won't really be abandoning her, will you?

MAE: I guess not. I feel much better having talked to you about this. Thank you for listening.

Note that Joan did not try to convince Mae that the decision to send her mother to a nursing home was a good one. She let Mae come to her own conclusion and helped her overcome her guilt.

11-48 What are the chances of success when a supervisor counsels an employee?

Success is impossible to predict. When the employee's problem is caused by a need to clarify his or her thinking, counseling can have immediate effect. You may have to hold more than one counseling session to build a sense of trust and help the employee work out the problem. When job problems are caused by deep-seated personal factors, the counseling session may have no effect at all. It may lead to a temporary improvement followed by a regression to the poor behavior. In such cases, professional help is needed.

11-49 When is it advisable to refer an employee to a professional?

If after initial attempts to help, you realize that the problem is beyond your expertise, suggest professional counseling. Some obvious cases are alcoholism, drug addiction, medical problems, depression, deep mood swings, and serious marital or family crises. Less obvious cases are constant worriers, rebellious people, and people who don't respond to your counseling.

11-50 How can I tell people to see the company shrink without making them feel that I think they are crazy?

Never suggest that employees need psychiatric help. Avoid using the term *psychologist, psychiatrist,* or *therapist.* Tell troubled employees that they might benefit from seeing a counselor who specializes in the matters that bother them. Talk about other people you know who were helped by such professionals. If you have an employee assistance program (EAP), explain how it works. Point out that nobody else in the company will have to know they are being counseled. If you do not have such a program, suggest private sources or nonprofit services. Your company's health insurance may cover such services. If so, explain that to employees.

11-51 You've mentioned employee assistance programs several times. What exactly is an EAP?

An employee assistance program is a company-sponsored counseling service. Many organizations have instituted such programs to help their employees deal with personal problems that are interfering with their productivity. Such problems include alcoholism, marital difficulties, depression, and other psychological concerns. The counselors are not company employees but independent contractors—usually specialists who provide this service to several organizations.

Here's how an EAP works: The company promotes the availability of the service to its people through the usual communication channels. Often a hot-line telephone number is provided.

The employee who has a problem calls the hot line. After a brief screening, the employee is referred to an appropriate counselor. All contacts initiated by the employee are confidential.

In addition, supervisors are advised (and sometimes trained) to recognize when counseling may be needed and to suggest to employees that they take advantage of the service. In some instances, the company may require that the employee assistance program be used as part of a disciplinary action. (For example, an alcoholic may be given the option of using the EAP to overcome the problem or be terminated.)

Although an EAP is expensive, organizations that have had such a program in place for several years report that it pays off. The program salvages skilled and experienced people in whom the company has made a major investment over the years.

11-52   What types of professional are included in employee assistance programs or are recommended to employees when no EAP exists?

Most programs include the following specialists:

- *Medical doctors.* MDs may deal with general medical problems or specific disorders.

- *Psychiatrists.* These MDs specialize in serious psychological and emotional disorders.

- *Psychologists or psychotherapists.* These people usually have an advanced degree in psychology or social work. They work with people who have less serious emotional problems. Most of the referrals made by supervisors will be to psychologists.

- *Marriage counselors or family therapists.* These specialists deal with marital problems and difficulties with children or other family members.

- *Financial counselors.* Since many of the worries people have are about money, financial counselors can help them work out payment plans with creditors, develop budgets, and live within their incomes.

11-53   We don't have an EAP. Some of my people bring me their personal problems and seek my counseling. I'm not qualified—nor do I have the time to be involved in their personal lives. How can I stop them from coming to me with these matters?

If their work is affected by personal problems, you must take the time to listen—carefully and empathetically. Your effort may help them become better producers. Even if the problems are not affecting their work, you must at least listen. Supervisors have an obligation, even if it is time-consuming, to hear their people out.

One word of caution: Don't get emotionally involved with your people's personal problems. Listen and gently tell them that you understand why they are troubled, but that you do not have any better answers than they have. Suggest that they think the problem out or discuss it with a family friend, counselor, or religious leader.

Another caution: Don't give personal advice according to how you "read" the case. You have heard only the employee's side of the story and may not have all the facts. Uninformed advice may only make the situation worse.

11-54   How can I get my people to separate their personal worries from their business life?

You cannot. You work with the total human being, not just the job incarnation of the person. All people carry their whole being to work. There is no way they can hang their troubles on the coat rack when they report to work, forget about them, and put them back on when they leave for home. Employees carry personal baggage all the time.

By letting employees talk to you about their troubles, you may alleviate the situation temporarily. But people are still going to be worried about the sick child, the bill collector, the cheating spouse, and the day-to-day trip-ups of life.

11-55   I can understand worrying about serious matters, but some people waste time brooding about trivial problems. I'm one of those people. What should I do?

A few years ago I made a study of trivial worries. I asked 40 people this question: "Is there anything worrying you today that is keeping you from concentrating on your work?" About 60 percent answered yes. Some of their problems—a very few—were serious, but the great percentage were trivial:

RITA: I'm planning a backyard barbecue for 50 people for next Sunday. I'm so worried it will rain. There's no way I can get 50 people into my house.

BENNY: My wife and I are going on a cruise next month. I had to send a check for $4000 to the travel agent. If one of us gets sick and we can't go, we forfeit 50 percent. I'm worried sick one of us *will* get sick.

Rita and Benny could save themselves a lot of worry if they asked two key questions:

1. If what I am worrying about should happen, what is the worst thing that will develop? Will I die? Lose my job? Destroy my marriage?

   RITA: What is the worst thing that would happen if it rained Sunday? I'd have 50 wet people in my house.

   BENNY: What is the worst thing that would happen if we couldn't make the cruise? We'd lose $2000. That's not peanuts, but at our income level, it wouldn't put us in the poorhouse.

2. Is there anything I can do *now* that might mitigate the worst that could happen?

   RITA: I'll set a rain date for the barbecue. If it rains Sunday, we'll have it the following Sunday.

   BENNY: I'll buy insurance. It would cost about $50. It's worth $50 for me not to have to worry about losing $2000.

Ask yourself these two questions and you too will worry a lot less about trivial matters.

One psychotherapist uses the following technique when her clients bring her trivial worries: She asks each one to write the problem down on a paper and seal it in an envelope. She holds the envelopes for several months. After that time, when her clients come in for regular visits, she returns the envelopes and asks them to read what they wrote. Then she asks: "Did it happen?" In 90 percent of the cases, what people were worrying about never came to pass. If we can accept the fact that most of the trivial matters we worry about will never happen, we are less likely to worry.

11-56 What do I do if one of my people refuses to go for counseling after I suggest it?

You should make a renewed effort to persuade the person to seek help. You cannot force anybody to go for counseling—except if it is used as an alternative to discipline. For example, the employee's excessive absenteeism is caused by alcoholism. You may give the employee the option of going for counseling or being fired.

11-57   If an employee is undergoing lengthy psychological therapy and continues to perform below standard, what should I do?

This is a matter for the company to decide. The employee may be protected by the Americans with Disabilities Act. Check with your medical and legal consultants on specific cases. If the employee is making a sincere effort to improve, it is a good idea to give him or her all the support you can. It may take time, but it probably will pay off.

11-58   One of my employees has a variety of emotional problems but refuses to go for professional counseling. His mood swings and unwarranted verbal attacks are destroying the morale of the department. When I tried to fire him, the arbitrator ruled in favor of the union. He has become impossible. What do I do?

There is little you can do without his cooperation. Peers may be able to help. If workers who are also union members bring the matter to the attention of the union, it will be less likely to back up the employee in future disciplinary procedures. If you have a good relationship with the union steward, suggest that he or she talk with the employee about undergoing counseling. If you cannot approach the steward directly, ask one of your people to do so. Should the employee continue to reject counseling, document each outburst and institute appropriate discipline.

11-59   Seida has been in and out of counseling several times. After a few sessions, she appears to be readjusted and does good, even superior work for a time. Then she regresses. What should I do?

Counseling has had a short-term effect on Seida. You and the counselors should encourage her to continue going, even though she appears to have overcome a problem. There are deeper troubles that have not been resolved.

11-60   I feel I could benefit by counseling, but I'm afraid if it gets out to others in the company, my advancement will be jeopardized. Can I really trust the EAP not to break the confidence?

There's no way to guarantee that your company will never learn about your counseling. In most organizations, management is not given access to EAP files. The EAP counselors bill in such a way that names of users are not identified. Of course, there can be slip-ups, and management may even pressure some contractors to divulge information.

Most EAPs do maintain confidentiality. However, if you know that your company is likely to snoop, it would be better to seek counseling outside the EAP and pay for it yourself. Your health insurance may cover it, but if the processing of claims goes through the company, again caution is advised.

11-61   My people bring me their personal problems, and I do take time to listen. Then they want my advice. How can I avoid telling them what to do?

It is very tempting to play "Dear Abby" and tell people how to cope with their problems, but it can be dangerous. Giving advice that leads someone to make a major life change—in marital status, child rearing, or some other area—is too serious a matter for any supervisor to tackle, especially off the top of the head. Poor advice can lead to tragic consequences.

Your role as counselor is to help people *think through* their problems so they can make decisions on a less emotional and more logical basis. Ask questions to clarify issues. Help define the positives and negatives. If commonsense solutions are not enough, suggest that people seek help from professional counselors.

12

Employee Evaluation

All people like to know how they are doing. Managers have an obligation to keep employees apprised of their progress or lack of progress on the job.

Most companies require a formal review at least once a year. However, appraisal should be an informal and continuous process. Supervisors should make it a regular practice to talk to their people about the good and bad aspects of their performance. The dialogue should be ongoing, as projects or assignments are made and completed.

When supervisors are asked what aspects of their work they dread most, the first is usually firing people; the second is making employee appraisals or evaluations. Like most people, supervisors are uncomfortable discussing negatives. This chapter explores the questions that supervisors are most concerned about in the employee evaluation process.

Purposes of Employee Evaluation

12-1   If I keep my people apprised on a regular basis of how they are doing, why is a formal evaluation necessary?

Formal evaluations provide a framework for discussing the overall work of an employee. They lead to corrections of deficiencies and improved performance. Formal counseling and coaching can give employees recognition for past work, reinforcement for increased skills, and enthusiasm for future improvements.

A formal evaluation program makes the appraisal process more objective and makes it easier to compare one employee with another. The program provides helpful data for promotion decisions and, in most companies, is the basis of salary or wage adjustments, bonuses, and other financial rewards.

12-2   What are some other benefits of formal appraisals?

Because of their formality, appraisal programs are taken more seriously than informal comments about performance. The formal evaluation establishes a baseline against which people can measure their own progress. It forces managers to look at each of their people in an objective and systematic manner. It encourages people to take affirmative steps to improve their performance and work toward more challenging goals.

12-3   What are some limitations of formal appraisals?

Both supervisors and employees tend to be uncomfortable about a formal, structured process. Some supervisors avoid making hard decisions and overrate poor performers rather than deal with unhappy people; others underrate good people because they are afraid these workers will become competitors. Many rating systems are poorly designed and create more problems than solutions. Any system is only as good as the people who are administering it.

12-4   What can I do to be a better evaluator?

The single most important ingredient of success is preparation. Train yourself in how to use the system so that you are committed to evaluating a person honestly, objectively, and with the best interests of the company and the employee in mind. More specific techniques of evaluation are described later in this chapter.

12-5   What criteria should be used in setting performance standards on which evaluations will be made?

Performance standards are usually based on the experiences of satisfactory workers doing that type of job over a period of time. They may be quantitative, qualitative, or intangible. All performance standards should meet these criteria:

- *Specific.*   The employee should know exactly what is expected.
- *Measurable.*   The standard must be judged against some measure. This is easy when the work is quantifiable; more difficult (but possible) when it is not quantifiable. Examples of nonquantifiable measures are completion of assignments on schedule, introduction of new concepts, and contributions to team activities.
- *Realistic.*   The standard must be realistic and attainable. Otherwise, people will not consider it fair and will resist working toward it.
- *Understood and accepted.*   All employees should know what is expected and should be in agreement that the standard is fair.

12-6   W. Edwards Deming, the guru of the quality movement, was very much opposed to performance evaluation. Why did he feel this way?

Because most performance reviews in the past were oriented to quantity, quality was ignored. A highly productive worker was one who produced the most material—so long as there were not too many rejected items. Deming believed that the emphasis should be on quality. Today most companies do factor quality into performance evaluation.

12-7   We use the job description as the basis for performance appraisals. Is this a good approach?

If the job description is accurate and includes performance standards, it is an excellent source on which to base evaluations. However, the descriptions are not always current. Jobs are constantly changing and job descriptions do not always follow. All job descriptions should be reviewed periodically and brought up to date.

12-8   How soon after an employee is hired should performance be reviewed?

Informal reviews should be made throughout the training process. Once the formal training is over and the worker is on the job, a follow-up review might be given after 3 months to make sure that the employee is performing properly. This review should be systematic, covering all the work that has been and is being done. Suggestions should be made for improvements, and additional training should be scheduled if needed. Employees should not expect salary adjustments at this time, unless it is policy to give raises to all satisfactory workers after training.

A second review may be given at the end of 6 months. This review should be more formal than the first, resembling the annual performance appraisal.

12-9   After the first year, should employees be evaluated more than once a year?

Most companies give one formal review each year. Some managers advocate semiannual or even more frequent reviews to act as continuing motivators for improved performance. This approach has its advantages, but most companies do not believe it is worth the added time and effort imposed on supervisors. If employees receive consistent informal counseling on performance, no more than one formal review per year is necessary.

12-10   How can progress be measured systematically during a performance review?

Base the review on the job description and performance standards. To measure progress, establish specific criteria for each standard—for example, quantity, quality, time, cost, and intangibles:

Quantity.   Number of items produced

Number of customers served

Number of cases handled

Number of invoices processed

Quality.   Number of rejected items

Percentage of reduction in rejects

Percentage of reduction in rework

Reduction in downtime

Time.   Number of missed deadlines

Time needed to answer inquiries

Turnaround time

Time needed to complete assignments

Cost.	Amount over budget
	Money saved on projects
	Reduction in cost per unit
	Reduction in overtime
Intangibles.	Reduction in absenteeism and tardiness
	Reduction in turnover
	Number of suggestions made
	Team participation

12-11 Other than job factors, what matters should be considered in evaluating an employee?

The appraisal is not only a way of evaluating performance. It is also a means of determining long-term potential and of helping employees grow and develop. Leadership ability, creativity, communication skills, and similar characteristics should be assessed—not against current performance, but in relation to future development. Employees who lack strengths in these areas should not be penalized. They should be guided toward improvements that will promote their advancement and/or personal growth.

12-12 I find that many employees resent being evaluated. How can I get them to accept it?

Most people are uncomfortable about being evaluated. Let your employees know that this is part of the job, and that everybody faces periodic formal evaluations. Even the CEO is evaluated by the board. Point out that performance evaluations have a constructive purpose. People do not see themselves as others do. An objective review of their work reinforces the things they are doing right and points the way to improvements as needed.

12-13 Is it a good idea to have employees rate themselves before they meet with the supervisor for the appraisal interview?

Yes. Many companies give a blank copy of the evaluation form to employees so they can rate themselves in the same manner that their supervisor will. People are generally honest with themselves. They know where they are strong and where they need improvement. This self-assessment makes it easier for employees to accept the supervisor's evaluation. When they come in for the review, they will have given serious thought to all the items being evaluated and will be able to discuss them rationally.

12-14 How do I deal with employees who work as best as they can, but still merit only average or just-below-average ratings?

One of the main purposes of the performance review is to reinforce what is expected on the job. Here is your chance to discuss the performance of middling employees and see what can be done to improve it. These employees are performing only as best as they *think* they can; with more effort or more know-how, they could improve. Arrange for additional training to remotivate them to desire to do better.

12-15 Are there any legal implications in the performance review process?

Yes. Several federal laws and various state laws must be considered. All the civil rights laws discussed in Chapter 3 apply to the appraisal process. You must be careful that your reviews do not even subconsciously discriminate because of age, race, sex, religion, national origin, or disability. If the evaluation may lead to a salary adjustment, you must also take into account the law mandating equal pay for men and women for equal work.

All criteria used in performance appraisal must meet the guidelines set by the Equal Employment Opportunity Commission:

- All standards must be tied directly to the job itself.
- All standards must be necessary for successful performance of the job and must not have an adverse impact on a protected class. For example, if a standard involves heavy lifting but lifting is only a small percentage of the work, most women will be adversely affected.
- All standards should be based on careful job analyses and validated against actual performance on the job.

To ensure compliance with the spirit as well as the letter of the law, the company should establish guidelines for all managers and supervisors and set up a training program to implement them. These guidelines should be reviewed by legal counsel, since there are many subtleties in civil rights law.

12-16 What record should be kept of the appraisal?

Documented records are the best defense against charges of discrimination (see Chapter 13). It is a good idea to keep a running log for all employees. Note all the positives and negatives that pertain to each worker during the year. It is not necessary to indicate routine matters. If the employee does not exceed or fall below standard, nothing need be mentioned. Note exceptions in performance:

Above standard	Below standard
Exceeded quotas on a project by 15 percent	Had to redo 12 assignments
Suggested an idea which saved the company $5000	Rejects were 10 percent above acceptable level

Always be specific. Saying "poor work" or "unsatisfactory performance" will not stand up if challenged.

12-17   I was appointed supervisor of my department 2 months ago. One of my people was due for a review at that time, but it has been deferred until I settle in. Another person is scheduled for a review this month. How can I honestly review my people's work when I have not supervised them for any length of time?

It is not possible to give a thorough review when you have had only limited exposure to an employee. If your predecessor is still with the company, she or he should be required to make the appraisal (or participate with you in doing it). If a work log was kept (see question 12-16), study it carefully. If neither of these options is possible, talk to others in the company who had an opportunity to observe the employee's work. Barring this, you will have to base your appraisal on the limited experience you have had with the employee. You might also try to postpone the appraisal until you have had more opportunity to observe that person's work.

12-18   Is it a good idea for more than one person to rate an employee?

If more than one supervisor works closely with the employee, it is helpful to obtain more than one evaluation. Often the immediate supervisor and the manager at the next level both have direct exposure to a worker. In some types of jobs, an employee may be assigned to work for various supervisors over a period of time. In such cases, it is advantageous to get all the managers who have significant exposure to the employee involved in the process.

Second appraisals minimize prejudice. They also broaden the horizons over which an employee is evaluated. One rater may see certain traits (good or bad) in the worker that another overlooks.

12-19   We've been thinking about instituting a system in which employees rate one another. Is this feasible?

Peer evaluation has had mixed results. Generally, it works better with professional, technical, creative, and administrative people than with rank-and-file office or plant personnel.

On the positive side, if peers rank one another, the combined ratings of all are likely to be more meaningful and certainly less subject to bias than the one rating by a supervisor. Peers see strengths and weaknesses in co-workers that the boss may overlook. On the negative side, peers may be rivals for promotion and may try to discredit a leading contender for advancement. Two close friends may rate each other higher than warranted. Finally, there are anticompany people who would never be disloyal to a co-worker by rating him or her low.

12-20   In our company raises, promotions, and other actions are decided on the basis of performance evaluations. Is this the best way of making such decisions?

If the review system is well designed and administered, performance ratings are probably the least controversial way of deciding on raises, promotions, and other personnel actions. However, factors other than those in the rating system may also be important. Leadership, creativity, ability to get along with others, communication skills, and similar characteristics may not be adequately covered in the performance appraisal. Yet they may be essential for the job to which the employee may be promoted. In such a case, the evaluation should be considered only as one of the components in making the promotion decision.

Trait Rating

12-21   What is the most widely used evaluation system?

The most widely used system to appraise employees is trait rating. Using a chart or scoresheet, the evaluator rates the employee on a series of traits. The usual traits measured are quantity of work, quality of work, knowledge of job, attendance, resourcefulness, creativity, and dependability. The rater checks a box indicating the evaluation of each trait, ranging from "excellent" to "unsatisfactory." Numerical values are given to each evaluation, and a score is computed for the employee. Usually the supervisor is also asked to write an overall view of the person being rated.

12-22   One of the problems I see in our trait system is that different supervisors interpret the ratings differently. One supervisor feels that to get a 5—our top rating—workers have to be perfect. Another supervisor gives a 5 to workers who are doing their very best, even if it is far from perfect. Is it possible to devise objective measures?

This is one of the most serious limitations of the trait system. The standards on which measurements are determined may not be consistent throughout the organization. Some supervisors have much higher or much lower standards than others.

It is easy to have consistent measurements for quantity of work, acceptable quality, and attendance. But it is difficult to set standards on such intangible factors as creativity, initiative, and cooperation. Except for quantifiable factors, you cannot depend on a written manual.

The only way for a company to overcome the "rating bias" is to carefully train all supervisors in the system. Through case problems, role-plays, and discussion groups, supervisors can be trained in how to measure performance factors. All training must be reinforced periodically. Many companies have found that measurements are very objective for the first few months after training, but over time supervisors revert to their old, subjective ways. Supervisors should be given a refresher course at least once a year.

12-23   My boss complains that supervisors give too many high ratings. He wants us to rate people on a bell curve. Will that help or hurt?

A bell curve—or more formally, a normal distribution curve—assumes that the group being rated is evenly divided: that it consists of a small number of superior and very poor workers, a little larger group of better-than-average and just-satisfactory workers, and a majority of average workers. If this is true, then the ratings in the department will fit the bell curve. However, very few departments have such a neat distribution. Requiring supervisors to rate people in this way is unfair to the very good workers who happen to be in a department of excellent workers and therefore are rated low by comparison. In another department they might be among the very best workers. Similarly, just-satisfactory workers in a department of substandard workers will be given higher ratings than they deserve.

12-24   I was told to avoid the "halo effect." What does this mean?

The halo effect, a common phenomenon in the interview process (see question 57 in Chapter 2), also extends to performance evaluation. If an employee has one very impressive trait, the evaluator assumes (incorrectly) that other traits are equally impressive. You are so impressed by the speed at which Helen works that you rate her higher on other qualities than she deserves.

The opposite phenomenon is the pitchfork effect. One negative trait so disturbs you that you rate the employee lower on other traits. Hari's poor lateness record causes you to rate him lower than he deserves on actual output. He is a knowledgeable, productive employee.

Once you are aware of this tendency, you can make a conscious effort not to distort your evaluations.

12-25   When I rate an employee, I tend to remember everything he or she has done in the past few months and forget what happened early in the year. How can I overcome this bias?

Psychometricians call this the *rule of recency*—and it is a common problem in all evaluation systems. People tend to remember more recent things and forget what happened earlier. As suggested in question 12-16 keep a log for all your employees. When evaluation time comes, review this log. It will enable you to consider the whole year, not just the recent past.

12-26   At my previous job, the boss was afraid to give anybody a top rating or a very low rating. So all of us received middle-range ratings. This was OK for the poor workers, but I resented not being given the higher rating I thought I deserved. Why do people do that?

Rating down the middle is a way of avoiding hard decisions. Many supervisors feel uncomfortable giving somebody a very high or very low score, so they give few or no "superior" or "unsatis-factory" ratings, a scattering of "good" and "just satisfactory" rat-ings, and lots of "average" grades.

The problem is exacerbated when companies require that supervisors write an explanation of all very high or very low rat-ings. Rather than go to the trouble of defending the ratings, the supervisor marks everyone in the middle. The problem can be remedied by having clearly defined criteria to measure each trait.

12-27   I am about to make my first evaluation of one of my people. On her past three evaluations, my predecessor rated her 4 on a 5-point scale. In my opinion, she should be rated 2 or at the most 3. Am I being too strict?

Perhaps your predecessor was too lenient or in some way favored this employee. You must "call them as you see them." Do not be influenced by previous ratings—even if you were the one who made them. People do change for better or for worse. Rate your people on how they performed during the period being measured.

12-28   I just don't like Nick. He's often nasty and disrespect-ful. However, his work is good. How can I avoid letting my dislike influence my ratings?

In a trait system, you should evaluate each trait as a separate item and not let other factors influence your judgment. Nick should be rated as high as he deserves in quantity, quality, atten-dance, and so forth, but should be rated low in cooperation and similar traits. Your narrative comments, if required, might reflect the disrespect. Be sure to give specific examples.

12-29   We do not use a bell curve, but I subconsciously com-pare my people against one another when rating them. Is this normal?

Yes. When people work side by side, it is natural to compare them. Comparisons are not unfair if people are being measured against the same criteria. However, your comparisons may be flawed if you have been overly influenced by the halo effect (see question 12-24) or a personal prejudice. Try to avoid comparisons by measuring each trait of a person against the standard rather than by ranking one person against another.

Other Evaluation Systems

12-30   We use the trait system. I find it OK for lower-echelon jobs but inadequate for technical, professional, and managerial jobs. What can I use instead?

There are many types of employee evaluation systems. The one most often used to evaluate technical, professional, sales, administrative, and managerial jobs is the *results-oriented system*. It can be used in any situation where results are measurable. Such a program obviously works best with quantifiable factors, such as sales volume, production units, and dollars earned, but it can be adapted to intangible areas such as creativity and goal attainment.

In a results-oriented system, the evaluators do not have to rely on their judgment of abstract traits, but can focus on what was expected from the employee and how close it came to being attained. The performance standards are established jointly by manager and employee at the beginning of the evaluation period and are measured at the end of it.

12-31   How do you grade the employee when using a results-oriented system?

Some companies dispense with grades in using this system. The supervisor writes a narrative report summarizing what has been accomplished and commenting on its significance. Other companies require the supervisor to rate overall performance on a numerical scale.

12-32   It seems that evidence of results, or goal attainment, is the key to results-oriented evaluations. Won't employees be tempted to set goals that are easy to reach to ensure higher evaluations at the end of the period?

That is why the goals are set together with the manager. It's the manager's job to encourage people to reach out and set goals that are attainable yet challenging. Some companies weigh the results on the basis of objective criteria. An easier goal ("Increase production by 2 percent") will be given less weight than a more difficult goal ("Design a complete revision of management development program").

12-33   I know how to measure quantifiable results, but how can I determine if intangible results are being met?

Even intangible factors have tangible phases that can be for measurement. For example, instead of indicating the goal as "improve employee morale," specify it in terms that are measurable: "reduce turnover by X percent" or "Decrease the number of grievances filed by Y percent." Some intangibles related to morale can be measured by time: "Complete the new manual by July 1."

12-34   All managers and technicians in my company must submit monthly progress reports. How would these fit in with annual appraisals?

The monthly reports must be designed in the same manner as the appraisals if they are to fit in. In a results-oriented system, the monthly report should list the results desired for that month (which will be congruent with the results desired for the year) in one column and then what actually was accomplished in a second column. Here is an example of a progress report:

Results desired: May 1	Results achieved: May 31
Open 3 new accounts	Opened 2 new accounts
Make service calls on 5 inactive customers; reactivate a minimumof 2	Called on 5 customers; reactivated 3
Hire a sales trainee	Interviewed 6 candidates and made offer to 1; waiting for her acceptance

At the end of the year, all 12 monthly reports should be reviewed and used as the basis for the evaluation.

12-35   What is meant by "behaviorally anchored rating scales"?

The *behaviorally anchored rating system* (BARS) is based on the concept that rating the behavior of an employee will provide a more objective view of performance than rating results. BARS criteria are based on critical incidents judged to be characteristic of the various levels of performance. For example, dependability is defined as the ability to meet commitments and deadlines with minimum supervision. A person who consistently meets these deadlines and needs little supervision earns a high score; a person who meets deadlines and commitments 90 percent of the time and needs only occasional supervision is rated average; and a person who meets commitments and deadlines less than 80 percent of the time and needs constant supervision is rated unsatisfactory.

Many companies find BARS an effective way of measuring employees, since the system focuses on actual behavior rather than on a subjective evaluation by the boss.

12-36   One of my friends works for a company that uses assessment centers to evaluate employees. What are they?

Assessment centers are highly sophisticated and complex evaluation mechanisms. Individuals are brought to a special assessment center for 2 or 3 days of intensive observation, interviews, testing, and counseling. A team of management specialists and psychologists makes the evaluations. The ratings are compiled from a variety of sources, including:

- Personal history statements
- Interviews by management representatives
- Observed performance in a series of situational exercises
- Analyses of projective and other psychological tests
- Peer evaluations by other assessers
- Personal impressions of the evaluators during the sessions

Testing is followed by a counseling session, at which each participant discusses his or her future with the company and how the data developed at the assessment center can be applied to personal development.

This is an expensive procedure and is used primarily by large organizations. Assessment centers do not replace the supervisor's evaluation of performance. They are designed to help identify future leaders for the company and to assist employees in their own self-development.

The Performance Appraisal Interview

12-37   How can I make performance appraisal meetings less stressful for my people?

When employees are slated for review, speak to them informally a few days before the meeting. Go to each one's work site and chat casually about the session. Mention that this is a routine part of the job and that everybody, including you and your boss, has an annual review. Give your employees a copy of the review form and suggest that they look it over so they will have an idea of what will be discussed. If company policy permits, have them evaluate their own performance and tell them to be prepared to present their own reviews at the meeting. Encourage them to bring up any aspects of the job or their own careers that they would like to discuss.

At the meeting itself, make the employee comfortable. You may want to use a conference room, since some employees may find your office intimidating. Make sure there are no interruptions or telephone calls during the meeting. Start the discussion on a noncontroversial subject, such as a personal interest or company activity.

12-38   Is there anything else I can do to help the employee prepare for this meeting?

In addition to furnishing a copy of the evaluation form, suggest that the employee think about the following:

- What do I like best and least about my job? Why?
- Are there any special problems that are keeping me from doing better work?
- What could I do next year that I am not doing now to improve my performance?
- What goals did I set at my last appraisal?
- How close did I come to achieving them?
- What goals will I set for the next year?
- What can my supervisor do to help me achieve my goals?
- What additional training should I take to improve my work?
- What additional training will help me advance in my career?

12-39   What should *I* do to prepare for the appraisal meeting?

Your key tool is the appraisal form that you have completed. Review it carefully. Note any special items, positive or negative, that you wish to emphasize. Review your log on this employee (see question 12-16). Think about the individual's personality. Is the employee sensitive, nervous, aggressive, belligerent? Prepare to deal with any personal characteristics that may cause problems on the job.

If part of your meeting involves goal setting, list those goals you would like the employee to set. If he or she does not bring them up during the meeting, you can suggest them.

12-40   Is there any best way to conduct the performance appraisal interview?

Norman Maier,* a specialist in the field of appraisal interviewing, suggests three different approaches to telling the employee about the evaluation. The first approach, the *tell-and-sell method*, focuses on communicating the employee's evaluation as accurately as possible. The supervisor seeks to inform the employee about how he or she is doing, gain acceptance of the evaluation, and finally get the employee to follow the plan outlined for self-improvement.

The tell-and-sell approach takes considerable skill. The supervisor must persuade the employee to change along the lines indicated in the review. Such an approach may be met, overtly or covertly, by resistance and even hostility. To ensure acceptance, supervisors must get at the motivation of their employees and tie in the evaluation with those motives. Supervisors can make improvement on the job more attractive by such extrinsic means as rewards for good work and threats of punishment for poor work or failure to correct undesirable behavior. In each situation, the new behavior is accepted, not for its own sake, but rather for the anticipated reward or absence of punishment.

Here lies the limitation of the tell-and-sell method: Employees may say they accept the evaluation, and may even carefully disguise their hostility. But after the conference, nothing really happens.

12-41   Tell and sell is what I do now. What other approach does Maier suggest?

The second approach, the *tell-and-listen method*, overcomes some of the problems of the tell-and-sell approach. Here the supervisor describes the results of the evaluation and then lets the employee respond. The first part of the interview covers the strengths and weaknesses as seen by the supervisor. The second part involves a thorough exploration of the subordinate's feelings about the evaluation.

*Norman R. F. Maier, *The Appraisal Interview,* John Wiley & Sons, New York, 1958.

Supervisors need to develop four key skills to succeed in this approach:

1. *Active and empathetic listening.*   The supervisor must accept and try to understand what the employee is really feeling and what his or her attitudes are.

2. *Making effective use of pauses.*   The supervisor must wait patiently for the other person to talk and not put words into the employee's mouth.

3. *Reflecting feelings.*   The supervisor responds to the other person's feelings to show understanding.

4. *Summarizing feelings.*   The supervisor indicates progress, demonstrates understanding, and emphasizes certain points.

Such an interview minimizes hostility and resentment because employees have a chance to express themselves openly, without pressure from the boss. They feel accepted and important; they are involved in solving their own problems and in clarifying any misunderstandings with their supervisor. On the negative side, employees may dominate the situation and not benefit from the supervisor's evaluation at all.

12-42   I can see where tell and listen has its drawbacks. Does Maier have an approach which he feels is best?

Maier's third approach to appraisal interviews is the *problem-solving method,* in which the reviewer becomes a helper rather than a judge of employees. Unlike other approaches, problem solving makes no provision for communicating the appraisal per se. It makes the assumption that the interest of both interviewer and employee is to improve the work being done. When employees accept the fact that the supervisor is there to help rather than to criticize, they are more than willing to discuss their difficulties.

The real objective here is employee development, not praise and/or disapproval. The function of the supervisor is to discover the interests of subordinates, respond to them, and help employees examine themselves and the job. The supervisor tries to forget his or her own viewpoint and instead view the job as the employee sees it.

Supervisors do not try to solve the problems presented; they refrain from making suggestions on their own. If employees offer ideas that seem impractical, the supervisor probes for real meanings. Even when the ideas are naive or superficial, the supervisor tries to encourage employees to seek and find their own solutions.

Like tell and listen, the problem-solving approach relies on nondirective techniques such as active listening, accepting, and responding to feelings. However, it goes one step further in that leadership of the discussion rests with the subordinate rather than with the supervisor.

The problem-solving approach motivates original thinking because it stimulates curiosity. It engenders intrinsic motivation because employees develop their own concepts of how to do a better job and are, therefore, committed to improvement. With genuine control over their own activities, workers are more motivated to achieve the desired results and gain a strong feeling of job satisfaction when the effort is successful.

12-43   The problem-solving approach sounds like a good theoretical concept, but it seems to me to be too time-consuming and roundabout. Also, it does not lend itself to evaluating the employee for raises or promotions. How is the method best used?

In Maier's view, problem solving will achieve the true objective of performance review—improved performance—better than any other approach and is worth the time it takes. Supervisors must be carefully trained in this method, which is quite different from traditional approaches. It is best used with people in professional, managerial, and creative positions. Problem solving is probably not feasible for lower-echelon jobs. Nor is it designed for salary adjustment or assessment for promotion. The approach must be supplemented by other techniques if it is used for such purposes.

12-44   Books like *The One-Minute Manager* advocate the sandwich approach in discussing employee appraisals. Sandwich in the bad parts with positive remarks. Good idea?

The advantage of sandwiching is that you reinforce the good things that workers do and show that you are aware of and appreciate them. Subsequent suggestions for improvement of weak areas are more likely to be accepted, because the first layer of praise has softened resistance to criticism. The final layer, additional praise and reassurance, makes the sandwich totally digestible: the employee leaves the meeting feeling good.

The drawback to the sandwich approach is that the employee knows it is being used and is thinking all through the initial praise: "When is it coming?" This negates the praise, since the employee is focused, not on what is being said, but on what is going to come next: the negative layer.

To overcome resistance, ask employees to describe their significant contributions, and comment on what they say. Then ask in what areas employees think they can improve. Use their ideas as the basis for your suggestions. End by expressing reassurance and confidence that employees can do what they have agreed to do. This makes a better sandwich.

12-45   What is the best way to discuss unsatisfactory performance?

Ask the employee to tell you what he or she can do better. If this does not bring out areas in which you believe performance has not met standards, spend some time clarifying the performance standards and pointing out specific instances in which these standards have not been met. Avoid general statements: "Your work has not been satisfactory." "You are too slow." Be as explicit as possible. Refer to production records and your log on individual performance and remind the employee of previous discussions you have had on the matter. Together develop a plan for improvements.

12-46   Is it a good idea to take notes during an appraisal discussion?

The evaluation form serves as a guide to the discussion. If anything comes up that is not covered by the form, you should make a brief note of it. It is not necessary or advisable to take detailed notes about what is discussed. Concentrate on *listening* to what is being said—not writing it down.

12-47   Suppose that, during the discussion, I realize that I have not considered some important points brought up by the employee. Can I upgrade my appraisal?

In most companies the appraisal isn't final until after the discussion. It is not uncommon for supervisors to learn something during a discussion that causes them to reconsider a rating or comment. The goal is an accurate appraisal, and there is no shame in correcting an initial rating. It is the right thing to do.

12-48   Should employees be permitted to rebut my reviews?

When raises and promotions are based on appraisals, employees have a great stake in what is decided. They should be given the opportunity to rebut what appears to them to be incorrect or biased information. Many appraisal forms have a section for such rebuttals. Employee comments are kept in the file with the review and are given consideration when actions based on the review are taken.

12-49   When I discussed Jim's appraisal with him, he agreed with everything I said. But from his subsequent actions, I don't think he really understood where he needs improvement. How do I deal with him?

Some people block out criticism and verbally or nonverbally acquiesce without fully understanding. You know your people, and if you recognize this pattern of behavior in Jim, make sure he does understand your comments by careful feedback. Have Jim repeat just what is required of him and ask him to write it down. This will avoid misunderstandings later on.

Other people will understand your recommendations very well and just say they agree, even if they don't, to avoid an argument. Then they will ignore the incident and continue performing in the same unsatisfactory way. Follow up on these people for the first few weeks after the review to reinforce what was decided and to ensure that it is being done.

12-50   My company wants people to set goals for improvement at the end of the performance review. How can I get them to set realistic goals and commit themselves to achieving them?

Let employees know before the discussion that they will be asked to set goals for the ensuing year. If they have done so over the past few years, use their previous goals as the basis for the new goals. Employees should be prepared to discuss what they did to achieve past goals, what problems they faced in meeting them, how the problems were overcome, and what goals they did not reach. This discussion should segue easily into setting goals for the next period.

For employees who are having a first review, goal setting will be a new experience. In advance of the meeting, give them examples of goals that other workers have set. Suggest that they carefully consider what goals they believe are important for continued growth and improvement. Be prepared to help employees set goals that are attainable but not too easily achieved. Help them recognize the importance of setting goals and obtain their commitment to achieve them.

12-51   How do I follow up on what has been agreed to at the evaluation interview?

Make a list of all the factors that should be followed up, and indicate what improvements are expected and the time frames for them. For example, the employee agrees to make a special effort to improve quality, as measured by a reduction in rejected items. Schedule a meeting a month later to cover what has been done in this area alone.

12-52   Suppose a raise is denied because of poor performance. Is it wise to suggest that if the employee shows significant improvement over the next few months, another review will be scheduled?

Unless you make the offer to all employees, problems can result. You give the opportunity to Joe because you believe it will be an incentive for him to improve, but you do not give the same opportunity to Maria because in your judgment she is too lazy. Maria now claims sex discrimination. To avoid problems, extend the opportunity to all your people, as described in the answer to the next question.

12-53   When I conduct performance reviews with my people, all they think about is how big a salary raise they are going to get. How can I get them to focus on performance?

Encourage your company to separate the performance review from salary adjustment by several months. At the first meeting, center the discussion on performance and offer suggestions for improvement. At the salary meeting at a subsequent date, focus on the improvements made. The employee will get a raise based on last year's performance, plus an incremental raise if improvements emanating from the review have been implemented. For example, you might offer a 5 percent base raise plus another 1 percent if suggestions for improvement have been realized.

12-54   We are under a salary freeze. No matter how good a rating my employees get, no salary adjustments can be made. How can I make the performance review meaningful to them?

Because salary adjustment has been the major component of most evaluation systems, salary freezes can negate the entire process. The only way to make the process meaningful is to sell your people on the importance of improved performance to the company's financial recovery so the freeze can be lifted. Here is your chance to put the emphasis on performance and on future growth rather than on immediate reward. Point out that when the freeze is over, the amount of the raise will be based on this appraisal.

12-55 How can I get employees with excellent reviews to commit themselves to doing even better work to fit our concept of continuing improvement?

All people should be motivated to work toward continuing improvement. The Japanese call this *kaizen,* and it is an integral part of Japanese management philosophy. All workers are indoctrinated to be committed to continuing improvement.

Let all your people know that continuing improvement is expected of them and that they will benefit by becoming even better workers. This approach will create a challenging and exciting work environment. The satisfaction of seeing the results of their efforts, and the recognition by management of their accomplishments, will motivate people to be committed to keep improving.

12-56 Merit systems are designed to encourage employees to excel. They often create an atmosphere of competition in the workplace. How does this affect a work environment in which it is essential that people work closely together to accomplish their goals?

Use a results-oriented evaluation system, in which people are measured against their own past accomplishments instead of against their peers (see questions 12-30 to 12-34). Cooperation should be one factor in the evaluation.

12-57 I am due for my own appraisal next week. Any suggestions as to what I can do to prepare for it?

1. *Review your performance.*   Be honest with yourself. Using a copy of the review form, score your own performance. Now you are prepared to systematically think about your achievements in the same way your boss has.

2. *Make a list of your accomplishments.*   In addition to scoring the review sheet or noting comments on the items to be dis-

cussed, list your major accomplishments over the past year. Include all the special things you have done to contribute to the success of the department.

3. *Consider your deficiencies.* None of us is perfect. You probably did some things that did not work out and have areas in which you know you can do better. Your supervisor is likely to bring these matters up at the review. Think about them and be prepared to suggest ways that you can overcome them.

4. *Listen attentively during the review.* Do not interrupt except to ask clarifying questions. Under no circumstances should you disagree or rebut at this point. Let the supervisor complete his or her comments before offering your own.

5. *Be constructive.* Of course, if you fully agree with the review, thank your supervisor. If you do not, here is your chance to make your rebuttal. If you have carefully reviewed your accomplishments and are cognizant of your deficiencies, you are ready to make your points. Start by thanking the supervisor for his or her support over the past year and then say: "I understand everything you said and I appreciate your frankness. However, there are certain accomplishments—ones which I am particularly proud of and for which you complimented me at the time—that you may not have taken into consideration." Then enumerate these items. If deficiencies are pointed out, do not make excuses for them. Instead, describe what you are doing to overcome them. Suggest that these efforts be considered before the evaluation is made final.

6. *Set goals for the future.* Review the goals you set at last year's appraisal. Discuss how they were reached or what the status of each of them is at this time. Build agreement with your boss on goals for the coming year.

13

Discipline

When you hear the word *discipline,* the first synonym that pops into mind is probably *punishment.* Look at that word again; you will see another word built into those letters—disciple.

Both words stem from the Latin *disciplina,* meaning to learn. If we were to look at our disciplinary efforts at work as learning activities instead of punishing activities, we would get a lot more out of discipline. Unfortunately, we cannot always succeed in getting people to learn, so from time to time we do have to resort to punishment. Every company has some disciplinary procedure to punish employees who do not perform satisfactorily or who violate the rules.

The final step in disciplinary action is termination. Every time we fire somebody, not only do we risk litigation but we cost the organization a bundle of money. Our entire investment in hiring, training, administering, and supervising that person is lost forever. We must make every effort to salvage employees in the earliest stages of the disciplinary procedure—long before the option of termination arises—by helping them *learn* to be more effective on the job.

This chapter explores the sensitive questions that arise in disciplining employees. The final step of the disciplinary system—termination—is discussed in Chapter 14.

Progressive Discipline

13-1   What is progressive discipline?

Progressive discipline is a systematic approach in which employees are given every opportunity to correct the problem involved. Before companies had such systems, employees could be fired for minor offenses or at the whim of the supervisor. Progressive discipline programs have enabled companies to work with their people to overcome problems and become productive workers. Supervisors are motivated to work with their people rather than to arbitrarily terminate employees. Progressive discipline also protects the company from charges of unfairness and costly litigation.

13-2   What are the usual steps in a progressive discipline program?

Virtually all such programs start with an informal (often called "oral" or "verbal") warning. If the problem continues, a more formal counseling session is held. The next step is a written warning, followed by a period of probation. If these actions do not alleviate the situation, more serious punishment follows—typically, one or more periods of suspension without pay. The final step is terminating the employment of the offender.

13-3   How soon after the offense is it best to give the first (informal) warning?

Immediately—with three exceptions:

1. *When other people are around.*   All disciplinary matters should be taken care of in private. Nobody should be embarrassed in front of co-workers.

2. *When the supervisor is mad.*   Unless you are calm, the warning will degenerate into a diatribe.

3. *When the employee is mad.*   Unless the worker is calm, no constructive solutions can result.

13-4   If it is a first offense, should I reprimand the employee or just have a casual chat, pointing out the problem and working toward a solution?

This depends on the situation. In the case of lateness, the "casual chat" should take place the first and/or second time the employee is late. The third lateness triggers the progressive discipline and should be done according to the book. (*Note:* This reprimand is still informal, but it is more than casual.) When the offense is less clearly defined in the policy manual, discretion is called for. Use casual discussions where appropriate before activating the progressive discipline system.

13-5   What is the most effective way of reprimanding somebody?

The objective of the reprimand is to make the employee aware that he or she has violated a company rule and that the infraction is of serious concern to the supervisor. The reprimand also gives the employee the chance to correct the situation.

The following acrostic of REPRIMAND summarizes how to make the most of the process:

R espect the employee. Don't criticize him or her as a person. Focus on the problem—on the *what,* not the *who.*

E nter the picture early. Reprimand the offender as soon as possible after the event. The longer you wait, the less effective the reprimand becomes.

P roceed in private. Never reprimand anybody in the presence of others. This causes bitterness and embarrassment—not only in the offender, but among those who witness the reprimand.

R eassure the employee. Let the offender know you have confidence that he or she will improve. Reinforce your position by maintaining an empathetic attitude throughout the procedure. Listen attentively, patiently, and with an open mind.

I nterrupt rarely and only to clarify. Never get into an argument. If the employee makes statements that are untrue, ask questions but do not contradict at this time.

M otivate the employee to want to change. Encourage the offender to come up with suggestions to resolve the problem.

A dopt a positive attitude. Do not show anger or any negative emotion. Be constructive.

N ever be sarcastic.

D ocument the incident. To protect your company in case of litigation, document the reprimand, even if it is informal (see question 13-8).

13-6   I've reprimanded lots of people in my time and they always have excuses—some of which get really wild. What do you do about excuses?

Listen. No matter how ridiculous the excuse may be, listen fully and do not interrupt or make comments other than an occasional, noncommittal "uh-huh" or "yes."

Why listen? First, the excuse may turn out to be acceptable. Most companies do have some permittable reasons for lateness or other infractions of rules. Second, even if the excuse is totally absurd, you must let the employee get it out of his or her system. This "catharsis" is important. Unless people can unburden their minds, they will be unable to take in anything you say. Whether it be an employee's tardiness, a co-workers' gripe, or a customer's complaint, until you hear out the entire story, anything you say will fall on deaf ears.

So listen to excuses all the way. When the employee has finished (assuming the excuse is not acceptable), comment: "But the important thing is that you comply with the rules."

13-7   How can I reprimand an employee without causing resentment?

Let's role-play a "how not to do it" example and then a good example: Office policy is that if an employee comes in late three times over a 6-month period, the supervisor must issue a reprimand. Sally has just come in late for the third time. Ken, her boss, confronts her:

KEN: (*Angry voice.*) Sally—late again! You know we have a deadline today. Of all the days to come in late, you pick today. Don't you have any sense of responsibility?

SALLY: (*Annoyed.*) I'm only 10 minutes late. I ran into a traffic jam and I couldn't do anything about it.

KEN: If you left early enough, you wouldn't have had traffic problems. The rest of us were here on time. You just don't have a sense of responsibility.

SALLY: I have as much sense of responsibility as anyone.

KEN: If you're late again, I'm going to have to suspend you.

Did that solve anything? The supervisor did everything wrong. The objective of the informal warning is to alert the employee that there is a problem and that it should be corrected. By using an angry tone and taking an antagonistic attitude, Ken defeats that purpose. Understandably, he is upset because of the impending deadline. Still, he should let himself cool down and then talk to Sally in a calm manner.

Let's listen in on how it might be done more effectively:

KEN: Sally, you know how important it is for all of us to be on the job at 8:30. We work as a team and unless the whole team is here on time, the work of the entire department suffers.

SALLY: I'm sorry, Ken. I ran into unusual traffic this morning.

KEN: We all face traffic in the morning, Sally. What can you do to make sure that you will be on time in the future?

SALLY: I'm usually here on time. I leave the house at the same time every day. I've been late only three times, and in each case, the problem has been unusually heavy traffic. I guess it is due to the construction on the highway.

KEN: Is there an alternative route you can take?

SALLY: No, but if I leave my house 10 or 15 minutes earlier I would probably miss that traffic.

KEN: That sounds like a good idea. You're a valuable member of our team and being on time will help us all.

Notice the difference. No anger, No recriminations. Just an attempt to solve the problem. This time Ken listens to Sally's story and asks for suggestions as to how the problem might be solved. He is constructive and positive in his approach.

13-8   How can I document an oral warning?

Every company should develop its own documentation policy and all supervisors should follow it. There are several ways to document an "oral" or "verbal" warning. (These two terms should really be dropped, since documentation is necessary. It is better to call the warning "informal.")

Some companies enter the informal warning in a departmental log in which records are kept of other matters such as production and attendance. This is usually considered adequate. However, conservative attorneys advise that it is better to use a document similar to the written warning notice, with a notation on the memo that it is a first or informal warning (see questions 13-15 and 13-16).

13-9   In our company the second step in progressive discipline is counseling. How does this differ from reprimanding?

Counseling is a more serious and more formal step than reprimanding, and it takes more time. Whereas a reprimand may be brief and conducted at the work site (provided it is private), the counseling session should be held in the supervisor's office or in a conference room. The purpose of the counseling session is to get the supervisor and employee to work together to resolve the problem. Because counseling is the second stage of discipline, the employee should be made aware that the behavior involved can no longer be looked at casually.

13-10   If counseling is more formal, it can't be done haphazardly. How can I prepare for such a session with an employee?

Get all the facts about the situation and as much information about the employee as you can. Review the personnel file. If the employee has had previous problems, study how they were handled and what was done. For example, if you are about to have a counseling session with Tony, check your file. You may note that you reprimanded him last month for failing to keep his workstation in proper order. You also notice that 3 years ago your predecessor disciplined him for failing to follow procedures and thereby causing significant damage to a computer file. Despite a reprimand and counseling, Tony stubbornly ignored the procedures until after a written warning. The same type of carelessness has recurred.

Get all the details of Tony's present offense. Exactly what has he done to violate procedures? In order to solve the problem, you must have specifics, not just a general feeling. If Tony has been with you for a while, you probably know a good deal about his personality and how he reacts to you. If you know he is very tense in discussions, prepare to spend more time developing rapport at the beginning of the session. If you have an easygoing relationship, you can be more direct. Now you are ready for the meeting.

13-11   Can you role-play a counseling session to give me a better idea of how to proceed?

Bring Tony into your office or a conference room. Have all relevant documents, statistics, or figures at hand. Start with some small talk, and then get into the subject as soon as you feel Tony is comfortable.

YOU: Tony, when we spoke last month, I thought we had an understanding that you would keep your workstation in order, as outlined in the procedures manual. What's happened?

TONY: (*Gives a lengthy excuse and winds down*)... And so long as I can put my finger on anything I want when I need it, why should I have to go through all the unnecessary work required by the manual?

YOU: I can see how your system works for you, but the reason the procedures have been established is to provide consistency throughout the company. Suppose you get sick or you're on vacation and we need something you have been working on?

TONY: Well, I hadn't thought about that.

YOU: It will also be much easier for you. Sure, you can find everything you need now, but things keep changing. When we start new programs, you'd have to organize them to fit your system. The standard system has facility for change built into it, so in the long run it's not only good for the company but better for you.

TONY: OK. But I have everything set up right now in my way. How can I change overnight?

YOU: I don't expect you to change overnight. Let's work out a timetable so you can get on track in the most expedient way. We'll meet a week from today to go over it.

Together you and Tony develop a plan of action and a timetable, including follow-up procedures. It's a good idea to put the plan in writing, and both you and Tony should sign the form.

13-12   We ask our people to come up with their own ideas as to how to correct their behavior. Is this a good idea?

Yes. People should be asked how they might solve their problems rather than have solutions imposed on them. When they participate in problem solving, they are more likely to comply with what has been agreed on.

13-13   When I ask people to come up with solutions to problems, more often than not they answer: "I don't know what to do." How should I proceed?

People may not have immediate answers, but after some thought they can come up with good solutions. If there is no crisis involved, ask them to think about the situation overnight or even longer. Of course, some people will never be able to suggest a solution, and some problems are just too complex. In such cases, you should offer at least one suggestion and then discuss how to implement it with the employee.

13-14   How do I document a counseling meeting?

Again, each company should establish its own documentation system and all departments should follow it. Many companies provide printed forms for this purpose. Other organizations document the counseling meeting by having the employee prepare a handwritten statement outlining what has been agreed upon. The two approaches could be combined in a printed document giving the formal data (e.g., date, description of the offense, names of employee and supervisor) and leaving a blank space for the employee's statement.

When you ask an employee to compose a personal account of what will be done to correct the situation, you build both understanding and commitment. Both you and the employee should sign the document. Give one copy to the employee and keep a second copy on file. Let the employee know that you consider this a commitment and express your confidence that it will be kept.

13-15   If the employee does not keep the commitment and repeats the infraction, what is the next step?

Let's go back to Tony in question 13-11. Together, you and he developed a written plan of action; both of you signed the document. Now Tony has failed to come through as promised. The next step is a disciplinary interview—a more formal and serious indicator that his behavior cannot continue. Document the incident with a written warning to Tony. Keep a copy in his personnel file.

> YOU: Tony, you agreed to follow our manual in organizing your materials. It's been 3 weeks since our discussion. Why haven't you complied?
>
> TONY: Well, I've been pretty busy and I didn't think that reorganizing the work was a high priority, considering all my other responsibilities.
>
> YOU: You wrote out a plan of action which we both signed. In it you agreed to start at once.
>
> TONY: OK, I'll get to it.
>
> YOU: Tony, this is not the first time that you have not followed an agreed-upon plan. I have written a formal reprimand and if you do not comply immediately, we will have to go to the next step in our disciplinary procedure. That is to put you on probation, Do you understand.?

A sample formal written warning is shown in Figure 13-1.

13-16 What about disciplining employees who do not meet production standards?

Whether the reason for discipline is poor performance or infractions of company rules, the same progressive measures should be used. In the case of meeting production standards, emphasis should be placed on specific ways to improve performance. Informal warnings and counseling are supplemented by training and coaching. If these steps fail, a written warning should be issued. A sample is presented in Figure 13-2.

13-17 How many written warnings should an employee be given before more serious action is taken?

Since both the informal warning and the counseling session have been documented, the employee has already had two chances to correct the behavior. The first formal warning is actually the third record of disciplinary action. It should be followed by more serious measures. All the remaining steps should be documented and kept on file.

13-18 If the written warning does not solve the problem, the next step is usually probation. How does this work?

Probation is a means of letting the employee know that the behavior must be corrected within a specified period of time or punishment will follow. What you are doing is giving the employee another chance. Most people will recognize that this is a serious step. Probationary periods vary from as few as 10 days to the more usual 30 days. Some union contracts specify even longer periods. If significant progress is made, the probation is lifted. If the offense is repeated after lifting, the probation may be reinstated. In some cases, the next step in the procedure may be invoked.

13-19 What kinds of real punishment can be administered if probation doesn't help?

Ever since flogging was abolished, supervisors have very limited options in punishing employees. The most usual punishment short of termination is suspension without pay for a specified period.

Memo for Poor Conduct

FROM: Supervisor (*name*)

TO: Employee (*name*)

[Copies to personnel and any other departments deemed appropriate.]

On (date), we had an informal discussion concerning _____

_____

_____

On (date) we had a counseling session at which you agreed to

_____

_____

Since you have not complied with this agreement, you are being given formal notice that if the above matter is not corrected by (date), additional disciplinary steps will be taken as specified in Section _____ of the policies and procedures manual.

Signed:

_____
(Supervisor's signature)

Acknowledged:

_____ Date_____
(Employee's signature)

Figure 13-1

13-20   How long should a suspension be?

Let the punishment fit the crime. For minor infractions, a day; for more serious ones, several days. However, make sure that you administer suspension in a consistent manner. When the same offense is involved, you cannot give more days of suspension to people you do not like and fewer to those you do like.

Memo for Poor Performance

FROM: Supervisor (*name*)

TO: Employee (*name*)

[Copies to personnel and any other departments deemed appropriate.]

The performance standard for _____ [specify employee's type of work] is _____units per _____ [if not quantifiable, specify the standard]. Your production has been _____.

In order to help you, today I gave you ____ hours of special coaching. The areas covered included _____

_____

Signed:

_____
(Supervisor's signature)

Acknowledged:

_____ Date _____
(Employee's signature)

Figure 13-2

13-21   I can understand how suspension punishes a worker, but doesn't it also punish the department? Losing the productivity of a skilled employee may be detrimental to the company.

This is a very sensitive issue, especially when we suspend good workers who happen to have infractions of minor rules. Are we cutting off our nose to spite our face? Can we make exceptions so we do not lose productivity? The issue becomes even more serious when the violations continue and the question of termination arises.

Unless the disciplinary system is administered equitably and consistently, it falls apart. If the rules are unrealistic, change them. For example, frequent lateness may be alleviated by instituting flexible hours. But if a rule is on the books, it must be enforced with all people. Variations lead to setting precedents, and if you waive a rule for a good worker, you may have to waive it for all or face litigation.

13-22   Suppose I suspend somebody for a day. She repeats the infraction several weeks later. Can I now suspend her for a longer period?

It depends on your company's disciplinary procedure. In most companies, the supervisor has no flexibility. You must adhere to company policy. Some companies do provide for more than one period of suspension before termination is required.

13-23   Marilyn has two problems: tardiness and absenteeism. In counting her violations for progressive discipline, do I consider them as two separate offenses or can I combine them to determine the appropriate step?

Infractions of company rules are usually combined when administering progressive discipline. However, if the offenses are spread over a long period of time, they may be treated separately. For example, Marilyn has two absences in May, and then a lateness in July, both are in a 6-month period, but you may want to consider them separately. If, however, the pattern of lateness and absences is intermingled over a closer time period, you should consider them as part of the same disciplinary unit.

13-24   What steps can I take to discipline a good employee for minor, but continuing infractions of rules without demotivating him from good production?

When you speak to the employee about the infractions, praise him for the good work. Discuss the reasons for the rules that are being broken and the importance of compliance. Reassure the employee that you truly appreciate his efforts and that his performance will be even more valuable if the rules are obeyed.

Affirmative Discipline

13-25   I've read about companies that don't punish at all. It's called affirmative discipline. What's this all about?

A number of companies have used affirmative discipline successfully over the past few years. The basic concept is that mature adults do not have to be threatened with punishment to behave properly on the job. If you can get your people to commit themselves to follow company procedures, they will do it willingly.

Traditional progressive discipline is based on punishment for infractions. The underlying concept is that the employee must pay for his or her crime. In traditional discipline, the employee often feels that the penalty administered has absolved him or her from the transgression. This attitude works against solving problems and can even promote repeat offenses. More important, punishment often causes resentment and hostility. Affirmative discipline is designed to eliminate both absolution and resentment.

13-26   What is the first step in affirmative discipline?

During the orientation process, all employees are made fully aware of the company's rules and policies. Each employee signs a statement indicating that he or she understands the rules and has made a commitment to comply with them. Upon completion of the trial period, the employee meets with the supervisor. The rules and policies are again explained and the employee renews the commitment.

13-27   What happens if a violation occurs?

If a rule is violated, the supervisor meets with the employee and discusses the situation. The employee is reminded of his or her agreement to be committed to company policy and is asked to assure the supervisor that both the rule that has been broken and the nature of the employee's obligation and commitment are understood. The meeting is documented by a memo signed by both parties.

If a violation occurs again, a second conference is held. The employee is asked to sign a special affirmation statement. The purpose is to show that the company takes rule infractions seriously and expects the employee to do the same.

If the employee violates a minor rule for the third time within a specified period, or breaks a major rule for the first time, the supervisor asks the employee if he or she really wants to continue with the company. If the answer is yes, the employee is asked to sign a document acknowledging that he or she has violated the specified rule but wants to continue to be employed. This is reaffirmed with an indication that, should the offense be repeated, the employee understands he or she will be terminated.

13-28   Is there no suspension or other interim punishment before termination?

In some organizations, the employee is asked at this point, to take a day off—with pay—to seriously consider whether he or she can live up to the commitment made to the company.

Why with pay? By paying employees to think about their commitment, the company is expressing confidence in them and in the system. When people are treated as adults, both the organization and the workers benefit. Employees who do not comply after suspension are terminated. Companies that use affirmative measures report a significant reduction in discipline problems.

Legal Implications of Discipline

13-29   Why is documentation so important in every step of the disciplinary procedure?

If an employee challenges a discharge, does not receive a hoped-for promotion, or claims discrimination or harassment on the job, the company must be able to defend itself. Proper documentation is the best defense. That is why even informal steps should be as carefully documented as later and more serious actions.

13-30   Is it necessary for the employee to sign the documents?

For legal reasons, it is advisable to require the employee to sign any document that relates to his or her discipline. Many an employee has claimed that he or she was never given notice of infraction and that termination is a complete surprise. When the company presents documentation (not signed by the employee), the employee may charge that the documents were created especially for the hearing and did not exist before. Obtaining the signature of the employee prevents such claims. Even in cases of informal documentation, such as notes entered in a log, it is wise to get the employee to initial the notation as acknowledgment.

13-31   What do you do if the employee refuses to sign a document?

If the employee refuses to sign the document, call in a witness. This person can be another supervisor or even a secretary or clerk. The offender is asked in the presence of the witness to sign the document. If the employee again refuses, write on the document "Refused to sign" and have the witness sign to affirm this. The witness need not be told what is in the document.

13-32   Should disciplinary actions for poor performance be documented in the same way as those for poor conduct?

Since the purpose of documentation is to protect the company, it is essential in any type of action concerning an employee. Documentation for poor performance should include a statement of actual performance as compared with standards or other criteria plus a notation on what you have done to correct the situation (see Figure 13-2). Remember that proof of what you have done to bring the employee up to acceptable performance can be a key point in winning a case.

13-33   Should an employee be given copies of disciplinary documents?

It is a good idea to give the employee a copy of every formal document. Copies of informal comments, such as notes in a log, need not be presented, but should be available if requested. Putting secret documents about an employee in his or her personnel file is not a good idea. Supervisors should be aboveboard with employees on matters related to their performance and conduct.

When a disgruntled employee confers with an attorney in anticipation of legal action, he or she may be discouraged from proceeding if the attorney concludes from the disciplinary documents that the company has a strong case.

13-34   Are employees entitled to see documents that are in their personnel file?

Employees of the federal government are guaranteed access to their personnel files under the Federal Privacy Act and the Freedom of Information Act. Some states have similar laws for state employees. No federal law gives this right to employees in the private sector, but some states have passed such laws. Check with your state's labor department to determine if employees are covered.

Many companies have policies that allow an employee to review his or her file and make copies of documents under supervision. Most companies will keep certain documents confidential, such as letters of reference from previous employers and medical and psychological reports.

13-35   How long should a written warning be kept in an employee's personnel file?

Some companies keep all disciplinary documents on file forever in case of possible litigation. Others remove documents when specific infractions are not repeated for a given period.

When new supervisors take over, they may be unduly influenced by the documentation in an employee's file. The record is important in the case of recent infractions, but supervisors should not prejudge employees on matters that occurred long ago. This is why some companies remove old documentation and either discard it or keep it in a file that can be accessed only by the personnel or legal department.

13-36   Is it legal to punish employees by reducing them in rank?

There is no legal reason that you cannot punish employees by demoting or transferring them. However, reducing rank is appropriate only for people who fail to perform the job satisfactorily (see question 13-57), not for people who exhibit poor conduct. If a person violates company rules, progressive discipline should be followed.

All cases of demotion must comply with equal employment laws. For example, you cannot demote an employee because you want a younger person to do that job.

13-37   Can I punish employees by docking their pay?

Docking pay is usually used only as punishment for lateness or absenteeism. Most companies will not pay hourly workers for time not worked. If they are not there, they get no pay—except for sick days, personal days, vacation days, and other special circumstances, as detailed in the union contract or company policy manual.

13-38   We have a union contract that specifies each step of the disciplinary procedure. The union insists on rigid compliance, and this causes a tremendous loss of productive time. What can we do to circumvent the process?

A union contract must be adhered to. If you have a good relationship with union leaders, they may allow minor variations to save time and trouble. However, most unions insist on strict concurrence. You have no choice but to comply.

Discipline on the Job

13-39   Why do employees resent discipline?

Nobody likes to be punished, and discipline is looked upon as a form of punishment. Even if you administer discipline in a diplomatic manner, it is resented. It makes people feel inadequate. The only way to make your disciplinary actions more positive is to treat your employees as adults. Instead of bawling people out, discuss their problems in a calm and rational way. Do not impose solutions. Enlist employees' cooperation by asking for input on how the problem can be solved. You will never entirely erase the resentment, but you can minimize and dissipate it.

13-40   It seems to me that it is better to establish programs to prevent problems that might lead to disciplinary actions. How can I adopt a preventive stance?

Here are some suggestions to help reduce disciplinary problems on the job:

- *Explain rules periodically.*   People tend to forget rules, particularly if they are not obvious ones like rules related to lateness or smoking. When an employee is hired, these rules should be explained at the orientation session. Just stating the rules is not enough; explain the rationale as well. When employees know the reasons for company rules, they are more likely to understand, remember, and abide by them. Hold periodic meetings (at least once a year) at which some of the rules are reviewed. You need not have a meeting dedicated to "rules review"; build in a brief discussion during regular meetings.

- *Have employees participate in making rules.*   When new situations develop, instead of imposing rules on your people, get their ideas and suggestions as to what rules should apply.

- *Be fair and diplomatic.*   Treat your people as adults. Don't interpret rules arbitrarily. When possible, give the employee the benefit of the doubt.

- *Be consistent.*   Make sure that you administer the rules in the same way for everybody. Don't be stricter with people you don't like than with people you do like.

13-41   I feel very ill at ease when I have to discipline some-body. Any suggestions on overcoming this?

Disciplining is part of the job. If you look upon discipline as a learning activity rather than a punishing activity, you will feel more comfortable administering it (see the introduction to this chapter). When the time comes to speak to an employee about performance or conduct, set your mind by reviewing the situation and the personality of the employee. Prepare to discuss the problem and to concentrate on how to resolve it—not on the penalties that may be invoked.

Tailor your discussion to the employee's personality rather than approaching everybody in the same way. If the person is sensitive, take a low-key approach. If the employee is antagonistic, steel yourself to handle it. Keep in mind that your objective is to improve the situation, not to punish the person. Your own attitude will become more positive and you will automatically feel more at ease.

13-42   How can I discipline a person and keep his or her loyalty?

By showing sincere interest in people as individuals, you demonstrate to your employees that you are concerned about them and wish to make them productive and valuable. Discipline, if necessary, should be administered only after off-the-record informal talks with employees over time. Your people should know that you are there to help them meet their own goals as well as become productive people. Your interest and attention over time will reduce the need for formal discipline. And when such action must be taken, it will be received in a positive way and will be accepted as constructive.

13-43   How much patience should I have in dealing with disciplinary problems?

A successful supervisor is a patient person. Some of your employees need a lot more time and reinforcement than others. Unless you are patient with them, you will demotivate them and lose their productivity completely. When disciplinary actions are necessary, take extra time at each step to make sure people understand what they must do to improve.

You cannot adapt your company's disciplinary system to meet each person's needs. For example, you cannot give one employee more "chances" than another, but you can be more patient before you institute various phases of the system.

13-44   How can I anticipate problems so the need for discipline may be avoided?

An alert and observant supervisor can often anticipate potential problems before they become subject to discipline. In cases of poor performance, be alert for any deviations from standards. For example, an employee has been in the department for about 3 years. She is a satisfactory worker—never great, but she meets her performance standards. Gradually her performance begins to decline, slowly and almost imperceptibly. You don't pick this up until her production is almost 20 percent below standard, which triggers the first step in your disciplinary system for poor performance. Had you been aware of the problem earlier, you would have been able to stem the decline before it reached the critical point.

The best way to avoid disciplinary action is to note early infractions of rules before they become subject to discipline and discuss them with employees. Don't wait until employees are late three times before talking to them about tardiness. Calling their attention to the importance of being on time at their first lateness—although not part of the formal disciplinary system—will let them know you take lateness seriously.

In cases where there are patterns of violations throughout the department (e.g., extending breaks or lunch hours), bring the matter up at a departmental meeting. This will alert your people to your concern and alleviate the need for disciplinary action.

13-45   Are there any circumstances in which I can waive disciplinary action for an otherwise good worker who violates company rules?

Exceptions can be made in exceptional circumstances. For example, one of your people has a temporary emergency at home and must take more time off than is usually allowed. The danger here is that any time you allow an exception to a rule, you set a precedent which others may use as justification for waiving the rules for them. To avoid this problem, specify in writing the reason for your decision whenever a rule is waived. Unless the circumstances are virtually identical, others cannot claim it as precedent.

13-46   Can a supervisor be a strict disciplinarian and still maintain good relations with his or her people?

There is a difference between being a strict disciplinarian and being a martinet. The martinet is unreasonable and expects unwavering obedience to rules and directives. This type of boss may run a tight ship, but is more likely to have resentful employees, high turnover, and perhaps sabotage.

Employees respect a strict disciplinarian who is fair in administering discipline, who has a degree of flexibility, and who is consistent in his or her actions. People know exactly what the boss expects of them in both performance and behavior. As long as discipline is perceived to be equitable and reasonable, strict enforcement will not be resented.

13-47   Some of my people extend their lunch hour. When I call them down on this, they stop for a while, but within a short time the pattern starts again. Any suggestions?

As discussed in answer to question 13-44, the good supervisor must anticipate problems before they become subject to disciplinary action. The next time someone extends a lunch break, remind the employee that everyone is expected to be back from lunch when scheduled and that people have agreed after previous discussions of this matter to come back on time. If the offense is repeated, reinforce the importance of following rules and describe the penalties that might ensue. If this too fails, take necessary disciplinary action. When employees understand that you will not tolerate continued misbehavior, they will not revert to unacceptable practices.

13-48   We have a strict no-smoking policy. Every once in a while I catch somebody sneaking a smoke. It's not a fire hazard, but it does violate the rule. How tough should I be?

Very tough. No-smoking rules are no different from any other rules. If you allow them to be ignored, there is no point in having the rule. In addition, no-smoking rules are often the result of state or local laws requiring companies to prohibit smoking except in designated areas. Allowing an exception is a violation of the law.

13-49   How can I keep cool when bawling out my people?

First, a good supervisor never *bawls out* people. A reprimand is not a bawling out. It is a calm discussion of the situation (see question 13-5).

You should never reprimand somebody when you are mad or upset. Wait until you have calmed down. True, employees can so rile you that you want to ream them on the spot, but all that will do is let you vent your anger. You may frighten employees into temporarily changing their ways. But you will not solve the problem and will only create resentment that is reflected in long-term behavior. When you are tempted to holler or scream, count to 10 or more to cool off. If possible, leave the room and don't return until you are calmer. Then talk to the culprit.

There are times when you may be so upset that you cannot control yourself. You lose your cool and holler and scream at a person. If you do this and get everything out of your system, quickly apologize and convert the tirade into a true reprimand: "What you did upset me and I blew up. I'm sorry I yelled, but it did get the initial anger out. Now let's look at this in a rational way." Then do it.

13-50 I am held responsible for maintaining the order of my department. To do this I must discipline people from time to time. However, my boss—the plant manager—does not always back me up. What can I do?

Unless your boss supports you, there is no way employees will be serious about following the rules. If they know your boss will overrule you, they may take advantage. Have a heart-to-heart talk with the plant manager about this. Sell the importance of having the boss support your disciplinary decisions. Of course, there may be times when you do make a poor or unfair decision and it should be overruled. This will be the exceptional case.

13-51 One of my employees has an attendance problem. She has two small children who are ill frequently, plus she is frequently out ill herself. She is on probation now, and with the flu and cold season on again she is taking more time off. She has had several written warnings about attendance. Ours is a small customer service department with extremely busy phones. When one person is out, it puts a strain on the other two employees to handle the phones along with their daily work. Under the circumstances, how can I fairly decide when further disciplinary action should be taken?

Even though you have sympathy for the employee, your main obligation is to your company. You are responsible for ensuring that your department functions at optimum capacity. With only two people to do the work of three, productivity is bound to fall. If the employee is absent again, your only choice is to take the next step in the disciplinary procedure. Continued absenteeism could lead to termination.

13-52   How do I deal with employees who have a variety of disciplinary problems?

Most disciplinary systems are designed to deal with a person who repeats the same offense (e.g., tardiness) over and over. The question of whether to treat each type of infraction as a separate disciplinary problem or to combine incidents is not clear-cut.

If the offenses are separated by a long period of time (several months), they are best dealt with as separate items. For example, Carla is late three times and is reprimanded; 2 months later, she violates a no-smoking rule. The offense should be treated as a new infraction, not a continuation of the first (tardiness). That is, Carla should be given an informal warning—not the second-tier punishment she would have received if she had been late again.

On the other hand, if Vince violates several rules within a short period of time, a pattern of behavior may be building. The situation should be corrected immediately, and the disciplinary steps may be combined. For example; two latenesses plus one absence over a 60-day period may result in a reprimand and one more infraction of any type is the next step—usually counseling.

Because of its legal implications, the decision as to whether to treat offenses separately or together should be made by the company and not by any individual supervisor.

13-53   What should I do with an employee who has been reprimanded many times and keeps coming up with unacceptable excuses?

Discuss exactly what the rules call for and what excuses (if any) are acceptable. Obtain good feedback to make sure the employee understands. The next time an infraction occurs, listen to the excuse and (if not acceptable) reinforce what was previously discussed. Take whatever disciplinary action is indicated.

13-54   Should an employee be disciplined for failure to meet performance standards?

The purpose of discipline is to correct behavior. If the behavior is in the form of poor performance, discipline is appropriate. However, look at discipline as a learning process rather than a punishing process. The first step (the informal warning) is accompanied by coaching and training. The objective is to bring the employee up to performance standards. The following steps (formal warnings, probation) are implemented with added training. If all this fails and the standards cannot be met, the employee may be suspended or even terminated. Be sure to document all the steps you take.

13-55   Iso really is trying hard, but he just can't master the technical aspects of the job. My boss says I should put him on probation and start writing up all his errors. Is this a good idea?

First make every effort to help Iso master the technical aspects of the job. You may give him personal training or send him to a technical school or seminar. You may call in a representative of the equipment manufacturer or software developer to help him overcome his problems. Document each of the steps you take to help Iso learn. This is a much better type of documentation than just writing up errors. If your actions are challenged, the court or hearing officer will be more impressed by your attempts to help than by a list of errors. After training, Iso's performance should be measured against standards.

If performance standards are not met, further action should be taken. To comply with your company's disciplinary procedure, you might put Iso on probation during the period of training or immediately after while you determine if the training has helped.

13-56   Is suspension appropriate for poor performance?

Although most companies do not differentiate between discipline for poor performance and discipline for poor conduct, there is a significant difference. The purpose of suspension is to punish the employee and let everybody know that violations of company rules are taken seriously. Latecomers or absentees may realize by the suspension that their behavior cannot continue or they will be discharged.

Suspension does not help in solving poor performance. Some companies replace suspension with a longer period of probation in which every effort is made to help the employee improve. If this fails, perhaps the worker can be transferred to a job he or she can do well. If not, the employee is discharged. If people cannot do the jobs they are paid to do, it is not fair to the company to keep them.

Many companies will keep long-term employees who have not been able to keep up with changes in technology or have slowed down. But this is a decision each organization must make for itself—based on its history, philosophy of doing business, and concern for its employees and its image.

13-57   Is reduction in rank an appropriate punishment for poor performance?

Many people are promoted into positions above their level of competence. They were good in their previous assignment, so they are promoted to a higher level, but cannot make the grade. It is far more advantageous for both the company and the employees to reduce such people in rank rather than discharge them. The company saves highly trained and skilled workers who now perform in jobs they can do well. In addition, the employees do not have to face the trauma of unemployment and seeking a new job.

13-58   How can I assure myself that I am handling a disciplinary situation satisfactorily?

By following a set procedure with each employee who is disciplined, you will avoid making many of the errors that supervisors make in disciplining. Study and use the guideline presented in Figure 13-3. Keep it in front of you during disciplinary discussions and make appropriate notes on it afterward.

Guidelines for Discipline

[*Complete before disciplinary interview.*]

Employee _____

Offense _____

_____

_____

Policy and procedures provision _____

_____

When offense occurred _____

Previous similar offenses _____

_____

_____

What I wish to accomplish _____

_____

_____

Things to keep in mind in dealing with employee _____

_____

_____

_____

Questions to ask at start of interview _____

_____

_____

_____

_____

_____

Figure 13-3

Figure 13-3 (Continued)

CHECKLIST

[*Keep in front of you during interview.*]

Am I calm and collected?   _____

Did I get the whole story?   _____

Am I really listening?   _____

Did I interrupt?   _____

Am I sarcastic?   _____

Did I emphasize the "what"?   _____

Did I encourage solutions from the employee? _____

Suggestions made by employee

_____

_____

_____

_____

_____

_____

Solution agreed upon _____

_____

_____

_____

Action taken after interview _____

_____

_____

DOCUMENTATION

Type of document _____

Date _____

14
Layoffs, Quits, and Termination

Sooner or later all employees leave a company. They may die or retire, but more likely the separation will be precipitated by a layoff, voluntary resignation, or discharge for cause.

Every time a person leaves a company, whether it be voluntarily or involuntarily, it costs the company a great deal of money. The entire investment made in hiring, training, administering, and supervising that person is lost forever. In addition, every time a person leaves, the supervisor has the added burden of either restructuring the work of those who remain or hiring and training a replacement. Supervisors must do all that they can to minimize the turnover in their departments.

Layoffs. In some industries work is done on a seasonal basis. When the production season is over, workers are laid off or furloughed. Most people working in such industries are aware of this and adapt their lives to account for it. They know that they will be rehired after the furlough and, since they collect unemployment insurance, do not consider it a significant problem.

Layoffs, however, are often more permanent. Business falls off and there is no need for as many workers, so some are laid off. If business improves, they may be called back, but there is no guarantee. People usually seek other jobs and are not available if recalled. In such cases, the company loses forever skilled people whom it has spent time and money training. Companies may close a plant or go out of business. In these cases there is no hope for laid off workers to be rehired.

Voluntary quits. People may leave a job for a variety of reasons. Sometimes it is purely personal: a spouse is relocated; people return to school or change careers. Often it is job-related: people are not making the progress they had hoped for at work; they need a higher salary; they are unhappy with working conditions, with their boss, with the job itself. In these cases, it is sometimes possible to reduce turnover by identifying recurring problems and correcting them so that future workers will not leave for these reasons.

Termination for cause. Some employees cannot do the job for which they have been hired and have to be discharged; others are satisfactory for a while, then fall below standard and are let go. Sometimes such people can be saved for the company by better training. Every effort should be made to do so.

Some workers are fired because of violation of company rules. The most common are continuing lateness or absences. Typically, progressive discipline is administered. Only after all the steps have been taken is termination effected. In some cases, an employee may be discharged without progressive discipline (see question 14-37).

In discharging a worker in this litigious age, supervisors must take the necessary steps to protect the company through good documentation (see Chapter 13). Here are some of the most frequently asked questions when workers leave.

Layoffs

14-1 Our work is seasonal and we furlough a number of people during slow periods. Most of them will be rehired next season. However, we cannot guarantee that everybody will be rehired. What can we do so we don't lose skilled people who seek other jobs while on furlough?

Unless you can guarantee that employees will be rehired, there is no way you can be assured that they will not seek other employment. In industries where furloughs are expected (e.g., construction during winter months), some people may look forward to the furlough as a vacation. Those who want to work, or people you want to keep, may join the cadre of skilled employees who are kept on during the slow period for maintenance. If your company has a history of rehiring all furloughed workers, your best people will return. They depend on your company as much as you depend on them.

14-2   My company uses seniority as the basis for layoffs. What do I do with high performers who have less seniority than marginal workers?

Unless there is a union contract that specifies layoffs by reverse seniority, a company need not follow this practice. Some companies which do not have unions have specified reverse seniority in layoffs as part of their procedures manual. In this case, the policy is tantamount to a contract and must be adhered to. However, if neither of the above is true for your company, you can lay off people in any order you want, including keeping better workers over poorer workers with more seniority.

14-3   We lay people off on a LIFO basis: last in, first out. However, only over the past several years have we hired significant numbers of African Americans and Hispanics. We are about to have the first layoff in several years. If we follow strict seniority, the policy will have an adverse effect on these minorities. Will this present legal problems?

The Civil Rights Act of 1964 specifically exempts companies which have established seniority systems for layoffs and rehiring from being charged with discrimination if those systems are followed. There is an exception, however. If a member of a protected class can show that he or she personally experienced discrimination that resulted in a lower seniority than had there been no discrimination, that person may claim protection. (For example, Louisa was hired in 1985. She might have been hired in 1980, but the company did not place women in that job category at that time. Louisa might claim that except for the discriminatory policy, she would have higher seniority. However, each case must be decided individually.

14-4   We have to lay off several people because of slow business. How far in advance should we let them know?

If your company has 100 or more employees, it is required to comply with the Worker Adjustment and Retraining Notification Act (WARN). This law applies when there is a mass layoff or plant closing. A mass layoff is defined as a layoff or reduction in hours at a single site that affects 500 or more full-time employees or 50 or more if they constitute at least 33 percent of the active full-time work force. Reduction of hours means cutting hours worked by more than 50 percent each month for a 6-month period or longer. Notice must be given to those employees at least 60 days prior to their final day of work. Since there are exceptions to this rule, check with your company's legal department.

14-5   We have a total of 300 full-time workers. Do we have to go through all that red tape if we are going to lay off people?

If you lay off more than 100—that is, 33 percent of your work force—you must comply. If fewer people are to be laid off, you are not required to give formal notice.

14-6   We are not covered by the law. How much notice is it advisable to give people who are to be laid off?

It is only fair to give them adequate notice so they can take whatever steps they need to prepare for the loss of the job. It is entirely up to the company.

14-7   We will close down one of our plants in 3 months. We have notified all the workers. Some of the people we really need to phase out the plant are looking for other jobs. I can understand this. Is there anything we can do to keep them until we are ready to close down?

Of course, the company cannot compel an employee to remain. Some may be concerned that by the time they are released, the best available jobs in the area will be taken by workers who left the company before they did. Companies facing this problem usually offer key employees some financial incentive to remain until the closing date. The incentive may be in the form of a bonus, an increase in separation pay, or some other means of encouraging people to work until the company is ready to release them.

14-8   When we lay off people, how long must we continue covering them for health insurance and other benefits?

Under the federal law know as COBRA, companies with 20 or more employees must give people the opportunity to maintain their health insurance after they leave the company. The former employee (or dependents) may opt to continue coverage at his or her own expense for a limited period. Employees who are laid off may continue coverage for 18 months; those who are disabled at the time of coverage, 29 months. During this period, the employee must pay the full premium at the same rate the company pays (which is usually considerably less than an individual's premium) plus a small administrative charge. Other provisions are made for surviving or divorced spouses of employees.

COBRA rights can be cut off before the usual time if:

■ The covered person does not pay the premium

■ The covered person becomes covered by another health plan

■ The employer terminates the health plan for all its employees

■ The covered person becomes eligible for Medicare benefits

As we enter the mid-1990s, the Clinton administration is considering major changes in health-care coverage. The results, when adopted, may change current laws significantly. In addition, several states have laws on continuation of benefits which are more advantageous to employees. Such state laws take precedence over the federal law.

14-9   When people are laid off, what steps should be taken in processing them out?

In most companies the personnel or human resources department will do the processing, so supervisors need not be concerned. Once the supervisor notifies employees that they will be laid off, they are sent to personnel for processing out.

In smaller companies or branches with no personnel department, the supervisor must become involved. Once the employee is told of the decision, the supervisor should be prepared to do the following:

1. Discuss the continuation of benefits (see question 14-8).

2. Present the final check.

3. Discuss separation pay.

4. Discuss callback procedures as appropriate.

5. Retrieve company property (e.g., keys, credit cards, tools, IDs).

6. Discuss outplacement as appropriate (see question 14-15).

7. Answer questions.

8. Wish the employee well.

14-10   Can I hold back all or part of the final paycheck until I get back company property the employee has?

In most states you cannot hold money owed an employee longer than the day on which she or he would normally be paid. For example, final paychecks are for the period ending one week before the normal payday. You lay the person off at the end of the workweek. Normally, you would give the employee all accrued pay at that time. If the employee does not return property, you can hold the check until the normal payday (one week later), but not longer.

14-11   How much severance pay are we required to pay laid-off workers?

Federal law does not require a company to pay laid-off employees any severance pay. Most union contracts include provisions for severance. Many companies voluntarily give severance pay to laid-off workers and sometimes to workers who leave because of inability to do a job—but not to those discharged for poor conduct.

The amount is generally based on length of service. One week's pay per year of service is fairly typical. However, the amount varies from company to company and often within a company by job category. It is not uncommon for higher-salaried workers to be given a larger amount than those in lower echelons. Management personnel often negotiate their severance pay as part of a termination deal. The company must be cautious here. Unless the employee is in a unique position (such as a higher-ranking manager), making a special deal may set a precedent. For example, you agree to give Charlie 4 months' severance pay; now everybody in job categories similar to Charlie's can claim entitlement to the same amount. A precedent has been set.

14-12   Are laid-off employees entitled to be paid for sick and vacation days they did not use?

In most companies sick pay means pay for days when a person is sick. The time is not paid for if it is not used. Vacation pay is another matter. If the company has an accrued vacation plan (e.g., employees earn one vacation day for each month employed, up to a stated maximum), accrued time must be paid for. On the other hand, if vacation time is not accrued (e.g., the company gives all employees 1 or 2 weeks' vacation each year), there is no obligation to pay vacation time if employees have not completed the year's work. Since state and local laws differ somewhat, check to be sure what is covered in your area.

14-13   How do layoffs affect a company's unemployment compensation taxes?

The rate of tax that is paid for unemployment insurance is based on the number of former employees who have collected benefits. So it is to the advantage of companies to keep turnover at a minimum.

14-14   Should we conduct exit interviews with people who are being laid off?

It is not too useful. The purpose of an exit interview is to learn why employees quit and at the same time develop information about their attitudes toward the job and the company that might help in reducing future turnover. When people are laid off because of lack of work, the company knows why they are leaving. Also, because most hope to be rehired, it is unlikely that they will say things about the job that are negative. (Exit interviews are discussed in questions 14-23 to 14-25.)

14-15   Our company is closing one of its plants. Is there anything we can do to help employees ease their search for new employment?

Some companies have outplacement services to help laid-off employees relocate. These services, although originally designed to counsel professional and managerial personnel, have been expanded to deal with all types of employees. Workshops are conducted in analyzing skills, determining in what job categories they can be used, preparing résumés, and identifying potential employers. These programs have been successful in helping laid-off workers find jobs more rapidly than if left on their own.

14-16   Are there any alternatives to laying off people?

Instead of laying off workers, some companies have established work-sharing programs. All employees share the work that remains after some jobs are eliminated by either working fewer hours each week or working full time alternate weeks. The hourly pay remains the same but, because of reduced hours, the payroll is decreased. Some states have amended their unemployment insurance laws so that employees can collect some unemployment benefits during the work-sharing period.

Work sharing enables companies to keep skilled employees during slow periods. The workers gain as well. Although they receive less total pay, they are better off than not receiving anything. More important, they maintain all benefits.

Another alternative to layoffs is to reduce everybody's pay, including management's, during slow periods. Workers will accept the reduction if they still net significantly more than they would from unemployment benefits. A third approach is to encourage older workers to retire early. Since a company cannot compel workers to retire, incentives are provided to make it worth their while. When high-paid senior employees leave, the payroll is reduced significantly.

14-17   Is there a best way to rehire laid-off workers?

If seniority is the basis of the layoff, most companies rehire in reverse order—that is, the more senior employees are rehired first. This may not be the most desirable approach. If there is no contractual obligation to do so, it might be more advantageous to rehire people according to the skills needed as work expands. For example, the company may need to rehire production workers before more senior employees in the shipping department. Whatever system is used, it should be explained to workers at the time of the layoff to avoid misunderstandings and discontent when people are rehired.

Voluntary Quits

14-18   How much notice can we require of a person who quits?

There is no legal requirement that any notice be given when a person decides to quit. Companies may request that some notice be given so they can make provisions to replace the employee, but such notice cannot be mandatory. The only clout a company may have in enforcing this request is the employee's concern that he or she may not receive a good reference if inadequate notice is given.

14-19   If an employee voluntarily quits, must we pay for unused vacation or sick days?

The same rule applies as in layoffs (see question 14-12).

14-20   Carol has told her co-workers that she intends to work only until her vacation and then quit, but she has not mentioned it officially to me. Can I discharge her before she quits?

Unless there is a union contract or specific company policy to the contrary, you can fire Carol any time you want to. However, it may not be the best way of dealing with the situation. Assuming that Carol is a good worker and you do not want to lose her, take her aside and let her know that you have heard she plans to quit. Determine the reason for her decision. If it is job-related, perhaps you can persuade her to stay. If it is personal, let her know that you would appreciate her giving you adequate notice before resigning.

If Carol is a just-satisfactory employee, let her know you are aware of her plans and start looking for a replacement immediately. You can let her go when you have found one. If vacation time is determined on an accrual basis, you will have to pay Carol for the accrued vacation time when she leaves. If it is not accrued, but is based on completing a full year or some other system, you need not pay her for the vacation time if she does not qualify. However, a serious morale problem will arise with other workers if you fire her without vacation pay just before vacation time. In this case, it might be better to let Carol follow her own schedule of leaving after her vacation.

14-21   Gabriel has given us notice. He will leave in 2 weeks. He has asked me for a written reference. He's been an average worker. Should I give him such a letter? If so, what can I say?

Although such letters were popular in the United States many years ago and are still used in some countries today, very few companies give written letters of reference to former employees. Tell Gabriel that he can refer prospective employers to your personnel department, which will respond to any inquiry about him.

Some organizations allow the immediate supervisor to give such references. However, because of legal problems, many firms require that references be given only by the personnel department. (See questions 69–82 in Chapter 2.)

14-22   Is it a good idea to let an employee who has given notice train his or her successor?

Usually not. Training should be conducted by the supervisor or a designated trainer (see Chapter 4). Often people leave because of dissatisfaction with the company or the job. If such people train their replacements, they will transfer this discontent to the new employees. Even if departing workers are not discontent, they may perform the job in ways that you do not wish new people to acquire. If you, the supervisor, do the training, you can be sure each new employee will learn to perform the job properly.

14-23   Are exit interviews helpful?

When an employee leaves voluntarily, it is important to learn the real cause of leaving. Often the reason given is superficial. The exit interview gives the company a chance to dig deeper.

Jon may announce that he is leaving because he will get more money in the new job. Although this may be true, it could be only a small part of his decision to leave. The exit interviewer must probe and learn what other factors, if any, precipitated Jon's search for a new job.

A very important benefit of exit interviews is that they may uncover problems within a department that have contributed to turnover. The company can then take action to alleviate the problems and reduce future turnover.

14-24   Should the exit interview be conducted by the immediate supervisor?

No. Since some of the problems related to the employee's departure may involve the immediate supervisor, he or she should not conduct the exit interview. Either a representative of the personnel department or the person who supervises the immediate supervisor should hold the interview.

14-25   What questions should be asked in an exit interview?

The exit interview should be a real interview—not just a series of questions. Its purpose is to uncover the employee's real reasons for leaving and additional information about the way in which the job and the company were preceived.

The interviewer should start out by building rapport. The employee should be put at ease, not made to feel that this is an interrogation. The question as to why he or she is leaving the company should not be raised first. A better start might be: "Tell me about the kind of work you have been doing in your most recent assignment." This will start the conversation going, but will also enable the interviewer to evaluate whether it is the kind of work that would be expected on the job. One reason people quit is that the job turned out to be different from what they expected.

Here are some specific questions that might be asked about the job:

- What did you like most about this job? What did you like least?
- How do you feel about your compensation?
- How do you feel about the progress you have made in this company?
- How do you feel about working conditions?

Here are some questions that might be asked about supervision:

- What did you like most about your supervisor?
- What did you like least?
- How did your supervisor handle gripes or complaints?
- How would you describe your supervisor's style of supervising?
- How do you react to that style?
- Does the supervisor tend to favor some employees or act unfairly to others?

Here are some questions to sum up the interview:

- If you could discuss with top management exactly how you feel about this company, what would you say?
- What does the job to which you are going offer you that you were not getting here?

If the questions asked thus far have not brought out the true reasons for the employee's leaving, the interviewer should be direct:

"Why are you leaving at this particular time?" A good exit interview may take half an hour or more. However, it is time well spent if it provides insight into how people feel about the company and uncovers negative factors (or reinforces positive factors) in the work environment.

14-26   Is it a good idea to make a counteroffer to an employee who quits to take another job?

It depends on how badly you need that person. If the departure will cause a hardship to the department, you may want to do everything you can to keep the employee. However, you take a big risk in making counteroffers. Almost always you must give that person a substantial salary increase. Not only will you put your compensation structure off balance, but you are giving a message to every other employee: if you want more money, get another offer and use it as a bargaining chip.

14-27   If an employee quits, can she or he collect unemployment compensation?

Usually not. Employees who leave voluntarily are not qualified for unemployment benefits. Therefore they do not affect the ratings on which the company's unemployment taxes are based.

14-28   Do employees who quit have the same COBRA rights as laid-off workers when it comes to maintaining health-care benefits at their own expense?

Yes (see question 14-8).

14-29   When an employee hands in a resignation, what should I do to make the transition smooth?

First agree on a departure date. If it is best for the company to keep the employee on the job for a period of time until you can arrange for others to do it, set a date for the resignation that will accommodate this schedule. On the other hand, keeping an employee who has given notice around longer than necessary can affect morale.

It is a good idea to request a status report on the matters the employee is working on at this time so you can arrange for others to take them over. Develop a list of vendors, customers, or other people outside your department with whom the employee interrelates so you can notify them of the change.

14-30   When do I tell my other employees that a person has resigned?

The chances are that they already know. The employee may have told them before telling you. In any case, as soon as you are notified, let the others know when the employee will leave and how it will affect their work. If they will have to do more work or work more hours until a replacement is hired, explain the new arrangement.

Firing Employees Legally and Tactfully

14-31 I've done all I can to salvage Ron. He's been absent more times than we allow. We've gone through all the steps in our progressive discipline. The next step has to be termination. How do I do it?

Ron should not be surprised when he is terminated after going through progressive discipline. At the penultimate step (usually suspension), Ron should have been told that if he were absent one more time he would be discharged. Therefore, he should expect it.

First, review all the documentation. Make sure you have followed all the steps required in your policy manual. Then bring Ron into a conference room and review the documents. You don't have to read every word, but summarize each of the steps taken.

Let's role-play a termination discussion.

BOSS: Ron, please sit down. Over the past 8 months we've had several discussions about your attendance. I have here the various documents relating to these discussions.

RON: I know I've been absent a lot, but when I'm here I'm a good worker. You told me that many times.

BOSS: That's why I'm sorry it has reached this point. Ron, there is more to a job than performing it well. As I've told you before, unless we can rely on our people being on the job, we can't meet our production standards and maintain our competitive edge. You've been given several opportunities to correct this situation. On October 10 you were given an informal warning and you promised me you would not be absent again. You were out the following Monday. At that time we had a counseling session. You then wrote a plan of action in which you committed yourself to being here every day. Three weeks later you were out again—and on a Monday.

RON: That's right, but as I told you, my girlfriend lives in Springfield and that's a 5-hour drive.

BOSS: We discussed that many times and it doesn't justify absence from the job. You've been on probation twice and you were suspended for 1 day in January and for 3 days last month. At your last suspension I told you that if you were absent again, the next step would be termination. We have no alternative but to let you go.

Note that there is no discussion or argument. When Ron brings up his good performance and his so-called excuse (the long drive from his girlfriend's town), the boss quickly dismisses these points. This is not the time for arguments, recriminations, or excuses. The damage is long past correcting.

14-32   Do you have any guidelines for preparing for a termination interview?

Figure 14-1 provides some guidelines for termination.

14-33   Is there a best place to conduct the termination interview?

It seems logical to conduct it in your own office. However, sometimes an employee may become upset and try to extend the interview with pleas for reconsideration. It is better to use a conference room. If matters get out of hand, you can always walk out and leave the employee alone. If you were in your own office, this could not be done as readily as it is not a good idea to leave the discharged employee alone in your office.

14-34   What do I do if an employee gives me a hard time at a termination session? I had an employee who ranted and raved and even threatened me.

Keep cool and try to calm the employee down. Let's role-play this type of situation. First, the wrong way:

BOSS: ... And despite all the efforts we've made to help you improve your performance, you still haven't met our production standards.

DORA: ... But I'm doing the best I can.

BOSS: I know you've tried, but production is measured against standards that all workers must meet and you have not met them.

Termination Checklist

Name of employee_____ Date_____

1. State applicable policy and procedures rule.

   _____

   _____

2. If poor conduct, list progressive discipline steps taken and
   dates.

   Informal warning   _____

   Written notice   _____

   Counseling interview   _____

   Punishments: _____   _____

                           _____   _____

                           _____   _____

3. If poor performance, list steps taken to improve performance and dates.

   _____   _____

   _____   _____

   _____   _____

   _____   _____

4. Have you reviewed all pertinent
   documents?   _____

5. Have you reviewed procedures in
   similar cases?   _____

6. Have you treated this case in the
   same way as similar cases in the past?   _____

7. Has this action been reviewed by
   your immediate supervisor?   _____

       the personnel department?   _____

       the company attorney?   _____

Figure 14-1

Figure 14-1 (Continued)

8. Are any claims pending against the
   company by this employee?   _____

   Workers' compensation   _____

   Other   _____

9. List any special factors that might
   be brought up in case this termination
   is challenged.   _____

10. Summarize the termination interview.   _____

    Date and hour   _____

    Witness's name   _____

    Position   _____

    Comments   _____

11. List final steps and dates.   _____

    ID returned   _____

    Keys returned   _____

    Company property returned   _____

    Security clearance cancelled   _____

    Final paycheck issued   _____

    Other actions   _____

    Files sent to personnel   _____

DORA: (*Voice rising.*) That's not fair. The real reason you're firing me is that you don't like me.

BOSS: (*Voice rising.*) *That's* not fair. I treat you like I treat everybody else.

DORA: (*Voice rising more.*) Not true. You hate me and that's why you're firing me.

BOSS: (*Voice rising more.*) Don't argue with me. Liking or not liking has nothing to do with this.

Now let's role-play how the situation might have been handled differently:

BOSS: ...And despite all the efforts we've made to help you improve your performance, you have not met our production standards.

DORA: But I'm doing the best I can. Last week I did better than the week before.

BOSS: I know you've tried, but production is measured against standards that all workers must meet. That's the only way we can stay competitive. And you have not met those standards.

DORA: (*Voice rising.*) That's not fair. The real reason you're firing me is that you don't like me.

BOSS: (*Calmly.*) Dora, you know that isn't true. I've tried very hard to help you improve. You have acknowledged this many times. There are many people who work well in some areas and not in others. I have a feeling that you probably could be more effective in another type of work. I know you've tried, but unfortunately there is a limit to how long we can keep people who do not meet production standards.

DORA: (*Calmed down.*) I did try, but it was too hard for me.

Notice that the supervisor did not lose her temper. If you have a low threshold for anger, make every effort to stay calm. Count to 10, 20, or more before responding. Don't get into arguments about the termination. The decision has been made and will not be changed.

If the employee raises his or her voice, lower yours. People respond to a raised voice by speaking even louder. By responding more softly, you disarm the other person and this has a calming effect. Once the employee is calm, you can continue your review of the documents and bring the meeting to a close. Never use a termination session as a means of telling off an employee. You may be glad to get rid of the person, but don't let this show in your words or actions.

14-35 Our company requires that a third party be present when somebody is fired. Is that a good idea?

Yes. The presence of a third party inhibits both you and the employee from losing your tempers and saying or doing inappropriate things. It also provides a witness so that the employee cannot later claim statements or promises were made that were not made.

After Agnes was fired for poor performance, she filed suit against the company for age discrimination. Her claim was that when she was terminated, the supervisor told her that the company needed younger people to meet production standards—a totally false claim. Had a third person been in the room when she was terminated, Agnes would never have brought up this claim, because she knows that it would be refuted by the witness.

14-36   Who is the best person to serve as a witness?

Ask someone from the personnel or human resources department. These people are trained in how to handle terminations. They also can be helpful in answering questions about benefits and other administrative problems regarding the separation. If such a person is not available, call in another supervisor as the witness. Most union contracts, specify that a representative of the union be present in addition to anybody the company may use.

14-37   Are there times when I can fire someone without going through progressive discipline?

Most companies allow for spontaneous termination under very special circumstances which are clearly delineated in the policy manual. These circumstances include such serious offenses as drinking on the job, fighting, stealing, and insubordination. Supervisors should resort to spontaneous termination only when they are sure they have irrefutable proof that the employee has committed a serious offense.

It is not always easy to prove these allegations. Shari was fired for coming in drunk. She certainly acted drunk, but even a police officer cannot sustain a charge of drunk driving unless breath or blood tests have been taken. You see Chuck shooting up in the men's room. Is this adequate evidence? Are you sure it was heroin? It may have been insulin.

Unless you are absolutely sure of your facts, do not discharge somebody spontaneously. If Shari appears drunk, send her home and write her up. She will realize that you mean business and that if she continues this behavior she will be fired. If Chuck appears to be using an illegal substance, suspend him until you can verify what it is. Then take appropriate action.

Caution: Do not let an employee who is impaired by alcohol or drugs drive. If an accident occurs, the company may be held liable. Call a taxi.

14-38   When I fire somebody after progressive discipline, I have a series of documents on file to back me up. If I fire somebody spontaneously, there is no documentation. How do I protect myself and the company?

Write a detailed report describing the circumstances leading up to the termination. Get written statements from witnesses as to what occurred. If you can, get the employee to sign a statement attesting to the accuracy of the report.

14-39   My company is paranoid about being sued over termination. Often employees get away with serious violations. How can I prevent someone I terminate from suing?

Under our legal system, anybody can sue anybody for any reason. No one is ever fully protected. However, most attorneys who handle this type of litigation work on a contingency basis. If they don't win, they get no fee. If you have prepared the termination properly and have all the documentation, it is unlikely that a lawyer looking at those documents would even take the case. It would be obvious that you have sufficient grounds to win.

14-40   We fired a woman who was caught stealing. She signed a confession and we thought that ended the case. Now she is suing us for unlawful discharge. How can she do this?

In similar cases, the courts have ruled in favor of the complainant on the grounds that the confession was obtained by duress. She may claim that you told her that if she didn't sign the confession you would prosecute her as a criminal. Rather than face that, she signed. Now she claims that she did not steal anything and it was a misunderstanding. You will now have to prove that she did steal. In such cases, the best protection is to have solid evidence to prove your case and to report it to the police.

14-41   I've read articles in the paper about terminated employees suing for defamation of character. How can they do that?

Such cases can emanate from many sources. An example:

When Al was terminated for violation of company rules, the supervisor asked a security guard to escort Al to his desk, make sure he removed only personal possessions, and then escort him out of the building. The security guard took Al by the arm and marched him to his desk; then marched him out of the building.

Al sued, claiming that this treatment gave the other employees the impression that he was a criminal and had been discharged for stealing or some other heinous offense. He won a substantial settlement.

Even in the case of a serious offense—such as stealing—the company must be cautious. Suppose that, to alert other employees to the risk of stealing, the company publicizes the case, naming the culprit and specifying the cause of termination. The employee might sue for defamation.

14-42   What steps can I take to avoid defamation charges?

1. Be certain of the facts. Conduct a thorough investigation. Consult with your human resources and legal departments or outside consultants or attorneys.
2. Be factual in talking with others or in describing the situation in writing. Give facts, not opinions.
3. Tell only those who need to know.
4. Avoid making examples of fired employees. Other employees will probably know what happened, and that is usually enough to serve as a deterrent.

14-43   I know bosses who make life very unpleasant for employees so that they will quit. They stop talking to them and no longer invite them to meetings. They even assign them unpleasant tasks. Many people who are treated like that will quit. Such cases are voluntary quits and people can't sue. Right?

Wrong. Making a person unhappy so he or she will quit can be interpreted by the courts as "constructive discharge"—that is, because of the treatment of the employee, the resignation is considered to be a termination rather than a voluntary action. Such employees may become so aggravated, they will sue. Perhaps more important, no effort is made to resolve the problem. Why is the employee being "forced" to quit? With progressive discipline, some answers may be found. If that fails, termination is the solution.

14-44   I have been told that we have to be particularly careful in firing people who are covered by the equal employment opportunity laws—women, minorities, older people, and disabled workers. If we fire people in these protected categories, aren't they more likely to claim that the real reason for their discharge was discrimination?

When people are fired, it is human nature for them to try to place the blame on somebody or something else. An older person may claim he or she was fired because of age, an Asian because of national origin, and so on. This does not mean protected groups have to be treated differently from others. They are expected to meet the same performance standards and obey the same rules.

Document each disciplinary step in the same way for all employees. Don't focus on documenting offenses of minority employees out of concern over litigation. If you have thorough documentation for a minority employee and nothing for a nonminority person, this alone is considered discrimination.

14-45   Our company requires 2 weeks' notice if somebody quits. Is it a good idea to give similar notice to a person you fire?

This is OK for layoffs, but not a good idea for disciplinary terminations. Not only should terminated people not be allowed to stay for 2 weeks; they should be removed from the workplace as quickly as possible. Such people may disrupt the work of others by talking to them and creating scenes. There are reports of terminated people who sabotaged equipment, destroyed computer files, or stole information that could be useful to competitors.

14-46   When I fire people, I am often more upset than they are. What can I do to prepare myself for the termination session?

Nobody should be surprised at being fired after progressive discipline. However, it is never a pleasant experience and some supervisors are nervous about it. Here are some suggestions to help you over the hurdles:

1. Use a conference room, not your own office (see question 14-33).

2. Review all the documents so you will be prepared to discuss them.

3. Review all that you know about the personality of the employee:
   - What problems have you had with this worker in the past?
   - How did the employee respond to previous discussions?
   - How has this person related with you in the past? With other employees?
   - What special personal problems does the employee have that you are aware of?

4. Review any problems you have had in firing other employees and map out a plan to avoid them.

5. Ask your personnel director for guidance on company rules that may apply.

6. Relax before the meeting. Do whatever helps you clear your mind and calm your emotions. You are not the employee's executioner; you are performing a necessary part of your job.

Keep in mind that you have done all that you can through the informal and formal steps to salvage the employee. You need not feel guilty about this final step.

14-47   What day and time is it best to fire somebody?

Traditionally, people are fired at the end of the workday on Friday. This is not really a good time. Of course, there is no perfect time for firing. Many companies find that it is best to discharge people early in the day and send them home. This alleviates the concern about terminated employees griping to co-workers as everyone leaves the facility. Some organizations feel that terminating people in midweek is best, since it gives them a chance to start looking for a new job the next day and not brooding about it over the weekend.

14-48   Once an employee is fired, how should he or she be outprocessed?

In most larger companies, fired employees are sent to the personnel department for processing. They are told their rights to continue medical coverage, how long they will be covered for benefits, their eligibility for unemployment, and so on. In addition, they are asked to return any company property that they may have. If there is no personnel department, the supervisor must handle the procedure. (see question 14-9 and Figure 14-1).

14-49   Must I pay an employee at the time he or she is fired?

State laws vary. Some states have different rules for voluntary versus involuntary separation. In general, employees who are laid off or fired must be paid at the time of termination; employees who quit must wait until the next regular payday. However, even if your state allows you to defer payment for involuntary separations, it is advisable to give fired workers their final check at the time of termination. In this way, you need have no future contact with these employees.

14-50   How much severance pay must I give an employee who is fired?

The same rules apply as when a person quits or is laid off (see questions 14-11 and 14-12).

14-51   Is it a good idea to allow or encourage employees to resign rather than be fired?

If people resign, it may look better when they seek another job. Some prefer this option. However, if people quit voluntarily, they forfeit their eligibility for unemployment benefits. Make this clear when the option of resignation is offered. In addition, be sure it is truly an option and not a forced resignation, which could be considered a "constructive discharge" (see question 14-43).

14-52   What do I tell the other workers when one of their peers has been terminated?

In most cases, everybody knows. People have observed the employee's behavior and performance over time. They are aware of the previous disciplinary steps that have been taken. You need not make an issue of it. Tell them that Val has been terminated. You do not have to explain or justify your action. If you have been fair in your treatment of Val, there will be no repercussions.

In a union situation where a termination is being grieved, it is not in the best interest of the company to explain your side to the other workers. Your arguments should be reserved for the hearing. If you are questioned by others, explain that because of the arbitration you are not allowed to discuss the matter.

Employment at Will

14-53   What is meant by "employment at will"?

Employment at will is a legal concept under which any employee is hired and can be fired at the will of the employer. The employer has the right to refuse to hire an applicant or to terminate an employee for any reason or no reason at all.

14-54   What federal or state law gives employers that right?

There is no statute on the books that has legislated employment at will. It is based on common law. From the beginning of this country's history, Americans have been guided by two kinds of law: legislated acts and common law. The former are the laws passed by Congress, the states, and local governments. Common law is based on accepted practices as upheld by court decisions. It has the same impact on our actions as legislation except that common law can be superseded by legislation and excepted by contractual agreement. Violations of common law are not criminal acts; they are torts, or civil wrongs, and are dealt with as civil actions or civil lawsuits.

14-55   What legislation has superseded employment at will?

Both federal and state legislation prohibits an employer from firing or refusing to hire somebody because of union activity, race, religion, national origin, age, disability, and a few other protections. This means that despite the common law concept of employment at will, a company may not violate these laws.

14-56   Our union contract clearly specifies under what circumstances people can be fired. How does this provision fit into the employment-at-will common law?

In addition to legislation superseding common law, parties can agree by contract to waive their common law rights. A union contract is an agreement to do just that. The company waives its rights to fire people at will. Employment at will can also be waived by private contracts. If an employer and employee agree that the employee will be employed for a specific period of time, the company has waived its right to fire that person until the end of the contract, except under circumstances specified in certain contractual provisions.

14-57   Does this mean we can make any deals we want with employees so long as we get them to sign a contract?

You cannot waive through contract a right that has been established under legislated statutes. For example, it is not legal to sign a contract in which employees agree to work for less than the minimum wage.

14-58   We don't have a union and nobody in our company has a contract. Does this mean that people can be fired at any time for any reason?

Not quite. An employer's use of employment at will is restricted not only by federal statutes—such as the National Labor Relations Act (prohibiting termination because of union activity) and the various civil rights laws—but also by a number of court decisions made at the state level over the past several years. These decisions vary from state to state, but the examples given in response to the following questions generally apply. Check with your attorney for specific applications in the states in which your company operates.

14-59 We don't have contracts with our people, but they all get copies of the rules and regulations and access to company policy manuals. Don't written rules have the same legal impact as a contract?

In several states, courts have ruled that a company policy and procedures manual is tantamount to a contract. Even though the manual is not a formal and signed agreement, the company has published it and employees are expected to follow it. The company is also expected to comply with the rules.

In one company, a supervisor was fired without having gone through progressive discipline. He claimed that when he had to fire somebody, he was required to follow the progressive discipline steps outlined in the manual; therefore, he should have expected the same treatment. The company's contention was that the manual was only a guideline—not a rigid procedure. The court ruled in favor of the employee. If a policy is published in the manual, employees should expect it to be followed.

14-60 What about oral commitments? If the manager who hires me assures me that the job is permanent and then fires me 6 months later, can I sue?

Many courts have ruled that oral statements on matters of employment are as binding as written contracts. One man who quit his job to work for another company was fired after less than a year. He sued, stating that he left his former job only because he was told during his hiring interview that he would be employed for life in the new company. The court awarded him a large settlement.

No supervisor should make any oral commitments to applicants about tenure of employment. In fact many companies print a "disclaimer" on the application form: "All employees are hired at will and no oral commitments are binding." Some even add that written commitments are valid only if signed by a senior officer of the company.

14-61 What steps should be taken to avoid legal problems and technical violations?

1. All supervisors should be thoroughly trained in company procedures concerning termination and should adhere to them.

2. No supervisor should ever make commitments concerning tenure or other employment conditions.

3. Written job offers should be prepared by the personnel or human resources department and screened by the legal department or company attorney.

4. The term "permanent" employee should be removed from company documents. Nobody is permanent. If the company must differentiate between temporary or part-time people and others, call the full-time people "regular" employees.

5. Even if the application for employment (see Figure 1-2) includes a statement that the company is an at-will employer, a similar statement should be included in the employee handbook and policy and procedures manual. Management should seek legal advice on how to word statements on application forms, in company manuals, and on other documents to guard against technical violations.

15

Time
Management

Supervisors are constantly complaining that there is so much work
to do and so little time to do it. In addition to their major function
of managing a department, most people in supervisory positions
spend a great portion of their working time in operational or nonsupervisory activities. The chief accountant, for example, will
spend more time in performing accounting functions than in
supervising staff.

Once promoted to management positions, supervisors are
measured, not on how well these operational activities are performed, but on how well the department is functioning. Since
there just aren't enough hours in their workday, supervisors must
learn how to manage their time effectively so all the work can be
done within the time available.

As supervisors, we first need to determine what we wish to
accomplish and how close we come to doing it. We must have
goals and plans to reach those goals. These plans should be both
long and short term. Then we must analyze our workday to see
what we are accomplishing, what is not being done that should
be done, and most important what is preventing us from doing
what we have planned to do. This chapter explores some of the
major factors involved in managing time.

Planning

15-1   In every seminar I've taken on time management, I'm told that it is important to have goals. What do goals have to do with managing time?

Unless we know what we want to accomplish, there is no way of measuring whether or not we are accomplishing it. In addition, the goals we set become the touchstone against which we can measure how effectively we are managing our time. We should ask this question about everything we do on the job: "Is what I am doing now helping me reach my goals?" If the answer is no, we are wasting our time.

Don't let this frighten you. The answer is going to be no a lot more often than it will be yes. This is because supervisors are often required to do many things that are not productive. For example, in a large organization, people spend an inordinate amount of time keeping records of what they do so other people know what they are doing. This may be important for control, but it doesn't add one bit to productivity. To manage our time more effectively, we must first determine if what we are doing is not goal-related and if possible, eliminate it; if this is not possible, we must reduce the amount of time it takes so we can devote more of our time to truly productive matters.

15-2   What guidelines can you offer so I can create goals that are meaningful both to me and to the company?

To make goals more than pipe dreams, you must strive to make them specific, attainable, and above all CLEAR:

C larify objectives.   Indicate in clear terms what you wish to accomplish. "To improve the quality of product produced in my department" is too vague a goal. Instead be specific: "By the end of this fiscal year, the number of rejects in my department will be reduced by 30 percent."

L imit their scope.   Unless goals have a reasonable chance of being achieved, setting them is meaningless. To ensure reasonableness, break the long-term goals into attainable subgoals.

Long-term goal.   "To develop a new health-care program for the company by the end of the year."

Intermediate goal.   "To have full information on alternative plans by the end of 6 months."

Short-term goal.   "To complete my investigation of the XYZ HMO by the end of this month."

E quate personal and company goals.   The goals you set for yourself or your department must be congruent with those of your immediate supervisor and of the company. Otherwise you will be wasting your time. No matter how commendable your goals may be, unless you are doing what the organization wants, you will not be productive.

A im for flexibility.   There are times when it is not possible to meet the goals that have been set. Don't be frustrated and give up. Review what has transpired, evaluate the situation, and make necessary adjustments. In some organizations you may be required to set three levels of goals. The middle level is the desired goal. The higher level is set so that if things are going faster than expected, you shift into that level. The lower level is set so that if obstacles develop, it is not necessary to give up; you just shift to that level.

R esist complacency.   Once you have reached a goal, set another that will make you stretch and continue to improve and grow.

15-3   I never have enough time in the day. How can I tell where my time is going?

Make a time analysis of your day. To do this, draw a chart similar to Figure 15-1. Break your workday into 15-minute segments and list in each box what you did during that time period. Keep a log for several days—preferably not consecutive ones, since you may be totally absorbed in a single project. Choose 2 days per week for 3 weeks and you will obtain a more comprehensive view of how your time is being spent.

15-4   What should I learn from the time analysis?

You will see where your time is actually being spent. People are often shocked to learn how much time they waste on such things as duplicating work, being overcautious by checking and rechecking work, chatting about nonbusiness matters with co-workers, and handling unnecessary paperwork. One very important result of time analysis is that people see how many interruptions interfere with planned work and where those interruptions are coming from. Most people know that they are wasting time; time analysis pinpoints the cause.

Time Analysis Worksheet	
Time Segment	Activities
8:00–8:15	
8:15–8:30	
8:30–8:45	
8:45–9:00	

Continue as above for the entire day.

Figure 15-1

15-5   I've tried to make a time analysis of my day by keeping a record of everything I do in 15-minute intervals. But I always get so busy that I forget to enter the data.

Many people give up when they forget to enter several segments. It is best, of course, if you make the entry at the end of the time specified, but you can enter it later. You may have to think back and may even miss something. Total accuracy is not as important as obtaining a good idea of how your time was spent.

15-6   One of my big interrupters is my boss. She tells me all about her personal problems. How can I enter this in the log without offending her?

It is not always necessary to show your log to your boss. The purpose of the time analysis is to help you get more control of your time. If, however, you know that your boss may ask to see it or even may inadvertently see it, you may want to enter this type of situation in a discreet manner (e.g., "Discussion with Betty"). You know exactly what it means, but Betty or anybody else seeing it could interpret it as a business discussion. Working smarter with your boss is the focus of Chapter 16.

15-7   Long-range planning is important, but in order to get my day-to-day work done, I must concentrate on short-term planning. What is the best tool to make sure that my daily work will be accomplished?

Almost every successful time manager uses lists (sometimes called "to-do lists") as the basis for day-to-day planning. Making a list of everything you plan to do ensures that you will not forget something.

15-8   I use a to-do list and try to follow it, but I'm constantly interrupted. I wind up with only half my list completed and sometimes really important things are not done. What's the answer?

The to-do list is the basic tool for day-to-day planning, but it is not an effective tool unless it is prioritized. One of the most famous industrialists in the United States in the early twentieth century was Charles Schwab, president of U.S. Steel Corporation. He attributed his ability to managing time to a suggestion made by one of the progenitors of modern management consulting, Ivey Lee.

When Lee proposed to Schwab that he could help him make U.S. Steel even more effective than it was, Schwab was skeptical. After all, Lee admitted that he knew nothing at all about the steel business. But Lee convinced him that certain principles were applicable to all businesses. He suggested that Schwab try just one of his ideas for a month. If it proved to have merit, Schwab could pay Lee whatever he felt it was worth; if it was of no value, no fee would be charged.

This approximates Lee's advice:

Every morning when you come in, or you may prefer to do this the preceding evening, make a list of all the things you wish to accomplish that day and put it in priority order. Then work on the first item on the list and don't leave it for the second until you have done everything you can on the first.

You'll be interrupted. No job is free from interruption. But once you have taken care of the interruption, get back to what you were working on. The big mistake people make is when interrupted, they forget what they were doing before and don't get back to it.

By the end of the day, you will probably not have performed everything on the list. But the important things were all accomplished. Take those that were not done, integrate them with new things which may have arisen, and make a new list—in priority order—for the next day. Continue this throughout the month.

At the end of the month, there will be items left that you never got to. You repeated them day after day. This is an indicator to you that they were not important enough for you to do. They either should have been delegated or not done at all. But the important items were all accomplished.

When they met at the end of the month, Schwab gave Lee a check for $25,000. He said it was the best advice he ever had. It worked so well for him that Schwab required all his subordinate managers to use it as well.

That's what you must do. Establish priorities and stick to them. You may never get all your planned work done, but this will ensure that the important matters are achieved.

15-9 Any other suggestions on using to-do lists?

Check off each item as you finish it. This has a dual benefit psychologically: it eliminates your concern about the item and, as you see the list getting smaller and smaller, it relieves stress and tension about having too much to do.

List only important items. Adding routine tasks not only makes the list longer than necessary, but creates the impression that you have too much to accomplish. The routine tasks are usually done almost automatically anyway. Keep the list where it can easily be seen. If you don't see it all the time, you will tend to forget it.

Do not get panic-stricken if you just can't see how you will complete all the items on the list. Review the list and adjust your priorities to meet the time available. Often items that originally appeared to be high priority can be reduced in rank because other matters have developed to make them less important.

Review the list at least once a day (more if circumstances change rapidly) and reprioritize when necessary. Then rewrite the list rather than crossing things out or renumbering. A neat list is easier to read, to follow, and to take seriously.

15-10   How can I set up a follow-up system so I don't spend so much time constantly checking my people's work?

Once an employee is properly trained, it should not be necessary to check work on a regular basis. When assigning an employee a new type of work, set control points and check only at those points. (See questions 14–18 in Chapter 5.)

If you are concerned with your people meeting deadlines, develop a system to trip your memory about the work you have assigned to your people. Here are two commonly used methods:

- *Desk calendar.*   List on the appropriate dates when assignments should be completed by each of your people. You may prefer to note items earlier than the due date so you can check progress.

- *Tickler file.*   Place a copy of the memo, letter, or report that initiated the assignment in a dated file folder. Each morning review the file for that day and the next several days to see what is due and, if desired, check progress. If there is no initiating memo, write a note to yourself about the project and place it in the appropriate dated file.

Interruptions

15-11   My biggest interruption is the telephone. I don't have a secretary to screen my calls. How can I cut down on these interruptions?

Most supervisors do not have secretaries. You have to pick up every call, since you obviously cannot guess who is calling and how important the call may be. Here are some suggestions.

Voicemail is now being used by many organizations. If you are away from your desk, taking another call, or busy with an important project, the voicemail takes a message for you. The advantages are obvious, but there are several problems as well. You may miss important calls. Or the call may be from your boss, who knows you are at your desk and gets annoyed if you do not answer personally. The solution is to check your voicemail frequently and return calls immediately. If a phone conversation lasts more than a few minutes, check your voicemail right after you hang up to make sure no important calls came through while you were talking. Also make it a practice to check your messages each time you return to your desk and periodically whenever you turn on the voicemail to attend to other matters.

Answering machines are similar to voicemail and give you the option of listening to the calling party's message before you decide whether to pick up. The major problem here is that you must still interrupt your concentration to listen to the message.

Another approach is to screen your calls rapidly as they come in. If you are engaged in a high-priority project and the call relates to a less important matter, politely tell the caller that you are unable to talk now and will call back. Give the caller an approximate time and ask if that would be convenient. Use discretion. It may not be a good idea to ever tell this to your boss or your boss's boss, or to an important customer. There are times when the interruption may be more important or politically expedient than the work you are doing.

15-12   Most of the calls I get or make are with people I deal with on a regular basis. We know each other so we spend a lot of time talking about personal matters before we get down to business. I know it is time-consuming, but the personal content of the calls helps lubricate the business relationship. Any suggestions?

Small talk is helpful in developing rapport and in showing personal interest in the person with whom you are speaking. Yes, you should spend some part of business conversations in personal chit-chat. But watch the time or it will overwhelm you.

The phone rings. The voice on the other end says, "Hi, this is Gil." You like this long-time colleague and you are happy to hear his voice. You respond with a hearty "Hi, Gil." And, since it's Monday morning, you are sure to ask: "How was your weekend?" Gil will likely tell you about his great weekend and you will want to tell him about yours. However, as interesting as your story may be, it will take a long time to relate. Instead, say: "Gil, I spent the weekend with our old pal Pat, who landed a great job at Acme. Right now I have a pile of work on my desk. Let's have lunch later in the week and I'll tell you all about it." Gil probably has a pile of work on his desk and he's just as anxious as you are to get to the business at hand.

Limit personal talk to 2 or 3 minutes. It *is* important, but keep it brief.

15-13   When I call people I am often put on hold. This seems to take an eternity. What can I do to make hold time more productive?

Most people do absolutely nothing constructive while on hold. They doodle, daydream, or just stare into space. Most jobs require some amount of clerical work which can be accomplished while on hold. Examples include entering figures in a production log, filling out report forms, checking tickler files, and reprioritizing to-do lists. Keep a folder next to the phone with some of the detail work you are required to do.

One salesperson kept all his sales statistics right by the phone. When on hold, he would fill out sales reports, call reports, or expense accounts, and even do some market research on prospective customers.

An office manager decided to keep her "on hold" folder filled with low-priority reading materials—newsletters, bulletins, brochures, and other items that she had to get to sooner or later. When she was on hold she caught up with all her reading.

The average hold is 3 to 5 minutes. If you could accomplish only 3 minutes' worth of work on 10 holds each day, you would complete half an hour's work that had to be done anyway.

15-14   I try to do other work while on hold, but I find it impossible to work when I have to hold the phone or squeeze it between my shoulder and my neck. How can I turn this time to my advantage?

Get a speaker phone. When you are put on hold, hang up the instrument and turn on the speaker. Now your hands are free. You can even get up and move around the office. When you hear the other person's voice, you can either continue the discussion on the speaker or, if you prefer, pick up the instrument and talk more privately.

15-15   I have friends, family members, and even colleagues who seem to have much more time than I do. They talk forever when they call me. How can I cut them off without being impolite or having them feel that they are not important to me?

Be diplomatically frank. Just tell them that you are unable to talk at this time, but will call them in the evening when you get home. When you speak to them at that time, or when you see them, assure them that you value their friendship but that sometimes it is inopportune to talk when you are at work. You might imply that your boss is getting strict about personal calls on the job.

15-16   My people seem to be making an inordinate number of personal calls. Every time I look at them, they are on the phone and not working. What can I do to stop this?

This is a problem in every company. When there is a phone on someone's desk, personal calls will be made and received. There are no easy answers and even complex approaches do not always work. Here are a few suggestions.

One company found that by clustering three desks around one phone, most business calls could be handled. This virtually stopped the use of the phone for personal matters. Since everybody in the cluster could overhear private conversations, employees were reluctant to make personal calls. Pay phones were installed in convenient places to accommodate the employees' needs.

Since clustering desks is not always feasible, a firm policy on limited use of the phone for personal matters should be instituted and enforced. Most companies will tolerate a limited number of personal calls. But if supervisors note that an employee is abusing this rule, the violation should be handled in the same manner as any other: informal warnings followed as necessary by progressive discipline.

15-17   How can a company monitor calls to determine if they are business or personal?

There are many ways companies can monitor calls. The simplest is to listen in on an extension phone. There are also a variety of electronic devices available that monitor calls. If employees are advised that calls are monitored, they will be less likely to use the telephone for personal matters.

Check the telephone bills. Some phone systems provide lists of all calls being made from each instrument, including the destination of the call and the time spent talking.

15-18   I'm so busy answering questions and solving problems from my people that I don't have time for my regular work. Any ideas on how this can be alleviated?

Keep an interruptions journal. Use a desk calendar, but instead of listing appointments, list interruptions. Every time one of your people brings you a problem, enter it in the journal, noting the time, the name of the employee, the type of problem, and how long the matter took. Do this for 6 or 7 weeks—long enough to find patterns for the interruptions.

Let's say you have six people reporting to you. When you study the patterns, you note that three of them rarely interrupt you with problems—and when they do the matter is usually serious. The other three are constantly bringing you problems. Two of these people have been in your department for less than a year. It may be that they are not yet fully or properly trained. (If so, you might give serious thought to this matter before training additional people.) By the nature of their problems, you know in what aspects of the job they need training and can get to work on those immediately.

The third member of this interruptive trio is Jerry, who has been in your department for 6 years. All through those years he has brought you an average of three problems a day. As you review these problems, you note that very few have been critical. They could have waited. It is time to take Jerry aside: "From now on I want you to hold all your problems until 4 p.m. Every day at 4, we will meet to discuss them."

Perhaps Jerry—not wanting to wait so long—will begin to solve his own problems. More likely, he will come to you at 4 sharp. But it is much less time-consuming to deal with three problems at one time than one at a time. More important, because the meeting is planned, you are not being interrupted.

15-19   My problem is my boss. I have to see her to solve some of my problems. Often when I call to ask for an appointment, she invites me to come right up. By the time I get there she is on the phone and I have to wait until she is finished. In the middle of our discussion, she gets other calls. I'm there for half an hour on something that should have taken 10 minutes. How can I conserve my time?

Can you consolidate your problems? Some problems do require immediate decisions, but many others can be deferred. If you can wait until you have two or three matters to discuss with your boss, you will save both your boss and yourself valuable time.

15-20   What about the times when my boss calls me to her office? I still sit there wasting valuable moments while she

answers the phone. Is it OK for me to suggest that she let her voicemail pick up these calls?

If you have a good relationship with your boss, you might make the suggestion. However, if you know your boss is sensitive about her authority—and, indeed, finds it ego building to be constantly called for information or advice—learn to bear with it.

15-21   I have an open-door policy. Any of my people can come into my office whenever there is a problem. This has proved good for morale and has helped my people, but it has been a major interrupter of my time. Should I modify my policy?

There are advantages and limitations to having an open-door policy. (See question 4 in Chapter 7.) One of the major limitations is that it encourages interruptions. One way of reducing interruptions is to limit your open-door hours. Your people will still feel free to come in with problems, suggestions, and complaints—at the designated times. By restricting your open-door hours, you will have adequate time for your other work.

15-22   By restricting the time I have available to listen to my people, do I run the risk of having them feel that I consider them less important than my other work?

Not if you make it clear from the beginning that they are your prime concern. However, the time in each workday is limited, and other matters must be taken care of in the course of running the department. Adequate time for your people should be provided, and scheduled accordingly.

15-23   I try to set time limits for appointments. Sometimes I schedule 15 minutes and it takes twice as long. Can I tell somebody "Your time is up" even if we have not completed the discussion?

It is not always possible to complete a matter in the time scheduled. Build in enough flexibility (by leaving some time between appointments) to accommodate for this.

When it becomes obvious that matters will take more than the scheduled time and the meeting cannot be extended, it is certainly proper to draw to a close and set a date to continue the discussion. Instead of making a brusque remark like "Your time is up," diplomatically close the session: "There is much more we must discuss before we can reach a decision. Unfortunately I have another appointment scheduled so let's continue this tomorrow. Will 11 be OK?"

15-24   I work in an open cubicle. People passing by often stop to chat. I don't want to appear to be unsociable, but it does interfere with my work. What do I do short of putting up a NO TALKING sign?

When someone walks by, you probably look up to see who it is. The passer-by looks at you. You make eye contact, and you nod or smile. You are being polite; the other person interprets it as an invitation to chat.

If it is possible, turn your desk around so that your back faces the aisle. By not making eye contact with these people, you obviate the invitation to come in and talk. If you cannot rearrange your work area, you will have to discipline yourself not to look up as people walk by.

15-25   Although purchasing is not one of my major activities, I do have to see salespeople from time to time. They come at inopportune moments and take too much of my time. How can I control this?

One way is to require all salespeople to make appointments before coming to see you. Refuse to meet with anyone who does not have an appointment.

Another approach is screening. Often you cannot know whether it is advantageous to see a "drop in" salesperson until you speak to him or her. If you invite the salesperson into your office, you will probably have to listen to the entire sales presentation and that could be very time-consuming indeed. Instead, go out to the reception area and speak to the visitor. Determine just what the sales pitch is. If it is a product or service in which you have no interest, terminate the interview immediately. A 3-minute screening interview in the reception area could save you a 20-minute (or longer) sales presentation.

15-26   Lou is a sports fan. He often comes into my office to talk about yesterday's games. I'm also a sports fan, and if I'm not busy, I don't mind. But when I am busy, how can I get rid of him?

When Lou comes in, stand up and walk out in front of your desk, blocking off any access to the side chair. Chat for a minute about the game and while talking, lead him slowly but directly to the exit.

15-27   Charlene is constantly bringing me her personal problems. I know that as her supervisor I should listen when she has a problem, but I don't always have the time to do so. How can I break the pattern?

Yes, supervisors have an obligation to listen when people bring them their personal problems. It can be very time-consuming. But there is an exception to every rule. Here is the exception to this rule: An employee who brings you personal problems every day would rather talk about her problems than do her work. You don't have to listen. Say: "Charlene, I know this is important to you and I do want to hear about it, but I have a deadline I must meet today. Why don't you come to see me right after work and we'll discuss it?" Such people rarely do.

15-28   Crisis, crisis, crisis! These fires must be put out. They are urgent but my other work must also be done. What can I do?

You must learn to differentiate between what is important and what is urgent. Important things are matters that help you reach your goals. Urgent matters are the fires that you must put out immediately to avoid irreparable damage.

Some crises are unavoidable: natural disasters such as hurricanes or extended power outages; unforeseen business problems such as supplier shutdowns or malfunctioning machines. You have to stop everything and put out the fire.

Sometimes, though, these crises might have been avoided with foresight. You knew that the supplier was having labor problems which might result in a strike; that there would have been no crisis if a substitute supplier had been lined up. The machine had broken before and was never properly repaired.

No matter how good you are as a manager, you will still face crises from time to time. The superior manager is one who anticipates potential crises and works to either eliminate the cause or make accommodations so that energies are spent, not on fighting fires, but on meeting the important objectives of the organization.

Handling Mail

15-29   My job requires reading and answering a large amount of correspondence. Any suggestions on how I can reduce the enormous amount of time this takes?

First, learn to read faster. Most people read approximately 200–300 words per minute. Courses in speed-reading have helped people increase this to 700–800 words per minute, or even faster, with full comprehension. Taking such a course will enable you to cut down significantly on the time it takes you to read—not only correspondence but all the other printed matter you must absorb on and off the job.

Second, get into the habit of reading a piece of correspondence *once* and taking action. Typically, you read a letter or memo to determine what should be done and then put it in a folder or pile on the desk for later action. When you finally get around to acting on it, you need to read it again. Instead, as you read the memo the first time, use the margin or a Post-It sheet to make notes about your response. When the time comes to answer the memo or take other action, you do not have to reread the entire message.

How much time will this save? It takes the average reader (not a speed-reader) 1 to 2 minutes per page to read a nontechnical letter and more for technical material. It takes only a few seconds to read Post-It notes. You can see how this time can add up for people who deal with a great deal of correspondence.

15-30   I am deluged with letters, memos, faxes, E-mail, and other paperwork. How can I organize my work so all these items can be handled?

As you read these items, make notes so you will not have to read them again (see question 15-29). Separate the items according to the action needed: "To be answered." "More information needed." "To be delegated." "To be filed."

Put the items in priority order and deal with the most important matters first. Don't fall into this common trap: You are working on an item and a letter or fax is given to you. You stop what you are working on and handle that new item. Unless the new item is urgent or of higher priority than others, put it in its proper handling order.

15-31   I don't have a secretary and I get a lot of interoffice memos that I must answer. Since I am not a fast typist, is it OK to respond in handwriting?

If you have a legible handwriting, it is often faster and more efficient to do that. Even better, instead of writing a new memo to respond to one you receive, just jot down a reply on the original memo. For example, you receive a memo requesting the inventory of a list of items. Instead of writing a new memo restating the items and showing the inventory, just write the amount of inventory next to each item on the memo you received and return it. If you need a copy, make a photocopy.

You can purchase multiple-page forms designed just for this purpose. The original memo and a copy are sent to the respondent; a third copy is kept by the sender. The respondent responds on the original, keeping the second copy with the response.

15-32   A couple of years ago we got faxes; now we have voicemail and E-mail. These are supposed to save time, yet I spend more time handling these "urgent" messages than I did before. How do I set priorities?

In determining what should be dealt with immediately or at a later time, focus on the content of the message, not the medium in which it was sent. Just because something came by fax or by electronic media does not mean it is more important than a letter or memo.

15-33   Much of my correspondence is routine. I think it could be answered by form letters in which I just checked off the appropriate response. My company thinks this is unprofessional and insists that I answer each letter individually. Who is right?

It depends on the type of image you wish to portray to your customers. If you want to impress them with your professionalism, form letters of this type will be a poor choice. Today with computers and word processors as part of almost every business, there is no need to use a check-off form. You can develop form letters for commonly occurring situations and then tailor the message to individual correspondents. The letters will no longer appear to be routine forms.

15-34   I receive copies of letters, memos, and reports for information only. I don't have to act on them, but it is important that I know about them. The problem is that they pile up on my desk until I get around to filing them and then it takes a long time to do the actual filing. What is the solution?

Dump them. Once you have read them, their purpose—to let you know what is going on—has been served. There is no need to keep them. In those few cases where it may be necessary to see a document that you have discarded, you can always get a copy from the department which sent it to you.

Not only does this save you (or your assistant) a great deal of filing time, but it saves the company valuable space. Many companies have warehouses filled with paper that they will never refer to again. Discarding copies of letters and memos that are sent to you just for your information and on which you take no action will reduce this wasted cost.

Meetings

15-35   In our company we spend an inordinate amount of time at meetings. I am often required to attend meetings that are a total waste of my time. Any way this can be alleviated?

People are invited to meetings because they have expertise in the areas to be covered or because the subjects under discussion affect their work. However, quite often people are invited to meetings simply because of their position. The general manager calls a meeting of all department managers—and even if the agenda doesn't concern you, you have to go.

Some companies have tried to avoid this problem by leaving the decision on whether to attend a meeting up to each person. A day or two before the meeting, a proposed agenda is circulated among all the people in a designated group (e.g., all department managers). It starts with a comment: "If anything on the agenda affects your work or you wish to contribute to this subject, please attend. Otherwise you need not come."

The danger of this approach is that some people who should be there opt not to attend. Before starting such a program, you should conduct a thorough orientation so that everybody knows what is going to be done, how the program will be implemented, the reason behind the concept, and what is expected of each person.

If people who should attend a first meeting do not come, counsel them to make sure they understand that they are needed. It may take several meetings before the system works smoothly, but once established it will save a lot of people a lot of time attending meetings that do not truly concern them.

15-36   My meetings often last a lot longer than scheduled because some of my people digress from the agenda. How can I tell them to stop?

It is important to adhere to an agenda or meetings will go on interminably. There are occasions when an unexpected situation may force the agenda to be set aside, but unless it is urgent, insist on strict adherence to the agenda. If another matter is introduced, point out clearly that although you understand people's concern over that matter, it cannot be raised at this time. Suggest that it be discussed privately after the meeting or put on the agenda for the next meeting.

15-37   Is it a good idea to have quick, informal meetings with colleagues when we meet casually in the hall or other parts of the building, or should business discussions be restricted to more formal meetings?

Matters which concern only two or three people need not be restricted to formal meetings. Much can be accomplished in informal chats in the normal course of the workday. Meetings should be reserved for situations in which several people must get together or when time schedules of the participants must be coordinated.

15-38   I was told that the way to keep a meeting brief is to make everyone stand during the session. Is this a good idea?

If your main objective is brevity, this is fine. However, the purpose of many meetings is to discuss and resolve tough problems. A more comfortable arrangement may be more conducive to serious discussions.

Personal Barriers to Efficient Use of Time

15-39   When things are going along well in my personal life, I keep things moving along on the job. But when I am

worried about some personal matter, I just can't concentrate on my work. How can I leave my personal worries at home?

It is human nature to worry. As noted in question 11-54, you can't ignore what's happening in your total life. Most mature adults can cope with worrying. But it does stop them from fully concentrating on their jobs. In the middle of the day, they may stop and think about a problem at home, then shake it off and get back to work.

However, occasionally problems will overwhelm people and significantly interfere with their performance. These may be medical problems, family problems, alcoholism, addiction, or depression. Such problems cannot be ignored. Professional help is often the only solution.

15-40   We have an employee assistance program for help with personal problems. I've never used it. How does the program work?

An employee assistance program (EAP) is a company-sponsored counseling service. (See question 2 in Chapter 9 for details.)

15-41   Our company does not have an EAP. There are times when I feel counseling would benefit me, but private counseling is too expensive. What can I do?

Many health insurance policies will cover all or part of the cost of counseling. Check your policy to determine if you have this coverage. Counseling at moderate cost is available in most communities through community services and by many religious organizations.

15-42   Some of my people have slowed down on their jobs, complaining that the work has become boring. The result has been lost motivation and reduced productivity. What can I do to make their jobs less boring?

Some jobs are basically boring. Even jobs which are not basically boring can become boring when people do the same work over and over for many years. There is an entire field devoted to making jobs less boring. It is called *job enrichment*. Experts in this field study jobs and determine ways in which work can be made more interesting to the workers. This usually requires total restructuring of the work.

Sometimes supervisors can make jobs less boring without calling in the experts. One approach is to cross-train people so they can perform a variety of jobs, not just one. Another is to periodically change assignments within the department After several months of the same work, a change of assignments can alleviate boredom. Give people who are bored special projects. In many companies opportunities open for a person to work on a special assignment.

A word of caution: Not everybody becomes bored doing routine work. Some people prefer to do the same thing over and over. They are comfortable working in a set pattern, and changing the pattern will hinder rather than help. (See question 8-34.)

15-43   I'm so tired toward the end of the day I can't think straight. No matter how carefully I plan my schedule, sometimes I just haven't the energy to do it. What can I do?

Have you had a thorough medical examination lately? Fatigue may be caused by medical problems. If you are in reasonably good health, determine if the work you do is exhausting you physically or mentally. Physical fatigue can be cured by rest. You may have to take more breaks during the day and get more sleep at night. Rest does not necessarily help mental fatigue. One way to overcome mental fatigue is by exercise. Plan a long walk during lunch instead of eating; go swimming or jogging; play a sport after work. People with regular regimens of exercise are less likely to become mentally fatigued.

15-44   Sometimes the pressures of my job are so great that I feel I am going to break down. How can I cope better?

When the stress on a job begins to overwhelm you, take a break. If you can, get away from the workplace. Get out of the building. Walk around the block or around the parking lot. In 10 or 15 minutes you will feel the stress dissolve and you will be able to face the job with new energy.

You might also try exercise. This doesn't mean getting up in the middle of a crowded office and doing jumping jacks. There are many excellent relaxation exercises you can do without being obtrusive. Read books or take programs in relaxation to help you learn to reduce stress.

Change pace. Most people work on more than one project at a time. If the pressures are too great on a current project, stop for a while and work on something else. When you get back to the first project, your mind will be clearer and solutions that once evaded you will become evident.

15-45   I am a procrastinator. I know that I keep putting off things that I don't like to do. They must be done. Is there any solution?

You are no exception. Most people put off doing things they don't like. If you don't like something, there is a strong probability that you don't do it well. When you finally get to do it, you are tight against a deadline. Now you not only have postponed the action but are more likely to fail. You must make a concerted effort to do exactly the opposite of what you have been doing. Do the thing you like least first. Not only will you be more likely to succeed because you have more time, but you will have the psychological advantage of getting it out of the way so you can concentrate on work you like.

Some procrastinators need help to overcome "the stall." Sometimes they ask another procrastinator to become a partner in the effort. Each one keeps a copy of the other's calendar, in which are listed the planned starting dates for various assignments—with notations as to projects which are disliked. Each monitors the other's activities and reminds or even nags the other to start assignments that have been stalled because of procrastination.

Other procrastinators give themselves a reward if they meet starting, interim, and final deadlines on projects they dislike. One health-conscious supervisor allowed himself an ice cream sundae only on days when he started or finished an assignment he would have formerly stalled.

Time Management on the Job

15-46   My boss keeps giving me more and more work. I've reached the point where there is just no time to do it all. What can I do to let her know enough is enough?

Before you approach your boss, make an analysis of the jobs you are doing. Which are really important? How much time are you devoting to each project? What priorities has the boss assigned to each of your assignments? What can you delegate to your subordinates? What can you do to make your own work more efficient? If after this analysis, you still feel that you have more work than you can handle, meet with the boss, review with her the results of your analysis and try to work out together what part of your work she can take away from you or put in a lower priority category so you can defer it until you have more time.

15-47   I'm frequently asked to serve on committees or take on special assignments. I've always accepted because I'm afraid if I refuse, it will be held against me. How can I say "no"?

There are times when we must say "no" or we will become so bogged down with "extra" work that we cannot do our own jobs effectively. On the other hand there are special assignments we should take because they can lead to achieving our job or career objectives.

Listen carefully to the description of the activity. If it is one that you do not want to accept, diplomatically decline: "I know this is an important project, but at this moment I am involved with several other projects and as much as I would like to help, I just haven't the time to do it." Specify the other projects.

If you do accept a reasonable amount of extra work and have earned the reputation of being a cooperative person, declining to take on projects you don't have time for will not adversely affect your career. Unless you learn to say no and not feel guilty about it, people will take advantage of you.

15-48   A good deal of my work requires concentrated thinking. I must insulate myself from interruptions. How can I do this when people barge in or telephone when I am trying to think?

Many people set aside an hour or more each day for uninterrupted thinking. They let it be known to colleagues, bosses, subordinates, telephone operators, and others that during those hours, they are incommunicado. Phone calls are picked up by voicemail or a secretary; the door is closed and, except in emergencies, this think-time is honored.

For most people, the boss is one of the big interrupters of the day. It is important that employees discuss this matter with the boss and ask for his or her cooperation in not calling them during quiet hours.

15-49   How do I let my people know when they are not managing their time properly?

Speak to them. Point out specific situations you observed in which employees demonstrated poor time management. Work with them on time management techniques. Start by having them make a time analysis of their day. Discuss how they can make better use of the wasted time that shows up in this analysis. Suggest that they attend a seminar on time management.

15-50   I spend too much time covering for my people when they are on vacation. They each have 20 vacation days a year. When I take off, I feel guilty. My work doesn't get done! Solution?

You shouldn't be doing the work of subordinates who are on vacation, ill, or out for any other reason. This work should be spread among the other people in the group. All employees should be told that filling in for absent employees is part of their job. As a supervisor, you must make sure that all staff members are trained to do the work of others. You should assign this work when a vacation is scheduled or when unplanned absences occur. If you do not have enough people, you may have to do some of the work yourself, but that should be an exception rather than the usual practice.

There is no reason for you to feel guilty about taking your own vacation. You have earned that right. Before you leave, make sure that all work is assigned and whoever is in charge in your absence (one of your staff or perhaps your boss) knows just what has to be done. Enjoy your vacation. Forget the job until you get back. In most jobs some matters may have to be deferred until you return, but the great portion of the work usually gets done. Like most people, you will find it a humbling experience to realize that you are not indispensable.

15-51   I am a shift supervisor. I have several managers over me who cover different aspects of the business. I am confronted all day by these bosses with "I need you to do this." How can I manage my day?

Working for more than one boss opens the door to conflict. Each one wants you to give his or her work first priority. Unless there is some coordination of priorities, there will be chaos.

Often situations like this arise when staff specialists deal directly with a line supervisor instead of working through that supervisor's immediate boss. The production manager orders the line supervisor to do one thing; the quality assurance manager gives another order; then the distribution manager wants to change a priority.

Unless you can get all orders to be funneled through your boss (e.g., the plant manager), you will have to bring everyone together and work out a plan of action. These managers understand that you cannot do everything at once. To achieve desired objectives, they will work with you to bring about a reasonable compromise.

15-52   As a working supervisor, I must do a good deal of the same work that my people do. This has caused a morale problem, because my people think I am goofing off when I leave the workbench to do administrative tasks. Any suggestions?

The administrative work is part of your supervisory function. Even though it may not appear to be as important as getting out production, it is necessary. Working supervisors are not expected to put out the same amount of production as their colleagues. You do not have to justify your function. However, remind your people from time to time that unless the paperwork is done, the job is not finished.

15-53   Whenever I give Kerry a new assignment, he asks, "Will it interfere with my break?" Can I ask him to change his break time to do the assignment?

Some states and localities have laws requiring that people in certain job categories (e.g., working at computer terminals) take breaks at specific intervals for health or safety reasons. Also, some union contracts specify times for breaks. In such cases, you cannot request changes. In other situations, you may make any changes needed to get the work out. A polite request to take the break later or even skip it is permissible. Of course, it is not a good idea to do this too often.

15-54   As a salesperson, I waste a tremendous amount of time waiting to see prospects. How can I use that time productively?

Plan for those waits. Take along paperwork that can be done without spreading out all over the reception area. Study marketing reports about prospects or customers you are scheduled to visit that day. Plan calls for later in the day and review product information and price lists.

Many salespeople today carry laptop computers and can accomplish a good deal of work while waiting. Others carry cellular telephones and make business calls.

16

Your Boss and Your Career

Probably the most important person in your job life is your immediate boss. He or she can make your job easy or tough, your life pleasant or unpleasant, your career successful or unsuccessful.

Over and over again in seminars on supervision, questions are raised about this delicate area of dealing with the boss. Just as in dealing with subordinates, there are no magic formulas. Bosses are people and people differ one from the other. To deal effectively with the key person in your job life, you need to learn as much as you can about the boss and tailor your approach to her or his individuality.

Keep in mind that when dealing with your subordinates you always have as a last resort the ability to exert your power: "Do this or else disciplinary action will be taken." You cannot resort to orders with your boss; more important, the boss can use his or her power over you. You must be diplomatic. You can negotiate; you can try to sell your ideas; possibly you can maneuver around some situations. The following sections answer the most frequently asked questions on this delicate relationship.

The Relationship Between
You and the Boss

16-1   What are the key things I should know about my boss?

1. *Know your boss's style of work.*   Learn early in your relationship with your boss the style in which he or she works. For example, information is a basic requirement to all jobs, but how that information is submitted to a manager should conform with the style that manager prefers. You learn that one vice president prefers detailed reports with statistical tables and footnoted narratives; another executive prefers seeing graphs and charts rather than reading statistics; still another likes to read a one-page summary with backup material to study if interested. You must submit information to these executives in the form they prefer or you will antagonize them.

This is also true of oral reports. The marketing manager and the sales manager ask you the same question: "What is the status of the Southwest marketing analysis?" To the sales manager, you respond: "It will be completed tomorrow afternoon." That is the right response for him. If you gave the same response to the marketing manager, it wouldn't do, because you know that she prefers more detail. To satisfy her, you respond: "We have completed parts A and B. We're working on part C and we have run into some problems. The report will be completed by tomorrow afternoon." You then describe the problems and what you are doing about them.

Two different bosses; two different responses.

Another aspect of work style is dress. If your boss wears tailored clothes and you prefer more casual outfits, you may not be taken seriously by that boss. You needn't imitate his or her style of dress, but it's a good idea to be more conservative in your choice of clothes at work.

2. *Know your boss's job goals.*   What does your boss want to achieve in this job? If you can help him or her reach these goals, you will be the type of employee every boss wants. Beverly works for Kevin, the human resources director. One of Kevin's long-range goals for the department has been the computerization of personnel records. He has been unable to sell this to his boss, the executive vice president. Although Beverly knows little about computers, she begins to study and learn as much as she can about this subject. She takes courses, reads articles, and attends

seminars. By doing this, she is able not only to help Kevin develop the necessary tools to sell this concept to his boss, but also to develop a wealth of knowledge that will help her in her own career development.

3. *Anticipate your boss's needs.*   By discussions and observation, you can learn what is of significant concern to your boss. By keeping abreast of what is happening in these areas, you can prepare material that will be needed by the boss. When he or she requests it, you will have it ready and available.

16-2   Do I have to be a "rubber stamp" to get along with my boss?

Some bosses do like to have people around them who agree with everything they say and do. Successful managers welcome dissent because it helps them clarify their own thinking. Of course, any dissent should be diplomatic. It isn't necessary to antagonize when you disagree.

Ivan always found something to disagree with at work. This attitude cost him two previous jobs. When he took his current job, he resolved not to be so critical, but his nature overcame him and before long he was again vociferously expounding his disagreements.

When his boss called him in for a private conference, Ivan expected to be fired again. However, this boss took a different tack: "Ivan, you can drive people crazy, but you do something for me that nobody else does. You make me think and reevaluate what I have often taken for granted. You provide a service I need. If you learn to do this more diplomatically, you can be a valuable employee."

16-3   How can I disagree with my boss without upsetting her?

1. *Do it privately.*   It is not a good idea to disagree with the boss in front of others. When Steve's boss proposed a marketing plan for the new product, she was so enthusiastic about it that most of the staff caught her excitement and accepted it uncritically. Steve saw some flaws in it, but felt it was not expedient to express them at that time and dampen the group's enthusiasm. He waited until the next day and then met with the boss privately.

2. *Ask questions.*   Steve started the discussion by expressing his agreement with the key part of the plan. "However," he continued, "I have some questions." He then stated his objections—not in the form of dogmatic statements, but as questions. "What would happen if thus and thus developed?" In this way he let the boss know his concerns without making her feel resentful.

3. *Present a positive plan of action.*   Before Steven went in to see the boss, he gave her plan serious thought and developed a few alternative steps that might solve the questions at issue. In this way instead of the disagreement being seen as negative, it was viewed as a positive approach.

4. *If you are wrong, admit it.*   Suppose, however, that the reservations Steve had about the plan were wrong. When Steve posed his questions, the manager's response proved her right. Steve now could thank her for clearing up the point. However, if Steve had made a major issue of it, he would now have to admit that he was in error. Don't be afraid to admit that you are wrong. Your supervisor will appreciate the fact that you gave serious consideration to the plan.

5. *Don't make an issue of minor matters.*   If you agree with the significant aspects of what your boss suggests, but disagree with some of the details, it is better to go along. Save your disagreements for important issues.

16-4   What do you do as a supervisor when your boss does not follow through? You have been to him with a problem and after sufficient time he has not responded.

Ask again. If after a reasonable time the boss has not given you an answer, there is nothing wrong with following up. Pursue the matter informally the next time you see him or more formally, if called for, by memo. There may be legitimate reasons for his not giving you an answer. If you don't ask, you won't know.

16-5   How do you deal with a boss who takes credit for your ideas?

Some bosses take credit inadvertently. They get so enthusiastic about an idea from one of their people that after a while they truly believe it is their own idea. If you feel that this is what has happened, a heart-to-heart talk with the boss might persuade him to acknowledge what he has done and to stop taking credit in the future.

Some managers make a practice of stealing the ideas of their people, and when confronted they will deny it: "I've been working on that idea for a long time; it's not original with you." If you work for such a person, protect your new concepts by submitting them through the suggestion system rather than bringing them directly to your boss. If this is not appropriate for the type of idea you have, submit it in writing to your boss with a copy to his or her boss.

16-6   My company has hired a new executive from outside the organization who will be my immediate boss. What can I do to get started on the right foot with this person?

Keep in mind that the new boss is a stranger to the company (and maybe the community) and is feeling his or her way into the new situation. Anything you can do to ease the transition will be appreciated. Offer to answer any questions on work in progress or on the background of matters the department is handling.

Until the new boss becomes more familiar with the work being performed, try to solve most problems on your own. At this point you probably have more knowledge of the work than the newcomer.

By observation and questions, find out the new boss's style of managing. Reshape your style to conform to it (see question 16-1).

16-7   My boss makes promises to me and my people and then doesn't keep them. How can I get him to keep his word?

Nobody trusts a boss who fails to keep promises. This is particularly true when people rely on the boss's word. Discuss the matter privately with your boss. If you cannot change his mind, at least get an explanation to give your people. Perhaps he has overstepped his own authority in making certain promises and has been overridden by a higher executive. If this is the case, try to gain access to the decision maker and persuade him or her to concur.

16-8   I have a great boss. I really appreciate what she has done to help me in my work. How can I thank her without appearing to be apple polishing?

Thank her sincerely. Be specific. Instead of saying "You're a great boss," specify what she did to help you: "The shortcuts you showed me have saved me a tremendous amount of time on the project. I really appreciate it."

Let your boss know when she is doing a good job. Her boss may not be appreciative. Ask her questions about a good decision she made. Ask how she arrived at that decision, what problems she had to solve, and how she solved them. Showing a sincere interest in these matters helps you learn from your boss and at the same time express recognition of her achievements.

16-9   My boss is constantly criticizing me. He tries to be constructive, but I can hear the disapproval in his voice.

Accept it as part of the job. Criticism is part of the learning process. We cannot learn unless our mistakes are pointed out. We cannot control the way our bosses criticize us, but we can control how we take it. Look at it as a learning, not a degrading, experience.

Don't take it personally. Remember it is not you, but what you have done that is being criticized. Most bosses offer criticism, not to debase others, but to help them correct a situation. Unfortunately, some bosses simply lack tact. You are not stupid or inept. It is the work that was criticized—not the human being who did it. Keep your emotions out of it.

Find good in being corrected. Truly mature people can learn from even the most malicious criticism. If your boss's criticism makes you aware of unperceived weaknesses, faults, or errors, despite your initial hurt, you can learn from it. Focus on the lesson—forget the method.

Remember that the boss wants you to succeed. A supervisor is measured on the success of his or her department. If you do not succeed, it will reflect on the supervisor. The boss's approach to criticism may have been wrong, but the long-term objective benefits both of you.

16-10   My boss is a gregarious guy. He is constantly "visiting" me and takes my time with small talk. How can I get him to let me do my work?

It's not easy to tell your boss to shut up and go away, but it must be done—in a diplomatic manner. After a few minutes of chatting, look at your watch and say, "Bob, you want me to complete this report by 2 o'clock. If I don't work on it now, I won't finish it on time." Bob will get the hint.

16-11 My boss frequently tells me he agrees with me or says he will provide something but then doesn't do it. How can I know if he is serious or doesn't really think it's a good idea?

There are people who, rather than disagree and perhaps have to argue a point, pretend that they do agree and then ignore what they agreed to do. If this is your boss's style, try to pin him down by asking for specifics. If he agrees to provide your department with materials, ask for specific time frames when each delivery will be made. If materials are not received when promised, follow through immediately. If the boss agrees to change a procedure, write a plan of action immediately after your discussion and send it to him for approval. If he does not approve, you will know when he fails to sign the plan.

16-12 Is it advantageous for an employee to maintain a personal relationship with the boss—as opposed to it being to a boss's advantage to maintain close ties with an employee?

It depends on the nature of the personal relationship. Being close friends with a boss may work in favor of the employee but may cause dissension in the department because of the perception of favoritism. Even if the manager does not favor you, others may think that he or she does.

A good (not close) personal relationship exists when you can freely discuss matters with your boss without the barrier of formal communications. This is developed by mutual respect. It is not necessary to socialize with the boss on a regular basis. You can go to lunch once in a while without it being interpreted as favored treatment—particularly if the boss lunches occasionally with other employees as well.

You can have a closer relationship with your boss than it is advisable to have with your people because both of you represent management. The higher up in the hierarchy you go, the more likely you are to have a close personal relationship with the person at the next higher level.

Policy

16-13 What can I do when I have responsibility and accountability for a project but am not given the authority needed to pursue it?

Somebody once described responsibility without authority as the definition of hell. First, ask for whatever authority you need. Be specific. For example, don't say: "I need authority to spend additional money on this project, if necessary." Instead, indicate under what clearly defined circumstances the authority will be used. Point out that any authority requested is for this project only and not a permanent change in your established power.

If the authority is not given, you must work within the limits that you have. When special factors develop that require decisions you are not authorized to make, refer them to your boss. If he or she responds that it is your job to make the decision, ask at that point for the authority to do so. Should this situation arise often enough, the boss will be glad to give you the needed authority— if for no other reason than not to have to deal with each little item that develops.

16-14   What do you do when you don't agree with a decision made by the boss?

First, try to sell the boss on how you think the matter should be handled (see questions 16-2, 16-35, and 16-36). If you do not succeed, you must abide by the decision and do your best to make it work. Perhaps the boss's decision was right. Your idea may not have been the best. No matter how wrong you may think the boss's approach is, do not try to sabotage it to prove you are right. Sabotage can lead to more serious problems on the job and will certainly not help you in your relationship with the boss.

16-15   I have observed some problems (such as poor communication between departments) that need to be solved for the long term in my company. However, my boss turns down any suggestions and refuses to recognize that such problems exist. What should I do?

When presenting the suggestions to your boss, do it indirectly. Ask a question about the situation rather than calling it a problem. Request his or her ideas on how to handle it. Here is an example of the *wrong* approach:

YOU: The people at the distribution center are holding up my shipments because of the red tape of paperwork. We could overcome the problem if they faxed us the forms instead of using interoffice memos.

BOSS: That would cost too much money. We usually get interoffice mail the next day. That's time enough.

You can argue all day, but the boss still won't see a problem. Now let's look at an effective approach:

YOU: I'm having a problem in getting materials from the distribution center on time. Any ideas on how we might expedite this?

BOSS: Have you talked to the distribution people about it?

YOU: Yes. They say it's the paperwork. They can't send the order unless they have a requisition. I send every requisition via interoffice mail, according to company policy. It takes at least a day and sometimes two days for them to get it.

BOSS: Can we fax it to them?

YOU: You'd have to change the policy. Do you have the authority to do that?

BOSS: Sure. I'll do it right away.

Assigning Work

16-16   How can I stop my boss from delegating work directly to my people without consulting me first?

Speak to the boss about it. Point out that the raison d'être of your job is to relieve your boss from having to handle these matters so he or she can concentrate on more important issues. Assigning work to the rank and file is your job. Also reiterate that you are responsible for your people's work. In order to maintain control, you need to have all assignments channeled through you.

16-17   How do I let my boss know that the goals established for the department are unrealistic?

Make sure you have all the data to prove that they are unrealistic. Review the budgets, the time factors, other priorities given to you and your people, resources available, and so on. Don't be antagonistic or challenge the boss: "These goals are ridiculous. There's no way we can meet them."

In a calm way, discuss the specifics of the goals that have been set and, using the research you have done, indicate what you can reasonably expect to accomplish. Ask the boss for suggestions on your priorities: "So, as you see, we cannot do everything in the time we have. In what areas do you think we should concentrate?"

16-18   I make a decision that I pass to my subordinates and they start work following my instructions. Then my boss

tells me she wants things done differently. Even if I don't agree with her, I have no choice but to follow the revised instructions. How do I break the news to my staff?

You tell them that after further consideration, it has been decided to change the method being used. Concentrate on the changes and certainly do not express your disagreement. If questions are raised, respond in positive terms: "When Sue and I reviewed the project, we thought that this approach would work better."

16-19   My predecessor ran this department with eight people for several years. The work has increased and I need more people. How can I request additional personnel without appearing to be less efficient than my predecessor?

Your major argument is that the amount of work has increased. Be prepared to show (if true) that the productivity of each of your people has increased and that they are working at optimum capacity. To meet your present workload, you either need more people or must be prepared to have your people work overtime, which may be more expensive. By presenting facts and figures, you can show that the need for increased staff is not a negative factor.

16-20   My boss is reluctant to delegate. How can I get him to let me do the work I know I am capable of doing?

The reason bosses fear delegation is their concern that if they don't do it themselves, it will not be done right (see Chapter 5). To overcome this, you have to prove that you are trustworthy and can accomplish superior work. Start by performing your current activities in an exemplary manner. As your boss develops confidence in you, he will be more likely to give you new assignments. When a new project is discussed, ask that it be given to you. This is an excellent way to show how you handle a job from its onset to its completion.

Another approach is to determine the types of work your boss doesn't really like to do and volunteer to take it off his hands. He will appreciate not having to do it, and you will set a precedent for taking on additional types of assignments in the future.

If the boss is reluctant to delegate a project that you really would like to do, suggest that you work on it together. The boss will maintain control the first few times this is done. After performing the work with you, he will see that you are capable of doing it and will be more willing to delegate it to you in the future.

16-21   My boss overworks me. She keeps giving me jobs and every one is "high priority." I'm stressed out. Any suggestions?

There are times when work can overwhelm anyone. Many industries have seasons when everybody is overworked (e.g., accountants during tax time). If you are in such a business, you must be prepared to be overworked. However, if overwork becomes a constant demand, it can lead to stress and burnout.

Before confronting the boss, see what you can do to make your work easier. Can you work smarter rather than harder? By analyzing the job, you may be able to eliminate some work, simplify other work, delegate assignments, or develop more efficient systems.

If reanalyzing the job is not sufficient, make a list of all the things you are working on, the time frames and deadlines expected, and other pertinent information. Meet with your boss and go over the list with her. Develop a program on how the workload can be accomplished most effectively. Some work might be deferred. What appeared to be a high priority last week is no longer as urgent. Some work might be assigned to other people. Additional personnel may be assigned if appropriate.

16-22   I supervise a branch office. My boss is at company headquarters in another city. This causes communication problems, since I cannot always get the information I need to do the job. How can I get timely answers from the boss?

In this day and age of electronic communication, it is not too difficult to get answers to questions rapidly. If you worked at company headquarters, you could drop in on the boss whenever you had a problem. In your remote location, use the telephone for matters which just require speech and the fax machine when detailed material must be studied. If the boss isn't available when you call, leave word on voicemail or have the boss paged. Have his or her car phone number on your speed-dial.

Since it is still helpful to have personal contact with your boss from time to time, arrange to visit the home office periodically and invite the boss to visit your branch. Extend an invitation to informal meetings such as the branch Christmas party or an award presentation. Keep the boss advised of problems as they develop so he or she will not be surprised by bad news and can anticipate your sharing good news.

16-23   I just discovered that I made a major error in my projections for next year's production. I'm afraid to tell my boss, but it must be done. How can I let him know about the error with the least amount of damage to myself?

There's no way you can escape telling him. Do not do so on the telephone (unless you are in a remote location) or when you meet the boss casually somewhere in the building. Ask for a private meeting. Prepare for the meeting by going over all the facts and the data. At the meeting get right to the point. Tell him what you did, how it happened. Don't make excuses. Accept the blame. Don't put the blame on your subordinates. You are the supervisor and are responsible for errors made by your people.

If the boss gets upset, stay calm. Start with: "I can understand that you are upset about this; I'm upset too." Then explain what you plan to do to correct the error: "I've already started the recalculations and should have the correct figures by Friday." If you do not have a plan of action to correct the problem, you may ask for help: "Any ideas you have that will help me develop the right figures would be greatly appreciated."

End on a positive note: "I plan to work day and night to get this corrected and I promise you that this time there will be no mistakes."

Personality Problems

16-24   I'm a college graduate and have been supervising my department for less than a year. My boss worked up from a secretary's position and has no college background. She sees me as a threat and is manifesting this by the way she deals with me. How can I overcome her fear?

When discussing your work, talk in objective terms. Instead of saying, "I did this" or "I had an idea and it worked," just discuss what the problem was and how it was resolved. Do not refer to your own initiative or intelligence. In the long run, the work will speak for your ability.

In talking to your boss, comment about the value of her long experience in helping you deal with the job and refrain from making statements about college courses that were useful on the job. Become a supportive aide. Anticipate the boss's needs and be ready to give her useful information at the time she needs it. Become an indispensable staff member and in time her fear of you will be replaced by respect and cooperation.

16-25   My boss has his favorites in my department—old cronies he has known for years. What should I do when he favors them over better workers in my group?

Your boss may not realize that he is favoring friends. Call it to his attention and tell him that you can understand his interest in these old friends, but that giving them favored treatment lowers the morale of the others.

16-26   I know I am doing a good job, but my boss never acknowledges it. She treats me with disdain and my people see this. What should I do?

Unfortunately, there are people in positions of power who look at all those of lower rank as inferiors and treat them accordingly. There is no way you can change the personality of your boss. Keep doing a good job. Your people will respect you for it. As they note that your boss treats everybody with disdain, they will not let that affect their respect for you.

16-27   My boss treats all the management-level people with respect, but looks down at rank-and-file workers. He behaves toward them as if they were an "underclass." My people resent it and this is reflected in low morale and high turnover. How can I help?

You cannot change your boss's personality. Try to get your people to accept him as he is. They don't have to like him, but they should respect his position. Get them to think of you as the buffer between them and the big boss. Earn and keep their respect. If your boss's attitudes or actions lead to a complaint, talk to him about the specifics of the complaint—not his general attitude. By dealing with individual grievances rather than his management style, you will alleviate the problems in your department.

16-28   Is there anything I can do to get my supervisor to stop using profanity when he talks to me and my people?

There is no excuse for using profanity on the job. Some men have the mistaken notion that using profanity makes them macho.

Some women use profanity to prove they are as tough as their male counterparts. Neither rationalization makes sense.

It is not easy to get a person to change what might be a long-time habit of interjecting expletives in every sentence. If you do not feel comfortable calling it to his attention, discuss it with your boss or the personnel manager. They have more clout than you and can make it clear to your boss that such language is not to be used. Women have brought charges of sexual harassment against companies in which such language is used by bosses or co-workers. (See question 37 in Chapter 3.)

If you have an easygoing relationship with your boss, informal conversations about his language may solve the problem. Some groups set up a penalty system. Every time one of the group uses an expletive, he or she puts a quarter in the penalty box. The money is used for a social event from time to time.

16-29   How do you tell your supervisor, who feels his management techniques are the best, that his ideas are contrary to the better management techniques popularized in seminars and books?

A question like this comes up in almost every seminar. Participants complain that no matter what good ideas they learn in the seminar, they cannot implement anything that is contrary to the boss's point of view.

You cannot change anybody's philosophy or managing overnight. Try to implement new concepts in bite-sized pieces. Take one new approach and use it in the way you manage your people (e.g., by encouraging them to participate in decisions concerning their work). As the results begin to show up in higher productivity, reduction of turnover, and the like, your new approach will speak for itself.

If your boss is open-minded enough to listen to new ideas, but resists them, show him or her passages from books on management and discuss them. Point out that these ideas are not based on some esoteric theories, but come from the experience of very successful supervisors in a variety of industries. Sell the idea by suggesting that the boss try out the concept on a specific project.

16-30   What do you do when you have a good group of hardworking people, and your manager comes in on a somewhat regular basis and berates them?

Stick up for your people. Let your manager know what they have accomplished. Show him or her facts and figures to back up your arguments. No matter how good a group may be, minor or occasional errors will be made. If the boss ignores the good work and rebukes your people for the errors, speak to him or her about it. Point out that their good work far outweighs any minor errors and that you will take responsibility to work with them to eliminate or reduce mistakes.

Some people do not realize how demoralizing a public bawling-out can be. Have a heart-to-heart talk with the manager. Try to persuade him or her to speak to you about these matters and let you deal with your people. The discussion may cause you some discomfort, but the result in higher morale and better work from your people will make it worthwhile.

16-31   I am a department manager. My boss and I have an excellent working relationship. I like my position and I have been promoted twice in 3 years. The problem is that my boss's boss dislikes my boss and projects this dislike on to me as well. He has shown this nonverbally in facial expressions and actions. The situation is hard for me to deal with. What can I do?

Let your boss's boss get to know you as an individual, not as an appendage to your boss. It will take time and patience. Despite his attitude toward you, go out of your way to cultivate him. Learn about his concerns and interests and keep him informed about developments in these areas. For example, if you learn that he is particularly concerned about quality, send him copies of articles you have read that cover the topic. If you attend a meeting of a trade or professional group in which the subject has been discussed, send him a note reporting on some of the ideas that were presented at the meeting. Don't overdo your reporting, but occasional reminders will soon separate you in his mind from your boss.

16-32   My boss has a habit of walking around the department stopping at each person's desk and checking the work being done. This annoys me. I know it isn't personal. She does this to everybody, but it makes me very nervous. What should I do?

One reason supervisors walk around is that they are afraid the work will not be done properly unless they constantly check it. Instead of waiting for the boss to look over your shoulder, bring your work to her after you have completed a segment of the assignment. Now when she makes her tour of the department, she will bypass you, since she has already checked your work. This will alleviate the annoyance of her looking over your shoulder.

In addition, once she recognizes that your work is usually fine, you can bring your work to her less often, since she will have developed more trust in you.

16-33   My boss is very permissive. He believes that subordinates should work out their own problems. This is fine under most circumstances, but there are times when I have questions on how to accomplish assignments. How can I bring them to him without having him interpret this as a sign of my incompetence?

Before starting a new assignment, work up a detailed plan of action as to how you intend to proceed. Meet with the boss—not to ask questions—but to review the plan with him before you proceed. He will be impressed by the thought you have given the assignment, and in the discussion will probably answer some of your questions before they are even asked. Presenting your plan of action will also give you the chance to bring up other questions without your appearing to lack competence. Instead, you will be seeking clarification of the ideas you have presented.

16-34   My boss used to be the supervisor of my department. I was hired from the outside to replace her when she moved up. My people still go to her rather than me when they have a problem. I've talked to her about it, but she says, "I was their supervisor for so long, it's just a habit; they'll get over it." It's a year now and they still do it. How can I get them to come to me?

It's time to speak to the boss about it again. Let her know that her interference is not only impeding your role as supervisor, but is keeping her from doing the more important work her current job demands. Insist that she politely refuse to handle these problems and refer the employees to you. If she does this just a few times, the message will be clearly conveyed (see question 16-16).

16-35   I understand the importance of "selling" ideas to higher-ups. How can I prepare to sell my ideas to my boss?

Selling ideas is not much different from selling a product or service. Here are some of the steps good salespeople take to prepare for making a sale:

1. *Clarify your ideas.* Research the information you may need to make your point. What have other companies done? What do experts say? Think carefully about the drawbacks of your ideas and be prepared to show how the advantages will outweigh the limitations.

2. *Decide what you offer.* From your analysis of the subject, determine what this concept will do that others will not. Use examples where possible of how the idea has worked before either in your company or in others.

3. *Determine what's in it for the boss.* Every salesperson knows that the main concern of any buyer is "What's in it for me?" How will the company benefit by accepting your idea? Can you demonstrate cost effectiveness? Increased productivity? Higher quality? You know your boss. What does he or she want from the job? If your idea will give the boss more recognition by top management, point this out. If the boss is particularly concerned with reaching a specific goal, show how your approach will help.

4. *Develop evidence.* Statistics, facts, and examples all serve as evidence. If appropriate, prepare charts or graphs, summarize reports from others who have had a similar idea, and submit other pertinent material.

16-36 Once I've prepared, what should I do to make the sale?

Follow the steps in any good sales presentation:

1. *Get the boss's attention.* Ask a question that will elicit a positive response. "Carlos, I know how concerned you are about increasing productivity. If there is a way of doing this without adding more personnel, you would want to know about it, wouldn't you? The only response Carlos could make is yes. You have his attention.

2. *Ask questions and listen for responses.* Most people are so anxious to sell their ideas that they do not listen to what the "buyer" really wants. Do not presuppose that your boss's objectives are the same as yours. Ask good questions to bring out how the boss sees the problem and what his or her real interests are. Listen to the responses so you can tailor your presentation to meet the boss's real concerns.

3. *Present evidence.* In your preparation, you have developed a good deal of evidence. Use it now to show the boss just how

your idea will help solve the problems he or she is most concerned about. You know how your boss likes to receive information (see question 16-1). Present it in the form that is most acceptable.

4. *Deal with objections.*   Salespeople like objections. It helps them determine what the prospect really wants and enables them to face up to that and increase their chances of making the sale. Your research should prepare you for the objections likely to be presented, and you should be ready to counter them. You will gain more insight into your boss's concerns. Use that insight to sharpen your presentation.

5. *Close the sale.*   There are several approaches to closing a sale. Probably the most appropriate in selling an idea to the boss is to ask for help in evaluating the concept.

Divide a paper into columns. Head one "negatives" and the other "positives." Immediately list the major objections that have been brought up in the "negative" column and write the counteracting arguments in the "positive" column. Add to the "positive" column all the additional benefits that have been discussed. If you have done your homework, you should have many more positives than negatives.

Then state: "Let's look at some of the reasons that may cause you to hesitate to accept this idea and weigh them against the reasons in favor of going ahead. In your opinion, which side weighs heavier?" The answer has to be the positive one.

Once you have obtained agreement that your concept is viable, say: "Inasmuch as you agree that this is a good idea, I would like to discuss how it can be implemented." If your boss must sell the concept to higher-level executives before it can be adopted, suggest that you will be happy to assist in that presentation.

16-37   How do I motivate another supervisor over whom I have no authority to complete tasks which are essential for me to complete my part of the assignment?

Just as when dealing with a boss, you can never say do it or else. But unlike your boss, a peer has no power over you. It is important to maintain good relations with peers so that a cooperative atmosphere develops in which each is willing and even anxious to help the others. Sell your peer in the same way you would sell your boss.

If this approach fails and you realize that you will not meet your deadline as a result, you can go to the person who supervises both of you and ask for intervention. This is a last resort. Make every effort to work out differences between the two of you and avoid involving the boss.

16-38 How can I improve communications with a boss who has limited knowledge of my area of responsibility?

Often managers are required to supervise people in specialties different from their own. The situation is difficult both for the supervisor and the employee. Your boss is probably just as ill at ease as you are when discussing matters in which expertise is lacking. Be patient. Explain as best you can the nature of what you are doing and how it fits into the work of the department. If highly technical matters are involved, suggest that a technical expert be consulted when needed. The expert could be another person within the organization who knows the field, a consultant, or a representative of a manufacturer or supplier of the equipment involved.

A boss who has confidence in the capability of specialized subordinates, usually lets them make decisions on technical aspects of the work and limits management to administrative and policy matters.

Your Career

16-39 I've risen as far as I can in my company. When is the right time to move on to another organization?

Changing jobs is not necessarily the best move to make. If you are a valued employee, the company does not want to lose all the time, money, and energy it has spent in training and developing you to the point which you have now reached. Speak to the human resources people and discuss the matter with them. There may be plans of which you are not aware that may increase your opportunities for advancement.

You may have gone as far as you can in your present job or department, but there may be other jobs within the organization to which you can be transferred. A lateral move may not give you immediate advancement, but it can be the first step on the ladder of a new career path. If no such opportunities can be developed, explore the job market in the areas in which you wish to work. If possible, do not leave one job until you have obtained another.

16-40   The changes in technology and management planning will make my job superfluous within the next few years. What can I do to deal with this?

Don't wait for the axe to fall. Discuss the matter *now* with management. Ask what you should do to prepare yourself to be of value to the company as these changes develop. What courses should you take to learn new technology? What assignments can management give you to enable you to gain experience in aspects of the work that will be needed?

Most companies would prefer to retrain people they know and trust than replace them with technically qualified strangers. They will pay tuition to schools and colleges, send you to special training classes, and provide on-the-job training. Let them know you are willing—indeed eager—to learn.

16-41   I've been a supervisor for about a year and I hate it. I enjoyed doing my technical work and now I spend most of my time in administrative matters. Can I ask to return to my old job without jeopardizing my career?

Many very good workers prefer doing work in their specialized fields rather than supervise others. There is no shame in wanting to do the kind of work you enjoy. Talk to your boss. It would not be a surprise. He or she probably has observed this and, since most people who do not like a job do not do it well, you may not be performing up to expectations in the new job. By returning to your old job, not only will you be happier, but you will be doing better and more productive work for the company.

As for the future, if the only advancement is via the administrative and supervisory route, you will be limited in your promotional opportunities. However, more and more companies are developing programs to compensate and recognize nonsupervisory personnel for good performance that does not require them to be supervisors.

16-42   I do good work, but so do my co-workers. What can I do to stand out against the tough competition for advancement?

Doing good work is important, but it is not enough. To stand out against tough competitors, you have to reach out and do more than is just expected of you. Volunteer for special assignments. Come up with suggestions and programs for improving quality, increasing production, reducing costs, or developing new business. Take risks. The only way a turtle can move forward is to stick its neck out of the shell.

16-43   I work in a family business. Other than marrying into the family, what can I do to move up when all the top jobs are held by family members?

In a small family business, you may have to marry in to become a top manager, but there are probably key positions that can be filled only by qualified outsiders. Many nonfamily members hold such jobs in family-owned businesses. Indeed, owners of such companies often recognize that their sons or daughters are not as competent as other employees who have talents that are more important to the organization than family ties. These outsiders do get promoted to highly responsible positions.

16-44   There are lots of opportunities in my company, but my boss is holding me back by not giving me a chance to show my capabilities. The powers-that-be don't even know I exist. How do I get noticed?

Here are some suggestions on how to become visible so that executives other than your own boss will know your capabilities:

- *Be competent in your work.* If you are incompetent and visible, it works against you.
- *Speak up.* One of the most effective ways of making yourself known to the executives in your organization is to participate actively in the meetings. Try to overcome any discomfort about speaking in public. This is one of the most common fears people have. It can be overcome by training and practice.
- *Show interest in other people's goals.* If you learn that one of the executives in your company has a special interest, make a practice of sending articles on that subject to him or her.
- *Volunteer.* From time to time companies have special projects for which volunteers are sought. These projects may be directly linked to the job, such as researching for information about a new process or piece of equipment. Sometimes they may be peripheral to the business, such as chairing a fund-raising drive for a favorite charity. By volunteering for such assignments, you

get to know and be known by managers who otherwise would never have the opportunity to see you in action.

- *Become active in professional associations.* Just being a member is good, but participation is even better. Darlene attributes her rapid rise in the company to her activities as a member of the program committee of the local chapter of the American Marketing Association. When asked to find a speaker for one of the association's meetings, she suggested the vice president of marketing of her company. She had never spoken to this man before and he had only a vague idea of her work as a lower-level marketing staff member. To orient him about the meeting, Darlene met with him before the meeting, sat next to him, and introduced him at the meeting. From then on Darlene was no longer just a name on the roster of the department. Her initiative led to better assignments and to career advancement.

- *Write for trade publications.* If you have the talent to write, send contributions on matters relating to your field to appropriate journals. Be careful not to write anything that might divulge company secrets or proprietary information. Most companies require that any articles relating to the company be screened by appropriate executives to ensure that proprietary material is not released. Once an article is published, to be sure that the executives you want to impress see it, send them copies.

Competence and professionalism are basic to success. Still, no matter how effective you may be, if you are not known to decision makers, you will be overlooked. By planning and implementing a program for your own visibility, you will increase your opportunities for career growth significantly.

Afterword

I can sum up how to be a successful supervisor in three words:

KNOW YOUR PEOPLE

Know each of your people as an individual. Know their strengths and limitations, their likes and dislikes, how they act and react. Learn their patterns of behavior.

Tailor the way you deal with each of them to his or her individuality rather than trying to get them to conform to your personality.

If you do this, you will find that your people respect you because they see that you respect them. They will be motivated by you because you are using what is of concern to them to reach them. They will make your job easier. They will make you look good to your boss. They will give you more satisfaction in your job and perhaps, though I cannot promise this, enable you to gain self-actualization by being a supervisor.

Index

Absenteeism, 301–305, 307–308, 379, 388–389
Accents, 156–157
Accommodations for disabled persons, 81–82
Accountability:
  delegation and, 141–142, 144
  instilling in subordinates, 16
Advertisements for applicants, 27–29
Advice giving, avoiding, 344
Affirmative action, 101–102
  motivation and, 227
Affirmative discipline, 379–381
Age(s):
  diversity among employees, 300
  salary differentials and, 226
  (See also Age discrimination)
Age discrimination, 76, 80, 99–101
  termination and, 413–414
Age Discrimination in Employment Act (ADEA) of 1967, 71, 76, 80, 99, 100
Aggressiveness, 266
  (See also Anger)
AIDS, 83, 261
Alcohol abuse, 82–83, 258–260, 303
Americans with Disabilities Act (ADA) of 1990, 71, 81–84, 225–226, 255–256, 260–261
Anger, 254–255, 257, 321, 327–328
  disciplining and, 387–388
Appearance:
  of applicants, 50–51
  dress codes and, 97, 310
  overconcern with, 311–312
Applicants (see Employee selection)
Application forms, 30–31, 33–35, 99
  retaining, 106
Aptitude tests, 54
Arbitration, 317–320
Arrest records, 84–85
Articulation, 155–156
Assertiveness, speech and, 157–158
Assessment centers, 358

Attendance (see Absenteeism; Tardiness)
Attendance awards, 302
Attire worn by employees, 97, 310
Attitude(s), communication and, 165–170
Attitude problems, 14, 244–251
Authority:
  delegation of (see Delegation)
  fear of, 273
  lack of, 450–451
  overstepping, 293

Behaviorally anchored rating system (BARS), 357–358
Benefits:
  attracting applicants and, 29–30
  employees over age 65 and, 100
  following layoffs and quits, 398
  motivation and, 210–211
Biases, 165–170
Bickering, 321
Body language, 158–159
Body odor, 255
Bona fide occupational qualifications (BFOQs), 76, 80
Boredom:
  alleviating, 438–439
  motivation and, 238, 243
Bosses (see Superiors; Supervisors)
Brainstorming, 199
Branches, supervising, 281–282
Break(s):
  extended, 287, 387
  time management and, 443
Breaking in, 2–5
Busybodies, 261–261, 264, 272–273, 300, 313, 330

Calendars, 426
Careers, 462–465
  goals for, 215–218

Case studies, 119–120
Change(s):
　making, 21–22
　opposed by union, 331, 333
Change management, 289
Changing jobs, 462–463
Child care, 86, 88–89
Civil rights (see Equal employment
　　opportunity laws)
Civil Rights Act of 1964, 70
Cliques, 274–275
Clothing worn by employees, 97, 310
COBRA, layoffs and quits and, 398
Communication:
　controlling conversation and, 297
　customer complaints about, 312–313
　delegation and, 138–140
　formal, 170–172
　with subordinates (see Downward
　　communication)
　with superiors (see Upward commu-
　　nication)
　by telephone (see Telephone calls)
Comparable worth, 87–88
Compensation:
　comparable worth and, 87–88
　complaints about, 327
　conflict related to, 296–297
　docking pay as disciplinary action
　　and, 383
　Equal Pay Act of 1963 and, 71,
　　87–88
　in help-wanted ads, 29
　of laid-off workers, 399–400
　motivation and, 209–211, 226, 233,
　　235–238
　negotiating, 64–65
　overtime pay, 2
　performance evaluation and, 352,
　　365–366
　severance pay, 399, 415–416
　terminations and, 415–416
　(See also Benefits)
Complaints, 262, 322–336
　from customers, 312–313
　about other employees, 322
　of overwork, 284, 286
　about supervisors, 324, 326–327
Compliments:
　to subordinates, 322
　to superiors, 448–449
Computers for training, 129
Confidence, lacking, 252–253
Conflicts:
　among employees, 294–301
　resolution of, 314–322

Conflicts (Cont.):
　with superiors, 446–447
Confrontation for conflict resolution,
　321
Contests as motivators, 213–214
Contract(s), restrictive covenant, 67–68
Contracted employees, motivating,
　239–240
Control, delegation and, 140–142
Conversation, controlling, 297
Cooperation:
　lack of, 272, 280
　obtaining, 175, 267–268, 274,
　　290–291
Counseling, 336–344, 438
　in progressive discipline, 372–375
Counteroffers, 68, 405
Creativity, developing, 197–203
Criminal records, 84–85
Crises, 433
Criticism:
　of coworkers, 295
　of subordinates, 166–169, 172,
　　251–252, 271, 449
　by superiors, 457–458
　of supervisors, 262, 270, 278
Cross-training, 124–125, 133–134
Cultural differences, 93–96, 159
　(See also Immigrants; Minorities;
　　Work force diversity)

Deadlines, 140, 141, 282–283, 289
Decision(s), questioning of, 275
Decision making, 252–253
Defamation of character:
　references and, 63–64
　termination and, 412–413
Defensiveness, 168, 251–252, 313
Delegation, 135–150
　communication and, 138–140
　control and, 140–142
　day-to-day problems in, 143–150
　encouraging from superiors,
　　453–454
　encouraging in subordinates, 145
　importance of, 135–138
Demotions, 291–292
　disciplinary, 383, 391
　of supervisors (see Supervisors, for-
　　mer, who have stepped down)
Diction, 157
Disability insurance, 265
Disabled persons, 71, 81–84, 225–226,
　255–256, 260–261
　firing, 413–414

Discipline, 368–392
    affirmative, 379–381
    legal implications of, 381–384
    preventing need for, 384, 386
    progressive, 369–379
Disputes, mediating, 315–317
Documentation:
    of disciplinary procedures, 375,
        381–383, 411
    of performance evaluations, 350–351
    of warnings, 372
    (*See also* Note taking)
Downsizing, motivation and, 222–223,
    238–239
Downward communication, 151–184
    attitudes, biases, and emotions and,
        165–170
    feedback and, 163–165
    listening and, 160–163
    nonverbal, 158–160
    order giving, 176–177
    problems with, 170–175
    speech and, 155–158
    word choice and, 152–155
    written, 177–184
Dress codes, 97, 310
Drug abuse, 260–261
Drug addicts, 82–83

Early retirement, 100–101
Education:
    communication and, 157
    downward communication and,
        152–153
    importance of, 31–32
    for management positions, 125–126
    motivation and, 236–237
Emotions:
    communication and, 165–170
    (*See also* Anger)
Empathy, 163
Employee assistance programs (EAPs),
    245, 259–260, 339–340, 343–344,
    438
Employee selection, 23–69
    giving information to applicants and,
        41–43
    hiring decisions and, 47, 50–53
    job specifications and, 23–24, 25
    offers and, 64–69
    problem applicants and, 43–45
    record keeping and, 46–50
    references and, 56–64
    screening applicants and, 30–41
    sources of personnel and, 24, 26–30

Employee selection (*Cont.*):
    testing and, 53–56, 98–99
Employment at will, 67, 416–419
Employment services:
    employment agencies, 26, 55
    school-affiliated, 27
    state, 26
Employment testing, 53–56, 98–99
Empowerment, 229–232
Equal employment opportunity laws,
    70–106
    affirmative action and, 101–102, 227
    age discrimination and, 71, 76, 80,
        99–101, 413–414
    Americans with Disabilities Act, 71,
        81–84, 225–226, 255–256,
        260–261
    complaint handling and, 102–106
    criminal records and, 84–85
    cultural differences and, 93–96
    dress codes and, 97
    employment testing and, 98–99
    hiring friends and relatives of
        employees and, 96
    legal and illegal questions and, 71,
        76–80, 86–87, 98
    marriage of employees and, 96–97
    penalties for violating, 105
    religious discrimination and, 81
    sex discrimination and, 76, 85–93,
        263–264
    smoking and, 98
    terminations and, 413–414
Equal Pay Act of 1963, 71, 87–88
Equipment:
    return of, 312, 399
    theft of, 264–265
Errors, reporting to superiors, 455
Evaluation (*see* Performance evaluation)
Exceptions, 306
Excuses:
    for absenteeism and tardiness, 308
    reprimands and, 370–371, 389
Executive Order 11246 of 1965, 71
Executive Order 11375 of 1967, 71
Exit interviews, 400, 403–405
Eye contact, 159–162

Fatigue, 439
Favoritism:
    avoiding appearance of, 276,
        278–279, 288, 293–294
    complaints of, 329
Fear:
    of authority, 273

Fear (*Cont.*):
  of superiors, 455–456
Feedback, 163–165, 183
Fees, of employment agencies, 26
Firing employees, 259, 395, 406–416
  (*See also* Employment at will)
Flexibility, improving, 292
Flextime, 305–307
Follow-up systems, 426
Followership, of applicants, assessing,
  37
Forgetting, 312
Formal communication, 170–172
Friends as employees, 9–12, 96, 274
Fringe benefits (*see* Benefits)

Gender separation of jobs, 227,
  247–248
Goals, 215–218
  for performance improvement, 364,
    366
  results-oriented performance evalua-
    tion systems and, 356–357
  time management and, 421–422
  unrealistic, 452
Gossip, 300
Grammar, 157
Grievance(s) (*see* Complaints)
Grievance procedures, 323–326,
  330–333
Gripes, 322–336

Halo effect in performance evaluation,
  354
Handicapped persons, 71, 81–84,
  225–226, 255–256, 260–261
  firing, 413–414
Help-wanted ads, 27–29
Hiring decisions, 47, 50–53
Housekeeping, 309, 310–311

Ideas (*see* Creativity; Suggestions)
Illness:
  AIDS, 83, 261
  feigned, to use up sick leave,
    308–309
  sending employees home due to,
    308
Immigrants, 93–96, 153–154, 228
  (*See also* Cultural differences; Work
    force diversity)
Incentives, monetary, 210
Independence, fostering, 298–299

Instruction manuals, 128–129
Instructions, retention of, 285
Insurance:
  disability, 265
  (*See also* Unemployment compensa-
    tion)
Intelligence of applicants, assessing,
  35–36, 53–54
Intelligence tests, 53–54
Interactive computer programs for
  training, 129
Interpersonal problems, 311
  conflict resolution and, 314–322
Interpersonal relations, 294–301
  with superiors (*see* Superiors)
Interruptions, 441
  listening and, 161
  by other departments, 287–288
  time management and, 423–424,
    426–433
Interviews:
  of applicants (*see* Job interviews)
  exit, 403–405
  listening in, 162
  performance appraisals and,
    358–367
  termination, 407–411, 414–415
Investigation bureaus, for reference
  checking, 63

Japanese management style, 208–209
Jargon, 154
Job applicants (*see* Employee selection)
Job descriptions, 23–25
  outdated, 111
  performance evaluation and, 347
Job enrichment, 214
Job instruction training (JIT), 111, 114,
  116
Job interviews:
  background in, 32, 35
  beginning, 32
  excessive talking by applicant in, 43
  interviewer's talking in, 37–38
  minimizing time required for, 30
  with multiple interviewers, 52–53
  with nervous applicants, 32
  probing for details in, 43–44
  questions in, 31, 38–39, 40–41, 71,
    76–80, 86–87, 98
  summary sheet for, 47–50
  by telephone, 44–45
Job offers, 64–69
Job security, 3, 220
Job specifications, 23–25

Kaizen, 366

Labor unions (*see* Unions)
Language:
  body, 158–159
  downward communication and,
    152–155
  foreign, 153–154, 156–157
  immigrants and, 94–95
  inappropriate, 91–92, 309–310,
    456–457
Lateness:
  to work, 305–309
  (*See also* Deadlines; Unfinished
    work)
Laws (*see* Equal employment opportu-
    nity laws; Legal issues)
Layoffs, 394–401
  alternatives to, 401
  motivation and, 222–223, 238–239
  notice of, 397
Laziness, 218–225
Leadership style, of applicants, assess-
    ing, 37
Legal issues:
  discipline and, 381–384
  employment at will and, 416–419
  equal employment opportunity laws
    and (*see* Equal employment
    opportunity laws)
  performance evaluation and,
    350–351
  references and, 63–64
  termination and, 411–414
Letters, 179–182
Lie detector tests, 84–85
Line supervisors, 275–276
Listening, 160–163, 166
  in performance appraisal interviews,
    360–361

Mail, handling, 434–436
Management:
  demands of, 288–289
  training for, 125–126
Management style, 273–274
  of co-supervisors, 271
  developing, 14–16
  domineering, 297–298
  Japanese, 208–209
  motivation and, 214–215, 239, 242
  of superiors, 457–459
  Theory X, 206–208
  Theory Y, 207, 208

Manipulative employees, 256, 266–267
Marriage:
  between employees, 96–97
  marital problems and, 256–257
Maslow's theory, 205–206
Maturity, of applicants, assessing, 36
McGregor's theory, 207–208
Mediation, 315–317
Medical examinations, preemployment,
    65–66, 83–84
Meetings:
  time management and, 436–437
  upward communication in, 194–197
Memos, 179–181
Mentors, 118
Merit systems, 366
Minorities:
  affirmative action and, 101–102
  employment testing and, 98–99
  firing, 413–414
  handling problems involving, 269
  layoffs and, 396
  motivating, 227
  (*See also* Equal employment oppor-
    tunity laws; Women)
Money:
  motivation and, 209–210
  (*See also* Compensation)
Morale, 13, 240–243
  working supervisors and, 443
Motivating employees, 13
Motivation, 204–240, 284–285
  of diversified work force, 225–228
  goals and, 215–218
  of peers, 461–462
  principles and techniques for,
    204–215
  problems with, 232–240
  productivity and, 218–225, 226
  team building and, 229–232
Mumbling, 155–156

Neatness, of work area, 309, 310–311
Needs, motivation and, 205–206
Negativism, 244–250, 263, 294–295
  morale and, 240–241
Nervous applicants, interviewing, 32, 35
Newspaper ads, 27–29
Nonverbal communication, 158–159
Nosy employees, 261–261, 264,
    272–273, 300, 313, 330
Note taking:
  during job interviews, 46–47
  during performance appraisal inter-
    views, 363

Note taking (*Cont.*):
  (*See also* Documentation)

Off-the-job training, 112
Offers, 64–69
Offices, sharing with subordinates, 12
On-the-job training, 112–115
  for management positions, 125–126
Opportunity as motivator, 213
Oral commitments, employment at will
  and, 418
Order giving, 173–174, 176–177
Orientation of new employees, 127–128
Outplacement services, 400
Overtime, 286–287
  pay for, 2
Overwork, 222–223, 440–441, 454
  complaints of, 284, 286
  motivation and, 237–238

Paperwork, 3
Peer evaluation, 352
Perfectionism, 269–270
Performance:
  average, 329, 350, 402–403
  improvement of, 366
  substandard, 289–290, 343, 350, 363,
    382, 389–391
Performance evaluation, 345–367
  assessment centers for, 358
  behaviorally anchored rating scales
    for, 357–358
  interviews and, 358–367
  monthly reports and, 357
  of new employees, 66
  by peers, 352
  preparing for, 359–360, 366–367
  purposes of, 346–362
  results-oriented system for, 356–357
  self-evaluation for, 349
  trait rating for, 352–355
Performance tests, 54
Permanent employees, 66
Personal problems, 251–257, 266, 433,
  438
  counseling and, 336–344
Personality(ies):
  of applicants, 50–51
  communication and, 168
  customer complaints about, 312–313
  morale and, 242
Personality conflicts, references and, 58
Personality problems, with superiors,
  455–462

Personality tests, 54
Physical energy of applicants, assessing, 36
Planning, 19
  time management and, 421–426
Policies, 450–452
  complaints about, 335–336
  employment at will and, 418
Polygraph tests, 84–85
Practice, training and, 116
Pregnancy, 88
Pressure, 277, 439–440
Probation, 376
Problem employees, 244–280
  alcohol and drugs and, 82–83,
    258–261
  attitude and, 244–251
  boss-subordinate relations and,
    270–280
  personal problems and, 251–257
  problem people and, 261–270
Problem-solving method for performance appraisal interviews,
  361–362
Procedures, getting employees to
  follow, 291
Procrastination, 440
Productivity:
  boredom and, 438–439
  increasing, 13–14, 175
  motivation and, 218–225, 226,
    232–233
  substandard, 376–378
Profanity, 91–92, 309–310, 456–457
Progressive discipline, 369–379
  termination following, 411
  termination without, 411
Promotions:
  advantages and disadvantages of,
    2–3
  announcement of, 4
  changing old habits and, 3
  motivation and, 234–235
  obtaining, 463–465
  performance evaluation and, 352
  (*See also* Demotions; Supervisors
  former, who have stepped
  down)
Protected classes, 102
  firing people in, 413–414
  (*See also specific classes of
  employees*)
Psychological problems, 255–256, 266,
  343
  referring employees for professional
  help for, 339

Quality of work life, 243
Quits, voluntary, 395, 401–406
    coercion and, 413
    encouraging, 416
    notice of, 401–402

Recognition as motivator, 211–213
Reference(s), for average workers,
    402–403
Reference checking, 56–64
    investigation bureaus for, 63
    by telephone, 58–62
    written references and, 63
Regional supervisors, 21
Rehiring, 401
Rejecting applicants, 68–69
Relatives as employees, 96, 257
Religious discrimination, 81, 301
Reports, 177–179, 182
    obtaining, 189–190
Reprimands, progressive discipline
    and, 369–372
Resentment:
    delegation and, 143–144, 145–146
    of disabled employees, 83
    of discipline, 384
    overcoming, 5–9, 246–247, 270
    of performance evaluation, 349
    reprimands and, 371–372
Resignations (see Quits, voluntary)
Resourcefulness of applicants, assess-
    ing, 36–37
Respect:
    gaining, 6–7, 250–251
    lack of, 277–278
    morale and, 241–242
    for subordinates, 7
Responsibilities, 2
    (See also Accountability; Authority)
Restrictive covenant contracts,
    67–68
Results-oriented performance evalua-
    tion systems, 356–357
Résumés, screening, 30
Retaining employees, 236
Retirement, motivation and, 222
Retirement age, 100–101
Retraining, 127, 463
Reverse discrimination, 101–102
Roaming employees, 292
Role playing, 118–119, 121
Romances between employees, 93,
    96–97
Rule of recency in performance
    evaluation, 354

Salary (see Compensation)
Sandwich approach for performance
    appraisal interviews, 362–363
School-affiliated employment services,
    27
Screening applicants, 30–41
Selection (see Employee selection)
Self-confidence, lacking, 252–253
Self-discipline, lacking, 278
Self-evaluation, 349
Semantics, 154–155
Seniority, layoffs and, 396
Severance pay, 399, 415–416
Sex discrimination, 76, 85–93, 263–264
Sexual harassment, 89–92
Sick leave, abuse of, 308–309
Sick time, layoffs and quits and,
    399–400
Skills:
    learning from subordinates, 8
    needed by supervisors, 2
    of trainers, 117
    training and (see Training)
    of workers, evaluating, 291
Sloppiness, 309, 310–311
Smoking, 98
    violation of prohibition of, 387
Socializing with subordinates, 10–11
Special assignments, 441
Speech, 155–158
Speed, 282
    (See also Deadlines)
Stability of applicants, assessing,
    39–40
Staff reductions, 22
Stammering, 156
Standard operating procedures, 183
State employment agencies, 26
Stealing, 264–265
    unlawful discharge suits and, 412
Street language, 91–92, 309–310,
    456–457
Subordinates:
    communication by (see Upward
        communication)
    delegating to (see Delegation)
    learning about, 17–19
    learning skills from, 8
    number of, 19–20
    sharing offices with, 12
    socializing with, 10–11
    as trainers, 116–118, 130, 132–133
Substance abuse, 82–83, 258–261
Suggestions, 276–277
    presenting to superiors, 451–452
    from subordinates, 185–188, 190–195

Suggestions (*Cont.*):
  (*See also* Creativity)
Superiors, 444–462
  disagreeing with, 446–447, 451
  personality problems with, 455–462
  policies and, 450–452
  relationship with, 445–450
  work assignments and, 452–455
Supervision:
  excessive need for, 262–263
  learning techniques for, 4
Supervisors:
  former, who have stepped down,
    16–17, 237, 264, 463
  multiple, 271, 442–443
  past, checking references with,
    57–64
  regional, 21
  subordinate, 186–188
  team leaders compared with, 20–21
Suspensions, 377–379, 381, 390–391
Swearing, 91–92, 309–310, 456–457

Tape recordings:
  of job interviews, 46
  for training, 120–122
Tardiness, 305–309, 379
Team building, 229–232, 252, 288, 297
Team leaders, supervisors compared
    with, 20–21
Telephone calls, 172–173
  at home, 277, 328
  as interruption, 426–431
Telephone job interviews, 44–45
Telephone reference checks, 58–62
Telephone skills, training in, 122
Tell-and-listen method for perfor-
    mance appraisal interviews,
    360–361
Tell-and-sell method for performance
    appraisal interviews, 360
Temper (*see* Anger)
Temporary help, motivating, 235–236
Termination (*see* Firing employees)
Termination interviews, 407–411
  preparing for, 414–415
Testing, 53–56, 98–99
Theft, 264–265
  unlawful discharge suits and, 412
Theory X, 206–208
Theory Y, 207
Tickler files, 426
Time analysis, 422–423
Time clock, punching cards for others
    and, 307

Time management, 420–443
  interruptions and, 426–433
  mail handling and, 434–436
  meetings and, 436–437
  personal barriers to efficient use of
    time and, 437–440
  planning and, 421–426
To-do lists, 424–426
Tools:
  return of, 312, 399
  theft of, 264–265
Training, 107–134
  continuing, 123–134
  employees as trainers for, 116–118,
    130, 132–133, 403
  methods for, 114, 116, 118–122
  motivation and, 221–222, 232
  off-the-job, 112
  on-the-job, 112–115, 125–126
  by quitting employees, 403
  retraining, 127, 463
  schedule for, 113–116
  of supervisors, 123–124
  systematic, 107–113
  team building and, 232
Training meetings, 130–132
Trait rating, 352–355
Trust, 169
  lack of, 246, 268, 271–272

Unemployment compensation:
  layoffs and, 400
  voluntary quits and, 405
Unfinished work, 299–300
  (*See also* Deadlines)
Uniforms, 97
Unions:
  disciplinary procedures and, 383–384
  employment at will and, 417
  grievance procedures and, 330–333
  motivation and, 224–225
Upward communication, 185–203
  creativity and, 197–203
  at distances, 454–455
  from individuals, 185–190
  in meetings, 194–197
  suggestion systems and, 190–194
  when superior lacks expertise, 462

Vacation time:
  covering for employees and, 442
  layoffs and quits and, 399–400
  scheduling, 293

Veterans, affirmative action and, 102
Veterans Readjustment Act of 1974, 102
Video equipment for training, 120–121
Visual impact in training, 120–122

Wages (*see* Compensation)
Warnings, 369, 372, 376, 378, 383
Weaknesses of applicants, probing for, 39
Wellness programs, 303
Witnesses in termination interviews, 410–411
Women:
    affirmative action and, 101–102
    discrimination against, 76, 85–93
    firing, 413–414
    motivating, 225

Women (*Cont.*):
    as supervisors of men, 272, 278–280
Word whiskers, 155–156
Work assignments, 281–294
    superiors and, 452–455
Work force diversity, 93–96
    motivation and, 225–228
    (*See also* Immigrants; Disabled persons; Minorities; Women)
Work habits, 309–313
Work schedules, changing, 283–284
Worker Adjustment and Retraining Notification Act (WARN), 397
Working papers, 99
Written assignments, 138–139
Written communication, 177–184
Written job offers, 66–67
Written references, 63

About the Author

Arthur R. Pell, Ph.D., is a nationally known author, lecturer, and consultant. He has written more than 35 books, including *How to Sell Yourself in an Interview, Getting the Most from Your People,* and *Managing through People,* and has edited the revised version of *How to Win Friends and Influence People* for Dale Carnegie and Associates. He currently speaks to groups under the auspices of Dun & Bradstreet Business Education Service and estimates that 10,000 people attend his Successful Supervision Workshop annually.